Words
of the Inuit

CONTEMPORARY STUDIES ON THE NORTH

ISSN 1928-1722

CHRIS TROTT, SERIES EDITOR

Words
of the Inuit

A Semantic Stroll
through a Northern
Culture

LOUIS-JACQUES DORAIS

UMP

UNIVERSITY OF MANITOBA PRESS

Words of the Inuit: A Semantic Stroll through a Northern Culture
© Louis-Jacques Dorais 2020
Foreword © Lisa Koperqualuk

28   27   26   25   24   2   3   4   5   6

University of Manitoba Press
Winnipeg, Manitoba, Canada
Treaty 1 Territory
uofmpress.ca

Cataloguing data available from Library and Archives Canada
Contemporary Studies on the North, ISSN 1928-1722 ; 7
ISBN 978-0-88755-862-7 (PAPER)
ISBN 978-0-88755-864-1 (PDF)
ISBN 978-0-88755-863-4 (EPUB)
ISBN 978-0-88755-914-3 (BOUND)

Cover image: Carving, dog sled and hunter. McCord Museum
N-0000.68.1.
Cover design by Marvin Harder
Interior design by Jess Koroscil

Printed in Canada

The University of Manitoba Press acknowledges the financial support for
its publication program provided by the Government of Canada through
the Canada Book Fund, the Canada Council for the Arts, the Manitoba
Department of Sport, Culture, and Heritage, the Manitoba Arts Council,
and the Manitoba Book Publishing Tax Credit.

Funded by the Government of Canada | Canada

Contents

Foreword

BY LISA KOPERQUALUK

There are so few non-Inuit able to communicate in my language that each time I converse with one who speaks Inuktitut I am usually doubly impressed. With the linguistic structure of our language being so different from English and French, we understand the challenge non-Inuit face when learning Inuktitut. Louis-Jacques Dorais is probably the only ethnolinguist/ anthropologist who has such a deep understanding of the Inuit language. He has dedicated most of his life to studying Canadian Inuktitut and teaching it to many students wishing to gain a glimpse of our world and better understand our culture. As I read through Louis-Jacques's book, I see that it brings to light our culture and world view through a stroll among our words and concepts.

When I first met him in the 1980s, Louis-Jacques was assisting the Kativik School Board on a linguistic project related to Inuktitut teaching. Little did I know that one day he would become my director for graduate studies at Laval University in Quebec City. I began my graduate studies with confidence that I would have exemplary guidance, for he knew the Inuit communities in Nunavik and their history, and had delved into our language for a long time.

Even now, I turn to him when I have a question about a specific word. For example, for a chapter in a book about the first bowhead whale hunt in 100 years in Nunavik, published by Avataq Cultural Institute, I needed an explanation for why *arvik* (bowhead whale) ended with a *k*, while in Nunavut it was spelled *arviq*, ending with guttural sound *q*. I had to find the justification of why, in Nunavik, we said it that way, so that readers of other dialects would not regard it as a mistake. It is interesting and also good to know how our language travelled and to see the path in which its pronunciation evolved, and to have the explanations that help us understand how that happens.

Oftentimes, an Inuk will be told by a parent or someone important in their lives as a way of encouragement, "*Kajusigit!*" which basically means "Continue" or "Don't give up!" When my grandfather told me this after I had recounted some particular struggle, I took it simply to mean, "Keep on going, carry on." Somehow, at that time, his words did not seem like particularly strong encouragement. Our elders in Nunavik and elsewhere use this expression when they really wish to encourage someone not to give up on whatever their endeavour might be. It seems that the deeper meaning, which my grandfather probably understood when he said it to me, really suggests, "Be strong, persevere." I think both my examples above answer Louis-Jacques's question of up to what point are etymological studies really significant and socially useful, for understanding the origins of our words is immensely helpful, particularly for those whose work has to do with Inuktitut and/or writing.

This book can be read likewise by an Inuktitut speaker, as well as by a learner or non-Inuktitut speaker, and all will be enriched by it. So much more can be learned about our way of thinking by analyzing Inuktitut in the way Louis-Jacques demonstrates. The study of Inuktitut rests not only in understanding its linguistic structure; a deeper study of our language reveals much more about the Inuit world view. It is this ethonolinguistic approach that brings about very interesting instances where our perception of the world can be better understood.

The chapter dealing with *sila* and *nuna* thus reveals the true meaning of these Inuit concepts to the reader. The word *sila* itself captures different layers of meaning, such as the one of the "cosmological regulator" of the universe, *Silaup Inua*, which I enjoyed learning of when I first was introduced to this distinct Inuit concept. And then there are internal and external *sila*, and their link to a person's mental capacity, wherein a wise and reasonable person is full of *sila*, is *silatujuq*. Louis-Jacques allows us to meander thoughtfully through the path he uncovers, layer by layer revealing this and other Inuit concepts such as *nuna*, earth or land.

Like many other Indigenous languages, we are at a crossroads where many in our communities are seeing our languages slowly deteriorating. We need to make decisions on protecting our language. Work is being done in our institutions to help protect our language, such as with the Inuktitut Language Commission and the Inuktitut language authorities in Inuit Nunangat; but these efforts go hand-in-hand with knowledge of linguistics and semantic understandings of Inuktitut. *Words of the Inuit* is definitely a resource that must become part of every library in Inuit Nunangat and all schools teaching Inuktitut and Inuit culture and history.

Acknowledgements

For several years, I had entertained the idea of delving more or less systematically into the meanings of Inuit words, in order to decipher the underlying significations many of them hid behind their immediate meaning. Besides anticipating the sheer pleasure of researching a fascinating area of Arctic Indigenous semantics, I wished to bring to light some of the symbolic images underlying Inuktitut, as well as other Inuit languages and dialects.

Many of these images are embedded in words dating back two or three millennia, when the ancestors of all modern Inuit and Yupik groups spoke the same language, called Proto-Eskimo by linguists. Because of changes in pronunciation and meaning that occurred over time, the relationship between these predecessor terms—and the images they convey—and current Inuit words is now obscure to a majority of people. However, there exist linguistic techniques for recovering the links between past and present language. My guess was that if Inuit speakers were made aware of the buried richness—accessed through linguistic analysis—of the words they commonly use, it could support their efforts to reconnect with an identity often undermined by the overwhelming and often brutal influence of the contemporary globalizing world.

My project began to materialize in 2015 when, after three years of retirement, I was asked by former colleagues at Université Laval's Department of Anthropology to teach a one-time semester course on the relationship between Inuit language and culture. In order to set up this course, I had to elicit the words that seemed the most culturally significant for speakers of Inuktitut and begin to look for their basic meanings and context of use. This left me with lexical materials that I started to put into book form in early 2017. From the beginning, I settled upon the title *Words of the Inuit*, inspired by my ethnolinguist colleague John Steckley's book *Words of the Huron*, a thorough description and analysis of the Huron-Wendat lexicon. Between 2007 and 2012, John and I had collaborated with the Wendake

First Nation of Quebec on a project aimed at revitalizing the then-dormant Wendat language, in order, so the Wendake people said, to strengthen their identity through using their ancestors' words (Dorais 2014).

The subtitle to this book (*A Semantic Stroll*) came later on, when I realized that instead of being formatted as a dictionary or a handbook, my work would consist in leisurely, albeit structured, intellectual explorations of words and meanings. Due to the subject matter—lexical and semantic analyses and reconstructions that often could be only tentative—what mattered most was the plausible underlying significations elicited through words, rather than the phonetic and morphological details of one or another specific term. Once again, my primary goal was to provide Inuit—as well as interested non-Inuit readers, of course—with the semantic raw materials that would allow them an in-depth reflection on the richness of their linguistic and cultural heritage and identity.

This book results from my involvement of over fifty years with Inuit as a researcher, *inuuqati* (companion), and *tiguaq* (adopted relative). I owe a special debt to the people of Quaqtaq, a small community of northeastern Nunavik (Arctic Quebec), who welcomed me for the first time in 1965, when I was a twenty-year-old anthropology student (see Introduction). They taught me their language and their way of life, and literally educated the child I then was, completely ignorant of how an *inuusuttuq* (young adult; literally, "one striving to become a human being") should behave. I am also grateful to those Inuit who later in my life helped me to increase my knowledge of their *uqausiit* (words) and *piusiit* (customs), as well as to the organizations that funded my research over the years, the Social Sciences and Humanities Research Council of Canada in particular. To all of them, "*Nakurmiimarialutuinnaq*"— "Genuine, big, and complete thanks."

Many thanks, too, to the colleagues whose insights on Inuit and other Indigenous societies helped refine my intellectual outlook. Regarding the present book, Professors Bernard Saladin d'Anglure, Frédéric Laugrand, and Christopher Trott, as well as two anonymous reviewers, must be specially thanked for their insightful suggestions. Chris Trott in particular accompanied me through the entire creative process, from the initial book proposal to the final editing steps, when a fine publishing team (including Jill McConkey, Glenn Bergen, and freelance copyeditor Maureen Epp) took over at the University of Manitoba Press. And last but not least, a big *nakurmiik* to Lisa

Koperqualuk, a first-rate intellectual, activist, and educator from Nunavik, who kindly agreed to add a foreword to my book.

Finally, almost five decades ago I had the chance to meet and marry a young Vietnamese woman who introduced me to East Asian civilization, a very different world from that of Inuit but at the same time, strangely similar on some points—the fact, for instance, that like humans and animals, souls and spirits belong to nature (Dorais 2007). This explains why a number of brief comparisons between Inuit and Vietnamese language and culture are found throughout the book.

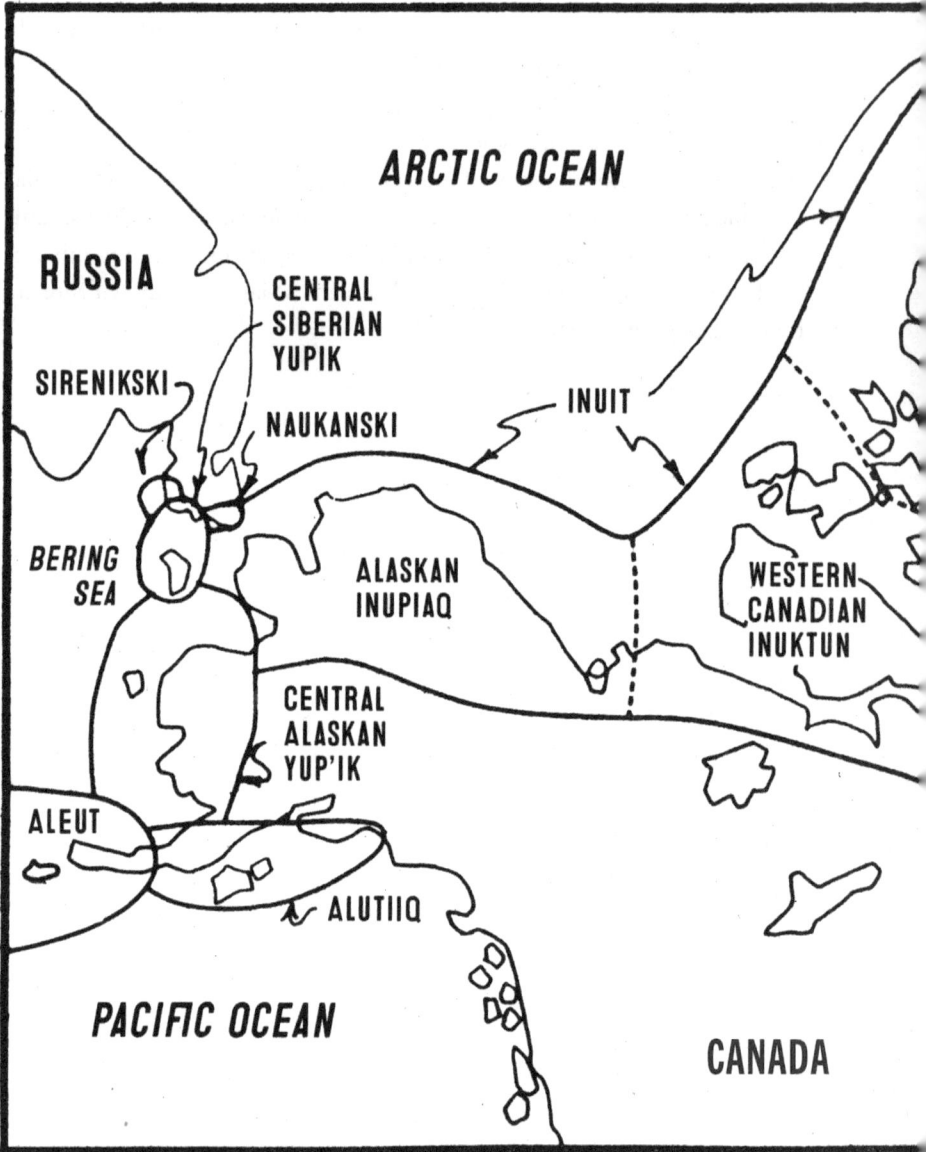

ARCTIC OCEAN

RUSSIA

CENTRAL
SIBERIAN
YUPIK

SIRENIKSKI

NAUKANSKI

INUIT

BERING
SEA

ALASKAN
INUPIAQ

WESTERN
CANADIAN
INUKTUN

CENTRAL
ALASKAN
YUP'IK

ALEUT

ALUTIIQ

PACIFIC OCEAN

CANADA

Map 1. The Eskimo-Aleut World
Adapted from Dorais 2017a, 9, with permission from NAC Media.

GREENLANDIC
KALAALLISUT

ATLANTIC

OCEAN

EASTERN
CANADIAN
INUKTITUT

HUDSON
BAY.

— LANGUAGE BOUNDARIES
- - - BOUNDARIES OF INUIT DIALECTAL GROUPINGS

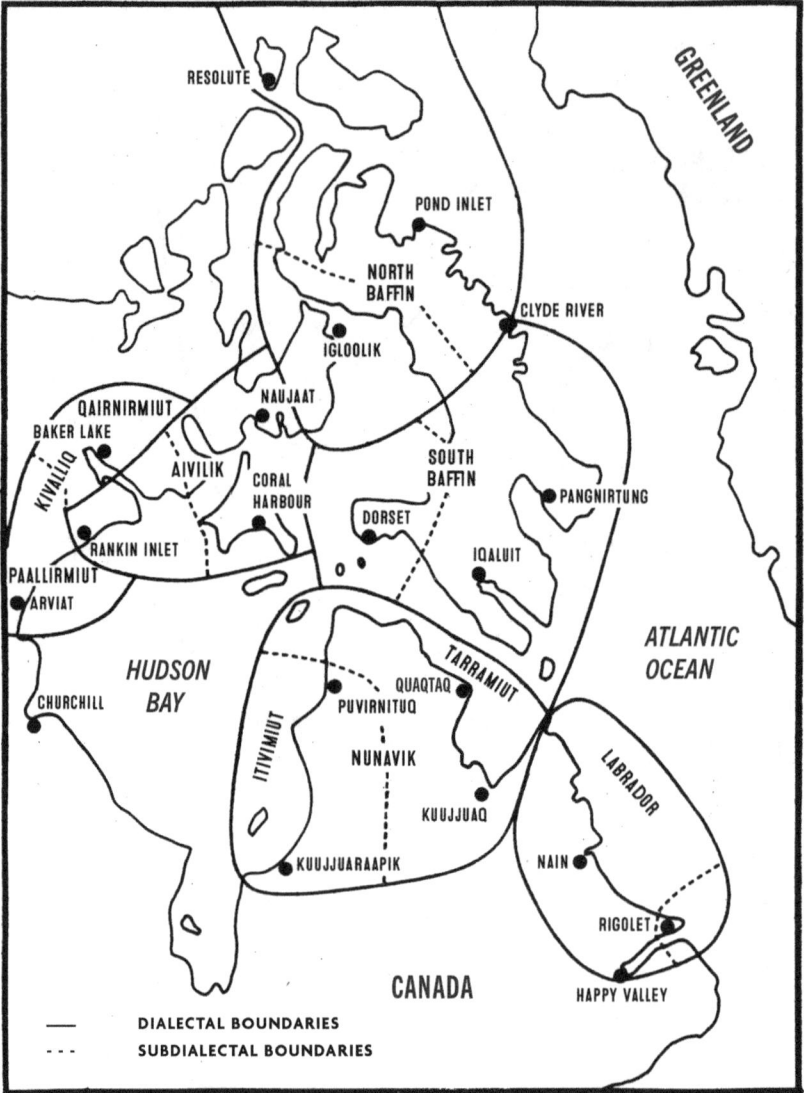

Map 2. Eastern Canadian Inuktitut
Adapted from Dorais 2017a, 133, with permission from NAC Media.

Words from the Past: A Stroll through Inuit Semantics

Uqartuq—Inuk sulinirarsuni isumaminik uqatuarami tagga uqartuq piujumik piunngitumilluuniit.

He/she talks—Because a person, affirming that he/she is truthful, always speaks his/her own idea, thus this person says something good or bad.[1]

TAAMUSI QUMAQ (1991, 101)

This book is about a fascinating language whose speakers are considered to be truthful, even while using words that may hide an underlying meaning. I first encountered this language over fifty years ago, when I started spending summers in the Arctic as a young undergraduate student in anthropology at the Université de Montréal. In 1965 and 1966, I was given the opportunity to conduct fieldwork for my upcoming MA thesis (on Inuit community organization) in Quaqtaq, a small village of 100 people or so, in northeastern Nunavik (Arctic Quebec; see Map 2).[2] All residents were Inuit, except for a Belgian Catholic missionary and a teacher from Saskatchewan who was away on his summer vacation during most of my visits.

At that time, only one Quaqtaq adult spoke any English—acquired during a three-year stay at a southern Canadian hospital—although several children had started learning it in the government school, established there in 1960. This is why, at first, I spent most of my days with the kids, walking through the village and entering their homes with them. Their parents treated me as a big child, and they were right to do so because I was completely incompetent in their language and culture. Despite my initial ignorance, however, this first summer in Quaqtaq (May–September 1965), which included a one-month stay at the nearby hunting camp of Airartuuq, allowed me to participate as best I could in the daily life of the local people, asking "*Suna una*"—"What is this?" as often as I could, in order to learn as many words as possible. But by the end of the summer, I was still unable to speak Inuktitut.

On my way to Quaqtaq, I had stopped in Kuujjuaq to meet with Father Lucien Schneider, who had been working for several years at compiling a dictionary and writing a grammar of the Nunavik dialect. When I returned to Montreal, Father Schneider obligingly gave me a stencilled draft copy of his grammar. With this in hand, and with the help of a basic dictionary of the western Hudson Bay dialect—which included a list of the syllabic writing characters—published in Ottawa ten years earlier by Father Arthur Thibert, I started to write letters in Inuktitut to Inuit patients being treated for tuberculosis at the Roberval sanatorium, north of Quebec City. On average, I was able to send six or seven different letters every Monday and received answers from my correspondents by the end of the same week. In early January, one of them wrote, "Your first letters did not make any sense, but now, I am starting to understand you."

This is how I learned Inuktitut. When I returned to Quaqtaq in May 1966, someone asked me, "How come when you left for Montreal last fall, you did not speak our tongue, but after a winter down South, you are almost fluent?" I had now mastered the basic grammar of the language, but I needed to greatly increase my vocabulary. This was the beginning of a lifelong involvement with Inuit and their language. My doctoral research on the words used by Nunavik and Labrador Inuit for designating a number of objects introduced by *Qallunaat* (people of European origin or descent), as well as subsequent projects conducted during forty years of teaching at Université Laval in Quebec City—including an introductory course in spoken Inuktitut I taught almost yearly—gave me the opportunity to visit a large number of Inuit communities, among them Quaqtaq, where I had acquired an adoptive family who welcomed me to their home every time I went back.

Surface Meaning and Underlying Signification

One aspect of Inuktitut I found particularly striking was the fact that in contrast with languages like English or my native French, many Inuit words could be understood in two different ways. Behind their immediate meaning—the name of the thing, person, idea, or event they were meant to denote—hid, so to speak, a second signification, an underlying definition of or comment on the object or concept being designated. This hidden meaning became apparent when analyzing the linguistic components of the words.

For example, soapstone, the raw material from which many pieces of Inuit art are carved, is called *qullisajaq* in Nunavik.[3] This word can be analyzed as follows:

qulli(q)-(t)sa(q)-jaq[4]

seal-oil lamp – that can be used for – piece of

"a piece of something that can be used for [making] a seal-oil lamp"

Indeed, before the advent of kerosene and later, electricity, Inuit cooked their meals, lit their homes, and heated their igloos and tents with seal-oil lamps made out of soapstone. Hence the name given to this material.

Here is another example. The words *piujuq* and *piunngituq* mean "good" and "bad," respectively.[5] But they may also be understood as follows:

pi-u-juq

thing – to be – he/she/it

"he/she/it is something"

pi-u-nngi(t)-tuq

thing – to be – not – he/she/it

"he/she/it is not something"

This suggests that at some underlying level of Inuit semantics (semantics refers to the meanings expressed through words, word-parts, and grammar), the concepts of "good" and "bad" are understood as an opposition between "being" and "not being." The mere fact of existing would be considered good, while non-existence would be equated with evil.[6] It may therefore be surmised that since *piujuq* and *piunngituq* can be understood both ways, there exists, at a deep semantic level, a link between the two sets of meanings these words convey.

Of course, this is only speculation. Inuit speakers are usually not aware at first of such an equivalency between being and being good, even though they are perfectly capable of recognizing the component parts of their language and of undertaking a practical analysis of the rules for combining them. This shows up, for instance, when they create words for new concepts, as will be seen shortly. However, as with speakers of any other language, very few individuals know the underlying logic that generates the rules allowing them to make up new sentences every time they speak, as well as the hidden meanings buried, so to speak, in the antecedent forms of the words they use on a daily basis. Some specialized linguistic training is therefore necessary for broadening the knowledge Inuit speakers have of their own language, thus enabling them to discover deeper dimensions of Inuktitut and other Inuit dialects.

Something else I discovered when learning Inuktitut was that most words denoting objects and ideas introduced into Inuit culture as a consequence of contact with *Qallunaat* also bore two levels of meaning. In a majority of cases, analysis of the component parts of these words disclosed an underlying description of the practical function or physical look of the denoted concept, as in *timmijuuq* ("that is in the habit of flying," i.e., an airplane) or *kiinaujaq* ("that looks like a face," i.e., money). In some other cases, however, the original meaning of a pre-contact word was applied or extended to a newly introduced concept, as in *ataniq* ("family head," i.e., the king or queen of England) or *atuartuq* ("he/she follows a visible track," i.e., he/she reads). Only completely new terms borrowed from another language, mostly English (e.g., *kaapi*, "coffee"), did not bear two semantic levels. Such words were very few in number.[7]

It was my interest in this phenomenon that led me to focus my doctoral research on what I called modern Inuktitut, words designating newly introduced objects and concepts in Nunavik and Labrador (Dorais 1983). By comparing the underlying meanings of over 2,100 new terms used in various cultural contexts (clothing, motors, medicine, etc.), I sought to understand how, within each context, these meanings—and thus the words that conveyed them—generated a structured discourse demonstrating how Inuit speakers envisioned different contemporary aspects of their culture (Dorais 1977). Later, I applied the same method to semantic contexts more embedded in the pre-contact Inuit world view, such as customary law (Dorais 1984a), animal names (Dorais 1984b), and gender relations (Dorais 1986).

Constructing Inuit Words

The ease with which a large number of Inuit terms, whether new or pre-contact, can be parsed (divided) into meaningful components comes from the polysynthetic structure of the language. Most words result from a process of construction, so to speak, combining a number of concepts that many other languages would express by way of a whole sentence, or at least with more than one word. This happens because Inuit words are usually made up of several morphemes (the word-internal units of signification), each morpheme having its own well-defined meaning. To a lesser degree, this also occurs in English, where for instance the word "houses" includes two morphemes: house- ("dwelling") and -s ("plurality"). In Inuit, however, the specific and often very concrete meaning of each morpheme, as well as its pronunciation, is preserved within all words to which it belongs, as in the *qullisajaq* and *piujuq* examples quoted above, while in English, a term like "houses" is generally perceived as an indivisible unit. This explains why it is easy to parse Inuit words into meaningful parts.

The Appendix to this book presents a relatively extensive grammatical description of Nunavik Inuktitut, the principal Inuit dialect discussed throughout the following chapters. It is important, however, to say a bit more here on how Inuit words are constructed. In Inuktitut, as in other Inuit dialects, words consist of a base—a morpheme that always occurs at the beginning of the word—plus a variable number of added morphemes (from zero to six or more) called affixes, which almost never appear in word-initial position. Some of these (the derivational affixes) are optional. They specify, modify, or transform the meaning(s) conveyed by the base and by each affix that may precede them, and many have a "heavy" signification, translating as full English words. By contrast, the grammatical endings (inflections) are compulsory affixes (one per word) that must generally occur at the end of a word,[8] in order to express its grammatical function as a noun, verb, or other part of speech.

This means that most Inuit words are semantic complexes that combine in an original way the separate meanings of their base, derivational affixes, and ending. Here are a few examples (in Nunavik Inuktitut), with the bases shown in bold type and the endings in italics:

1. **Sini**gusut*tuq*

   sini(k)-gusuk-*tuq*

   to sleep – to need – *third-person singular indicative*

   "He/she needs some sleep"

2. **Illu**jualiurumalaar*tugut*

   illu-(j)jua(q)-liu(r)-ruma-laar-*tugut*

   house – big – to build – to want to – future tense –
   first-person plural indicative

   "We will want to build a big house"

3. **Nuna**kkuujuu*q* **una**

   nuna-kku(t)-u(r)-juu-*q* / **una**

   land – through – to go – usually – *singular number /*
   this one

   "This (is) one that usually goes by land [i.e., a car]"

4. **Angiju***mik* nunakkuujuuqar*tunga*

   angiju(q)-*mik* / **nunakkuujuu(q)**-qar-*tunga*

   something big – *singular direct object* / **car** – to have
   – *first-person singular indicative*

   "I have a big car"

5. **Tupi**alun*nut* **tiki**lau*ravit* **quvia**su*git*

   tupi(q)-aluk-*nut* / **tiki(t)**-lau(r)-*ravit* / **quviasu(k)**-*git*

   tent – big – *to them* / **arrive** – past – *because you /*
   rejoice – *second-person singular imperative*

   "Because you (one) arrived at the big tents, do (you)
   rejoice!"

These examples illustrate several salient characteristics of Inuit words, bases, and affixes:

1. The global meaning of a word may be different from, although related to, the sum of its morphemes, as with *nunakkuujuuq*, "one that usually goes by land" (ex. 3), which functions as a base ("car," ex. 4).

2. Word-bases can begin an utterance, but as a general rule affixes cannot, even when they translate into English as full words or phrases, as with *gusuk-* (ex. 1), "to need" and *liur-* (ex. 2), "to build."

3. The same idea can be conveyed by an affix or by a base, but the two have different forms, as in the case of affixes *-jjuaq-* (ex. 2) and *-aluk-* (ex. 5), "big," versus the base *angiju(q)-* (ex. 4), "something big."

4. Affixes (with any required inflections) can never constitute a whole utterance, except in some instances of colloquial speech (see Appendix), while complex words (base + affix/es + ending) and inflected verbal bases (*quviasugit*, ex. 5, "do rejoice!") do.

The Inuit language is thus fundamentally different from English. However, when acknowledged, this difference does not constitute an obstacle to communication. Once the internal logic of Inuit words and the meaning of some basic morphemes have been understood and assimilated, the language becomes quite easy to follow.

Morphosemantics

The methodology of deciphering the underlying signification of a word through the semantic analysis of its morphemes is called morphosemantics. In addition to serving as a tool for ethnolinguists eager to research semiotics (the system of cognitive signs and symbols undergirding a language and the culture it expresses), morphosemantics is currently used in the computerized classification, parsing, and translation of scientific terms, medical terminology in particular (Namer and Zweigenbaum 2004).

In the Inuit language, a number of words, as well as most word-bases and affixes, cannot be broken down into components meaningful in current speech, even when they have more than one syllable. Some decades ago, it was proposed that this is because the Inuit language had changed over time, evolving from a monosyllabic to a polysyllabic structure. The agglutination of formerly significant monosyllables would have generated the polysyllabic morphemes that are functional in today's language. Etymological research— in this context, comparing homophonous syllables in order to elicit their smallest common meaning—could allow us to parse polysyllables that are semantically indivisible for current speakers into monosyllables that might have been meaningful to Inuit ancestors (Collis 1971).

The idea that the Inuit language was originally monosyllabic has now been abandoned, if it ever was taken into serious consideration. Nevertheless, parsing often yields interesting semantic results. As seen above, this is the case with the word *piujuq*. Subdividing it into three morphemes that happen to be monosyllabic and whose underlying signification ("it is something") is not always acknowledged by modern speakers (for whom *piujuq* may only mean "it is good") constitutes a good example of etymological morphosemantics.

The parsing of *piujuq* accords perfectly with the current grammar of Inuktitut, but this does not happen with every word. For instance, in my morphosemantic analysis of gender relations (Dorais 1986, 176; Dorais 2016, 68), I postulate that the underlying meaning of *ui* ("husband") is "swelling, protuberance," while that of *nuliaq* ("wife") is "little female in heat," two significations that would elicit a rather graphic description of marital relationships. My semantic postulate is based on a hypothetical—and thus debatable—etymological reconstruction of the morpheme *ui* and the disyllable *nuli-* (see Chapter 4). This reconstruction may or may not be accurate, but if it is, it illustrates the assertion of Bach (2009) that in polysynthetic languages, the etymology of what he calls "derivational items" (word-parts) may disclose meanings that have become opaque to current speakers because of lexicalization—the agglutination of separate morphemes, each with its own meaning, into one morphologically and semantically indivisible word (see Dorais 2017b).

Over the years, research in Inuit ethnolinguistics has shown that morphosemantics is very useful indeed for analyzing neologisms—words denoting objects and ideas introduced by *Qallunaat*. Apart from my *Uqausigusiqtaat* (1983), studies on neology in Inuktitut include, among others, dissertations by Cancel (2011), Harnum (1989), and Saint-Aubin (1980), as well as articles by Therrien (2000) and Graburn (1965). Outside Canada, Enel (1982) has researched neologisms in the Inuit dialect of West Greenland, and Berge and Kaplan (2005) have studied aspects of lexical development in Alaska and elsewhere following contact with Europeans. In a more recent paper, Sadock (2017) discusses the role that lexicalized morpheme clusters play in defining the West Greenlandic lexicon, neological or not.

Methodological Issues

When applied to the general, basic pre-*Qallunaat* vocabulary, morphosemantics often tends, as we just saw, to generate seductive but etymologically and semantically questionable significations sometimes rejected by native speakers. As a matter of fact, the most productive way to investigate the wider meanings of Inuit words—both surface and underlying—seems to be one based on the assumption that the lexicon constitutes a total linguistic phenomenon. Words are explainable as proceeding from a mix of grammatical, semantic, semiotic, etymological, sociolinguistic, and other factors, and they are related to each other within significantly structured lexical arrangements. Therefore, they must be understood in terms of their use in actual speech acts (and hence in terms of their cultural and social substratum), as well as through their links with morphological and/or semantic cognates (related forms) and correlates within and beyond the arrangements being studied (Dorais 2016, 74).

As far as Inuktitut and related dialects are concerned, this type of lexicological analysis—where morphosemantics constitutes one tool among several for understanding specific semantic and cultural domains—has yielded more encompassing and productive results than morphosemantics alone. It has generated a number of publications, most of them by French ethnolinguists, such as Therrien's study of the human body (1987) and her reflections on the link between semantics and mental concepts (2002), Randa's dissertation (1994) on the ethnozoology of Igloolik Inuit, Bordin's analytical lexicon of anatomical terms in Inuktitut (2003), Tersis and Mahieu's semantic analysis of some East Greenlandic affixed morphemes (2006), and Cancel's analytical survey of the language used in the public sphere in Nunavut (2011). These studies show that the lexicon has the potential to open a door into Inuit thought and culture. By inserting morphosemantic analysis into a more general examination of relationships between the meanings of words and the cultural context of their use, this type of ethnolinguistic approach allows us to take a closer look at various aspects of the world view of Inuit.

This is precisely what readers are invited to do in the following chapters. The present book is designed as a kind of stroll through the cultural semantics of Inuktitut, that is, through the words and concepts by which contemporary Canadian eastern Arctic Inuit understand and express their culture. It consists in an intellectual walk around the lexicon of Inuktitut, a stroll where words serve as keys to open up Inuit culture and world view. The book includes six chapters, dealing with words for the environment and the land; animals and subsistence activities; humans and spirits; family, kinship, and naming; the human body; and socializing with other people in the contemporary world. Our stroll ends with a reflection on the usefulness for modern Inuit—especially the young—to know about the underlying significations embedded in their language and culture. It is followed by the already mentioned Appendix, which offers a short and hopefully approachable description of the polysynthetic structure of Inuktitut, useful for understanding the very basis of Inuit cognition.

It must be noted that because the present work is not intended to be a study in linguistics, I do not provide readers with a full morphemic analysis of the words whose significations are discussed in the book. Rather than systematically identifying and translating every one of the Inuit morphemes contained in these words (as I did with the *qullisajaq*, *piujuq*, and other examples quoted above), I am content to render the literal meaning of each word as precisely as possible, without adding unnecessary linguistic details. I do provide, however, a practical semantic tool in the form of a Glossary, found at the end of the book. The Glossary lists in alphabetical order each of the more than 1,400 Inuit words discussed throughout the book, together with their current meanings and, when decipherable, their possible underlying significations or etymological links.

Proto-Eskimo Etymologies

Most significations under study here have to do with etymology. Those that do not stem from a straightforward parsing of words into currently used morphemes (synchronic etymology; see the *piujuq* example above) are elicited via a reconstruction of their original meaning (historical etymology). We saw that in some cases, such a reconstruction results from a semantic comparison between potentially cognate syllables and/or syllabic groupings—for instance, *nuli-* (possibly "female in heat") + *-aq* ("small") = *nuliaq* ("little female in heat"); currently "someone's wife." In other cases, however, it is possible and semantically productive to draw on etymological analyses going back further in time, to the era of the Proto-Eskimo language.

Proto-Eskimo (henceforth PE) is a hypothetical reconstruction of the common tongue heard some 2,000 to 2,500 years ago in central western Alaska and shared by the ancestors of those who now speak the Yupik languages (see below) and Inuit dialects. In many cases, PE can disclose hidden significations that would remain inaccessible if morphosemantic analysis limited itself to the current state of the language. Consequently, a large number of PE etymologies appear in this book. All are drawn from the invaluable *Comparative Eskimo Dictionary* (2010) compiled by Michael Fortescue, Steven Jacobson, and Lawrence Kaplan (henceforth cited as Fortescue et al. 2010).

In the mid-1980s, these three scholars, who specialize in Inuit and Yupik linguistics, started to elicit sets of word-bases and affixes drawn from their own field notes and files, from the archives of the Alaska Native Language Center (University of Alaska Fairbanks), and from published dictionaries representing all principal Inuit and Yupik language areas. They then undertook a comparison of the dialectal variants of each of these vocabulary items, looking for systematic differences in sound and similarities in meaning. This allowed them to locate regularities in sound change as well as slight variations in signification. This information was projected back to reconstruct a single root for each item, hypothesizing it as the plausible PE form of the word-base or affix under study, in terms of sound and meaning.

By way of example, in current Inuit dialects and Yupik languages, the following words are found:

akuq	mouth of a river, lower flap of parka (Greenland Inuit)
akuq	tail of a woman's parka (eastern Canadian Inuit)
aku	lower part of garment (western Canadian Inuit)
akuq	lower part of garment (northern Alaskan Inuit)
aguq	skirt (western Alaskan Inuit)
akuq	root of plant (Central Siberian Yupik)
akuq	root, skirt (Naukanski [eastern Siberian] Yupik)
aku(q)	skirt, lower part of garment (Central Alaskan Yup'ik)
akuq	skirt (Alutiiq [south-central Alaskan] Yupik)

Comparison between the sounds and meanings of each of these words has allowed Fortescue et al. (2010, 15) to reconstruct a PE root *aku(r)*[9] that would have meant "space between" or "lower part." This root could have been related to the PE base *akkir-* ("to lift up").

A few words that are now homophonous derive from two or more different PE roots. For example, *sijjaq* means both "beach" and "fox den" in Nunavik Inuktitut, although etymology shows that in the first case, *sijjaq* derives from PE *cinðar* ("beach, shore"), while in the second, it comes from *sitijjaq* ("big mouse hole"). This does not preclude the possibility that some speakers might still see a semantic link between the two meanings (dens can be found on beaches), but such an assumption would not rest on a sound linguistic basis. Homophony is relatively rare, though, and words that yield several different English translations—thus seeming to be homonyms—must usually be considered as one and the same lexical item whose overall meaning encompasses a number of separate *Qallunaat* concepts. As shall be seen in the next chapter, the term *sila* ("outside, weather, air, intelligence, etc.") is a good case in point.

Because the *Comparative Eskimo Dictionary* is my unique source for eliciting PE etymologies with some linguistic reliability, several of my analyses depend on the credibility of its data. This should not be a problem, though, since the work of Fortescue et al. is authoritative, widely recognized for its high scientific value and methodological rigor. Whenever the authors are not absolutely sure about an etymological reconstruction, they qualify it with words and phrases of caution (such as "perhaps" and "possible relationship to") that I have transferred to the present book when quoting the *Dictionary*.

Some Epistemology

One important epistemological question arises at this point: To what degree are etymological reconstructions, those going back to PE in particular, actually significant and hence socially useful for contemporary Inuit? Even though the lexicon of Inuktitut and other Inuit dialects derives directly from PE, modern speakers are not usually aware of the archaic forms of their language, and if they are, they cannot always decipher them.

My answer to this question is that the lack of intelligibility between PE and the current Inuit language mostly concerns pronunciation rather than grammar and semantics. For example, the Inuktitut word *ui* stems from PE *ugi*, although the meaning remains the same: "husband." In some cases, the modern signification of a vocabulary item may differ from its meaning in PE, as in the *aku(r)* example above, but a semantic link can generally be found between the two, as with the PE word-base *kayu-* ("to be strong") that has become *kajusi-* in Inuktitut ("to carry on with something; to persevere"). Indeed, resorting to etymology is particularly telling in this case, because it shows that the original signification of "persevering" is "to start to [-*si*-] be strong," perseverance thus being considered as a form of moral—and perhaps physical—strength. Instances of this type are numerous, where a partial discrepancy between the meaning of a modern word and that of its PE etymon (etymological root) illuminates the underlying signification of the former expression.

The linguist Anthony C. Woodbury has signalled the historical stability of the languages descended from PE. Their lexical and grammatical structure remains essentially the same as that of their common ancestor: "In [Fortescue et al. 2010], modern [word] bases in the daughter languages are reconstructed as bases (or bases plus suffixes) in Proto-Eskimo; while modern suffixes [affixes] are reconstructed as suffixes (or suffix clusters), not as bases" (Woodbury 2017, 550). This stability corroborates my answer to the question raised above. Because the linguistic differences between PE and its derivative languages are largely superficial, most semantic concepts and semiotic images expressed through the original tongue should remain relevant to modern speakers, thus contributing to a deeper understanding of their world view and a strengthened cultural identity.

Still, a caveat must be introduced here. From a strict linguistic perspective, any hypothesis about the origin of a word may be considered conclusive if, and only if, it is supported by a solid etymological analysis such as that proposed by Fortescue et al. in the *Comparative Eskimo Dictionary* or, as far as synchronic etymologies are concerned, if it results from parsing words into currently used morphemes (as in the *qullisajaq* and *piujuq* examples above). Otherwise, such hypotheses must be deemed to rest on mere informed guesswork. They can in no way be considered conclusive and historically valid.

Nevertheless, in my opinion, these "good guesses" may still be valuable to modern Inuit speakers. Despite their lack of a scientific linguistic basis, they stem from apparent similarities between morphemes. These similarities suggest possible—albeit unproved—semantic links that can encourage speakers to contemplate plausible underlying meanings of the words they use, even while knowing that such speculations are not necessarily historically grounded. This is why a number of etymological guesses, identified as such in the main text as well as in the final Glossary of Inuit words, are to be found throughout the book.

Dialects and Orthography

As hinted at earlier in this Introduction, the Inuit language comprises a number of dialects—regional forms of speech that possess their own characteristics but are largely intelligible to speakers of the other dialects. Inuit is also related to several languages that are likewise descended from PE but with which intelligibility is much lower. All these languages (collectively known as Eskimo) plus the more distantly related Aleut tongue (Unangam Tunuu) form the Eskimo-Aleut (or Eskaleut) linguistic family.

Map 1 shows the geographical distribution of Eskimo-Aleut languages. One of them, Sirenikski, is now extinct (its last speaker died around 1990 in the village of Sireniki, northeastern Siberia), but six are still alive, though severely endangered in some cases. These are listed from west to east (Dorais 2010, 28–29):

Aleut: Aleutian Islands and Alaska Peninsula (to the southwest of Alaska)

Central Siberian Yupik: northeasternmost Russia, St. Lawrence Island (Alaska)

Naukanski Yupik: easternmost tip of Chukotka (northeasternmost Russia)

Central Alaskan Yup'ik: southwestern Alaska

Alutiiq Cupik (Yupik): south-central Alaska

Inuit: northern Alaska, Canadian Arctic, Greenland (Kalaallit Nunaat)

The Inuit language constitutes by far the most important form of Eskimo-Aleut, both in geographical range (extending across the North American Arctic) and number of speakers (approximately 100,000 in 2016, including 42,000 in Canada, and more than 50,000 in Greenland).[10] Together with Greenlandic, the Inuktitut dialects (see below) are still very much alive. The language is changing, of course, as it has done for several centuries, but it was and still is able to take on modern life, making use of its grammatical and lexical resources to talk about the contemporary world in its own terms, as shall be seen in Chapter 6. Inuktitut and Greenlandic cannot be considered endangered yet, but some caution is necessary. The Alaskan and western Canadian Inuit dialects, as well as Labrador Inuttut, have stopped being passed on to children for the past three or four decades, and among speakers of Inuktitut, bilingualism might too easily become dominated by English.

The Inuit language can be subdivided into four groups of dialects. Their names—as well as those of some individual dialects—end with the cognate affixes *-titut*, *-tut*, *-tun*, or *-sut*, "[doing or talking] like." Thus, to speak Inuktitut is "to talk like Inuit" (Dorais 2010, 28–29):

Alaskan Inupiaq (Inupiatun): three or four dialects (northern Alaska)

Western Canadian Inuktun: Inuvialuktun/Siglitun (Inuvialuit area of the Northwest Territories), Inuinnaqtun and Nattilingmiutut (Kitikmeot region of the Nunavut territory)

Eastern Canadian Inuktitut: see below

Greenlandic Kalaallisut: three dialects (West, East, and Polar Greenlandic)

Inuktitut is a group of six closely related forms of speech spoken in the eastern Canadian Arctic.[11] It includes the following dialects (Map 2):

Kivalliq: western Hudson Bay (Kivalliq region of Nunavut)

Aivilik: northwestern Hudson Bay (Kivalliq region of Nunavut)

North Baffin: northern Baffin Island (Qikiqtaaluk [or Qikiqtani] region of Nunavut)

South Baffin: southern Baffin Island (Qikiqtaaluk region of Nunavut)

Labrador: Nunatsiavut (northern Labrador) area of Newfoundland and Labrador

Nunavik: northern part of Quebec

Nunavik Inuktitut comprises two slightly different varieties (or subdialects): that of northeastern Arctic Quebec (also known as Tarramiut), and east coast of Hudson Bay (western Nunavik or Itivimiut subdialect). Two of the most salient characteristics common to both varieties have to do with pronunciation. Together with South Baffin and Labrador dialects, Nunavik Inuktitut transforms many consonant groupings (e.g., *kt, gv, bl*) into geminates, or doubles (*tt, vv, ll*). For example, the word "Inuktitut" is pronounced *inu*kt*itut* in North Baffin but *inu*tt*itut* in Nunavik. Moreover, in contrast to most other Inuit dialects, Nunavik does not allow a syllable starting with two consonants to be immediately followed by another syllable of the same type within the confines of a word. This explains why, in the first example at the beginning of this Introduction, when the affixed morpheme *-tsaq-* is added to the word-base *qulli(q)-*, it loses its initial *t* in order to prevent two consonants (*ts*) from following the double consonant (*ll*) already occurring in *qulliq*. In the other Inuktitut dialects (with the exception of Labrador), where this so-called law of double consonants does not apply, what has become *qullisajaq* in Nunavik is pronounced *qullitsajaq* or *qulliksajaq*.

Most words discussed in this book belong to the Nunavik dialect of Inuktitut, more pointedly to its northeastern variety, the one I am acquainted with. If allowance is made for slight differences in pronunciation, often entailed by the gemination (doubling) of consonant groupings and the law of double consonants, a majority of Nunavik words also occur in other Inuktitut dialects. Throughout the book, I sometimes—though not in a systematic way—mention the North Baffin renditions of terms, either by quoting them right after their Nunavik version (*uppik/ukpik; pitsiulaaq/pittiulaaq*) or by putting in square brackets those letters that Nunavik deletes because of the law of double consonants (e.g., *tilli[k]tuq*). This applies to both the words discussed in the text and their listing in the Glossary.

My personal knowledge of the language has provided the largest part of the lexical data set out here, but these have been systematically checked against relevant published materials, namely Father Lucien Schneider's grammar (1972–76), list of affixed morphemes (1979), and Inuktitut-English dictionary (1985), compiled during the 1950s when Schneider was a missionary in northeastern Nunavik. For comparison's sake, I have also consulted the multidialectal (Aivilik, Kivalliq, North Baffin) lexicon of Alex Spalding (1998), a former Hudson's Bay Company trader fluent in Inuktitut.

Two monolingual dictionaries of definitions in Inuktitut were particularly useful for eliciting how Inuit speakers conceptualize their language. *Inuit uqausillaringit* [The genuine words of Inuit] was compiled over several years (1978–86) by Taamusi Qumaq (1991), an elder from western Nunavik.

Qumaq only spoke his native tongue and had never been schooled, but his mother had taught him to write in Inuktitut using the syllabic script. He thus was a genuine Indigenous intellectual grounded in traditional and contemporary Inuit knowledge, who took a deep interest in the structure and semantics of Inuktitut and defined words in relation to his own experience when using them (Dorais 2017b, 138–39). For this reason, his work was for me an indispensable source in understanding which defining traits stand out when a native Inuk speaker analyzes his or her language.

The other dictionary, *Uqausiit tukingit* [The meanings of Inuktitut words], was compiled by a team of North Baffin elders led by Elisapee Ootoova (2000) and coached by local educators. Its definitions, generally shorter and more synthetic than those of Qumaq, are especially interesting from a comparative standpoint.

In this book, the spelling of Inuktitut words largely abides by the rules of the Canadian Inuit Standard Orthography (so), adopted in 1976 by Canada's national Inuit organization, Inuit Tapirisat of Canada, now Inuit Tapiriit Kanatami (Dorais 2010, 180–81). However, I have incorporated a few minor modifications. The so consonant groupings *qp*, *qt*, *qs*, and *qq* are written here as *rp*, *rt*, *rs* and *rq*. By contrast, I keep the so geminates *ll*, *jj*, and *rr* rather than adopting the current Nunavik spellings (*tl*, *tj*, *qr*).

The Standard Orthography accurately transcribes the way Inuktitut speakers pronounce their language. Most Inuit consonants sound as they do in English, with the following exceptions:

q is a uvular stop sounding a little harder (i.e., from farther back in the throat) than Spanish *j* ("J*uan*") or German strong *ch* ("*Achtung!*")

j sounds like English "y" when standing alone between vowels, and like "j" (as in "*Jane*") in clusters

g is pronounced as a continuant (i.e., without a hard stop), somewhat like the letter *gamma* (γ) in Greek

r sounds like the French *R*

There are only three vowels: *a* (as in "marble"), *i* (as in "sleep"), and *u* (as in "June"). When written *aa, ii,* and *uu*, the vowels are long (pronounced with a rather strong emphasis). Groups of more than two vowels (e.g., **aai*) are not allowed.

Seven unfamiliar graphic symbols show up in some words I quote, whether Proto-Eskimo roots or words from dialects other than Nunavik. These are *c* ("ts"); ð and ə (which sound like "th" and "e" in "the"); & (which sounds like "l" without the vocal cords vibrating, as in the Welsh name "Lloyd"); *ġ* (R); *ñ* (as in Spanish); and *ž* (which sounds like a mix between English "r" and French "j"). Nevertheless, I have taken the liberty to use SO graphemes (namely *g*, *ng*, and &) for transcribing three of the non-SO symbols (□, ŋ, and ł) found in Fortescue et al. The (*C*) in parentheses that appears in a few PE roots marks the presence of an undetermined consonant in that position.

Readers should not be surprised to find that some Inuit word-parts translated in a certain way one place in this book may appear with a slightly different translation elsewhere. This is because Inuktitut word-bases and affixes contribute to the construction of a number of different polymorphemic terms. Consequently, the choice of expressions for translating these word-parts into English often depends on the overall meaning of the word within which they are used. This shows that, like morphosemantics and etymology, translation is far from being an exact science.

The latter statement points to the fact that the semantic and etymological analyses found in the present book cannot be considered final. As already discussed, morphosemantic reconstructions are often hypothetical, and Fortescue et al. insist that many morphological and etymological links between Proto-Eskimo roots presented in the *Comparative Eskimo Dictionary* are merely speculative. For these reasons, our perambulation through Inuit words is just that: a series of strolls. The book cannot be seen as a treatise on Inuit semantics, nor as a scientifically definitive compilation of the hidden meanings of words. True enough, all underlying significations proposed in each stroll have plausible bases as far as I know, whether stemming from etymology or informed guesswork, but in some cases, other renditions are equally possible. These significations should therefore be considered primarily as food for thought, glimpses into the symbolic images conveyed by words. My hope is that an awareness of these images will help Inuit to reconnect with their deepest identity, and *Qallunaat* to better understand a fascinating northern culture.

CHAPTER ONE

Words for Speaking about the Environment and the Land

PE cila or **ci&a** "(spirit of) weather or outside world."

PE nuna "land."

FORTESCUE ET AL. (2010, 84 AND 262)

Our stroll starts with words describing the cosmological and geographical environment that has surrounded Inuit since the arrival of their Asian ancestors in the North American Arctic, around 5,000 to 5,500 years before the present. These words are organized around two basic terms, *sila* and *nuna*, which were already in use some 2,000 to 2,500 years ago, when the forebears of contemporary speakers of the Yupik languages and Inuit dialects were living in central western Alaska and shared a common tongue, Proto-Eskimo (PE for short). *Sila*, then pronounced *cila* [*tsila*], seems to have been the name of the spirit who regulated the functioning of the entire cosmos, but the word also denoted—as it still does—the outside world in general, as well as its climatic conditions.[1] The physical nature of the cosmos was thus viewed as inseparable from its supranatural agent.[2] As for *nuna*, it conveys the idea of "solid ground, land" in PE as well as in all contemporary Eskimo-Aleut languages.[3]

Among historical Inuit, those encountered by explorers and early ethnographers, the cosmological regulator was often called *Silap* (or *Silam*) *Inua* ("the Person of the *Sila*"). In some areas (northern Baffin Island, for instance), the shamanic name of *Silap Inua* was *Naarjuk* ("Big Belly"), a giant baby who provoked storms when he loosened his diaper and farted (Saladin d'Anglure 2018, Chapter 3).

Sila

One of my earliest memories of hearing the word *sila* goes back to my first summer in Quaqtaq, during the month I spent in the hunting camp of Airartuuq. On most evenings after supper, I would start to toss balls with Charlie, the eldest son of my Inuit hosts, inside their tent. After a few minutes, Charlie would suggest, "*Silami?*"—"In *sila*?" and we would exit the premises to carry on with our game outside. This is how I became acquainted with one meaning of the word *sila*.

Another meaning I soon learned was when people spoke about weather. They would say, for instance, *silarqituq* ("*sila* is beautiful") when the weather was good, and *silaluttuq* ("*sila* is bad") if it was raining.[4] When I inquired about the pending arrival of an airplane—a big event in the 1960s—I was often told, "*Silarqituarpat*"—"Provided weather is good." I also understood that the air we breathe was called *sila*.

The word *sila* can thus be translated in different ways, but it encompasses one overall concept, that of a regulated externality. Therefore, it may be said to stand at the very basis of Inuit thinking about the environment, defined here as the surrounding milieu, perceptibly and tangibly natural as well as supranatural—that is, natural in another way, comprising various forces and beings often intangible and/or invisible. Beyond its immediate presence, mostly felt through climatic phenomena, *sila* constitutes the fundamental principle that regulates the seasons, the movements of the heavenly bodies, and those of animals (Saladin d'Anglure 1993).[5] No wonder that when the Western concept of "the world, the universe" had to be translated into Inuktitut, it was called *silarjuaq*, "the super-*sila*," or all-embracing externality.

For Inuit, human beings are also regulated by *sila*, and they thus constitute an integral part of the environment.[6] According to traditional northern Baffin cosmology, when a newborn baby takes a breath and utters its first scream, a bubble (*pullaq*) of the ambient air is encapsulated within its body. A miniature of the baby, surrounded by this air, stands at the centre of the bubble, which is released and bursts out at the person's death. With the homunculus encompassed by air borrowed from the larger *sila* (the atmosphere), this internal bubble constitutes a microcosm, thanks to which *sila*'s macrocosmic externality becomes internalized in every individual (Saladin d'Anglure 2018, chap. 3). The mental capacities of each person are influenced by the size and, possibly, the quality of their internal *sila*. Hence the words *silatujuq* ("who has much *sila*"), *silakittuq* ("who has little *sila*"), and *silaittuq* ("who has no *sila*") for distinguishing between wise, not so wise, and stupid individuals. In this way, one's abilities for acting in a reasonable way are linked to *sila*.

Another, perhaps more contemporary way of understanding the mental dimension of *sila* is the interpretation of the word *silatujuq* given by Betsie Annahatak, a Nunavik educator: "One who has a big world" (2014, 28). A person full of wisdom will be able to understand the interconnections of all beings in the world (*sila*), while a *silakittuq* ("small world") individual will have a limited perception of this interconnectedness.

The Seasons

The seasons of the year constitute a major manifestation of *sila*. In northeastern Nunavik there are six of them, divided according to various climatic events (Saladin d'Anglure 2013, 31):

ukiuq	winter (November to early May)
upirngasa(a)q[7]	spring ("the incoming *upirngaaq*"; May to late June)
upirngaalaaq	early summer ("the very small *upirngaaq*"; early July)
upirngaaq	summer[8] (mid-July to the end of August)
ukiatsaq	early fall ("the incoming *ukiaq*"; September)
ukiaq	fall (October)

According to their terminology, the seasons are divided into two groups, the *uki-* (of unknown etymology) and the *upi-*. During the former, the land and water progressively freeze, becoming covered with snow and ice from late October to early May. The latter are characterized by the progressive thaw of the land, lakes, and sea, whose snow and ice cover has completely disappeared by the month of August.

The words *ukiuq* and *ukiaq* are semantically related, the latter meaning "lesser *ukiuq*." Since winter lasts as long as all other seasons combined, it is no wonder that in Inuktitut the term *ukiuq* also applies to a whole year. For instance, one may be asked, "*Qatsinik ukiuqalirqit?*"—"How many winters do you have?" ("How old are you?"). When language specialists had to translate the word "Arctic," they chose the term *Ukiurta(r)tuq*, "the one where winter lasts for a long time."

The word-base *upi-* might be related to PE *upət-*, "to get excited, surprised, or to rush about."[9] With the addition of the affix *-rngaaq* ("one that does it for the first time"), the word *upirngaaq* ("summer or spring") would thus mean something like "which is surprised—or surprising—at first," perhaps an allusion to the sudden thawing conditions after eight or nine months of fall and winter freezing.

Rain, Snow, and Ice

We have seen that *sila* can affect people, either positively or negatively: *silarqi(r)tuq* ("*sila* is beautiful") when the sun shines; *silaluttuq* ("*sila* is bad") when it rains. Rain itself is called *surujuk* (possibly related to the base *sujuk-*, "to deteriorate"), while hail is *natarqunaq*, where the word-base *natarquq* ("cartilage") is followed by the affix *-naq*, which according to Fortescue et al. (2010, 457) means "something resembling." Hailstones would probably be likened to cartilage because of their firm, but crisp, texture. Extreme atmospheric humidity can generate fog (*tatsiq*), which is dispersed by wind (*anuri*). During summer, thunderstorms may occur (*kallu*, "thunder"; *qaummalak*, "which gives light once," i.e., lightning), but they are infrequent in the Arctic.

The prevailing winds play—or used to, before the advent of GPS devices—a crucial part in finding one's way when travelling and/or talking about directions. Consequently, they have been given names of their own. In northeastern Nunavik, there are four major winds (Saladin d'Anglure 2013, 23): *uanniq* (etymologically, "from down there," northwest wind); *nigiiq* (east wind); *qavannganiq* ("coming from inside [from inland?]," south wind); *atuarniq* ("following a path," north wind). In other areas of the Arctic, similar names may be used, but they do not necessarily refer to the same directions.

When it stops raining, an *ajagutaq* may appear in the sky, "a means for separating two parallel objects" (e.g., the runners of a sled); in other words, a rainbow that splits the sky (between sun and rain?). Outside of Nunavik, the rainbow is sometimes named *kataujaq* ("which looks like the doorway of a snow house").[10] Clouds are called *nuvujait* (singular, *nuvujaq*), a term that recalls the word *nuvuk* ("cape, point") but that is actually a modern rendition of the Proto-Inuit[11] *nuviya* and is etymologically related to *nuvə-*, "sinew thread." This means that clouds could have been envisioned as pieces (*-jait*) of thread in the sky. However, this does not preclude the possibility that some contemporary speakers of Inuktitut see a similarity of form between the words *nuvujaq* and *nuvuk*, and perceive clouds as capes or promontories floating in the sky, like the aerial islands in the 2009 movie *Avatar*.

From September on, rain changes to snow. The "one hundred Eskimo words for snow" is a well-known although often misunderstood example of how a language enables its speakers to make very fine distinctions among sets of semantic categories that characterize important cultural elements (Kaplan 2003; Dorais 2010, 135–36). For some unknown reason, people who cite this example often assert that the allegedly large number of Inuit words for snow ends in a two, variously claiming thirty-two, fifty-two, or even 102 different words for defining various types of snow (Steckley 2008).

Actually, in Nunavik Inuktitut—and the situation is the same in other dialects—I know of only seven words whose unique function is to denote a particular form of snow:

qanik	falling snow
masak	wet falling snow
aputi(k)	snow on the ground
pukak	crystalline snow on the ground
aniu	snow for making water
mannguq	melting snow
sirmiq	melting snow used as cement for the snow house[12]

However, Inuit are able to distinguish between at least twenty-five—and probably many more—different snow conditions (Dorais 2010, 135–36), expressed by way of dedicated terms (such as *qanik*, above) or through semantically more encompassing words whose meaning denotes a certain type of snow when used in specific contexts:

illusaq	material for a house, i.e., snow fit for making a snow house
maujaq	soft ground, i.e., soft snow on the ground
kinirtaq	something compact, i.e., damp, compact snow[13]
aqilluqaaq	very tender material (e.g., cooked meat), i.e., drift of soft snow
piirsituq	it carries things away, i.e., there is a blizzard of snow

It is plausible that some of the dedicated terms listed above may be etymological derivatives whose literal meaning is no longer decipherable to most current speakers. For instance, the word *aputi(k)* ("snow on the ground") might comprise the PE word-base *apə-* ("to become covered in snow") plus the affix *-un* ("a means to do it"). The literal, etymological meaning of *aputi(k)* would thus be "a means to cover with snow," a rather tautological definition, I admit.

Ice is as important as snow to Inuit, and their language allows them to make a very large number of semantic distinctions between different types of frozen water (Gearheard et al. 2013, chap. 7). A dictionary of terms related to sea ice in the Inupiatun dialect of Wales, Alaska, includes more than 110 entries (Weyapuk and Krupnik 2012).[14] Ironically, even if there probably exist more semantic distinctions for ice than for snow, only the alleged "one hundred words for snow" are commonly heard about, possibly because in *Qallunaat* minds, Inuit are primarily identified with snow (e.g., snow houses) rather than ice.

As was the case with snow, some of the distinctions for ice resort to dedicated words, while others make use of more general terms that apply to ice when employed in specific contexts. Here are a few examples of dedicated ice words in Nunavik Inuktitut:

siku	sea ice
nilak	freshwater ice
tuvaq	ice floe
piqalujaq	iceberg
qainnguq	ice that adheres to the shore

Once again, some of these seemingly mono-morphemic words that cannot be parsed into smaller meaningful units may derive from etymologically more complex terms. This is the case with *piqalujaq*: its Proto-Inuit form (*pəqaluyak*) might be related to PE *pəqu-* ("to bend or be bent"), according to Fortescue et al. (2010, 279). An iceberg would be seen as a piece of ice progressively deformed by its ongoing thawing. As far as the word *qainnguq* ("adhering shore ice") is concerned, it could be linked to PE *qa(C)əru(r)*, "[birch] bark" (Fortescue et al. 2010, 301), possibly because shore ice breaks away from land like birch bark detaches itself from the tree.

In the same vein, Inuktitut has several words for speaking about temperature, cold or warm. Something freezing is *qiujuq*, and if I say "*Qiujunga!*"—"I am freezing," it means I am very cold indeed. Any deeply frozen solid material (earth, meat, fish, etc.) is called *quaq*, a modern freezer being a *quaqauti* ("container for frozen things"). *Qiujajuq* ("he/she freezes repeatedly") means that someone is cold because the temperature has become *qiujanartuq* ("that makes one being cold") or *ijjilirtuq* ("that gets coldness," i.e., "that is very cold"). The *qiujajuq* individual may then exclaim, "*Ikkii!*"—"How cold!" A body or object that is progressively cooling down is said to be *nillatuq* or *nillijuq*, and a cooling atmosphere is *nillinartuq* ("that makes one become colder").

Conversely, someone who is hot is said to be *urquusiurtuq* ("who searches after warmth"), and the temperature is *urquujuq* ("that is warm") or *kiappaluttuq* ("that generates a feeling of warmth").[15] This person might exclaim, "*Urquuq!*"—"How hot!" In the Arctic, of course, despite global warming, this exclamation is still mostly heard inside an overheated house rather than outside of it. The word *urquujuq* literally means "it is an *urqu*" (i.e., a spatial position sheltered from the wind), prototypical warmth thus being directly linked to a manifestation (the wind) of *sila* ("weather").[16] The term *urqu* ("leeward side") may derive from PE *uqər* ("lee, shelter") + *-qur* ("associated with"), thus meaning "associated with a shelter" (Fortescue et al. 2010, 413). A hot object or a feverish person is *uunartuq* ("that makes one being burned"), and if I touch such an object, I am allowed to scream, "*Atataa!*"—"Ouch!" Boiling water (*tirtituq*, "it boils") is *uunartuq*, too, which is not the case if water is *nirumittuq*, "tepid" (etymologically, "soft and warm").

Light, Darkness, and the Heavenly Bodies

Because of its function as the ordering principle of the universe, *sila* regulates the alternation between light and darkness, day and night, the sun and the moon and stars. According to a myth from Igloolik in the northern Baffin Region, the world was formerly in perpetual darkness. As a result, life was extremely difficult for humans and for some animals (Rasmussen 1929, 253). One day, the fox and the raven were talking together. The fox, who hunts at night, was comfortable with obscurity, but the raven was not. The raven shouted, "*Qau! Qau!*"—"Light! Light!" The fox replied, "*Taaq! Ta-aq!*"—"Darkness! Darkness!" From then on, day alternated with night. According to Saladin d'Anglure (2018, 52), who relates this myth, "the raven's cry *Qau!*, which means 'day, daylight' in the Inuit language also means 'forehead' and is the root of *qaumaniq*, 'light,' or aura (the one that surrounds a shaman) and *qaujimaniq*, 'knowledge.'"

Light is thus understood by Inuit as manifesting in at least three ways: physically (*qau*, "daylight, dawn"), mentally (*qaumaniq*, "the fact of diffusing light," i.e., shamanic enlightening knowledge),[17] and intellectually (*qaujimaniq*, "the fact of having become aware," i.e., acquired knowledge).[18] Its opposite, *taaq* ("darkness, obscurity"), derives from PE *tarər-*, which is related to *tarniq*, "human soul" (etymologically, "being dark" [Fortescue et al. 2010, 363]), *tau* (derived from *taru*), "human being" in the special language once used by shamans, and *tarraq*, "shadow."

Sila's control over light and darkness has generated the alternation between day and night. *Ullu(q)* is the period of time, longer or shorter according to the season, when there is light.[19] Nowadays, in all Inuit dialects, the words for "evening" and "night" are *unnuk* and *unnuaq*, respectively, but in PE—and still now in the Yupik languages—*unnuk* denoted the daily period of darkness, while *unnuaq* ("small *unnuk*") only referred to early morning, when light is about to appear. Morning itself is called *ullaaq* ("small *ullu[q]*"). Since contact with Europeans became prevalent, the word *ullu(q)* has been used for denoting the twenty-four-hour day, hence *ullumi* ("in *ullu[q]*"), "today." In Nunavik Inuktitut and several other Canadian dialects, the word for "tomorrow" is *qauppat*, literally, "when there will be light"; while "yesterday" is *ippa(k)saq*, literally, "which will become [a period of time that occurred] some time ago."

Daylight comes from the sun, *siqiniq*, a woman holding a torch who is pursued by her incestuous brother, according to an important myth (Saladin d'Anglure 2018, chap. 4). The brother is the moon, *tarqiq*, who was the special protector of women in shamanic times. The word *tarqiq* also means "month," either traditional (lunar) or modern (calendar). *Siqiniq* and *tarqiq* move across the sky, *qilak*, a word that also denotes the vault or dome of the snow house and the roof of the mouth, as well as the Christian heaven. Etymologically, *qilak* derives from PE *qilag*, "sky." It is homophonous with the verbal base *qilak-* ("to weave, to tie" [PE *qilag-*]). One might thus postulate that the firmament is considered to be inseparable from (tied to) *nuna*, the earth, or that it weaves a net over *nuna*. The sky is also home to the stars and planets, *ulluriat*.[20]

The literal significations of some of the words just mentioned disclose interesting links with modern astrophysics. *Siqiniq* means "splashing, exploding" (more specifically, "sprinkling" in Nunavik Inuktitut), which evokes solar nuclear explosions as well as the radiation they emit. The *ulluriat* (singular *ulluriaq*) are "emissions of daylight," that is, elements that radiate. The native Alaskan linguist Edna Ahgeak MacLean (1990, 169) translates the Iñupiaq word *uvluġiaq* (*ulluriaq*) as "pathway for light," thus stressing the fact that light is in motion. As for *tarqiq*, it derives from PE *tanqir* ("light, moon"; Fortescue et al. 2010, 360), but modern Inuktitut speakers may understand it as "beautiful obscurity" (*ta[a]q-* ["darkness"] + *-rqiq* [as in *sila*rqiq, "nice weather"]), a meaning verging upon poetry.

Arctic nights are also illuminated by the northern lights, particularly frequent and spectacular at these latitudes. They are called *arsa(r)niit* (singular *arsa[r]niq*), "games of ball." This apparently strange name stems directly from traditional Inuit cosmology. Before Christianization, the souls of those who had died suddenly went up to the sky, where they spent part of their time playing soccer with a walrus skull (Saladin d'Anglure 2018, 56). People looking at *arsa(r)niit* are thus watching the reflection of the ball games of the dead. They can try to communicate with these spectral players by whistling at northern lights and imitating their dance movements, but the heavenly souls might feel challenged and cut off the heads of those who upset them.

Nuna

Next to *sila*, *nuna* is the other basic term summarizing Inuit thinking about environment. The word is well-known to non-Inuit in its modern meaning of a bounded territory, politically defined or not, because the names of such territories generally start with—or include—the noun base *nuna*-: Nunavut ("Our Land," the northern Canadian autonomous jurisdiction established in 1999), Nunavik ("Huge Land," Arctic Quebec), Nunatsiavut ("Our Beautiful Land," northern Labrador), Inuit Nunangat ("Land of the Inuit," the Inuit homeland, i.e., the areas of Canada ancestral to Inuit), and Kalaallit Nunaat ("Land of the *Kalaallit* [Greenlanders]," the self-governing island of Greenland).

As is the case with *sila*, the etymology of the word *nuna* is unclear, although its second syllable, -*na*, might well be the same one found at the end of nominal localizers in their singular basic form (see Appendix): *u*na ("this one"), *pan*na ("that one up there"), and so forth; it also occurs at the start of locative questions like na*ni* ("where?") and na*mut* ("whereto?"). Such a speculative morpheme -*na* could thus be demonstrative ("that, there"), pointing at a specific spatial location. The etymological semantics of *nuna* might then be hypothesized to include the idea of being positioned in space (i.e., within *sila*).

The Inuit concept of *nuna* includes much more than the ethnic and political significations just mentioned. In its most basic usage, it means "earth" and denotes dry, solid land, as opposed to *imaq* or *imiq*, "water," and especially to *tariuq* ("[the] salty [one]") or *imaaluk* ("big water"), the sea. More specifically, however, *nuna* is understood as those land areas inhabited by humans.[21] In the spring and summer of 1968, my colleague Bernard Saladin d'Anglure and I visited all the villages in Nunavik to survey Inuit place names, land use, and occupancy.[22] The question we asked in order to find out if a specific location was or had been inhabited was *"Nunagijaulaursimava?"*—"Was it ever had as a *nuna*?" Uninhabited places were said to be *nunagijaunngituq*, "which is (or was) not had as a *nuna*." In former times, it was hazardous to venture into *nunagijaunngitut* zones, far from habitation and devoid of human footprints, where one was liable to meet with spirits (Saladin d'Anglure 2018, 122).[23] This relation between land and human occupation had nothing to do with territorial ownership—a concept introduced by governments during the 1970s. Rather, it stemmed from the understanding that the primordial role of *nuna* is to be home to sentient beings and the resources they need for living, as expressed by Taamusi Qumaq in his definition of the word *nuna* (1991, 394):

Nuna   *Aulajuittuq. Taimannganialuk inuit uumajuillu nunangat, pirurvingat tuquvigivatsugulu. Nuna pirurtulik, imalik, niqilik, inulik amisurjuanik, ajjigiinngitunik tauttungit. Uqausiqaqatigiinnginiq tatattuq.*

Land   It cannot move. For a very long time, it has been the
                nuna of people and animals, the place where they
                grow and also the place where they die. *Nuna* has
                plants, water,[24] food, many people whose physical
                appearances are different [from others']. It is filled
                with languages unintelligible to each other.

For Qumaq, *nuna* is an all-inclusive space that gives life to people and animals and produces in abundance everything they need to exist. The people belong to a large variety of races ("different physical appearances") and
speak various languages, although sharing a common humanity.

It is worth mentioning that while Qumaq defines *nuna* as immobile
(*aulajuittuq*) and thus firm and solid, his definition of *sila* (1991, 462) starts
with the assessment of its emptiness: "*Silatuinnaq pitaqanngituq*"—"*Sila* by
itself has nothing [is void]." The definition then mentions the fact that *sila*
allows people to breathe and gives them the ability to see far away (because
of its emptiness). The two basic elements of the global environment, *sila* and
nuna, are thus seemingly considered as opposites—the former void and ethereal, the latter firm and solid—but complementary. Sentient beings need
both *nuna*, to find a home, and *sila*, to survey what lies beyond their immediate confines. This distinction between *sila* and *nuna* ripples throughout
Inuit cosmology, mythology, and daily practices in ways far too numerous
to be discussed here.

Inhabiting *Nuna*

Since *nuna* is primarily understood as inhabited, the most common way
to inquire about a person's abode is to ask him or her, "*Nani nunaqarqit?*"—"Where do you have [your] *nuna*?" The answer might be "*Kuujjuaq
nunagijara*"—"I have Kuujjuaq as [my] *nuna*," or "*Taunani qallunaani nunaqartunga*"—"I have [my] *nuna* down there among *Qallunaat* [non-Inu-
it],"[25] or "*Tariup akiani nunaqartunga*"—"I have [my] *nuna* across the sea
[in Europe or Africa]." The semantic extension given to one's *nuna* may vary
according to the context of the question.

As already mentioned, political developments that have occurred since
the 1970s—Indigenous territorial claims in particular—have added a new
dimension to the word *nuna*: that of a land partly or totally owned and

administered by its Aboriginal occupants.[26] We have seen above that the names of most Inuit-held territories include the morpheme *nuna* (Nunavut, Nunavik, etc.). *Nuna* also refers to the larger jurisdictions (provinces, states, countries) known to the Indigenous inhabitants of the Arctic. For example, *Kanata* (Canada), *Kupaik* (Quebec), *Manitupa* (Manitoba), *Alaasika* (Alaska), and *Amirika* (the United States) are all *nunait*.[27]

Before Inuit became a sedentary people—in Canada, this mostly occurred during the 1950s and '60s—all of the camps they occupied at different seasons of the year were considered to be *nunait*. With the creation of sedentary villages, a specific term had to be coined in order to distinguish between permanent and temporary settlements. In the eastern Canadian Arctic, the word chosen for "village" was *nunalik* ("which has a *nuna*," or "there is a *nuna*"), to underline the fact that such a location was an established and organized community, often with its own municipal administration, that was indeed an inhabited land deserving to appear on maps (*nunannguat*, "imitations of the land"), where the former seasonal camps were not shown at all.

One effect of this semantic evolution was that *Nuna*, "the Land" with a capital L, has become a strong symbol of Inuit identity and political rights. Nowadays, *Nuna* is often seen as somewhat antithetical to the *nunaliit*. The Land is the preferred place for practising the hunting, fishing, camping, and other activities that define Inuit culture, while villages are dominated by *Qallunaat*-inspired institutions (the schools, cash economy, government, electronic media, etc.) and are seen as fraught with drugs, alcohol, and other undesirable elements. In Nunavik, most individuals highly valorize *maqaivvik*, the "place where one goes out of the village" in order to experience the genuine Inuit way of life. This is the Land at its best: the traditional hunting and fishing locations once used as seasonal camps. When staying at the *maqaivvik*, people leave their problems aside and the young can reconnect with the culture of their grandparents (Dorais 1997, 88–92).

There exists a very practical affix for designating the dwellers of a particular *nuna*: *miut* (singular -*miuq* or -*miutaq*), "inhabitants of." It can be added to any place name (that of a camp, village, city, province, country, etc.), as in *Iqalummiut* ("people of Iqaluit [the capital of Nunavut]"), *Kupaisitimiut* ("people of Quebec City"), or *Kanatamiut* ("Canadians"). Besides "*Nani nunaqarqit?*" another way of asking people were they live is "*Nani*miu*nguvit?*"—"You are an inhabitant of where?"

The meaning of -*miut*/-*miuq* also extends to people who stay temporarily at some place. If, for instance, I meet someone whom I know to be a visitor to my village, and ask that person where he or she is staying, the answer might be something like "*Aanniavim*miu*ngujunga tagga*"—"For now, I am a -*miuq* of the hospital," or "*Miajikku*miu*ngujugut*" ("We are -*miut* of Mary's family"). Actually, when the semantic context allows it, this affix may refer to anyone or anything occupying a specific location, as in "*Quaqauti*miu*ngulirtuq aisikirimtara*"—"My ice cream is now a -*miuq* of the freezer." In some Inuit dialects (but not in Nunavik as far as I know), a fetus is called *ilu*miu*(ta)q* ("dweller of the [body's] inside [*ilu*]"). Etymologically, -*miut*/-*miuq* derives from PE -*miru*, which could result from combining the locative case of the nominal declension, -*mi* (see Appendix), with the affix -*ngu*, "to be" (Fortescue et al. 2010, 455); -*miuq* would thus mean "one who is there." In modern Inuktitut, however, there exists a distinction between the affixes -*(ng)u*-, "to be something" (like *ser* in Spanish), and -*it*-, "to be somewhere" (cf. Spanish *estar*). The latter morpheme always follows the locative grammatical ending, as in *nuna*miit*tuq*, "he/she is on the land."

Describing *Nuna*

Physically, *nuna* comprises a variety of elements (hills, lakes, rivers, shores, etc.) that help shape its different landscapes. These elements can be made up of water (*imaq* or *imiq*) or of solid materials such as rock (*ujaraq*), soil (*ijjuk*), clay or mud (*ma[r]raq*), or sand (*siuraq*). According to Fortescue et al. (2010, 120, 142), the words for "water," *imaq* and *imiq*, derive from two separate PE roots: *ima(r)* ("contents of something, especially of the sea") and *əmər* ("fresh water"). This explains why the first term generally refers to salt water—including its sea-dwelling creatures if *imaq* is perceived as "contained" in the sea—and the second to drinkable water.

Etymologies can also be suggested for the solid materials enumerated above. The word *ujaraq* might presumably be related to PE *uyag*- ("to stretch neck, to emerge from some place"), followed by the passive ending -*raq*. It could thus mean "what has been made to emerge, to protrude." *Ijjuk* (*ibjuk* west of Hudson Bay) comes from PE *(n)əvður* ("sod"), while *ma(r)raq* could be related to PE *maqə*- ("to ooze") and *maqu*- ("to suppurate") (Fortescue et al. 2010, 211). As for *siuraq*, it might be an alternative form of *sivuraq*,[28] a stable surface extending in front of something, such as a beach of sand. Although *siuraq* looks somewhat similar to *sijjaq*, the appellation for "beach, shore," this latter term is actually related to PE *cingə(t)-*, "to shove" (the water back?) and *cingig*, "point of land" (Fortescue et al. 2010, 88–89).

Intimately linked to *nuna*, the *nunajait* (singular *nunajaq*), "pieces of *nuna*," consist of all the small things that can be found on the ground. These include lichens, moss, and plants (*pirurtuit*, "those that grow"), as well as detached objects such as small stones and bits of animal feces. Edible plants— most of them berries, *paurngait* ("those firstly fastened down [i.e., newly or temporarily attached to the soil?]")—have their own names: *arpik* (Arctic raspberry), *kigutangirnaq* ("which makes one lose his/her teeth [because of its acidity]," Arctic blueberry), *kimminaq* ("which makes one grit his/her teeth [because it is sour]," huckleberry), *qunguliq* ("being sour," wild sorrel), and so on. Someone who gathers edible *nunajait* (and also shellfish, in Nunavik) is a *nunivattuq* (etymologically, "one who prowls about the real—or big—*nuna*"). Bigger objects also grow out of *nuna*: bunches of willow or other shrubs (*urpik*; possible etymology, "real shelter"), and in the southernmost Inuit territories, trees (*napaartuit*, "those that stand up"). The word for "wood," locally grown or driftwood (*tijjaluk*; etymologically, "drifted ashore") is *qijuk*. In Nunavik, this term also applies to any form of solid fuel (e.g., seal or whale blubber).

A partial list of elements shaping the landscape includes the following:

nuvuk	cape, promontory (also, the tip of any pointed object)
tikiraq	point of land ("that looks like an index finger [*tikiq*]")
qairtuq	high rock ("that has nothing on top [that is only rock]")
kangirsuk	bay, cove ("that looks like a location nearer to land")[29]
qarqaq	hill, mountain ("high area")
tasiq	lake ("that stretches out")
qikirtaq	island (related to *qikar-* [?]["to stay there doing nothing"])
kuuk	river ("that flows")

As already mentioned, water (*imaq, imiq*) belongs to *nuna* when it is perceived as a home and provider for men and animals, but at the same time, it is semantically opposed to *nuna* as solid ground. We saw that the sea is called *imaaluk* ("big water") or *tariuq* ("[the] salty [one]"),[30] the latter term also meaning "table salt" in Nunavik. *Imaq* can be *itijuq* ("deep") or *ikkatuq* ("shallow"), with a shoal being called *ikkaruq* ("that becomes shallow"). The sea is subject to tides, either rising (*ulittuq*, "it [the shore] becomes covered") or running out (*tinittuq*; possibly related to PE *tənu-*, "to push down"). When it is windy, there can be *maliit*, shattering waves (presumably related to Yupik *ma&əg-*, "to be close, to press up against") or *ingiuliit*, swells (perhaps, "to form ridges back and forth" [Fortescue et al. 2010, 153]).

The water/land opposition has a strong symbolic value. This translates directly into traditional practices and representations concerning animals. In older times, for instance, it was strictly forbidden to cook and eat sea and land mammal meat together; this taboo also extended to fish versus land mammals, as well as seabirds versus land birds. Whenever possible, separate plates and utensils had to be used for handling animal flesh belonging to each of the two domains. In spite of this division, some important species of sea and land mammals had their symbolic equivalent in the opposite category (Randa 2002). For example, the walrus with its tusks was considered to be the marine equivalent of the antler-bearing caribou.

In Inuktitut, words denoting elements of the landscape are extensively used as place names. Before GPS was introduced, toponymy allowed travellers to learn about the physical features they would encounter when travelling on a sled, snowmobile, or boat. Place names may also reveal something about the natural resources available at different locations. Here are a few examples:

Kuujjuaq (the administrative centre of Nunavik): "The huge river"

Kangirsujuaq (a Nunavik village): "The huge bay"

Qamanittuaq (village of Baker Lake, Nunavut): "The huge widening in a river"

Kinngait (village of Cape Dorset, Nunavut): "The hills, the mountains"

Iqaluit (the capital of Nunavut): "The fish"

Imilik (a camp on Ungava Bay, Nunavik): "There is freshwater"

Airartuuq (a camp on Ungava Bay, Nunavik): "Where edible roots are plentiful"

Pangnirtuuq (a Nunavut village): "Where bull caribou are plentiful"[31]

Taking One's Bearings

When travelling or hunting, it is essential to ascertain one's position in space and that of one's game. In Inuktitut, location can be expressed in relation to oneself or to something else. The Appendix shows that there exists a specific lexical class, localizers (and their subclass of nominal localizers), consisting of words that identify well-defined spatial positions or entities positioned in specific portions of space. These positions are defined in relation to the speaker unless the words denoting them are preceded by *ta(q)-* (the only prefix in Inuktitut), which indicates that the speaker is referring to a point in space already mentioned in the conversation. In Nunavik Inuktitut, there are ten localizers. Here are examples of each of them in the locative case, together with their associated nominal localizer:

uvani	here very close
una	this one close to me
maani	here
manna	this one
ikani	there
inna	that one
avani	there away
anna	that one farther away
pikani	up here
pinna	this one up here
paani	up there
panna	that one up there
kanani	down here
kanna	this one down here
unani/samani	down there

unna/sanna	that one down there
qamani	inside
qanna	this one inside
kiani	here outside
kinna	this one close outside

This system is fairly simple. It subdivides space into a limited number of domains, according to three pairs of criteria: proximity/distance, height/depth, and internality/externality. The fact that an entity is more or less easily perceptible can influence the estimation of its distance: an object that is equidimensional (whose length is more or less equal to its width) and/or immobile may be deemed closer than a non-equidimensional and/or mobile one (Dorais 2010, 147–48).

In a practical way, localizers allow speakers to identify immediately the portion of space or the entity they want to point out. For example, if I am in a canoe and see an eider duck flying not too far away, all I have to say is, *"Mitiq pinna!"*—"A duck, this one up here!" and provided my hunting companions are aware of my position in the canoe, they will immediately know where to look in order to try shooting at the bird.

Space can also be delimited in reference to people or entities other than the speaker. This is the case with the geographic directions. In most areas of the Arctic, in addition to the orientation of the prevailing winds (see above), there are two crucial directions for Inuit: seaward and landward. The former is always considered to lie downward (*ununga* or *samunga*, "toward down there") and the latter upward (*paunga*, "toward up there"), relative to the position one occupies. If the seashore happens to be in an easterly direction, as is the case in eastern Baffin Island, east is *unani* ("down there") and west is *paani* ("up there"). But if the coast faces west, as in the area of Greenland lying across from Baffin Island, the directons are reversed (Fortescue 1988).

There are specific names that correspond to "north" and "south." Both Nunavik and Labrador, the southernmost regions of the Inuit world, experience the rising and setting of the sun all year long, in contrast with more northern regions that have twenty-four-hour daylight or quasi-darkness during some periods of the year. This relevance of the daily alternation of light and obscurity may explain why, in Nunavik Inuktitut, the north is called *tarranga* ("its shadow") and the south, *siqininga* ("its sun"), as in *"Munriali*

Kuujjuap siqininganiittuq"—"Montreal lies in the sun [to the south] of Kuujjuaq," or *"Inuit nunangat tarratinniituq"*—"The land of Inuit lies in our shadow [to our north]." In Kuujjuaq, near southernmost Ungava Bay, the Hudson Strait Inuit were traditionally called the *Tarramiut* ("people of the shadow [north]") and those from the east coast of Hudson Bay, the *Itivimiut* ("people of the other side [of the Quebec-Labrador peninsula]"). Their designation for themselves (and for Inuit of Labrador) was *Siqinirmiut* ("people of the sun [south]").

Because the *Qallunaat* concepts of east and west as fixed orientations, independent from the direction of the sea, are now known to Inuit (cf. *tammariikkuti*, "what is used for preventing one from getting lost," compass), words have been coined to name them. In Nunavik, Schneider (1970b, 170 and 282) records *siqiniup nuivinga* ("where the sun appears," east) and *nipivik* ("where the sun sets," west).

In all Inuit dialects, there exists a series of words, mostly nouns with a possessive ending, that express different positions in relation to the speaker or to someone or something else. Here are a few examples, with the third-person singular locative ending (*-ani/-ngani*):

ataani	under ("in his/her/its underside")
qulaani	over ("on his/her/its upper side")
saangani	facing ("in a position facing him/her/it")
tunuani	behind ("at his/her/its rear")
saniani	beside, near ("at his/her/its side")
akiani	across ("in a portion of space opposing him/her/it")
itiviani	on the other side ("on his/her/its other side")
sivuani	at the front, before ("in his/her/its forepart")
kinguani	at the back, after ("in his/her/its hind part")

It is noteworthy that *akiani* applies only to the opposite side of a void space (e.g., *tariup akiani*, "across the sea"; *arqutiup akiani*, "across the road"), while *itiviani* denotes the other side of a solid space (e.g., *qarqaup itiviani*, "on the other side of the hill"). When travelling, *akiani* usually refers to the shore opposite one's point of departure when starting to cross over water, while *itiviani* often signifies one's intended point of arrival when crossing over a peninsula. As for *sivuani* and *kinguani*, they express both space and time. In the case of time, these words refer to the past and the future, respectively. My ancestors are thus in front of me (*sivurani*, "in my forepart") and my descendants at my back (*kingurani*, "in my hind part").[32] As shall be seen in the following chapters, some of these positional words have other, more specialized meanings.

Conclusion

This first stroll through Inuit semantics has introduced us to the vocabulary of the environment, a domain that forms the very basis of Inuit life. We saw that words linked to this domain are organized around two fundamental concepts: *sila* and *nuna*, the first of which is defined by the lexicographer Taamusi Qumaq as a void (*pitaqanngituq*, "it has nothing") and the second as a solid mass (*aulajuittuq*, "it cannot move").

In its more concrete meanings, *sila* translates as the outside, weather, air, and other related concepts, hence its alleged emptiness. Beyond that, however, *sila* acts as the grand master of Inuit cosmology: it regulates the seasons, the movements of the heavenly bodies and those of the animals, as well as human intelligence and wisdom (*silatujuq*, "who has much *sila*," i.e., who is intelligent and wise). Nowadays, the role of *sila* as the primordial operator may have been superficially replaced by imported religious and scientific views, but this function is always present, at least at an underlying semantic and symbolic level, in the words that define the natural phenomena it regulates.

Such words include the names of the seasons, among which spring and summer are described as "surprising" (*upi-*), probably because of their sudden advent after a cold and long winter. The vocabulary of the environment also includes the numerous appellations for different forms of water, snow, and ice. Some of these terms are solely dedicated to a specific type of frozen water (e.g., *qanik*, "falling snow"; *siku*, "sea ice"), but many others are understood as dealing with snow or ice when used in the proper context (e.g., *maniittuit*, "those whose surface is uneven," referring to broken pieces of ice heaped up on shore).

Celestial bodies also belong to *sila*. Their origins, as well as that of day and night, are explained in a few founding myths, and their very names may describe their hidden nature: *siqiniq* (sun), "splashing or sprinkling"; *tarqiq* (moon), "light," or possibly "beautiful darkness"; *ulluriat* (stars), "emissions of daylight"; *arsaniit* (northern lights), "ball games [of the dead]."

Within *sila*, *nuna* constitutes the immediate environment of human beings. It is both their home—properly speaking, an uninhabited location is not called *nuna*—and that of the faunal and other resources they need for ensuring their subsistence. Etymologically, the second syllable of *nuna* might refer to the concept of being located somewhere. Basically, the word denotes solid ground and for this reason, its meaning is opposed to that of *imiq/imaq*, "water." But on another level, both sea and fresh water are part of *nuna* because they are home to indispensable resources—and also to people who travel, or even camp, on sea ice and frozen lakes.

Nuna is shaped into different landscapes, whose components are often named by way of words that describe what they look like, such as *qarqaq*, "high area" (hill), or *kuuk*, "flowing" (river). There also exist elaborate sets of terms that allow people to find their way when travelling, or to point out objects in a very precise way. These include localizers, words that apportion space according to criteria of proximity, height, and interiority (e.g., *uvani*, "here very close"), and nouns with a possessive ending that denote various types of spatial relations (e.g., *tunua*, "his/her/its rear part, its back").

In its capacity as home and provider, *sila*-regulated *nuna* has become a strong symbol of identity for Inuit. It also forms the very basis of their territorial and political claims. This explains why most of their lands are now given names that include the word or word-base *nuna*. This term sums up all their territory can offer in terms of natural resources and subsistence activities. In the next chapter, we will examine how Inuit speak about the most important of these resources, game animals, and about the hunting and other *nuna*-related practices that most of them consider the epitome of their cultural identity.

CHAPTER TWO

Words for Speaking about Animals and Subsistence Activities

Uumajuq—Inutuinnaungittuq uumajuq anirnilik. Silamut anirsaarunnatulimaaq uumajuq tuqunganngituq. Uvvaluunniit iqaluit silamut anirsaarunnangittut imaup iluani anirsaarutiqarmigamik uumajut.

Animal—Not being actually human, it is alive, it has breath. An animal that is not dead can breathe completely, because of the air. In addition, fish that cannot breathe air are animals [are alive] because while in the water, they too have a breathing apparatus.

TAAMUSI QUMAQ (1991, 83)

Sila and *nuna* are populated by *uumajuit* (singular *uumajuq*)—animals—among other creatures, and even engender some of them. In Igloolik and other Inuit locales, the *silaat* (singular *silaaq*, "lesser *sila*"), considered to be *sila*'s children, are very large animals, generally whitish or, less frequently, brownish, that may look like caribou, bearded seals, polar bears, or other large creatures. Killing them is forbidden, under pain of dying prematurely (Saladin d'Anglure 2018, 68–69). *Silaat* are males. Their female equivalents are the *pukiit* (singular *pukiq*, "white belly fur of an animal"). Both types of creatures are born from *silaaksait* or *pukiksait* (*silaat/pukiit* "to be"), large eggs that come out of the ground (Saladin d'Anglure 2018, 68–69).[1] *Nuna* thus hatches the children of *sila*.

Like human beings, all *uumajuit* are sentient individuals endowed with their own understanding of their environment. They even possess forms of knowledge inaccessible to humans, except perhaps to the shamans of yore. For example, game animals perceive the moral behaviour of hunters and refuse to get caught by those who are not generous enough to share their catch with other people. Indeed, animals have always maintained a very special relation with Inuit. For centuries, even millennia, they were their principal providers of food, clothing, and raw materials for making tools, utensils, and hunting gear. Nowadays, despite tremendous changes in material culture, game still constitutes a reliable and nutritious source of food for Inuit. And as we saw in the preceding chapter, travelling and camping on the land in order to hunt and fish lies at the very basis of modern Arctic Indigenous identity.

In this second stroll, we will see how Inuktitut classifies the various species of animals known to its speakers, and how encounters between hunters and their prey are recounted in the language. We shall also examine the vocabulary pertaining to different aspects of subsistence activities: hunting, fishing, and trapping techniques; names of weapons and other land-related equipment; country food and raw materials; cooking, eating, and sewing utensils.

Uumajuit

As hinted at by Taamusi Qumaq's definition of the word *uumajuq*, cited above, animals are characterized by the fact that like human beings, they are breathing creatures, existing either in the open air or in the water. But they are not human. The general meaning of *uumajuq* is "it is alive/one that is alive." In the singular, the two meanings of the word *uumajuq* ("it is alive" and "animal") cannot be distinguished except through context, but in the plural, at least in Nunavik, a morphemic distinction exists between *uumajut* ("they are alive") and *uumajuit* ("animals"). Animals are thus defined as animated beings. However, this meaning of the word *uumajuq* does not apply to humans as such. A living human person is said to be *inuujuq*, "he/she is a human/one who is a human" (i.e., "he/she is alive"), never *uumajuq*.[2] Despite this difference, though, both animals and people are animated by the same organ, *uummati* (the heart), "what gives life to a creature," a word whose base, *uuma-*, is also found in *uumajuq*. Whether animal or human, life thus proceeds from the same source.

According to Qumaq's definition, an animal is said to be *inutuinnaungittuq*, a word I translated above as "not being actually human." The word-base *inutuinna(q)-* can be rendered as "genuine person," which *uumajuit* are not. However, Qumaq's wording may mean that if animals are not genuine or real human beings, they might be considered persons of another kind. In *inutuinnaungittuq* (literally, "it is not a genuine or real person"), the meaning of the word depends on the position of the affix *-tuinna(q)-*. If this position shifts, the signification changes, as with *inutuinnangittuq* ("really, it is not a person"), *inuunngituinnatuq* ("really, it is a non-person"), and *inuunngitutuinnaq* ("it is just not a person"). Qumaq's choice of the first wording is thus significant. I already mentioned the special power of animals to recognize the social ethics of those who hunt them and their refusal to approach avaricious hunters. This implies that game, especially caribou and sea mammals, choose to get caught by Inuit. They offer themselves—*tunijut*, "they make a gift of themselves"—to those who are generous and share their catch with their companions (*ningirtut*, "they share the game they have caught"). In former times, the souls of captured *uumajuit* were known to return to their kin in order to report on the generosity (or lack thereof) of the hunter who had caught them. When I was in Airartuuq in 1965, I often watched the wife of my host pour a few drops of fresh water into the mouths of seals that were brought to the tent for flensing, in order to show them her gratitude for having offered themselves to her husband. The rationale of her action was that since sea mammals have only salt water to drink, they appreciate the opportunity to quench their thirst with some fresh water.

This behaviour, shared by all families I knew, is symptomatic of the respect Inuit have for animals. They consider animals as persons of a sort that must be appreciated and well treated. Oftentimes, I have heard hunters state, "*Uumajuit nakurijavut inuugutituarilaujugattigit akunialuk*"—"We are thankful toward animals because for a long time, they were our only means for staying alive." Inuit love hunting and fishing, but most of them consider it improper, and even utterly wrong, to catch more than what one needs for family and community. Game must be shared with other Inuit, but generally not sold to them.[3] People should not play with animals, like chasing a caribou or a fox in a snowmobile, just for fun. Some years ago, Nunavik hunters opposed biologists who wanted to put GPS collars on caribou in order to track their migrations, judging that this would be disrespectful to the animal.

Uumajuit are thus considered to be sentient beings that maintain an intimate relationship with Inuit. They are not human, having their own ways of knowing, behaving, and above all, a willingness to offer themselves as prey. In the distant past, as seen in the Igloolik myth of the fox and the raven (see Chapter 1), animals were able to talk and to communicate with humans (especially with shamans), but as far as I know, this is not the case anymore. *Uumajuit* are thus persons in a sense, but their personality is collective, shared by all members of a same species. This is why they do not have, and are not given, personal names, in contrast to humans and dogs—the latter belonging to a very special category of animals, as shall be seen later on.

Western zoology classifies animals into different genera and species, according to various anatomical and physiological criteria. Inuit do the same, although their classification is mostly based on obvious behavioural traits of the *uumajuit*.[4] In Nunavik Inuktitut, six principal classes of animals are given names[5]—the equivalents of the families and genera of the zoologists. These are the *puijiit, pisuttiit, timmiat, iqaluit, tininnimiutait,* and *qupirruit*. A generic term, *nirjutiit* (singular *nirjuti*, "means for eating"), applies to all large game animals.

Puijiit (Sea Mammals)

Puijiit (singular *puiji*) include all marine animals that must breathe fresh air out of the water. Literally, the word *puiji* means "one that has the habit of appearing [out of the water]," from the word-base *pui-*, "to appear" (like an object one is searching for that comes into sight). When a *puiji* moves visibly in the water, or when a land animal swims or walks on the bottom of a lake or river with its back visible, it is said to *puijju-*, "appear once and for some time [in water]." A human swimmer is a *puijjurartuq* ("one who swims repeatedly"). However, only *puijiit* and polar bears (as well as some birds, and of course human divers) can *arqa(r)-* (etymologically, "to go down repeatedly") or "dive into water." Interestingly, a bird or airplane that loses altitude in order to land is also said to *arqa(r)-*, air being considered here as analogous to water.

The prototypical *puijiit* are seals, whose heads bob completely out of the water when they breathe, but in Nunavik, walruses and whales are also classified as *puijiit*—things may be different elsewhere.[6] Qumaq (1991, 199) defines the word *puiji* as applying to any marine animal that must breathe air, and his definitions of the walrus and the orca (killer) whale mention explicitly that they are *puijiit*. In Inuktitut, there is no generic word for "seal"; nor is there one for "whale." Each species belonging to the *puijiit* has its own specific name.

In Nunavik and the eastern Canadian Arctic, the most common type of *puiji* is the *natsiq* (*nattiq* in several Nunavut dialects), the ringed seal (*Phoca hispida*).[7] Etymologically, its name (PE *nayyir*) might be related to *nay(ə)qur*, "head" (*niaquq* in modern Inuktitut) and/or *nayangar-*, "to nod," perhaps because of the animal's head bobbing out of the water (Fortescue et al. 2010, 244). *Qisik*, the skin of the *natsiq* (and of other seals), was used for sewing summer clothing as well as for making *kamiik* (Inuit boots), and before Brigitte Bardot's and Paul McCartney's campaigns against seal hunting, it constituted prime merchandise for bartering with traders. A young *natsiq* less than a year old is called a *natsiaq* ("small *natsiq*"), while an older one shedding its baby fur is a *saggalak* (from *saggatuq*, "it [the skin] shows up as if it had been scratched out").

Much larger than the *natsiq*, the *ujjuk* or *ugjuk*, depending on dialect, the bearded or square flipper seal (*Erignathus barbatus*), is also quite common. Its name is possibly related to PE *ugət-* ("to get up on something"). The hide of the bearded seal was formerly used for making tents, covering kayak and *umiaq* (large open boat) frames, and cutting out leather thongs (*atsunaaq* or *ak&unaaq*) and boot soles. An *ujjuk* less than one year old is a *tirillu* or *tiriglu* (possible etymology, "bad game animal"). The animal is called *pualulik* ("one with mitts") when it is between one and two years old because its fore flippers then look as if they were covered with fur mitts. An old *ujjuk* is a *sijjalijjaq* ("one that makes waves repeatedly [when moving at the surface of water]"). In Igloolik and perhaps elsewhere in the Inuit-speaking area, the *ujjuk* was called *mak&ak* in the shamanic language. This word might derive from *malik&ar-*, "to search for waves." The English word "mukluk," for Inuit fur boots, is a mispronunciation of *mak&ak*. It originates in western Alaska, where *mak&ak* is the bearded seal's common name in the Yupik languages (Fortescue et al. 2010, 203). The North Baffin shamanic vocabulary had thus preserved a PE word, long obsolete in current Inuktitut.

Other species of seal, found less frequently in Nunavik and eastern Nunavut, include the *qairulik* (harp seal, *Phoca groenlandica*) and the *qasigiaq* (harbour or freshwater seal, *Phoca vitulina concolor*). The name of the former animal can be glossed as "that has bark [on it]" (Fortescue et al. 2010,

301), maybe because of the colour and shape of its hide. As for the word *qasi-giaq*, it means "the fact of being speckled," referring to the multiple spots on the animal's fur.

Any young seal or other young animal is called *piaraq* ("young thing"). In northeastern Nunavik, this word also applies to human children. A mother from western Nunavik who had been ignorant of this particular meaning of *piaraq* once told me how insulted she felt when asked by an easterner, "*Qatsinik piaraqalirqit?*"—"How many young animals [children] do you have?" to which she replied, "*Uumajuunngilat nutarakka!*"—"My children are not animals!"

An adult seal is an *attuq* (etymologically, "big thing") and a rutting male, a *tiggaq* (related to PE *təgəg-*, "to be hard or stiff"; Fortescue et al. 2010, 367). An adolescent seal—or any adolescent animal—is a *tiqituraq*. This latter word might derive from the PE verbal base *tərig-* ("to be alert, furtive") and mean "a small one that is alert." Both *tərig-* and its cognate noun *tərig* ("game animal") have been quite productive as far as zoological terminology is concerned (Fortescue et al. 2010, 374–75). *Tirillu* could also be a derivative of *tərig*, and as we shall see below, the names of two other species of *uuma-juit* seem etymologically linked to these bases.

Apart from some whales, the *aiviq* (walrus, *Odobenus rosmarus*) is the largest of the *puijiit*. Its name might be related to PE *ayag-*, "to thrust or push with a pole [a tusk]" (Fortescue et al. 2010, 66). The hide of the walrus (*kauk*; nowadays, this word also applies to elephant hide) was never really useful, but its two ivory tusks, *tuugaak* (singular *tuugaaq*), served as raw material for making harpoon heads (*tuukkaq*; related to *tuugaaq*) and items like knives, needles, and the bottom part of sled runners. Walrus ivory was also used for carving small human- or animal-like amulets and clothing ornaments. With the arrival of *Qallunaat*, it became a major trading item and is still present in contemporary Inuit art. The word *tuugaaq* may be understood as "something that is poked head-on repeatedly" (Fortescue et al. 2010, 378). This meaning probably alludes to the fact that walruses use their tusks for digging clams, their preferred food, out of the sea floor.

Inuktitut distinguishes between at least four or five species of whales or, more properly, cetaceans. Two of them are not hunted: the *aarluk* (orca or killer whale, *Orcinus orca*) and the *tikaagullik* (an orca-like whale although less aggressive, possibly a subspecies of *Orcinus orca*).[8] The word *tikaagullik* is a contraction of *tikaagutilik* ("which has a *tikaaguti* [small peg of ivory fixed on the side of a harpoon handle to prevent loss of grip]") because the dorsal fin of the animal (*anguuti*, "a means to make it move on in water"; the word applies to all whale fins) resembles a peg or knob. The tail of any species of whale is called *sarpik*. One might speculate that this term relates to the verbal base *sarpik-* ("to point one's feet outward, to stand splay-footed"), a posture that shows some similarity to the shape of a whale tail.

The *arviq* or *arvik* (bowhead whale, *Balaena mysticetus*; the word might be related to the PE verbal base *arvər-*, meaning "to go down, to dive" [Fortescue et al. 2010, 50]) was for many centuries a major provider of food and raw materials to the ancestors of present-day Inuit. They used *surqaq* (baleen) for various purposes. The animal's *tulimait* ("ribs," singular *tulimaq*; the word refers to the ribs of any large animal) served as beams for supporting the earthen roof of semi-subterranean winter houses (*qarmaq*; possibly related to PE *qarə-*, "to come up [into a house]"). At the end of the nineteenth century and the beginning of the twentieth, large-scale whaling by Scottish and American ships almost exterminated the *arviq* in the eastern Arctic.[9] Nowadays, bowhead whales are rarely seen and hunting them is forbidden. In 1994, however, the community of Igloolik took the lead in reviving a whale hunt (see Kunuk 2002), even though it was officially illegal. The Canadian government protested at first but finally granted Inuit special permission to organize collective *arviq* hunts—one whale every two years at first, now three per year—across Nunavut and Nunavik, in order to help present-day people reconnect with their ancestral culture.

The most common type of whale is the *qilalugaq*. Around Baffin Island, this word denotes the narwhal (*Monodon monoceros*), a spotted (white with blackish markings) dolphin species whose males bear a long protruding helical tusk (called *tuugaaq*, like the walrus tusk). The word *qilalugaq* (or sometimes, *qinalugaq*) also applies to the beluga whale (*Delphinapterus leucas*), a completely white dolphin without a tusk. This might mean that the narwhal and the beluga are considered by Inuit as two varieties of the same species. In order to distinguish between them, the former is often called *qilalugaq tuugaalik* ("*qilalugaq* that has a tusk") or just *tuugaalik*,[10] while the latter is *qilalugaq qakurtaq* ("white *qilalugaq*") or just *qilalugaq* (especially in Hudson Bay, where the narwhal is absent). In Nunavik, where the narwhal is extremely uncommon, it is called *allanguaq* ("imitation of ornamental spots"), the word *qilalugaq* being reserved for the beluga. The term *allanguaq* refers to the spotted skin of the narwhal. As for *qilalugaq*, one might hypothesize that it includes the base *qila-* ("a short period of time"),[11] but the remainder of the word (*-lugaq*) is unclear. This could be analyzed as *-lu(k)-* ("bad") + *-gaq* ("small"), but the combined meaning of these elements ("a bad little short period of time") would not make much sense as zoological terminology. Note that a baby *qilalugaq* is called *qilalukkaanaq* ("something resembling a small beluga or narwhal").

According to an often-recalled myth, the narwhal got its tusk when a mother who had abused her blind son was drawn into the sea while holding a harpoon line attached to a whale (Laugrand and Oosten 2008, chap. 6). Her long hair, entwined around the line, became a spiralled tusk and she was transformed into a *qilalugaq*. This creature is known as *Lumaajuq* ("the one who shouts *Lumaa*") because of the cry heard by hunters when they happen to meet her.[12] More prosaically, the narwhal tusk formerly served as a tent pole or was broken into pieces for making various implements. Nowadays, however, it proves much more lucrative to sell it to a rich buyer.

The edible skin (actually, the dermis) of both the narwhal and the beluga whale is called *mattaaq* or *maktaaq*, often transcribed into English as "muktuk." The much tougher skin of the *arviq* is called *mattaq* or *maktaq*. So *mattaaq* means "lesser *mattaq*" (*matta[q]-* + *-aq*, "lesser, small"). According to Fortescue et al. (2010, 209), *mattaq/maktaq* might be etymologically linked to PE *mangir-* ("to gnaw") and possibly derived from *mangirtaq* ("which is gnawed"). Whales (and seals) also provide Inuit with blubber (*ursuq*). In former times, blubber was used as fuel for traditional oil lamps, or later on, for the makeshift stoves—constructed from a metal barrel cut in half—found in summer tents.

Pisuttiit (Land Mammals)

All four-legged *uumajuit* that live on the land are called *pisuttiit* or *pisuktiit* ("walkers," singular *pisutti*). This zoological category includes large and mid-sized animals (caribou, muskox, wolf, fox, etc.) as well as small mammals, the *pisuttiapiit* ("little *pisuttiit*"): hare, weasel, lemming, and so on. In the same way that the word *puijiit* refers to that genus's most salient feature, the ability to appear suddenly out of its habitat, *imaq* (water), and become visible to hunters, the *pisuttiit* are defined by their most obvious characteristic, that of being walking creatures that roam *nuna* (land). These two genera provide Inuit with their most fundamental marine and land resources.

Tuttu or *tuktu*, the caribou (*Rangifer arcticus*), may be considered as the prototypical *pisutti*. It is found all across the North American Arctic, where it forms migratory herds whose patterns of migration are generally predictable—a place used regularly by caribou herds to cross a river or lake is called a *nalluq* ("wading in water"). In some areas, herds are so huge that in the shamanic language, *tuttuit* were dubbed *nunaup kumangit* ("lice of the earth"). Etymologically, *tuttu* derives from PE *tuntu*, a word possibly related to *tunnu* ("back fat of caribou"; connected to *tunu*, "the back"), which could mean "much fat" (Fortescue et al. 2010, 382). In former times, the hairy hide of the caribou (*tuttujaq*, "piece of *tuttu*") served for both blankets (*qipiit*) and bed sheets. The latter were called *qaaq*, "that on top," because they were placed over a mattress made of branches and dried moss (*alliaq*, "the one under") and/or a matting of willow and dwarf birch (*qilattait*, "those bound together"). Above all, *tuttujaq* provided the primary raw material for sewing winter clothing. This is why a major *tuttu* hunt was conducted at the end of summer, to leave women with enough time to sew their family's clothes. To do so, they used thread made of caribou (or beluga) sinew (*ivalu*). Caribou antler (*najjuk* or *nagjuk*; related to PE *nayət-*, "to get caught or snagged") was useful for fabricating various utensils. A *tuttu* less than one year old is a *nurraq*. According to Fortescue et al. (2010, 265), this word might share a common root with PE *nurar(ar)*, "nephew/niece of a woman."[13] A yearling is called *nukatugaq* (possibly, "a younger one that is eaten") and an adult male caribou is a *panniq* or *pangniq*.

The muskox (*Ovibos moschatus*), *umimmak* or *umingmak* ("big whiskers"), is mostly found in the northern Arctic, but in the mid-1960s a few animals were brought to Nunavik, where they have thrived since and are occasionally met by Inuit hunters. The muskox horn (*najjuk/nagjuk*) probably had the same uses as caribou antler. In spite of its name, the muskox is a big sheep; its wool (*qiviuq*; possible etymology, "that curls back") is very silky and there have been attempts at selling it in southern Canada, either raw or as knitted wear. According to Randa, because caribou and muskox both have *najjuk* (whether antler or horn), traditional Inuit considered them as symbolic substitutes for each other. Analogously, among sea mammals, the tusk-bearing narwhal was seen as a substitute for the walrus (Randa 2002, 76).

Unlike the preceding species of *pisuttiit*, the *amaruq* or wolf (*Canis lupus*) is not eaten. Wolves follow the caribou and muskox herds. According to a southern Baffin elder I heard speaking at a language symposium in Iqaluit in 2010, the word *amaruq* could be connected to the verbal base *amar-* ("to carry on one's back") because wolves like to carry their prey on their back. Indeed, *amaruq* derives from PE *amaqur*, where the syllable *-qur* possibly means "something associated with" (Fortescue et al. 2010, 24, 467). *Amaruq* could thus be understood as "associated with carrying something on its back."

The same individual also mentioned that the *qavvik* or *qagvik* (wolverine, *Gulo gulo luscus*) got its name because it often climbs on some elevation (*qavvituq*, "it climbs") in order to jump on its prey. According to Fortescue et al. (2010, 317), however, the word *qavvik* (PE *qatvig*) could be related to *qatə*, "deep or loud voice," in reference to "the deep growling sound the animal makes." Wolverines are found across the Arctic but in very small numbers. As far as I know, they are not eaten. It is noteworthy that in some parts of Greenland, where the *qavvik* is unknown, the cognate term *qappik* denotes a mythical beast (Fortescue et al. 2010, 317). This means that the memory of the wolverine and its name has survived there in a symbolic form.

The *atsaq* or *ak&aq* (black bear, *Ursus americanus*) is rarely seen by most Inuit because it dwells in the southernmost parts of the Arctic. With global warming, however, encounters with this animal are said to be increasingly frequent in areas where they formerly did not occur. Some people in southern Nunavik assert that *atsaq* meat is edible, but I have met individuals who refused to eat it.

Smaller than the preceding *pisuttiit* but larger than the following ones, the *tiriganniaq* or *tiriganiaq* (fox) is found everywhere across the Arctic. Inuit distinguish between two major types of fox: *tiriganniaq qakurtaq* ("white *tiriganniaq*" or Arctic fox, *Vulpes lagopus*) and *tiriganniaq kajuq* ("brown-red *tiriganniaq*" or red fox, *Vulpes vulpes fulva*). The word *tiriganniaq* starts with a derivative of the PE root *tərig* ("alert, furtive game animal") already encountered in the terms *tiqituraq* and perhaps *tirillu* (Fortescue et al. 2010, 374–75). *Tiriganniaq* could thus mean—but this is partially guesswork—"one that is trying [*-niaq*] to look like [*-ar-*] a furtive game animal [*tərig-*]." Foxes dwell in dens (*sijjait*, singular *sijjaq*). This word is homophonous to that for "beach" (*sijjaq*) mentioned in the preceding chapter. However, the two appellations do not seem related. Etymologically, the name of the den would be derived from the noun base *siti-* ("lemming or mouse hole") + *-jja(rittu)q* ("that has or is a big one"). The den of the fox could thus be defined as a "big animal hole," while, as already discussed, the word for "beach" would be linked to PE *cingə-* ("shoving") or *cingig* ("point of land").

Before the arrival of *Qallunaat* traders, the skin of the fox (*tirigannia-jaq*, "piece of fox") was practically useless, except for adding a fur trimming to parka hoods or for sewing baby clothing. However, when commercial concerns such as the Hudson's Bay Company started opening stores in the Arctic—as early as the late eighteenth century in Greenland and Labrador and as late as the 1900s in northeastern Canada—fox skin became the most important trading item and remained so until the mid-twentieth century. The flesh of the fox is considered edible but is only eaten in the absence of anything else, mostly by men on their traplines.

The *pisuttiapiit* ("little *pisuttiiit*") include a number of small fur-bearing mammals and rodents (e.g., *avinngaq* or lemming,[14] conjecturally, "one that starts to divide itself"; *ujjunaq* or shrew mouse, "that looks like a bearded seal [because of its whiskers]"; *nunivakkaq* or long-tailed mouse, "one that is picked up from the ground"). Among them, the *tiriaq* (weasel or ermine, *Mustela erminea*) bears a name derived, once again, from PE *tərig-* and meaning "one that looks like a furtive game animal." On the basis of their appellations, the weasel and the fox would thus be considered analogous species—a smaller one (*tiriaq*) that "looks furtive" and a bigger one (*tirigan-niaq*) that "tries to look furtive" but, it may be suggested, has problems doing so because of its larger size.

As was the case with the fox, the weasel, and other fur-bearing *pisutti-apiit*—the mink or *kuutsiuti* ("one concerned with rivers," *Mustela vison*); the otter or *pamiurtuuq* ("with a big tail," *Lutra canadensis*)—became really sought after only when the fur trade appeared. One fur-bearer mostly found on the southern fringe of the Arctic, the muskrat (*Ondatra zibethica*), bears a name—*kivgaluk* (west of Hudson Bay), *kiggaluk* (Labrador), or *kivvaluk* (Nunavik)—that poses an interesting semantic problem. Its base, *kigga(q)-/kivga(q)-*, means "messenger, helper" (possibly related to PE *kəvəg-*, "to lift [a load]"). According to Fortescue et al. (2010, 189), the last syllable, *-luk*, stands for the affix *-kuluk*, "dear little." But why would the muskrat be called "dear little messenger?" Fortescue et al. wonder if this could be because it is seen as a "little messenger moving to and fro between water and land" (2010, 189). Another, related suggestion (Frédéric Laugrand, personal communication) is that the word might allude to the fact that muskrats travel ceaselessly—in order to get food—between their lodge and the bank of the river in which the lodge is built.

The only *pisuttiapik* that is generally eaten—and whose fur was used for baby diapers and infant clothing—is the *ukaliq* (Arctic hare, *Lepus arcticus*).[15] In the novel *Sanaaq* by Mitiarjuk Nappaaluk, the *ukaliq* is said to possess seven anuses, so that when you see one running, you just need to shout, "*Itingit, itingit!*"—"Its anuses, its anuses!" The animal will be so ashamed that it will immediately stop and sit down in order to hide its anuses, an ideal position for being shot at. I witnessed this technique once in Nunavik, and it actually worked.

Timmiat (Birds)

The word *timmiat* or *tingmiat* (singular *timmiaq*, "one that flies repeatedly"; cf. *timmijuq*, "it takes off repeatedly [is flying]") denotes all species of birds, although the smaller ones are often called *qupanuat* (singular *qupanuaq*, perhaps "small fancy trim" [Fortescue et al. 2010, 346]), a word that refers more specifically to the migratory snow bunting (*Plectrophenax nivalis*). Even though *timmiat* cannot be considered staples of the traditional Inuit diet, they played, and still play, an important part as seasonal alternatives to the more basic sources of food, caribou and *puijiit*. In spring and fall, when migratory birds reached or departed the Arctic, their flesh and eggs (*manniit*, singular *mannik*) were—and still are—truly welcome.

Edible migratory birds include, among others, the following species:

mitiq	eider duck (*Somateria mollissima*)
nirliq	Canada goose (*Branta canadensis*)
kanguq	snow goose (*Chen hyperborea*)
tuullik	common loon (*Gavia immer*)
qarsauq	red-throated loon (*Gavia stellata*)
appaq/akpaq	thick-billed murre (small bird nesting in cliffs; *Uria lomvia*)

The word *nirliq* might be related to the verbal base *nirlur-* ("to raise head" [Fortescue et al. 2010, 253]), an accurate description of geese feeding, raising their heads repeatedly in order to watch their surroundings. As for *appaq*, Fortescue et al. (2010, 21, 23) suggest it could be etymologically connected to PE *aləg-* ("to wipe, sweep"), the link between the two words being ethnological: *appaq* skins were formerly used for cleaning purposes. Sweeping tent floors was done with the wing (*isaruq*, "something attached in order to extend limbs") of a *naujaq* (seagull, *Larus argentatus*) or *naujavik* ("big *naujaq*," glaucous gull, *Larus hyperboreus*). These two migratory birds are not generally edible, although their eggs are.

There exist two species that are closely related but do not share the same adaptive behaviour. In Nunavik, the *aqiggiq* (rock ptarmigan, *Lagopus mutus rupestris*) is found in the North between May and October, while its larger cousin, *aqiggivik* ("big *agiggiq*" or willow ptarmigan, *Lagopus lagopus*), remains in the country all year long. Both species are edible.

A few other species spend the whole year in the Arctic:

pitsiulaaq/pittiulaaq	black guillemot (*Cepphus grille*)
tulugaq	northern raven (*Corvus corax*)
uppik/ukpik	snowy owl (*Nyctea nyctea*)

Unlike the raven and owl, the *pitsiulaaq* is edible. Its name ends with an affix (*-laaq*) denoting something very small. So the guillemot would be defined as a "very small *pitsiu-*." The only morphologically plausible, although highly conjectural, reconstruction of the base *pitsiu-* I can think of is *pitsiut* ("a means for making it do something"). This does not make much sense, but *pitsiulaaq* might refer to the limited width of the bird's gape (the inside of a bird's open mouth, its "means for making it swallow"), which is prominently red at breeding time. By contrast, *tulugaq* can be easily glossed as "one that gives blows [*tulur-*] repeatedly [*-ga(r)-*] with its tusk, fang, or (in this case) beak [*siggu(k)*; this word also means "muzzle"]."

Other species of *timmiat* known to Inuit are a small number of migratory or resident birds of prey, such as *kiggavik*, the generic name for falcons (e.g., peregrine falcon, *Falco peregrinus*). In present-day Nunavik and Baffin Inuktitut, this name can be tentatively glossed as "big messenger [*kiggaq*]." It is tempting to oppose this hypothetical big messenger to the "little messenger," the *kiggaluk* (or *kivvaluk*) or muskrat. The former travels between *qilak* (the sky) and *nuna* (the earth), while the latter does the same between *nuna* and *imaq* (water). However, according to Fortescue et al. (2010, 179), *kəði-*, the possible PE etymon of *kigga-* in *kiggavik*, is different from *kəvg-*, the etymon of *kiggaluk* (cf. North Alaskan Iñupiaq kiž*gavik* vs. kiv*galuk*), meaning that the name of the falcon would not have anything to do with messengers. The PE word-base *kəði-* means "alone, only." If this etymology stands true, *kiggavik* could thus mean "the big solitary." This does not exclude the possibility, though, that modern speakers of Inuktitut might guess the meaning of *kiggavik* to be "big messenger." Whatever the case may be, the *kiggavik* was an important spirit in shamanic times (Frédéric Laugrand, personal communication) and its name may have conveyed this importance.

To conclude this survey of birds, both migratory and sedentary species build nests (*ullu*, nest; etymologically, "place for tying up"; this word is *not* related to *ullu[q]*, "day[light]") and incubate (*ivajuq*, "it incubates") in the Arctic. Besides laying eggs (*manniit*) that Inuit gather in the spring (*pikiut-tuq*, "he/she gathers eggs;" from PE *pəkyu*, "egg"), the *mitiq* (eider duck) female stuffs her nest with down (*quniguq*, "that usually curls on itself"), which is collected in order to pad winter clothing or, more frequently these days, to sell for money.

Iqaluit (Fish)

Properly speaking, the word *iqaluit* (singular *iqaluk*) only refers to fish of the trout and (in Alaska) salmon families. In the Canadian Arctic, it applies more particularly to Arctic char (*Salvelinus alpinus*), a giant trout that may reach the size of a small salmon and is often dubbed *iqaluppik/iqalukpik* ("the very best *iqaluk*"). In Inuktitut, no generic appellation exists for fish belonging to other families. This is why in the present-day language, any type of fish tends to be called an *iqaluk*. It is interesting to know that in the East Greenlandic dialect (Dorais 1984), a lexical distinction is drawn between the *kapurniakkat* ("those captured with a three-pronged spear," trout and salmon) and *aalisakkat* ("those captured with a fishing line," all other species of fish).

Salmon thrives in the waters of Alaska, where it is generally designated by a cognate or derivative of *iqaluk* (Fortescue et al. 2010, 154–55): *iqa&uk, qaluk, aqaluk, aqalugžuaq* ("huge *aqaluk*"). In Greenland and Labrador, salmon is called *kapisilik* or *kavisilik*, "that has scales," and *iqaluk* refers to Arctic char. A fish scale is a *kavisiq*, a word related to the verbal base *kapi-* ("to sting"), maybe because of the sharp edge of scales. Outside these regions, the Atlantic salmon (*Salmo salar*) is only found in the southernmost part of Ungava Bay (Nunavik) and its name, *saama*, has been borrowed from English.[16] Interestingly, in Nunavik and the rest of the eastern Canadian Arctic, *kavisilik* or *kapisilik* denotes the whitefish (*Coregonus clupeiformis*), which is not an *iqaluk*, properly speaking. This might indicate that when the ancestors of present-day Labrador and Greenland Inuit reached the Atlantic Ocean about 800 years ago and "discovered" salmon, they applied to this scaly fish an already existing name that they found relevant: "one that has scales."[17]

Trout and other commonly eaten fish also include the following:

nutilliq	speckled (brook) trout (*Salvelinus fontinalis*)
isiuralittaaq	grey (lake) trout (*Salvelinus namaycush*)
ivitaaruq	red trout (*Salmo trutta*)
uugaq	polar cod (*Boreogadus saida*)
kanajuq	sculpin (*Oncocottus hexacornis*)

Proto-Eskimo or Proto-Inuit etymologies can be proposed for some of these words:

nutəm- ("from the beginning") + *-liq* ("the most") = *nutilliq* ("the oldest one")

isi(q)- ("smoke, steam") + *-urar-* ("small") + *-lik-* ("to have") + *-taaq* ("added") = *isiuralittaaq* ("with some [colour of] smoke on it")

ivita(aq)- ("reddish earth") + *-aruq* ("small) = *ivitaaruq* ("little red earth")

It might be tempting to gloss the word *uugaq* as "one that has been burned" (*uu[t]-* ["to burn"] + *-gaq* [passive]). However, the PE form of *uugaq* is *uðu-kar* (Fortescue et al. 2010, 392) and has nothing to do with the root for "burning," *ugut-*.

In former times, fish, especially Arctic char and other species of trout, were an important supplemental food in winter. Char caught during fall, when it ascended the rivers, was cached (*qinniq* or *qinnivik*, "stone cache"; possibly related to Proto-Yupik *qəngžur-*, "to gather"), and some families who wintered inland relied on fish caught from under lake ice to ensure their subsistence. Nowadays, many Inuit, especially women, love to go fishing in all seasons. Besides the flesh of fish, the roe (*suvak*) is eaten, a special dish (*suvallijaq*, "made with *suvak*") being prepared by mixing roe with seal oil and berries before freezing it all.

Tininnimiutait (Shellfish)

Tininnimiutait (singular *tininnimiutaq*) are "those that inhabit the *tinin-niq* [running-out tide]," that is, the marine beach areas uncovered at low tide. They include shells and crustaceans, but also seaweeds such as *kuanniq*, an edible alga. In Greenland, *kuanniq* designates the angelica, a large um-belliferous plant whose form might be reminiscent of seaweed. According to Fortescue et al. (2010, 195), this word is presumed to be a loan from Old Norse *hvonn* (plural *hvannir*), "angelica." In Canada, however, *kuanniq* means "edible seaweed" all over the eastern Arctic, and it is difficult to un-derstand how a medieval Viking word could have entered Inuktitut in areas as far away as the northwestern shore of Hudson Bay.

Most *tininnimiutait* were and are eaten, raw or cooked, as a dietary supplement. Here are a few species, with the very descriptive significations of their names:

uviluq	mussel (*Mytilus edulis*) ("that opens like an eye")
ammuumajuq	Arctic clam (*Mya truncata*) ("looked down at from above")[18]
ajuarnaq	barnacle (*Patella sp.*) ("that looks like an abscess")
siupiruq	periwinkle (*Littorina sp.*) (conjecturally, "big ear")
kinguk	small shrimp (*Pandalus sp.*) ("that moves backward [?]")
pujjuuti	any crustacean with claws ("something used for pinching")

Qupirruit (Bugs)

This last category of *uumajuit* includes all insects, worms, spiders, water beetles, and other small flying or creeping creatures. *Qupirruit* (singular *qupirruk*) are the only type of *uumajuit* that are not normally eaten—except for the *kumak* (louse; possibly related to PE *kuməg-*, "to scratch") and its *irqiit* (nits), which some individuals used to crunch with their teeth when delousing someone else. Etymologically, *qupirruk* seems to mean "something associated with splitting lengthwise" (*qupi-*) (Fortescue et al. 2010, 347). The rationale of this meaning is far from clear, but it is interesting to note that the etymological signification of the English "insect" is precisely "something that is split, or cut into parts" (because most insects are clearly divided into a head, a thorax, and an abdomen).

Many Inuit women feel uncomfortable or even terrified when encountering *qupirruit* such as larvae, maggots, and bumblebees. Their attitude may be linked to a myth in which an unfaithful woman was eaten by maggots (Saladin d'Anglure 2018, 125), and also to the fact that insects were often deemed to control life and death. They appeared to be immortal because they or their larvae hibernate all winter long, coming back to life in spring (Laugrand and Oosten 2012).

Here are a few names of *qupirruit*, together with their underlying significations, once again quite graphic:

kitturiaq/kikturiaq	mosquito ("that bites repeatedly")
pillitajuuq	flea, sand-hopper ("that has the habit to hop repeatedly")
aasivak	spider ("large *aasi*" [cognate of PE *aður-*, "to crawl" ?])
auvvik	caterpillar (etymologically, "place for crawling")
qitirulliq	maggot ("that has something associated with the middle part [of the rotting flesh where it thrives?]")
nuviuvak	fly (Proto-Inuit, "one that hangs around very much")
igutsaq	bumblebee ("that strives to sting")
milugiaq	black fly ("one that goes sucking out")

New types of *qupirruit* have appeared since the arrival of *Qallunaat*. Reptiles (*parngusuut*, "those that usually crawl"), for instance, mentioned in the Bible or seen on television, are classified as bugs. In Nunavik, this includes snakes, *nimiriat* ("those that wind themselves around") and crocodiles, *qupirrualuit* ("big bugs").

A Semantic System

The combined meanings of the six genera of *uumajuit* known to Nunavik Inuit form a semantic system that classifies animals according to their respective habitats. Three classes of species are defined as occupying specific portions of *sila*:

> *Iqaluit* (fish) are dwellers of *imaq* (salt or fresh water); the prototypical species of *iqaluit*, Arctic char, actually moves between both forms of *imaq*, living in the sea during the summer and in lakes when winter comes; the word *iqaluk* is reminiscent of *irqaq* ("bottom of an expanse of water"), although it is highly improbable that both terms share the same etymology.
>
> *Pisuttiit* (land mammals) live on *nuna* (earth); their name, "walkers," implies the type of habitat they occupy.
>
> *Timmiat* (birds) spend a large part of their life moving across *sila* (here in its restricted meaning of "air"); hence their appellation, "those that fly."

The three remaining genera are defined as overlapping different habitats:

> *Puijiit* (sea mammals) live at the boundary between water, their usual habitat, and the air they must breathe in order to survive; this is expressed in their name, "those that appear out of water."
>
> *Tininnimiutait* (shellfish), "inhabitants of beach areas uncovered at low tide," live in the water at high tide and on land (the beach) the rest of the time; they thus occupy both *imaq* and *nuna*.
>
> *Qupirruit* (bugs) are found in all three zones: water (sand-hoppers and other water beetles), land (worms, spiders, body lice), and air (flying insects); this could account for a possible but highly hypothetical gloss

of their name, "those that are split [among various habitats?]"; their ubiquity could also partly explain why, as mentioned above, bugs were formerly thought to control life and death.

Despite the existence of *tininnimiutait*, which occupy a liminal marine/ terrestrial area, the boundary dividing *imaq* from *nuna* (*sinaa*, "its edge," i.e., the shoreline) marks a symbolic division between the two domains of land and sea. As we saw earlier, it was once strictly forbidden, under pain of severe bad luck, to cook and eat the flesh of *pisuttiit* together with that of *puijiit* and *iqaluit*. Nowadays, stories are told about encounters along the shore with benevolent marine beings. Some of these (*iqaluunappaa*, "half-part of a fish [mermaid]") are found stranded aground, rewarding with gifts those who put them back into water (Alasuaq 1981). Others (*taliilajut*, "who hide frequently") live on coastal reefs, rescuing Inuit who are about to drown. These stories tell, with a mirror effect, about re-establishing the temporarily disrupted division between *imaq* and *nuna*. In the first case, a marine being (*iqaluunappaa*) is sent back to its element by a terrestrial creature (an Inuk), while in the second, a drowning Inuk can return back to dry land because he or she is rescued by a denizen of the sea (*taliilajuq*).

Hostile beings can also be encountered along *sinaa*. In July 1969, when visiting Killiniq (Port Burwell), a now-abandoned village at the northeastern tip of Ungava Bay, I was told by a resident how a few years earlier, he and other people had seen a giant monkey-like creature walking out of the sea. My informant had been very afraid, seizing his gun in defence until the creature reached the high-tide line and receded back into the water, unable to progress on land beyond the beach area.

In spite of the *imaq/nuna* division, there exists a major trespasser of the boundary between sea and land. This very special *uumajuq* is the polar bear (*nanuq*). It can swim and dive in the water as easily as it walks and runs on land. Like another *uumajuq*, the dog (*qimmiq*), it does not fit easily into any one of the six genera already described. For different reasons, both animals play a very important part in the Inuit imaginary.

Nanuq (The Polar Bear)

*Pisuttulu qimmiqanngimata isumalirpuq sapirnangittut
qimmiqanngimamik. Tamaanilu sivuningani utarqilirpuq tuqujumalugit
nirijumalugillu. . . . Taakkua inuit qanigijanganni nanuq utarqivuq
tirlilirpata aivigijumalugit. Qaujimagami qaujijaurqaaruni
tuqutaujunnarami pitsiarasuarpuq. Qaujijaurqaarani tikigunigit
saalagijunnaramigit utarqivuq taqatsiarilugit.*

And it [*nanuq*] thinks that because these [men] who walk do not have
dogs, the situation is not hopeless, since they have no dogs. And here,
before them, it is waiting, wanting to kill and eat them. . . .
The bear waits close to these people, wanting to go and get them when
they will be unaware [of its presence]. Because it knows that it can
be killed if it is discovered first, it tries to act in a proper way. Since it
can be victorious over them if it reaches them without having been
discovered first, it waits, presuming they are very tired.

—Markoosie (2011, 145)

Like Inuit and in contradistinction to other *uumajuit*, polar bears (*nanuit*, singular *nanuq*; *Thalarctos maritimus*) live at the juncture between land and sea.[19] They can walk and stalk prey on solid ground, but are also skillful swimmers and divers, expert at hunting sea mammals in water or on the sea ice. According to Randa (1986), they are considered to be both *pisuttiit* ("walkers," i.e., land mammals) and *imarmiutait* ("sea dwellers"). Their fat is called *ursuq*, like that of sea mammals. In the southern zones of the Arctic, where black bears (*atsait/ak&ait*) cohabit with *nanuit*, the most salient semantic difference between the two species has to do with their status as *pisuttiit*. In the Inuinnaqtun dialect, for instance, *akhait* (*atsait*) are *nunaup aulajuit* ("the land's mobile [walking] ones"), while polar bears are *sikuup aulajuit* ("the mobile ones of the sea ice") (Rasmussen 1932, 108).

Nanuit can hunt in organized groups. They go after the same prey animals as those sought by Inuit, who often consider polar bears as fellow hunters (Laugrand and Oosten 2015, chap. 7). Stronger than human beings—they kill animals with their bare paws—their cleverness is equal to that of men. As seen in the quotation above, drawn from Markoosie's novel about a tragic bear hunt, *nanuq* is able to understand the whereabouts of its prey and to reflect on the proper course of action to take in order to kill before being caught. Written in Inuktitut by an airplane pilot originally from Nunavik but living in Resolute Bay (northern Nunavut), *Angunasuttiup naukkutinga* first appeared in 1969–70 in a Canadian government magazine (*Inuttituut*) and was published in English translation in 1970 under the title *Harpoon of the Hunter.*[20]

In his narrative, which has the merit of describing the bear hunt from the standpoints of both the men and the animal, Markoosie does not differentiate between the words he uses when speaking about Inuit and about *nanuq*. The bear knows (*qaujima-*), thus having access to the light (*qau*) that makes people aware of their environment (cf. Chapter 1). It wants to reach well-defined goals (*tuqujumalugit nirijumalugillu*, "wanting to kill and eat them"). It also thinks (*isumalirpuq*), showing that it possesses *isuma* ("reason"), the mental faculty that characterizes mature human beings. Markoosie's equating the human mind and that of polar bears reflects what myths and traditional stories tell us about *nanuq*: beyond *isuma* and *qaujimaniq* ("knowledge"), it has access to *qaumaniq* ("shamanic light"). Thus according to Inuit symbolism, the polar bear is a powerful shamanic spirit (Saladin d'Anglure 2004). It is said to be left-handed (*saumik*), like shamans who used their left hand to conduct some rituals.

Despite its physical strength and supranatural capacities, *nanuq* has always been hunted by Inuit. Bear hunts may be organized when a polar bear is known to roam nearby, but the animal is most often met by chance. Up to the 1960s, collective hunts were organized on islands where *nanuit* congregated during summer—such as Akpatok in northern Ungava Bay—but this is a thing of the past. Nowadays, quotas are imposed on the number of bears the residents of a village are allowed to catch. Bear meat is eaten, and skins (*nanurait*, singular *nanuraq*, "that looks like a *nanuq*") were formerly used for sewing winter clothing, especially pants, or for making bed mattresses, but for several decades *nanurait* have instead been sold at a good price.

Qimmiq (The Dog)

Qimmiinut malittaq, marruunut, Kajualummulu, Qirnimullu.
Taimaguuq, arqutimini, aqiggisilirtuq; millurasualangasitsuniguuq,
qimmiinut pangalaarijausijut aqiggiit. Taimaguuq,

pangalaarinnilirmatik, qammatugululirquq imaak: "Au au
Kajualuk au au!"

She [Sanaaq] is followed by two dogs, Kajualuk and Qirniq. Then, it
is said, she sees some ptarmigans on her way; when she is about to start
trying to throw rocks at them, the ptarmigans begin being run after by
the dogs. Then it is said, because they are running, she starts shouting
lamely, like this: "Stop [*au au*] Kajualuk, stop!"

—Mitiarjuk Nappaaluk (1984, 1)

Until the demise of dog teams in the mid-1960s and the introduction of *Qallunaat* pet animals such as cats (*puusi*, from the English "pussy [cat]"), *qimmiit* or *qingmiit* (dogs) were the only domestic animal known to Inuit. As
such, they have always held a very special position in Indigenous society and
imagination. Dogs are *uumajuit* for sure, but because they share the lives of
Inuit, they have acquired something of their masters' sensibility and intelligence, so that hunters consider them as partners (Laugrand and Oosten
2015, chap. 6). However, a clear distinction remains between men and dogs,
and transgressions have dire consequences, as illustrated in the myth of the
girl who married her dog and, in some versions, was drowned by her father
and became *Kannaaluk* ("The Big One Down Here") or *Sanna* ("The One
Down There"), the mistress of the *puijiit* (Saladin d'Anglure 2018, chap. 5).

The PE form of the word *qimmiq* is *qikmir*, and according to Fortescue
et al. (2010, 331), it might be glossed as "one that is compelled to be shy or
respectful." Indeed, the role of the dog is to obey and assist its master, who
feeds it in return for its services. A *qimmiq*'s master is called its *inuk*, its
person. A dog cannot behave properly if it is not related to a human being,
and conversely, if this human is a hunter, he needs—or rather, needed—his
dogs to conduct the subsistence activities allowing him to feed and clothe
his family as well as his *qimmiit*. There thus exists a close relationship of reciprocity between man and dog.

The word *qimmiq* is possibly connected to the verbal base *qimuk-*, "to pull
something while in a harness," and to the PE root *qamur-*, "to pull." While
unproven, this connection highlights the best-known function of Inuit dogs,
at least in winter: to pull their master's sled (*qamutiik*, "the two [runners]
used for pulling"). A travelling equipage made up of a dog team, the sled it
is pulling, and the people and baggage on the sled is called *qimutsiit* ("those

that move when they [dogs] pull"). Formerly in summers, *qimmiit* carried a limited quantity of goods in a pack saddle (*nammauti*, "that is used for carrying something on one's back"), or they hauled *umiat* (open skin boats) along rivers (*ikurtut*, "they are hauled upriver").

Some familiar dogs hung around their masters and accompanied them on strolls, as illustrated in the opening quotation. Like the human members of their *inuk*'s household, *qimmiit* received personal names such as those used by Mitiarjuk: *Kajualuk* ("Big Brown") and *Qirniq* ("Black"). Some of these appellations were shared by men (e.g., *Taqulik*, "Who shows white spots over the eyes," now a patronym in Nunavik). *Qimmiit* understood their names, as well as the oral commands given them by their master when pulling a sled or otherwise (e.g., *au* or *aaa*, "stop!"; *rarara*, "make a left turn!").[21] Of course, the only way a dog could answer was by howling (*miuggutuq*, "it says *miu*"), moaning (*maaralajuq*, "it says *maa*"), or much less frequently, barking (*qiluttuq*, "it barks"). When a *qimmiq* died, its skin (*qimmisuk*, "lesser dog") was often used for making winter pants or trimming parka hoods. Fur sewn around a hood is called *nuilaq* (possibly related to *nui-*, "to appear"), and young dogs with a promising fur were sometimes named *Nuilaq*, an appellation that disclosed the fate intended for them.

When *Qallunaat* came to the North, Inuit learned about exotic domestic animals and had to find words for speaking about them. In northeastern Nunavik, the horse was called *qimmijuaq* ("super-dog") because it pulled vehicles like *qimmiit* did, and the cow became a *tuttuvaq* ("big caribou"),[22] in view of its size and its hoofs, split like those of a *tuttu*. By contrast, in western Nunavik, it was the horse that was designated in reference to its hoofs (*kukitualik*, "that has a single [i.e., non-split] hoof"), while the cow was defined through its principal function (*immuliurti*, "milk maker"). In both regions, the pig was named *kuukkusi*, a word borrowed from the Cree or Innu Algonquian language (cf. Innu *kukush*). Another Algonquian loan word, *pakaakuani*, for chicken (cf. Innu *pakakuan*), is used in northeastern Nunavik, but in the western part of the region, the bird is named *aqiggiujaq*, "that looks like a ptarmigan." *Kuukkusi* and *pakaakuani* are the only two words in Nunavik Inuktitut and, as far as I know, in any Canadian Inuit dialect, borrowed from a First Nations language. Another loan word used in Nunavik, *saugaq* ("sheep"), comes from West Greenlandic (where it is known as *sava*), through the Moravian missionaries in Labrador. *Sava* had itself been borrowed from Old Norse by the Greenlanders, during the Viking settlement of Greenland in the tenth to fifteenth centuries.

Subsistence Activities

Subsistence activities refer to the hunting, fishing, and trapping techniques aimed at capturing *uumajuit*, and using weapons and related paraphernalia (*piuliniagait*, "those objects that will serve to do something") to implement these techniques. Food and clothing produced by way of such activities are also related to subsistence.

In Inuktitut and other forms of the Inuit language, subsistence activities have generated a very rich and detailed vocabulary. Since the arrival of *Qallunaat*, however, especially during the last five or six decades, traditional subsistence techniques and implements have been increasingly replaced by wage work and global technology, so that a large part of the associated lexicon has become obsolete and tends to be forgotten. In this section, only a small sample of words for speaking about subsistence activities will be examined.

Encountering Uumajuit

In the preceding chapter, when discussing the concept of land (*nuna*), it was mentioned that in Nunavik, hunting, fishing, and trapping are conducted at the *maqaivvik* ("a place where one travels [out of the village or seasonal camp]"). These activities are thus known as *maqainniq*, "travelling on the land." The etymology of *maqait-* ("to be absent travelling") is not completely clear (although it seems to include the negative affix -*it*-), but a tentative literal signification could be "not to carry a kayak" (cf. *maqit-*,[23] "to carry a kayak on one's own shoulders" + -*it*-, "not to"). To travel (on water) would consist in actually using a kayak rather than having to carry it.

The most general terms for speaking about hunting, fishing, and trapping are *uumajursiutuq* ("he/she searches for animals"), *iqalunniatuq* ("he/she deals with fish"), and *mikigiarniatuq* ("he/she deals with traps"). A more specialized word for "one who hunts" is *angunasuttuq* ("he/she strives to catch game"). A full-time hunter is an *uumajursiuti* or *angunasutti* ("one who usually hunts"), while a fisher is called *iqalunniati* ("one who usually fishes") and a trapper, *mikigiarniati* ("one who usually traps").

In the case of sea and land mammals as well as birds, when going after an animal one has to look for it. This is expressed by adding to the name of the animal the affix *-siur-* ("to look or search for") that derives from *-si-* ("to encounter, to see") + *-ur* ("frequently"). To search for an animal would thus consist in being (or trying to be?) in frequent contact with it. Examples include *natsisiurtuq* ("goes looking for ringed seals"), *tuttusiurtuq* ("goes looking for caribou"), and *nanursiutuq* ("goes looking for a polar bear"). When an animal is found, there is an encounter with it (cf. the affix *-si-* above). For example, a man coming back from hunting sea mammals will be asked, *"Puijisivit?"*—"Have you encountered *puijiit*?" He might answer, *"Ujjunik puijisigaluarsunga, ujjungittunga"*—"Even though I have encountered *puijiit* [in the form of] bearded seals, I have not got them." The encounter allows the hunter to establish a direct relationship of predator versus prey with the animal. This is expressed thanks to the word *uumajurniatuq* ("he/she deals with an *uumajuq*").

When an encounter occurs, the *uumajuq* is usually caught, provided it is willing to give itself to the hunter. There is no specific word denoting the action of catching an animal. To tell about such an occurrence, a verbal ending is simply affixed to the name of the animal (see Appendix), as in *ujju*ngittunga ("I did not get bearded seals") above, *tuttu*tunga ("I got a caribou"), *nirli*tutit ("you got a Canada goose"), or *nannu*tuq ("he/she got a polar bear"). It is as if the finality of an *uumajuq*'s life—let us remember that the word *uumajuq* means "it is alive"—would be to offer itself to a worthy hunter, this act being implied in the very name of the species.[24] For instance, a *natsiq* ("ringed seal") would only fulfill its life goal (*uumajjuti*, "reason for being alive") when being *natsitaq* ("caught as a seal"), or "ringed seal-ed." In a way, animals thus act as intermediaries between humans and *sila*. In the words of the well-known Inuit ecological activist Sheila Watt-Cloutier (2016, 137), "The animals that are our country food connect us to the water and the land, to the 'source' of our life, to God."

Once its destiny is fulfilled, so to speak, the dead *uumajuq* becomes an *uumajuviniq* ("former *uumajuq*"). Because the very meaning of the word *uumajuq* is "it is alive," it would be contradictory to call a dead animal *uumajuq*. The *natsiq* caught in the example above is now a *natsiviniq*, one that was a *natsiq* once but is no longer such. If we follow the teachings of the shamans of old, it may be presumed that after the animal has offered itself to humans, it returns to the collective soul of its species and is born again as a *natsiaq* ("baby seal").

From the standpoint of the *uumajuit*, the different stages of these fatal encounters between game animals and human hunters can be summarized as follows. The stages are expressed in the passive voice because the words used are those of the hunter:

uumajursiutaq	"one that is searched for as an *uumajuq* [i.e., is hunted]"
uumajursiarijaq	"one that is an encountered *uumajuq* [i.e., is actually seen]"
uumajurniavigijaq	"one that is had as an occasion for dealing with an *uumajuq* [i.e., has become a prey]"
uumajurtaq	"one that is '*uumajuq*-ed' [i.e., is caught as an animal]"
uumajuviniq	"one that was an *uumajuq* once [i.e., is a dead animal]"

and maybe (cf. Spalding 1998, 194):

uumartuq	"one that comes to life again [i.e., revives]"

Encountering game animals may thus be considered a kind of ritual or drama in at least five acts, whereby *uumajuit* offer their bodies to those hunters willing to share them with their community. Once this sacrifice has been accomplished, animal souls are free to be reborn, thus perpetuating the cycle of life and death. For this reason, beyond its basic economic and social functions, hunting can truly be defined as "a symbolic activity enabling to bridge the gap between the visible and the invisible" (Therrien 1999, 30).

Hunting and Fishing Gear

Maqainniq entails the use of a complex equipment, adapted to each type of subsistence activity. *Puijiit* were generally hunted with a harpoon (*igimaq*, "that is thrown repeatedly," or *unaaq*, possibly related to PE *urnəg-*, "to go toward"), whose detachable head (*naulaq*, from *naulik-*, "to throw a harpoon"; or *tuukkaq*) was tied to a leather line (*ipiraq*, "that is tied"; or *aliq*) held in the hand of the harpooner. In winter, hunters waited for seal at the breathing holes these animals maintain in the sea ice (*alluit* or *agluit*, singular *allu/aglu*; etymologically, "place for getting out"), and when spring came, they stalked seals basking in the sun on the ice floe (*uuttuq*, "it [seal on ice] gets burned").

In late summer, caribou were the object of a collective hunt. Two parallel or converging rows of stone cairns (*inutsuit*, singular *inutsuk* or *inuksuk*, "that resembles a person") were built, and women and children shouted at the animals in order to entice them to run between the cairns. Men waited behind the *inutsuit* or at the end of the rows, killing the incoming caribou with a spear (*anguvigaq*, "small occasion or place for catching something") or a bow (*pititsi* or *pitiksi*, "that makes it receive something") and arrows (*qarjuit*, singular *qarjuk*; possibly from PE *qarəður*, "one that comes up or away" [Fortescue et al. 2010, 314, 439]). Smaller, three-pronged darts or spears were used for throwing at birds (*nuit*) or spearing Arctic char (*kakivak*, "that has the habit of stinging"). In summer, char were also caught with stone weirs (*saputiit*, "used for blocking something") that stopped fish swimming upriver. Another fishing implement was the line and hook (*aulasauti*, "used for trying to make it [the hook and its decoy] move").

The arrival of *Qallunaat* brought major changes to Inuit technology. Fish nets (*nuluat*, "the laced ones") were introduced, as well as steel traps (*mikigiat*, singular *mikigiaq*, "tearing something away with the teeth") for catching fox. The biggest innovation, however, was the introduction of guns (*qukiutiit*, singular *qukiuti*, "means for producing a loud noise")[25] and bullets (*sakkuit*, singular *sakku*, "projectile"), made available to Inuit since the late 1700s in some areas. Firearms progressively replaced traditional weapons, and harpoons and spears have long become obsolete. Ancient tools disappeared, too. For example, manual and electric drills took the place of the bow drill but kept the same name (*ikuutaq*, "a means for hacking"). The adze became an axe (*ulimauti*, "a means for fashioning something"), and stones formerly used for hammering were replaced by the hammer (*ujaratsiaq*, "good stone," or *kautaq*, "a means for hammering").

The old means of transportation, so essential to a semi-nomadic society, progressively disappeared when imported contrivances became available. The large open skin boat (*umiaq*; possible etymology, "something closed off [from water]" [Fortescue et al. 2010, 403]) was replaced by the motor boat (*umiaraa-luk*, "big *umiaq*") as early as the beginning of the twentieth century,[26] and from the 1920s on, the canvas canoe (*qajariaq*, "that is like a kayak") powered by an outboard motor (*qianngujuuq*, "that sounds like crying") started replacing skin kayaks (*qajait*, singular *qajaq*), the last of which disappeared from Nunavik in the mid-1960s. During the same decade, snowmobiles (*sikiitu*, from the trademark "Skidoo") took the place of dogs, although the new contrivances were still used to pull sleds (*qamutiik*). Finally, regarding dwellings, the tent (*tupiq*) started being covered with canvas rather than skins at the beginning of the twentieth century, and in Nunavik, wooden houses (*illujuat*, "super-residences") completely replaced the snow house (*illuvigaq*, "little big residence") by the end of the 1950s.

The Products of Subsistence Activities

The primary goal of subsistence activities is to produce food for men and their domestic animals. Among Inuit, the most basic type of food is *niqi* ("meat, flesh"), a word related to the verbal base *niri-* ("to eat"). In a parallel way, the prototypical beverage, water (*imiq*), the only one known to traditional Inuit, has generated the base *imir-* ("to drink"; cf. *imirtuq*, "he/she drinks"). Nowadays, the word *niqi* applies to any type of food, and meat, properly speaking, especially that of locally hunted animals, is called *niqituinnaq* ("genuine *niqi*"). An old Inuk who has not eaten *niqituinnaq* for a few days might say, "*Kaattunga*"—"I am hungry," even if he or she has eaten plenty of *Qallunaat* food.[27] This is why Inuit elders hospitalized in southern Canada are provided with country food sent from Nunavik or Nunavut.

The lexical distinction between *niqi* as a generic term for food and *niqituinnaq* ("meat") may have appeared when *Qallunaat* traders introduced flour during the eighteenth and nineteenth centuries. This new food item soon became an indispensable complement to meat, or even a replacement when game was scarce. In Nunavik, flour became considered a staple food and this was reflected in the vocabulary. Meat remained the "genuine *niqi*" (*niqituinnaq*), but flour was defined as another form of *niqi*: *niqitsajaq* ("*niqi*-to-be") in western Nunavik and *sanaugaq* ("something [*niqi*] that is manufactured") in the northeastern part of the region. Flour was mostly used for baking bread (*niaquujaq*, "that looks like a head") or, much more frequently, bannock bread (*panirtitaq*, "that has been dried"). The latter word refers to the way bannock is baked. Flour is mixed with water, seal blubber or commercial shortening (*punniq*, "coagulated fat floating on broth"), and baking powder (*pujjusiuti*, "means for making it [dough] rise"). This moist mixture is then baked in a saucepan or in the oven, until it has become dry.

Meat can be eaten raw (*mikigaq*, "that is bitten off"; the same word applies to raw fish and even uncooked greens), boiled (*uujuq*, "that has burned for a long time"), dried (*nikku/mikku* for dried meat; *pitsi/pipsi* for dried fish, the latter possibly related to PE *pipək-*, "to split lengthwise")—very practical as *taquat* ("travel food")—gamey (*igunaq*; possible etymology, "the fact of extracting oil from blubber"), or, much more rarely, smoked (*isiritsiaq*, "that has been exposed to a lot of smoke").

Beluga or narwhal skin, *mattaaq*, is eaten raw, boiled, or fried in a pan. The giblets of most sea mammals, as well as those of caribou, are edible too. *Tinguk* (liver) is particularly appreciated raw. It was formerly reserved for male hunters, who often carved it directly from a freshly killed animal, while women had the exclusive right to eat *kujapik*, the meat around the dorsal vertebrae of large *puijiit*. Caribou fat (*tunnu*) and the blubber (*ursuq*) of ringed seals are eaten too, and raw or dried meat is often dipped in rancid seal or beluga oil (*misiraq*, "repeated dips"). The latter dish has a yellow-brown colour, and the first time I was offered *misiraq*, convinced it was seal urine, I admired the way Inuit ate every part of the *natsiq*, even, I thought, its excrement.

When referring to the meat of any *uumajuq* except, seemingly, fish and shellfish, the already mentioned affix -*viniq* ("a former, or dead one") is added to the name of the animal: *natsi*viniq ("ringed seal meat"), *tuttu*viniq ("caribou meat"), *ukali*viniq ("hare meat"), *miti*viniq ("eider duck meat"), and so on. When attached to the name of any kind of food, another affix, -*tu(r)*- ("to make use of"), takes the meaning "eating or drinking something," as in *tuttuvinir*tutuq ("he/she eats caribou meat"), *mattaa*turtunga ("I eat *mattaaq*"), *aisikirimi*turtugut ("we eat ice cream"), or *imialut*utut ("they drink big water [alcohol]").

Traditional cooking and eating utensils included *ukkusik* (possibly related to PE *ugut-*, "to cook something"), a cooking pot carved out of soapstone, as was the *qulliq*, the seal-oil lamp over which the *ukkusik* hung. *Qulliq* means "the uppermost one" because traditional lamps were set on a base that made them higher than the surface of the snow or other shelf on which they were placed. There were also plates (*puugutait*, singular *puugutaq*, "used for holding something") and cups (*qajuuttait*, singular *qajuuttaq*, "a means for drinking *qajuq* [meat or fish broth, generally drunk at the end of a meal]"). There were no forks or spoons, but knives were essential for undertaking various tasks. Each man had his *savik*, a pointed knife, and every woman possessed—and still does—her own *ulu* (a word meaning "tongue" in the Yupik languages; see Chapter 5), a half-moon-shaped knife used for carving meat, as well as for taking the fat off a skin or cutting out a piece of leather. A wider knife, the *pana* (this word means "spear, lance" in PE and most Inuit dialects), was used for cutting blocks of snow when building an igloo.

Another important product generated by subsistence activities was animal skin or hide, either *qisik* (sea mammal skin) or *amiq* (land mammal skin). Formerly, all clothes (*annuraat*, singular *annuraaq*; related to PE *atǝ-*, "to put on") were made of skin and sewed by women (*mirsu[r]tuq*, "she sews"), with a needle (*mirquti*, "used for sewing") and sinew thread (*ivalu*; conjecturally, "something for oscillating or swinging while moving,"[28] a possible allusion to threading). Everyone possessed two sets of clothing, an inner (*iluppiaq*, "most inside") and an outer set (*silappiaq*, "most outside"). The *iluppiaq* was always made of caribou skin and the fur was turned toward the body, while the *silappiaq*, in seal or caribou skin, had the fur facing outside. Each set of clothing comprised four pieces (cf. Saladin d'Anglure 2013, 100–102):

iluppiaq	*atigi* (hooded tunic; PE *atǝkǝ*, "that is put on")
	qarliik ilupaak (inner pants)
	alirtiik ("lower area," i.e., stockings)
	pualuuk ilupiruuk (inner mitts; *pualuuk*, "mitts," is related to *puuq*, "bag")
silappiaq	*qulittaq* ("added upper [body] part," i.e., hooded parka)
	qarlikajaak (outer pants)
	kamiik (boots)
	pualuuk silapiruuk (outer mitts)

Outer pants worn in winter could be made of polar bear or dog skin.

Furs have long been replaced by imported fabric (*qallunaartaq*, "something related to *Qallunaat*"). The *atigi* is now made of duffle, and a linen or polyester *silapaaq* ("the outermost one") has replaced the *qulittaq*. Inuit wear shirts (*uviniruq*, "that touches the skin"), sweaters (*tasijuaq*, "that stretches"), skirts and dresses (*ulik*, "that covers"; or *qaummaq*, "garment [with an] edge"), shoes and boots (*kamialuuk*, "big *kamiik*"), and hats (*nasaq*, the name of the traditional hood). But they have preserved some important elements of their former attire. The modern *atigi* has kept its fur-trimmed hood, sealskin *kamiik* are still worn, and women have largely maintained the habit of carrying their babies in the *amauti* ("means for carrying someone on one's own back"), a parka with a very wide back pouch. Such pieces of clothing have now become symbols of contemporary Inuit identity.

Conclusion

Uumajuit ("animals") are primarily defined as living creatures (cf. *uumajut*, "they are alive"). They share with human beings a common source of life, the heart (*uummati*, "what gives life"), but as we shall see in the next chapter, humans are *inuit* (*inuujuq*, "he/she is an *inuk*/is alive"), not *uumajuit*. Despite this fundamental difference, animals are endowed with some parahuman characteristics and as such, they must be respected by Inuit. Some species, the polar bear (*nanuq*), for instance, are able to learn about their surroundings, decide what they must do in order to survive, and think about what they need to do in order to fulfill their goals. *Uumajuit*, at least those that contribute to the subsistence of Inuit (the *nirjutiit*, "means for eating"), also have suprahuman powers. They offer themselves (*tunijut*) as prey to hunters whom they know to be generous, thus displaying a level of knowledge close to that of shamans.

Encounters between hunters and game animals are described as comprising several stages, culminating in catching *uumajuit* that had first been searched for, encountered, and dealt with. Linguistically, this capture is expressed by adding a verbal ending to the name of the animal (e.g., *tuttutunga*; literally, "caribou-I did," or "I caught a caribou"). The noun denoting the animal's species thus becomes a verb, as if the finality of being an *uumajuq* resides in the act of being killed. This may explain why a dead animal cannot be an *uumajuq* anymore. It becomes an *uumajuviniq* ("former animal"), one that has once been a living creature and might be reborn (*uumartuq*) in order to offer itself again to a worthy hunter.

One *uumajuq* does not enter into this type of encounter, except as hunting partner, the dog (*qimmiq*). Dogs are born to be "shy and respectful," as implied in the probable etymology of the word *qimmiq*. They must obey their master (their *inuk*), pulling the sled and doing other tasks. In exchange for their services, they do not have to look for their own sustenance, unlike all other *uumajuit*, because they are fed by their *inuk*, except in summer, when unneeded dogs are sometimes transported to an island where they have to provide for their own livelihood, searching for young birds, small rodents, carrion, or other food. *Qimmiit* belong to their master's household, receive personal names, and are the objects of some affection.

Besides its etymological link with the concepts of shyness and respect, the word *qimmiq* might possibly relate to the word-base *qimuk-* ("to pull something"). If this stands true, dogs would be partly defined through their primary function of sled-pullers. More generally, those names of *uumajuit* whose etymology is decipherable often refer to a salient characteristic of the genus or species they denote. The generic terms for sea mammals (*puijiit*, "those that appear out of the water"), land mammals (*pisuttiit*, "the walkers"), and birds (*timmiat*, "those that fly") are cases in point. In a similar way, the names of the ringed seal (*natsiq*, "nodding head"), caribou (*tuttu*, "much fat"), raven (*tulugaq*, "that gives blows with its beak"), mussel (*uviluq*, "that opens like an eye"), and many others provide micro-descriptions of these animals. Such descriptive terms also denote a number of implements and products related to traditional subsistence activities, such as *igimaq* ("thrown repeatedly," harpoon), *mikigaq* ("bitten off," raw meat), and *mirquti* ("used for sewing," needle).

This stroll through words used for speaking about animals and subsistence, as incomplete as it is, confirms two lexical tendencies already observed in the preceding chapter: the existence of a very specialized technical vocabulary (e.g., the names given to animals of different age groups); and the fact that, as we just saw, many words consist of micro-descriptions of what they denote. Some terms, however, refer to another level of reality. For example, the name of the muskrat, *kiggaluk* ("little messenger"), seems metaphorical rather than strictly descriptive. Several technical terms convey such metaphors, albeit in an implicit, often unsaid way. In Inuit symbolism, for instance, objects with curved shapes, like the half-moon *ulu* knife and the rounded tail of the *amauti* parka, are associated with women, while pointed shapes, such as harpoons (*igimait* or *unaat*), the *savik* knife, and the prow of the kayak (*usuujaq*, "that looks like a penis") are related to men (Saladin d'Anglure 1977). According to Therrien (1987, 60), the snow house shares several physical and functional similarities with women (e.g., internality and relative permanency), while the kayak suggests characteristics of men (e.g., externality and movement). The next chapter, on humans and spirits, should open a door on this symbolic world.

CHAPTER THREE

Words for Speaking about Humans and Spirits

Inuk—Anirnilik, isumaqarvilik, tarnilik. Isuarturijaminik maligiarunnatuq uvvaluunniit maligumanngikuni maligunnangittuq. Amma angutik arnausunilu tuqusuittumik tarnilik inuk.

Human being—He/she has breath, a receptacle for thoughts, a soul. He/she may set about following what seems convenient to him/her, or not following it if he/she does not want to. And a human being, man or woman, has an immortal soul.

TAAMUSI QUMAQ (1991, 35)

**Inuk—Ukiuqtaqturmiutaq
Qallunaangunngittuq inuuvuq.**

Inuup timingatut aaqqiksimajut tamarmik inungmik taijaugivut.

Inuk/Human being

An inhabitant of the Arctic who is not a Qallunaaq is an Inuk.

Anyone whose body is shaped like that of an Inuk is also called inuk.

ELISAPEE OOTOOVA ET AL. (2000, 56)

Like the word *nuna*, now familiar to the general public thanks to names such as Nunavut and Nunavik given to Indigenous Arctic territories in North America, the term *inuk* (plural *inuit*), "person, human being," is also well-known. Over the past four decades, it has almost completely replaced the appellation "Eskimo" as an ethnic designation.[1] This may entail some degree of ambiguity, as shown in the two definitions above, one (Qumaq's) from Nunavik, the other from northern Baffin Island. In order to avoid such ambiguity, in this chapter and the following ones, the word *inuk/inuit*, in italics and with a small initial *i*, will always mean "human being(s)," while "Inuk/Inuit," with a capital "I" (and no italics) will refer to ethnic Inuit.

For Qumaq, the term *inuk* refers to all creatures, men and women, who in addition to breathing like *uumajuit* ("animals") have a "receptacle for thoughts" (*isumaqarvik*), that is, an intellect that allows them to think,[2] and an immortal soul (*tarniq*). Because they are able to cogitate (*isumajuq*, "he/she thinks, reflects on something"), *inuit* understand what is suitable or convenient for them (*isuartuq* or *i&uartuq*; etymologically, "that is well"), although they can decide if they will follow (*malittuq*, "he/she follows someone or something") that path or not. Besides intelligence (shared to some extent with polar bears and dogs), human beings are endowed with a free will that allows them to make a choice between good and evil. Each person has an immortal soul, presumably unlike animals, whose collective soul is shared by all members of a species.

For Ootoova and her collaborators, an *inuk* is first of all an Indigenous inhabitant of the (North American) Arctic, one who is not a white person (*Qallunaaq*). Secondarily, any individual shaped like an Indigenous *inuk* may be called an *inuk*, too. In the minds of the Pond Inlet (North Baffin) compilers of the *Uqausiit tukingit* dictionary, the prototypical human beings—at least those living in the Arctic—are thus the ethnic Inuit.

The same idea is implicit in Qumaq's definition of the plural word *inuit*, listed as a separate entry from the singular *inuk* (1991, 35):

Inuit—Taijaugusingat nunarjuamiut tauttuqatigiinngitut piusiqaqatigiigatillu uqausiqaqatigiigatillu. Taimaittuumata inuit nujaliit qirnitanik ammalu uviningit kajuit qakurtaungittut.

People—[This is] the appellation of the inhabitants of the whole world, who do not share the same look and whose customs, as well as languages, are different. Because it is so, [Inuit] people have black hair and their skin is brown, not white.

This definition is anthropological, whereas that of *inuk* was moral. This description insists on the racial, cultural, and linguistic diversity of human beings, but it singles out ethnic Inuit by highlighting what differentiates them physically from *Qallunaat* ("their skin is brown, not white").

Questions of Identity

This apparent ambiguity of *inuk/inuit*, a word that refers at the same time to humanity in general and to a specific Indigenous group, is due to the fact that like many other peoples—the Innu and Dene First Nations, or the Melanesian and Polynesian Kanak, for instance—Inuit did not have any special ethnic or national self-appellation. They simply thought of themselves as "people," human beings. In Inuktitut, the current way for a visitor to inquire if there is someone in the house he or she has just entered is to ask, "*Inuqarqa?*"—"Is there any *inuk* [person]?" At a more restricted level, local groups were—and still are—identified thanks to the affix *-miut* ("inhabitants of") added to the name of the place or area where they dwelt, or by the name of their family head followed by the suffix *-kkut* ("group, family of").

As we saw in Qumaq's definition at the opening of Chapter 2, one of the primary distinctions in Inuit thinking is the subdivision of breathing creatures into two different categories: people (*inuit*) and animals (*uumajuit*). Qumaq states explicitly that the latter are not "actually human" (*inutuinnaungittut*), even though they possess some near-human or suprahuman abilities. Besides animals, however, the universe (*silarjuaq*, "huge *sila*") includes other categories of non-human—or not fully human—sentient beings endowed, like *inuit*, with some form of *isuma* ("reason"):

tuniit	prehistoric paleo-Eskimo Dorset people (present in the Arctic long before the ancestors of present-day Inuit), presumed by some Inuit to still live far inland; the word might be related to the PE base *tunər-*, "strength, solidity" (Fortescue et al. 2010, 382)
tuurngait	shamanic spirits (see below)

inugagulli(ga)it, etc.   dwarves and several other types of
non-human beings

Inuit living in the southern regions of the Arctic have long been in contact
with individuals who look and behave like human beings but were formerly
considered as radically alien and therefore not fully *inuit*: the Algonquian
and Dene First Nations. In Nunavik and Labrador, Algonquian-speaking
Innu, Naskapi, and Cree are called *allait* (singular *alla*), "strangers," while
west of Hudson Bay, a distinction is made between *unaliit* or *unallit* (singular *unaliq*), "fearsome people" (Cree), and *irqiliit* or *itqilgit* (singular *irqilik*
or *itqilik*), "those with louse nits [*irqi(it)*]" (Dene). In Alaska, Dene are
known under names cognate to their Canadian appellation: *ingqilit, iqqil-
git*, or *icqilgit*.

Traditional thinking has been partly modified by Christian beliefs and
school education, but even now, many if not most Inuit consider *sila* to be
inhabited by several different categories of sentient beings with whom interaction is possible. Some of these beings, the *uumajuit*, can be encountered
by anyone. Others, like the *tuurngait* and *inugagulli(ga)it*, are much more
elusive. Their suprahuman powers enable them to become invisible whenever they want, and/or to be seen only by those—the shamans of yore, for
instance—who possess *qaumaniq* ("shamanic light"). As for the Cree, Dene,
and other First Nations, they are now considered to be full human beings, of
course. Furthermore, they are seen as fellow *nunalituqait* ("ancient holders
of the land") or *nunaqarqaatuit* ("those who held land before others"),
that is, Indigenous peoples. However, Inuit do not consider themselves as
belonging to Canada's First Nations because their culture, history, social
conditions, and natural environment are too different from those of other
Canadian Aboriginals.

From the sixteenth century on, and earlier in Greenland, Inuit had
increasing contact with creatures coming from *tariup akiani*, the other side of
the sea. These often big and hairy people, who sailed huge boats and possessed
a wealth of objects and foodstuffs unknown—but desirable—to Inuit, were
called *qallunaat* or *qablunaat* (singular *qallunaaq/qablunaaq*). This term
for referring to white Europeans seems to have appeared in Greenland, later
spreading to most of the Canadian Arctic.[3] Its most obvious meaning is
"prominent or frowning eyebrows," but according to Fortescue et al. (2010,
318–19), the word might also have been derived from the now-obsolete

Greenlandic verbal base *qallunaar-* ("to wither, become bleached"). Whatever the case may be, the term *qallunaat* defines white people through one salient aspect of their physical appearance: hairiness, or having a pale face.

In her novel *Sanaaq* (written in the early 1950s),[4] Nunavik author Salome Mitiarjuk Nappaaluk imagines—based on stories heard from elders during her youth—the first encounter between a small band of Inuit hunters and a group of Europeans:

> *Sunauvva ullaangulirtilugu umiarjuaraaluk tikittuviniq sinittilugit; Arnatuinnaq ullaakut takunialirtuq; takujariursuni imaililirtuq, tupaarsaisuni ilaminik: "Ilakkaa tupaliritsi! Sunaalukiaq saattini qikartualuk?"*

> Surpringly, at sunrise, while they were asleep, a huge ship has arrived. In the morning Arnatuinnaq goes out [of the tent] to have a look. Seeing [such a thing] for the first time, she behaves as follows: she wakes her companions: "My fellows, wake up! What is that big immobile thing facing us?" (Nappaaluk 1984, 26)

Arnatuinnaq's people are terrified when the ship blows its horn several times. Some sailors then come ashore:

> *Suli irsigaluarsutik, inuummata surquisiliramik, irsigunnailirtut. Itirtaulirqut qallunaanut; itirsimalirmata Aqiarulaaq imaililirquq qallunaanut: "Ai!" Sunauvva, tukisirqajanngimata, nillingittuluunniit; uqaviruutilirmataguuq, taikkua inutuinnait ajugailliutuvialuuqattalirtut.*

> While still afraid, when they realize that they [the sailors] are human beings [*inuit*], they are not terrified anymore. The *Qallunaat* enter [the tent]; when they are inside, Aqiarulaaq [addresses] the *Qallunaat* as follows: "Hi!" Surprisingly, because they do not understand, they [the sailors] do not even emit a sound. But when they start speaking among themselves, they, the genuine *inuit* [*inutuinnait*], are completely astonished.[5] (Nappaaluk 1984, 26)

The arriving *Qallunaat* are rapidly identified as human beings and as such, they are expected to speak Inuktitut (i.e., like *inuit*). But they do not understand that language, even though they seem able to communicate orally among themselves. Hence the astonishment of the "genuine *inuit*," who have encountered a form of humanity that is new to them.

Until the mid-twentieth century, in Arctic Canada at least, all non-Indigenous people were considered to be *Qallunaat*.[6] But once Inuit became familiar with people whose languages or physical looks were at variance, the word *qallunaat* became a generic term, with separate nationalities or races receiving specific appellations. In Nunavik, for instance, *qallunaat* include the following subcategories (the list is not exhaustive):

qallunaangajuit	mixed-blood Inuit ("part *qallunaat*")
qallunaatuinnait	Anglophones ("the only genuine *qallunaat*")
uiguit	Francophones ("[those who say] *oui-oui*")
jamait	Germans (from the English "German")
qirnitait	people of colour, blacks ("black beings")[7]
sainisiit	Chinese (from the English "Chinese")
inuujartuit	East Asians in general ("those who look like Inuit")

In northern Labrador, the word *qallunaangajuit* (*Kallunângajuit* in the local spelling) was long used as an ethnic appellation for those who were called "Settlers" in English—descendants of British fishermen and trappers who had moved to the area during the nineteenth century and married Indigenous women. In 2005, these people were part of the Nunatsiavut Agreement between the Labrador Inuit Association and the government of Newfoundland, and they are now considered to be fully fledged Inuit.

Qallunaatuinnait, the speakers of English, are seen as the prototypical *Qallunaat* ("only genuine *qallunaat*") because they were the first non-Indigenous people to maintain sustained contact with the Nunavik (and most other Canadian) Inuit. After some time, the Inuit language had to find a way to distinguish between human beings (*inuit*) in general—a type of creatures to which *Qallunaat* obviously belonged (see the extract from *Sanaaq*, above)—and ethnic Inuit, the Indigenous inhabitants of the North American Arctic.

In Canada and Alaska, this was generally done by affixing to the word-base *inu-* ("person") various morphemes that stressed the fact that ethnic Inuit do constitute the prototype of Arctic humanity:[8]

inutuinnait	"the only genuine people" (Nunavik, Labrador, eastern Nunavut)
inungmariit	"the complete people" (Nattilingmiutut speakers, western Nunavut)
inuinnait	"the genuine people" (Inuinnaqtun speakers, western Nunavut)
inuvialuit	"the big real people" (Mackenzie coast and delta, Northwest Territories)
inu-/iñupiat	"the real people" (northern Alaska)

Nowadays, some of these names—the last three in particular—have become quasi-ethnic regional designations, in Inuktitut as well as in English.

Being an Inuk

Fortescue et al. (2010, 150) suggest that the word *inuk*—and its Yupik cognates *yuk* and *suk*—might be related to the Proto-Aleut word-bases *ing(i)yu-* ("living body") and *ingisxi-* ("owner"). This means that the contemporary term *inuk* could possibly reflect a very old Proto-Eskimo-Aleut form, shared some 4,000 years ago by speakers of the language(s) ancestral to modern Aleut, Yupik, and Inuit.[9] *Inuit* (humans) and other creatures endowed with *isuma* would thus be defined as animated beings who can "own" other beings:

> Such ownership could be either physical (as in *qimmiup* inu*a*, "a dog's person" [i.e., master]) or spiritual (as in *sikuup* inu*a*, "the person of the sea-ice" [i.e., its resident spirit]). In other words, a person (embodied or spiritual) would be an animated animator, in contrast with animals (*uumajuit*, "those who are alive"), which are animated but do not "own" anything else. (Dorais 2010, 138)

Fortescue et al. (2010, 150) also mention that meanings of the word *inuk* that extend beyond and, metaphorically, below that of "human person" are attested in all Yupik languages and Inuit dialects. Such meanings include "resident spirit," as noted above, but also "animated occupant of a specific space":

a chick in an egg (e.g., *mannik* inu*lik*, "the egg has someone [an embryo] in it"), a seal in its breathing hole (e.g., *alluup* inu*a aulajuujaartuq*, "the inhabitant of the seal-hole seemed to move" [Spalding 1998, 26]), and so on.

In the case of human beings, the term *inuk* lies at the centre of a network of derivatives expressing the development, behaviour, and underlying nature of humanity. The ethnolinguist Michèle Therrien (1987) gives the following examples in Nunavik Inuktitut:

inuulirtuq	he/she is born ("starts to be a person")
inuujuq	he/she is alive ("is a person")
inururtuq	he/she reincarnates ("becomes a person")
inurqituq	he/she is a good individual ("is a good person")
inuluk	a bad individual ("a bad person")
inuttitut/inuktitut	Inuit language and customs ("[doing] like human beings")

More specifically, the different stages of human existence, expressed through derivatives of the word *inuk* or otherwise, describe the progressive achievement of full humanness. In northeastern Nunavik Inuktitut, life unfolds as follows:

piaratsaq, or *inutsaq*	human fetus ("future young thing," *or* "future person")
inuulirtuq	who is born ("who starts to be a person")
nutaraq	infant, baby ("new being")
piaraq	child ("young thing")
uvikkaq	teenager ("who has been lengthened [?]")
inuusuttuq	youth, young adult ("who is striving to be a person")
inummarik	mature adult ("complete person")
inutuqaq	elderly individual ("long-standing person")
inuviniq	deceased individual ("former person")

Human beings thus start as "future children or persons," before being born as new individuals who progressively grow and learn to be men or women, striving to become actual persons (*inuit*). Full humanness is only reached at maturity, when people are "complete *inuit*," and then "long-standing persons," elders who will die one day and be remembered as "former individuals." As will be seen in the next chapter, the cycle of life starts anew (*inururtuq*, "he/she reincarnates") when the names of these *inuviniit* are given to newborn babies. It should be noted that in Nunavut, an adult is called *innaq*. Etymologically related to Proto-Inuit *inəq-*, "to finish" (Fortescue et al. 2010, 145), this word evokes completeness, thus conveying the same idea as *inummarik* does. In eastern Nunavut, *inungmarik/inummarik* refers to a traditional Inuk, generally an elder, who knows the environment, language, and culture perfectly. As I was once told, "You can drop an *inungmarik* anywhere on the land, and he or she will be able to find his or her way back home without outside support."

Like animals, humans can be either male or female. A man or a male animal are called *anguti*, while a human or animal female is an *arnaq*.[10] The anthropologist Bernard Saladin d'Anglure (2005) has hypothesized that independently from their sexual orientation, some Inuit belong to a "third gender." This would include individuals named after someone whose gender is different from their own biological sex and who are raised until puberty as if they belonged to the gender of their namesake. Most shamans could have belonged to this "third gender." It must be said, however, that such a notion does not find any linguistic expression in Inuktitut, and speakers are not generally aware of gender categories other than male and female.

According to North Baffin mythology, the first two *inuit* were males, born from the earth. One took the other as spouse, so he became pregnant. When he was about to give birth, his companion sang a magic song, urging the man's penis to split in order to create a way out for the fetus; thence the advent of women (Rasmussen 1929, 252).

The most obvious etymology for the word *anguti* is "a means for catching something," from the verbal base *angu-* ("to catch") and the affix *-(u)ti* ("a means for"). However, Fortescue et al. (2010, 38) states that PE *angun*—etymon of the modern Inuktitut form—instead stems from *angə-* ("being big") plus possibly *-un* ("a means for doing"). This assertion is based on a morphological criterion: the modern Inuit forms of *angun* ("male") are never geminated (*angngun*), while those of *angu-* ("to catch") sometimes are, hence the alleged linguistic impossibility that the former be derived from the latter. From a semantic perspective, though, it is quite plausible, but unproved, that for speakers of Inuktitut and other Inuit dialects, *anguti* ("man") and *anguvaa* ("catches it [game, etc.]") are related, since the traditional role of Inuit males was to provide meat and furs.

Fortescue et al. do not propose any etymology for the word *arnaq* ("female"). I have suggested (Dorais 2016, 68) that this term might derive from *ar-* ("to move, to run")[11] + *-nar* ("to make it so"). So, *arnaq* could be guessed to literally mean "who makes something move, who agitates something." This derivation may not make much sense to contemporary speakers, but it is linguistically plausible, and in my article I tentatively concluded that at a deeper semantic level, if *anguti* is understood as "a means for catching something," *arnaq* could well be defined as the one who puts the catcher into motion.

In Nunavik Inuktitut, an old man is an *ittuq* and an old woman, a *ningiuq*. At the other end of the age spectrum, a boy is called a *surusiq* (*turusiq* on Hudson Bay), a word that perhaps derives from *su(uq)-* ("something") + *-rusiq* ("secondary"), a boy being a "secondary [male] thing"; or from *surur-* ("to become useful") + *-siq* ("the fact of"), a male baby becoming a boy when he starts being able to help out. A young girl is a *niviarsiaq*, for which I have proposed (2016, 69) "the nice one (*-siaq*) who has been knocked down backward (*niviar-*)," implying a graphic sexual meaning. According to Fortescue et al. (2010, 255), however, PE *nəvi(C)ar-* ("girl") is instead related to *nəvə-* ("clinging to") or *nəviuq-* ("hanging around near"), the modern term *niviarsiaq* thus meaning something like "the one who is made to cling or stay close to someone." This would perhaps allude to the fact that traditionally, girls did not normally ramble off by themselves as men and boys did.

In Inuktitut, there do not exist morphological and lexical differences in the way men and women speak. Individuals belonging to either gender refer to the same objects or notions using the same words. However, because men and women develop distinct gender-related skills and interests, the extent of their vocabulary in one or another field of knowledge reflects these abilities. For example, men are usually more familiar with the classification of animal species than women are, while women have a much more extended knowledge of plants.

Young children possess their own vocabulary.[12] They are addressed and they answer in "baby talk," as is the case with many or most other languages of the world. In Nunavik, this vocabulary includes the following words:

amaama	breastmilk ("*Amaamaa!*"—"I want milk!")
anaana	mother ("*Anaanaa!*"—"Mommy!")
apaapa	solid food ("*Apaapalirit!*"—"Eat!")
ataata	father ("*Ataataa!*"—"Daddy!")
ququ	animal, big or small ("*Ququ una!*"—"That's an animal!")
apa	to urinate ("*Apaa!*"—"I need to pee!")
a'aluk[13]	something dangerous ("*A'aluuk!*"—"Watch out!")

The first four words display a nice pattern of phonological and semantic harmony. All four consist of reduplicated syllables with the vowel *a*. Food items (*amaama, apaapa*) use bilabial consonants, while the appellations for both parents are articulated on dentals. The terms for "breastmilk" and "mother" include nasal consonants (*m* and *n*), whereas those for "solid food" and "father" display non-nasals. Nasals thus evoke milk—with an *mm* suckling sound—and its provider, the mother, while non-nasals denote solid food and its traditional purveyor, the father.

Thinking and Feeling

Isuma-, Thinking

The most obvious and visible—because of its physical nature—component of human beings is their *timi* ("body"), which will be the subject of Chapter 5. If physiological mechanisms (moving, breathing, digesting) are set aside, human life—*inuusiq*, "the fact of being a person"—embodied in one's *timi* is regulated by *isuma* ("thought, reason"), the already mentioned mental faculty that enables men and women to understand *sila* and determine how they should behave in order to relate optimally to their natural and social environments. Taamusi Qumaq, who states in his definition of the word *inuk* (above) that humans possess an *isumaqarvik* ("receptacle for thoughts"), insists on the power of *isuma* in spite of its immateriality: "It cannot be seen; because of a person's mechanism for thinking [*isumauti*], what he/she thinks without uttering a sound, [his/her] thought, can set many things in motion, even though it is just thinking" (1991, 45). Ootoova et al. (2000, 75) summarize the three functions of *isuma* in this way: "*Isuma* is a mechanism for being able to remember, being able to know, and being able to become aware [of one's surroundings]."

Children and young people acquire *isuma* in a progressive way. By observing their surroundings and listening to adults, they learn how to deal correctly with *sila*, animals, their fellow *inuit*, and suprahuman beings. It is only when a person uses *isuma* properly that he or she is considered to be an adult individual, an *inummarik* ("complete *inuk*"). This does not always have to do with age. I remember a man who had had several children with the same woman but refused to acknowledge any social and financial responsibility toward them. When he was fifty-four, however, he finally recognized he had been wrong, stating publicly (on the community radio) that he would marry the mother of his children and take care of his family. The reaction of his fellow villagers was to say, "At last, he has become an adult (*inummarik*)."

Some people have more *isuma* than others. They are said to be *isumatujuq* ("who has a lot of *isuma*") or *silatujuq* ("who has a lot of *sila*").[14] By contrast, stupid individuals are *isumaittut* ("without *isuma*") or *silaittut* ("without *sila*"). The etymology of the word *isuma* is unclear. It could be related to PE *cumig-* ("to be anxious or annoyed about something"), although some speakers of Inuktitut might instead guess that *isuma* derives from *isuk-* ("end, extremity") + *-ma* ("something done"). Reasonable thinking might thus consist in "having reached the end [of acquiring common sense?]." The problem with such an etymology is morphological: *isuk-* + *-ma* would normally yield **isumma*, not *isuma*, and the affix *-ma-* must be attached to a verbal base, while *isuk* is a noun. However, there is one derivative of *isuma* that takes a double *m*: *isummaniq*, "someone [e.g., a child] who is now able to think correctly," meaning one who has reached the end of the *isuma*-acquiring process. So, the etymology of *isuma* remains an open question.

While *isuma* allows *inuit* to connect efficiently with their natural and social environments, it also teaches them the limits of these relationships. When, despite one's optimal efforts, a situation has become insurmountable—in cases of death, fatal illness, or serious heartbreak, for instance—an intelligent person understands that it is useless hoping to remedy it. The situation is out of one's power (*ajurnatuq/ajurnartuq*, "it makes one powerless"), the individual facing it is totally impotent (*ajurtuq*, "he/she cannot do anything more"), and it would be counterproductive and self-deluding to go further. The current phrase heard in such situations, especially in case of death, is *"Ajurna(r)mat"*—"[It happened] because nothing can be done." Rather than being fatalistic, this phrase expresses a realistic appraisal of the limitations of human capabilities.

Mental Skills

Isuma enables people to make use of a number of mental skills. Four of them are particularly important: knowing, understanding, remembering, and speaking. As we saw in Chapter 1, the verb *qaujima-* ("to know," literally, "to have become aware") starts with the base *qau-* ("light"): to know is to be enlightened. Ignorance is expressed through the verbal base *nalu-* (possibly related to PE *nallir*, "which one" [Fortescue et al. 2010, 231]), as in *naluvaa* ("he/she ignores it") or *nalunartuq* ("that makes one ignorant," i.e., "that is difficult to understand").

What is known must be understood. In the eastern Canadian Arctic, the word-base for "understanding" is *tukisi-*, as in *tukisivit?* ("do you understand?") and *tukisinngilanga* ("I don't understand"). The literal meaning of *tukisi-* is "to encounter a lengthwise axis [*tuki*]." Understanding something or someone thus consists in centring one's own mind and one's source of knowledge along the same axis. Interestingly enough, in Canada's western Arctic as well as in Alaska, the base for "understanding" is *kangirsi-*, literally, "to enter [*kangir-*] a bay," while in Greenland, it is *paasi-*, "entering the mouth [*paa-*] of a fjord." In both cases, to understand is to penetrate the source of knowledge.

What is known and understood is remembered, *irqa(r)-*, as in irqa*paa*, "he/she remembers it." *Irqa(r)-* (PE *ənqa[r]-*) might be a near cognate of *irqaq* (PE *ətqaq*), "the bottom of an expanse of water." Remembering would be like looking for memories in the depths of the mind. Another word-base for "remembering" is *aulaji-*, connected to *aula-* ("to move [memories out from the depths?]"). A few Inuit have memories of their intrauterine life and of their birth (see Saladin d'Anglure 1977; 2018, chap. 15), but most people trace their earliest recollections to the days when they were carried on their mother's back. They might say, for instance, "*Ilitarsigiurtunga amartausunga*"—"I started to recognize things while being carried in an *amauti*."

The literal meaning of *ilitarsi-* ("to recognize") is "to enter in contact (-*si*-) with an *ilitaq* [something or someone that/who has been recognized]." The verbal base *ili(t)*- has two significations: "to recognize someone or something familiar" (as in "Ili*tarivinga?*"—"Do you recognize me?"), as well as "to learn something" (as in "*Kisitsigutiit* ili*takka*"—"The numbers, I learn them," i.e., "I learn arithmetic"). The difference between the two meanings might only be apparent. It is quite possible that learning consists in recognizing elements of knowledge that a learner has not deciphered yet, even if they are already present in his or her familiar surroundings. If this makes sense, *ilippaa* ("he/she learns it") could be glossed as "he/she finds it to be familiar."

Knowledge, understanding, and memory allow people to communicate orally with their fellow *inuit*. "Speaking, saying" is *uqar-*, as in *uqartuq* ("he/she speaks, says") and *uqausiit* ("which are used for speaking," i.e., "words, language"). As stated by Taamusi Qumaq in the quotation that opens the Introduction to this book, speakers are deemed to be sincere—*sulijuq*, "he/she speaks the truth, is right" (literally, "it produces something," i.e., truthful words entail constructive results). Some speakers are not truthful, however, either voluntarily or because of their ignorance (*sallutujuq*, "he/she lies or is wrong"). Making a mistake is a serious matter, and lying deliberately is much worse. This is why when people say they "know" (*qaujimajut*) something, it is because they have experienced it directly. Otherwise, speakers state that they have "heard" (*tusaumajut*) about something, often mentioning—or being asked—the source of this hearsay.

Ippi-, Feeling

Ideally, all "complete persons" (adults) endowed with *isuma* are expected to have a good knowledge of their surroundings, always tell the truth (or what appears truth to them), and be able to control their feelings. This should allow them to behave according to common sense, thus contributing to maintaining harmony within *sila* and human society. Such people are said to be *ajunngi(t)tuq* ("not without power"), able to act in a competent and efficient way. However, as hinted at by Qumaq (1991, 35) in his definition of the word *inuk*, all *inuit* possess a highly valued free will that enables them to take decisions: "[They] may set about following what seems convenient to [them], or not following it if [they do] not want to." This is reflected in the language. The current way of telling a person that he or she is left with a free choice ("as you wish!") is "*Isumannik*"—"[You may follow] your *isuma*." Since thought has no limit, the notion of something innumerable or available at will is often expressed through the word *isumainnaq*, "a genuine *isuma*" (i.e., a boundless idea).

Because they are endowed with free will, *inuit* can behave in different ways, good (*piujuq*) or bad (*piunngituq*), suitable (*isuartuq*) or unsuitable (*isuittuq*).[15] Their reason often enters into conflict with their sensations and emotions. Physical and emotional feelings, as well as the awareness of what is happening in one's surroundings, are generally expressed with a single word-base, *ippi-/ikpi-* ("to feel [e.g., a pain or emotion], to be aware of something"; as in *ippigivaa*, "feels it, notices it"). *Isuma* does not always coincide with *ippigijait* ("feelings"), although *ippigusunniq* ("the fact of feeling or being aware of something") provides *inuit* with raw materials for reflecting upon their physical, societal, and supranatural environment.

Lack of balance between *isuma* and *ippigijait* can lead to emotional and social disorders. The anthropologist Jean Briggs, who conducted in the 1960s a thorough study of emotions among the Utkuhiksalik Inuit of central Nunavut (Briggs 1970), has elicited names for eleven types of feelings. Most of these appellations also exist in Nunavik Inuktitut, with the same or closely related meanings. Affection, for instance, is expressed in several ways, including the following:

nalligusuttuq	feels concerned with the well-being of someone, loves someone (related to PE *nangət-*, "to finish it up")
piutsatuq	finds someone nice, values him/her ("considers him/her to be something good")
niviurtuq	is anxious about a loved one, wants to be with him/her (etymologically, "clings repeatedly to something")
ungajuq	wants to be with someone

Happiness (*quviasuttuq* and *aliasuttuq*, "he/she is happy, rejoices"; *quvianartuq* and *alianartuq*,[16] "it provokes joy, happiness") is often perceived as the lack of hatred and envy that entails moral well-being. There exist words for expressing unhappiness (*tutsimajuq*, "is sad"; *kavartuq*, "feels blue"; *painngutuq*, "is tired to stay alone," i.e., is homesick), but the most common way to inquire about someone's apparent sadness is to ask, "*Quviasugunnaiqit?*" — "Are you not happy anymore?" This implies that people are expected to be in a good mood, unhappiness being considered a deviation from desirable feelings.

In spite of this expectation for happiness, hatred and envy may sometimes occur, in one form or another:

uumisuttuq	dislikes or hates someone (related to PE *ugu-*, "heated up")
ninngatuq	is angry
qilingujuq	is sullen, sulks
suattuq	abuses someone with words, quarrels with him/her (literally, "raises voice")
tusujuq	is envious, covets someone else's property or spouse
tilli(k)tuq	steals something
sinnajuq	is jealous

Negative feelings can cause some individuals to become dangerous (*kappianartuq*, "fearful, provokes fear"; *kappiasuttuq*, "is afraid," etymologically, "is anxious"), up to the point that other people may fear for their life (*irsinartuq*, "frightful, very dangerous"; *irsijuq*, "is frightened, afraid of being attacked violently"; related to Proto-Yupik *ira-*, "to be horrified").[17] In traditional Inuit camps, when an active or potential murderer (*inuarti*, "one who gets at human beings") was discovered, the men would agree that one of them would kill this violent person and then take his widow and children into his own household.

Harmony

Generally speaking, any inadequate or incorrect behaviour or habit tends to jeopardize social harmony and break peace (*saimmainiq*, "the fact of feeling consoled, morally appeased"; etymologically, "being in a state of ease"). Such behaviour is thus considered undesirable and for this reason, feels offensive until it has been corrected and peace restored. Like their forefathers, modern Inuit believe that judicial procedures and sanctions, whether customary or regulated by the laws of *Qallunaat*, find their only justification in the fact that they aim at restoring harmony, by reminding people what is the best way to behave in society.

In the preceding chapter, we discussed the importance of sharing the products of hunting and fishing (*ningirtuq*, "receives his/her part of the game that has been caught"). Sharing belongs to a more encompassing moral obligation of supporting each other (*ikajurtuq*, "helps someone"), especially those who need it more.[18] Respecting this obligation ensures social harmony. This is why from an early age, children are taught to be helpful. In Quaqtaq once, as I was walking through the village with my adoptive father (Saali Tarqiapik, the head of the household where I lived), we saw his old uncle trying to move something heavy. My father asked me, "*Inuuvit?*"—"Are you an Inuk?" Ignoring the reason for his question and how to answer it, I replied, "*Aatsuk*"—"I don't know." He then said, "*Inuit ikajusuungummata apirijau-gatik, ikajulaurlavuk!*"—"Because the Inuit habit is to aid people without being asked, let us help him!"

Receiving shares of the catch or hunt and being aided by others induces a feeling of gratitude (*nakursatuq*, "he/she thanks"; etymologically, "finds it worthy of praise because it is good"). As mentioned in Chapter 2, this feeling extends to animals, who give themselves to generous hunters. When Inuit entered into contact with Christianity, they discovered that sharing, mutual aid, and gratitude, which formed the very basis of their moral well-being, connection with *sila*, and social harmony, were quite similar to the evangelical precept of loving one's neighbour. This is why some people consider traditional Inuit culture to be closer to Christian teachings than the modern *Qallunaat* way of life will ever be.

Harmony implies respect. Humans must respect other sentient beings, whether supranatural or animal; younger individuals must show reverence toward their elders; and people must treat each other in a respectful way. The word-base *ilira-* expresses this sentiment of high respect (cf. *ilirasuttuq*, "feels respect"). It is sometimes translated as "awe," but in my opinion, this word is too strong. Those who are *iliragijait* ("*ilira*-ed")—one's parents and community elders, role models, revered beings, and so on—cannot be treated with too much familiarity, but they are not openly feared, even though one can feel somewhat ill at ease with them; a possible meaning of the PE etymon of *ilira-* could be "to want to ask for something but not dare"

(Fortescue et al. 2010, 115). One or two generations ago, many Inuit considered the *Qallunaat* working in the North as traders, policemen, missionaries, or government personnel to be *iliranartut* ("sources of *ilira-*," i.e., "worthy of respect") because of their power over the Indigenous population and the penalties they could inflict. But this is not the case anymore. I remember an occasion when I was joking with some Inuit friends that after my college graduation, I could come back to the Arctic as an administrator for the federal government. One of them replied that I was not *iliranartuq* ("*ilira*-inspiring") enough to boss Inuit. I felt relieved.

At a lower semantic level, *ilira-* can simply mean that one feels embarrassed toward somebody else, for instance, for not having replied promptly to an email. Someone who feels really bad because he or she has done something wrong is *kanngusuttuq* ("he/she is ashamed"). By contrast, a person who does not manifest *ilira-*, whether an unruly child or a vicious adult, is said to be *uiviittuq*, "without mental ability" (Fortescue et al. 2010, 422).

The Suprahuman World

Besides being home to *inuit*, the world hosts a vast number of sentient beings endowed with *isuma*. Some are invisible, others become visible when they wish to, or can only be seen by those who possess shamanic light, *qaumaniq*. There also exist supra- or parahuman forces that regulate life. At the cosmological level, *sila* is one of these forces, whether it is envisioned as an impersonal power or, as already mentioned, as an anthropomorphic being—*Silap* (or *Silam*) *Inua* ("The Person of *Sila*"), or the giant baby *Naarjuk* ("Big Belly")—ruling over weather and the seasons.

Human Souls

At the individual level, each human being possesses three immaterial components (aside from *isuma*): *anirniq* ("vital breath"), *atiq* ("name"), and *tarniq* ("human-like shadow"). All three are considered by most authors as different types of souls.

Both *inuit* and *uumajuit* ("animals") have *anirniq*, whose literal meaning is "the fact of breathing out" (cf. *anirtirijuq*, "he/she breathes out repeatedly [i.e., respires]"). According to Fortescue et al. (2010, 30), the PE root *anər-* ("breathing out") might be related to *anə-* ("to exit, to come out"), and indeed, when human or animal beings breathe out for the last time, they die and their *anirniq* disappears. The breath soul thus plays a vital role in ensuring life. Catholic missionaries borrowed the word *anirniq* for translating the term "spirit," as in *Anirnialuk* ("Great Spirit [God]") and *Anirniq Piujuq* ("Good Spirit [Holy Spirit]").

Only humans are endowed with an *atiq* ("name"), although they can bestow names on dogs, and since contact with *Qallunaat*, on boats and ships. The same interrogative pronoun, *kina?* ("who?"), is used for asking about the name of a person (or dog) and of a boat, as in "Kina *una umiarjuaq tikit-turataaq?—Amundsen una*"—"Who is this ship who has just arrived?—It [is] the Amundsen." As far as humans are concerned, *atiq* is actually a soul because when the names of deceased persons are given to a newborn—or when someone takes another name in order to escape illness or some other misfortune—these persons are revived in the new bearer of their names. Names can also be transferred from individuals who are still alive, elders in most cases, whose life is then reinforced because it is shared with that of the young person(s) named after them. The transmission of name souls thus allows for a form of reincarnation (more on this in the next chapter). The PE root for "name," *atər*, might be related to *ata(ði)-*, "to be the same" (Fortescue et al. 2010, 55). The notion of shared personal identity—or at least of the name as embodiment of a person's self—would therefore be inseparable from the act of naming.

The term for the third soul, *tarniq*, also meant "shadow" in PE (Fortescue et al. 2010, 363). Only *inuit* and some forms of suprahuman beings possess a *tarniq*. In the preceding pages I have referred to the collective souls of animal species, but these are not called *tarniq*. Taamusi Qumaq (1991, 253) states explicitly, "Animals are said not to have *tarniit*; what serves as subsistence [food] for humans living on earth does not possess a *tarniq*." It is nevertheless possible that animals participate in a soul through the *inua* ("its *inuk*," i.e., the master spirit) of their species.[19]

According to Fortescue et al. (2010, 363), the PE form of *tarniq*, *tar(ə)nər*, derives from *tarər-* ("to be dark") + *-nər* (nominalizing affix). As mentioned in Chapter 1, *tarniq* is etymologically related to *taaq* ("darkness"), *tarraq* ("shadow, reflection [e.g., in a mirror]"), and *tau* ("human being" in the shamanic language).[20] The *tarniq* soul can thus be considered as a kind of shadow or reflection of the individual it inhabits.[21] According to Saladin d'Anglure (2013, 180), for traditional Nunavik Inuit, *tarniq* was a miniature replica of the person, not larger than a finger, that was found in the lower part of the body. According to the North Baffin people, this miniature was encased in a compressed air bubble, swallowed when the newborn baby uttered its first cries (Saladin d'Anglure 2018, 59).

At death (*tuqujuq*, "he/she/it dies")—in northern Baffin, when the bubble bursts out—the shadow soul survives the body.[22] From one region to another, pre-Christian beliefs varied as to the fate of *tarniq*, but generally speaking, the souls of those who had died suddenly (including women who had passed away while giving birth) went to the upper world (*qilak*, "sky"), a pleasant place where they played ball with a walrus skull. The other deceased went to the colder and darker nether world, situated underground (*alliq*, "the lower one") or at the bottom of the sea (*qimiujaq*, "that looks like a net-line [?]"). Christian missionaries used the word *tarniq* for designating the immortal soul that goes to heaven (*qilak*) or hell (*kappianartuvik*, "the huge terrifying one"), according to the good or evil existence a person has led.

Corpses (*inuviniit*, "former persons") are buried under rocks (*iluviq*, "tomb"; etymologically related to PE *ə&u-*, "to put in a certain way"), formerly with some of their personal belongings. *Tarniit* can come back to haunt living beings (*angirraniq*, "the fact of returning back home [i.e., ghost; also *ijuruq*]"), with whom the dead also communicate through dreams (*sinnatuumajuq*, "he/she dreams"; possible etymological meaning, "sleeps repeatedly" [Fortescue et al. 2010, 87]). Shamans could interact with deceased individuals, some of whom—particularly those from whom they had received their *atiit* ("names")—acted as their helping spirits. *Tarniit* are thus apt at joining the suprahuman world.

Tuurngait and Other Suprahuman Beings

Besides *tarniit*, the suprahuman world includes a large number of beings who possess *isuma*, as *inuit* do. But these beings are also endowed with supranatural powers inaccessible to humans, except to some shamans. One of these powers is to make themselves visible or invisible at will. Other special characteristics have to do with strength or sudden changes in appearance.

Tuurngait (singular *tuurngaq*) are, or rather were, the auxiliary or familiar spirits of the shamans, whom they helped in the accomplishment of their duties. *Tuurngaq* is a generic term, since shamans enrolled the support of all kinds of beings eager to assist them: spirits in animal or human form,[23] monstrous creatures, features of the landscape (e.g., a river), deceased individuals (especially former shamans), *atiit* (the souls of those from whom the shaman had got his names), and so on. According to Fortescue et al. (2010, 378), the literal meaning of *tuurngaq* might be "one who has been secured." This signification makes sense when it is considered alongside the name of the drum used by shamans for summoning their *tuurngait*: *qilaut(i)*. Although this word possibly derives from the PE root *qəla-*, "to invoke spirits" (Fortescue et al. 2010, 322), more recent speakers of the Inuit language may suppose that the meaning of *qilaut(i)* is derived from *qila(k)-* ("to weave, to tie") + -*ut* ("a means to"). The drum would then be an "instrument for weaving and securing" a tight link between shamans and *tuurngait*. With the drum, the shaman takes hold of the *tuurngaq*'s assistance, thus ensuring the implementation of the supranatural aid offered by the spirit. Since shamans were often bound with *atsunaaq* ("leather thongs") during seances, their physical bonds might have recalled the immaterial ties that made *tuurngait* into spiritual helpers.

For Christian missionaries, *tuurngait* were pagan and thus demonic creatures. In their preaching, the word *tuurngaq* took the sense of "devil." The chief of the Christian devils is *Tuurngaaluk* ("Great *tuurngaq*")[24] or *Saatanasi* ("Satan"). For many contemporary Inuit, especially Evangelical Christians, *tuurngaq* is still synonymous with "devil," but several people consider that in former times, some helping spirits assisted shamans in a positive way. In his definition of the word *tuurngaq*, Qumaq (1991, 241) states that before the advent of Christianity, God helped Inuit through those shamans who healed people thanks to divine aid. It could be added that for shamans, this aid took the form of beneficent—not devilish—spirits.

Besides *tuurngait*, there exist scores of suprahuman beings of different types, the list of which may vary from one region of the Arctic to another. In Inukjuak (western Nunavik), for instance, *tuurngait* are now understood as affluent human-like beings who live inside rocks some distance from the village. From time to time, they visit the community to do their shopping, wearing beautiful clothes and parking their brand-new snowmobiles in front of the general store (Ouellette 2000).

Other examples of suprahuman beings include *Sanna* ("The One Down There"), also known as *Kannaaluk* ("The Big One Down Here"), *Nuliajuk* ("Little Wife"), or *Imaup Inua* ("The *Inuk* of the Sea"). She is the mistress of *puijiit* (sea mammals) and resides at the bottom of the ocean, from where she controls the movements of seals, walrus, and whales.

Tarqiq, the moon spirit, is the protector of women, even though he once committed incest with his sister *Siqiniq*, the sun.

Ijirait ("who are made invisible") and *tarriatsuit* ("hidden ones") are beings that look like *inuit* but live in a parallel universe and make themselves visible only when they wish so. They may wed humans. In Kangiqtugaapik (Baffin Region), a man named Naujarlaq once married a *tarriatsuk* woman, with whom he had a girl child, while also wedding a human, who too gave him a girl. When the *tarriatsuit* converted to Christianity, they told him he could no longer visit them, but that his *tarriatsuk* and human wives and children would merge into each other. Naujarlaq was still alive in 1998, when the anthropologist Bernard Saladin d'Anglure travelled to Kangiqtugaapik in order to record his life history.

Inugagulli(ga)it ("the small ones provided with something that has to do with fingers and toes" [Fortescue et al. 2010, 150–51]) are dwarves who are extremely strong, despite their very small size—they can haul half a walrus by themselves. In 2009, a group of children and teenagers from Kangirsuk (Nunavik) spotted *inugagulligait* behind their community school.

Amautilialuk ("the big one with an *amauti*") is an ogre who captures people, puts them in his (her?) *amauti* (parka for carrying babies), and brings them back to his abode in order to eat them. Two *amautilialuuk* used to live near Quaqtaq (Nunavik), but they have not been encountered for over sixty years.

Uirsait ("would-be husbands") and *nuliarsait* ("would-be wives") are incubus and succubus spirits, respectively, that take the guise of a person's former fiancé or fiancée. They are met by forlorn lovers who walk alone far from the camp or village and are the only ones able to see them. It is said that some sixty years ago in Kangiqsujuaq (Nunavik), a woman was often seen strolling alone in the village, talking to herself with her arms extended sidewise, as if she was holding someone by the hand. She was just taking walks, chatting with the two invisible children she had had with her *uirsaq*.

Some of these suprahuman beings play an important part in traditional Inuit cosmology. This is the case with *Sanna* (often spelled *Sedna*) and *Tarqiq*, as well as with *Lumaajuq* and *Naarjuk*, mentioned in the preceding chapters. Such entities belong to mythology. They are known thanks to *unikkausiit* ("things that are to be told [myths, legends]") and *unikkaatuat* ("things told several times [stories]"). Both of these words derive from *unikka(r)-/unip-ka(r)-* (cf. *unikkatuq*, "tells a story"), whose underlying signification is "to make [someone] tell something" (Fortescue et al. 2010, 406). In Nunavik, visitors entering a home are routinely told: *"Unikkalaurit!"*—"Tell about something!" The *unikkausiit* and *unikkaatuat* explain, by way of oral narratives, how contrasts and alternations such as those between men and women, life and death, day and night, summer and winter came to be, and how people should behave properly in order to preserve harmony (Dorais 2010, 162–65).

Shamans and Missionaries

In pre- and early contact Inuit culture, the shaman (*angakkuq*) acted as a middleman—or middlewoman, since women too could become shamans—between the human and suprahuman worlds. A possible etymology of the word *angakkuq* (Fortescue et al. 2010, 34) links it to PE verbal bases meaning "to move about, to strain to get free, to sway." This may suggest that shamans commuted between different worlds: *inuit* and non-human; living and dead; masculine and feminine. Their *qaumaniq* ("shamanic enlightening knowledge"; see Chapter 1), acquired through years of ordeals and arduous training, enabled them to move freely across physical, social, and supranatural boundaries (see Saladin d'Anglure 2001).

As already mentioned, shamans enrolled *tuurngait* as their spiritual helpers. These assisted them in healing the sick, bringing good weather back, and fetching game in periods of famine. Shamans also provided people with *arnguat* ("amulets"; etymologically, "which look like hanging something"), as well as with advice about prescribed deeds (*piqujait*, "that are ordered, must be done") and taboos (*allirutiit*, "means for being forbidden from doing something"), alimentary or other. *Angakkuit* could also predict the future through *qilaniq* ("invoking spirits"),[25] a divination technique whereby a string was tied to a person's limb or to an object. A question (*apirquti*, "means for interrogating") was asked and the shaman pulled the string. If he/she was able to lift the limb or object up, the answer was positive (*angirtuq*, "says yes"). If not, the answer was negative.

Fetching game in periods of scarcity, as well as other special tasks, required that the shaman travel to other worlds. He—female shamans did not usually perform such feats—could, for instance, visit *Tarqiq*, the moon spirit, or travel to the bottom of the sea to try to convince *Sanna* to release the sea mammals she was holding back because of the non-observance of taboos. Such seances were public and generally occurred in winter. People would gather at night in a large ceremonial snow house (*qaggiq*). The *angakkuq* was tied up, the lamps extinguished—darkness contrasted with shamanic light (*qaumaniq*)—and the sound of the drum (*qilauti*) was heard, as well as the incantations of the shaman summoning his *tuurngait*. The *tarniq* of the *angakkuq* then left his body for another world. When it returned after some time, the shaman would explain what he had seen and eventually, which prescriptions or taboos had not been observed, urging the culprits of such offences to confess their fault (*uqausirivaa*, "he/she has it as words [puts his/her fault in words]"). During some seances, magic songs and formulas (*irinaliurutiit*, "means for producing a scream") were heard; these made use of a special metaphorical or shamanic language.[26] *Irinaliurutiit* were also sung or recited during private healing rituals, for which the shaman received a gift (*tunijjuti*, "a means for giving something").[27] They often consisted of fragments of old songs—such as *pisiit* or *ajajait*, men's personal chants—or of barely intelligible sentences that had been collected, it was said, at a time when animals were able to speak (Dorais 2010, 167).

Angakkuit could also send their *tuurngait* to harm or even kill people. The technique for casting a spell over someone was called *tuurnginiq* ("resorting to *tuurngait*") or *ilisiirniq* ("the action [of the *tuurngaq*?] of putting oneself into place"). Some non-shamans were able to use *ilisiirqutiit* ("means for casting a spell"), too. Spell casters (*ilisiirtut*, "those who practise *ilisiirniq*") survived the demise of traditional shamanism and during the 1960s, at least two of them were well-known in Nunavik. Nowadays, this form of sorcery is generally interpreted in terms of demonic possession and thwarted by Christian exorcism (*tuurnganik anititsigiaq*, "the action of chasing *tuurngait* [devils] away").

It was from the late nineteenth century on—much earlier in Greenland and Labrador—that Inuit came into contact with missionaries. For various reasons (described in Laugrand and Oosten 2010), Christianity was adopted relatively rapidly. It is noteworthy that in the eastern Canadian Arctic, Christian teachings were better accepted in regions where shamans and other local leaders had heard about them beforehand (when visiting trading posts, for instance) and introduced them to their fellow Inuit prior to being visited by *Qallunaat* clergymen. It did not take too long for missionaries of the Anglican (*ajuqirtuijiit*, "who teach for a long time") or Catholic (*itsirarjuat/iksigarjuat*, "who bow forward, their back turned on people")[28] persuasions to replace *angakkuit*. However, due to the small number of *Qallunaat* priests, many shamans became lay preachers (*tutsiatitsijiit*, "those who make people pray") in the seasonal camps, thus establishing a form of Inuit Christianity that still preserves much of the shamanic world view.

For some *angakkuit*, it was painful to get rid of their *tuurngait*, these "beings they had secured" through weaving intimate links with them. It was sorrowful for the *tuurngait* too. Zacharias Kunuk's feature movie *The Journals of Knud Rasmussen* (2006) illustrates this superbly—and very movingly, in my opinion—when the shaman Aua, whose family and camp-mates have decided to join a group of recently converted Inuit, realizes that his helping spirits are not needed anymore. He thanks them, explaining that they must go their own way now that he has stopped being an *angakkuq*, but they are reluctant to leave, demonstrating their attachment to him before finally agreeing to disappear forever.

With the advent of Christianity, Inuit became religious in the Western sense of the word. In Inuktitut, "religion" translates to *uppiniq/ukpirniq*, "the fact of believing," and religious individuals are *uppituit/ukpirtuit*, "those who believe."[29] I have sometimes heard Inuit state that religion did not exist before the arrival of missionaries. Relationships with the suprahuman world were part of daily life, not a separate phenomenon based on faith, as they are for *Qallunaat*. The historian of religion Mircea Eliade (1989, 127) considers that historically, faith is linked to the advent (or introduction) of a mono-theistic doctrine. It consists in a new revelation that is structurally different from "archaic religious experiences" based on practice and tradition rather than belief. The adoption of faith makes these experiences void, a situation that is reflected in the Inuktitut word for "converting," *saagiartuq* ("he/she looks at it [revelation] full face"), which expresses the need to turn away from traditional practices.[30]

After conversion, Inuit worshipped *Guuti* ("God")[31] and *Jisusi Kiristusi* ("Jesus Christ"). The ceremonial igloo (*qaggiq*) was replaced by the *tutsia-vik* ("place for praying [church]"), where people gathered at least once a week to say prayers (*tutsiatuq/tuksiartuq*, "prays, begs"), sing hymns (*inngi[r]tuq/imngirtuq*, "sings a hymn"; etymologically, "makes a loud sound"), and listen to a preacher. The cross (*sanningajulik*, "that has a cross-piece on it") super-seded shamanic *arnguat* ("amulets"), and Christmas (*quviasuvvik*, "time for rejoicing"; or *qitinnguq*, "that becomes the middle [of the year]") took the place of the winter solstice festivities during which *angakkuit* had officiated, as reported by Franz Boas (1964).

Because the Christian faith is based on the Bible (*allait ijjujut*, "the thick [*ijjujut*] writings [*allait*]"), missionaries had to teach Inuit to read and write. This process seems to have gone smoothly and efficiently, especially in the eastern Canadian Arctic where, with the exception of Labrador, a very simple syllabic writing system (*qaniujaarpait*, "the big [signs] that look like snowflakes") was introduced.[32] This system, akin to shorthand, had been devised around 1830 by a team of Wesleyan missionaries (James Evans and his Indigenous collaborators) for members of the Ojibway and Cree First Nations. In the late 1860s, it was adapted to Inuktitut at Fort George, on the Quebec shore of James Bay, by Anglican ministers who started teaching it to Inuit trading there. Syllabics spread quickly. Those who had learned it at Fort George and, later on, during visits to other missions, brought their new knowledge back to their camps and transmitted it to their family and friends (Harper 1985).

In Nunavik and some other parts of the Arctic (Greenland, for instance), the letters of the alphabet as well as the syllabic characters are called *allait* or *aglait* ("decorative patterns"). Accordingly, the verbal base chosen for translating the concept of "writing" is *alla(r)-* ("to draw or sew decorative patterns"), while "reading" is *allaniar-* ("to deal with decorative patterns [letters]") or *atuar-* ("to follow a visible track"). Elsewhere, "to write" is translated as *titirar-* ("to mark something with repeated dots"). A pencil or pen is an *allauti* or *titirauti* ("used for writing"), and in Nunavik, a sheet of paper is called *sikutsajaq* ("piece of future ice [freezing water]") because of a perceived similarity between paper and a thin layer of new ice.

One of the first pre-Christian practices to disappear was the respect of taboos. In the Baffin Region, Inuit who converted often got together to eat a forbidden piece of food (caribou lung, for instance) to mark the fact that they were renouncing their old habits. This ritual was called *sirqitiq*, from *sirqittuq*, "he/she crosses over from a less dangerous to a more dangerous terrain" (Spalding 1998, 136), as if those who embraced the new faith were not afraid to throw themselves into unknown waters. Christianity, however, possessed its own unavoidable taboo: the prohibition of work, travel, and other worldly pursuits on Sunday. In order to respect this proscription, Inuit had to modify their relation to time. They already knew about days (*ulluit*), lunar months (*tarqiit*), and years (*ukiut*), but they now learned that there existed weeks made of six working days plus Sunday.

Appropriate names were given to these new temporal subdivisions. In Nunavik, for instance, the workable week was called *pinasuarusiq* ("the fact of working"), while Sunday became *allitut* ("they respect a taboo") or *allituqartuq* ("there are people respecting a taboo")—it was even dubbed *sanattaili* ("forbidden to work!") in some Nunavut dialects. The working days were named accordingly, from *alliriirtut* ("they have finished observing a taboo," Monday) to *allingisungarvik* ("when, for the last time, they do not observe a taboo," Saturday), the intervening days being numbered (e.g., *aippangat*, "their second one," or Tuesday). The only exception was Friday, which is still called *niritsivik* ("time for feeding [people]"), a reference to the period when Indigenous workers of the Hudson's Bay Company were given their weekly ration of biscuits on that day. In North Baffin, it is Saturday that is called *sivataarvik*, "time for getting biscuits."

Inuit also had to learn about the hours of the day (*kaivallagusiq*, "the fact of revolving"; or *ikaurniq*, "going across something") in order to attend church services or be on time when working for *Qallunaat*. Hours from one to eleven were denoted by numbers followed by *-nngu(r)tuq* ("it becomes"), as in *"pingasu*nngutuq—it becomes three," that is, "it is three o'clock (a.m. or p.m)." Noon and midnight were called *qitiraliq* ("starting to be half of it [day or night]"). People soon acquired watches and clocks (*siqirngujaq*, "that looks like the sun [because it tells time]"), as well as calendars (*ulluit*, "days"). Thus beyond a strictly religious impact, the advent of Christianity transformed the modes of communication and the notion of time for Inuit, through literacy and the clock.[33]

Conclusion

Being an *inuk*, a human person, implies a variety of things. *Inuit* are breathing creatures (*anirniliit*, "they have vital breath [*anirniq*]") like animals, and like them they have a *timi* ("body"). This entails the mastery of all physical skills necessary to draw one's livelihood from *nuna* ("land") and *imaq* ("water, sea"), but also involves limitations linked to the fact of being constrained by *sila* (here in the restricted sense of "natural environment"). However, in contradistinction to animals (except perhaps polar bears and, to a certain extent, dogs), humans have access to *isuma* ("thinking") and possess an *atiq* ("name soul") through which their forebears can revive. They also have a *tarniq* ("human-like shadow") that survives the dead body. All of this might explain the etymology of the word *inuk* ("living body" and "owner/animator"): an animated being who is able to manage its surroundings; in other words, an animated animator.

These specificities of *inuit* endow them with at least four mental abilities stemming from *isuma*: knowing, understanding, remembering, and speaking. These skills enable people to behave themselves—and relate to *sila*—in a rational way, although a lack of balance between *isuma* and *ippigijait* ("feelings") can result in incorrect or undesirable actions that might compromise natural and social harmony.

In former times, breaks in the relationship between *inuit* and *sila*—potential causes of illness, bad weather, or the disappearance of game animals—were mended by shamans (*angakkuit*). Etymologically, the word *angakkuq* might refer to an ability to move and get free, suggesting that the shaman's principal chracteristic was the skill of travelling between different worlds. Thanks to their parahuman enlightening power (*qaumaniq*, "diffusing light") and the support of their helping spirits (*tuurngait*; etymologically, "those who have been secured"), whom they bound into a lifelong intimate relationship, *angakkuit* acquired powerful magical songs and formulas (*irinaliurutiit*) and/or entered into contact with various suprahuman beings. Magic and supranatural encounters enabled shamans to restore harmony and cope with unexpected situations affecting Inuit society.

One such unforeseen situation was the arrival of Christian missionaries (*ajuqirtuijiit*, "who teach for a long time")—starting in the late 1800s in most areas of the Canadian Arctic—who introduced the combined concepts of faith and religion (*uppiniq*). Many shamans became interested in the new teachings and rituals, bringing them to their fellow people and quite often becoming lay Christian preachers (*tutsiatitsijiit*) themselves. Even though *angakkuit* finally disappeared as a social category, their active role in promoting Christianity generated a unique form of religion that preserved a large part of the shamanic world view.

Christian knowledge was based on a written medium, the Bible (*allait ijjujut*). This means that missionaries had to introduce their flock to literacy. Inuit embraced it enthusiastically, so that in the eastern Canadian Arctic, almost everyone had become literate in Inuktitut less than thirty years after the advent of Christianity. The new faith thus brought in a mode of communication that was completely novel, as well as a relation to time unknown until then. Together with the development of commercial trade around the same period, these circumstances ushered in tremendous changes in the traditional way of life. In spite of that, Inuit preserved their identity of prototypical Arctic human beings (*inutuinnait*, "the only genuine *inuit*"), thanks in large part to the structuring role played, as we shall now see, by their naming practices and kinship system.

CHAPTER FOUR

Words for Speaking about Family, Kinship, and Naming

**Isuittuunirsaaluuqattalirmat piaraliutuinnatut
ataatalijanngitunik uqumaittuugunautillugit.
Katujjisuni arnalu angutilu piunirsaumat piaraliritsuni
qanurtuularigiaqaliratta. Katititaummaituulutik
piarqiutuinnariaqanngimata nuliariinniq
pinnguatuinnaugalaanngimat, atuutitsialugu
pijariaqaraluarmat uigiinniq nuliariinniq.**

It is really inconvenient when [women] with children
whose father is not present appear to bear a heavy load.
Since it is better when a woman and a man join together
to take care of children, this is what we should really
wish for. Those who will not get married together should
not have children with each other, because forming a
couple is not a game at all. Having a husband, having a
wife should be done in a proper way.

LOUISA KULULAAQ, (2008–2009, 14)

This quotation from *Pirurpalianirmuulingajut unikkaatuat* (Tales aimed at growing), a booklet written in 2008–9 for her community school by Louisa Kululaaq, an elder from Quaqtaq (Nunavik), expresses the author's views on the family. First, normal family life is based on the presence of a man and a woman. When fathers are absent, their children's mother must "bear a heavy [*uqumaittu(q)*] load."[1] Second, both spouses should take care of their children; childrearing is not an exclusively feminine task. And finally, procreation is not desirable if the would-be parents do not plan to get married some day. Louisa Kululaaq's views agree with what is reported in ethnographic literature about Inuit kinship. Most families are nuclear (a father, a mother, and their children); such families are expected to endure for long ("those who will not get married together should not have children," in Louisa's words); and kinship is bilateral, that is, recognized on both the mother's and father's sides ("a woman and a man [should] join together to take care of children").

When I was an undergraduate student in anthropology, one of our compulsory readings was Lewis Henry Morgan's classic work, *Systems of Consanguinity and Affinity of the Human Family* (1870). In that book, all existing types of family organization were divided into a limited number of typical systems. One of these was dubbed the "Eskimo" kinship system—which, by the way, is the one currently found in modern Western societies—characterized by bilaterality, the absence of matrilineal or patrilineal clans or other closed kin groupings (i.e., accessible only through genealogical descent),[2] the predominance of the nuclear family, and the fact that, unlike many other systems, the words designating a person's uncles, aunts, and cousins are different from those used for denoting one's father, mother, and siblings. Louisa Kululaaq's views on contemporary families are congruent with Morgan's description and thus reflect an "Eskimo" form of kinship structure.

In this chapter, we will stroll through some of the vocabulary heard when Inuit speak about that structure. As shall be seen, the lexicon of family relationships includes domains that extend beyond mere kinship terminology. These comprise adoption, relatives often considered as symbolic, and above all, a naming system that may entail a rearrangement of the whole structure.

Kinship Terminology

All languages have words that denote the links relating an individual (dubbed *Ego* in anthropological parlance and in the following pages) to other persons, through "blood" (actually DNA and genes), matrimony, or adoption. However, the extent and contents of this terminology may vary considerably between languages. For example, while English differentiates between nephews and nieces on the one hand, and grandchildren on the other, this is not the case in Italian and Vietnamese. In these unrelated languages, both categories of relatives are called *nipoti* (Italian) or *cháu* (Vietnamese). This may seem strange to English speakers—in English, nephews have nothing to do with grandchildren—but there is an underlying logic in the Italian and Vietnamese terminology. *Nipoti* and *cháu* denote the only two types of relatives belonging to a generation younger than Ego's that are genetically linked to Ego through only one individual (Ego's sibling or child).[3] Hence the homonymy of family positions that are considered in English (and Inuktitut) as separate types of kin.

As we shall now see, the structure of kinship terminology in Inuktitut is relatively similar to its English equivalent, although there exist significant differences between them. Since the Inuit terminological system shows some dialectal variations, one specific version will be presented here, the one in use in northeastern Nunavik.[4]

Defining Family and Kinship

It may seem surprising at first, but in Inuktitut (as well as in Inuit and Yupik, generally speaking), there is no specific word for "relative" or "kin." Nor is there a term for "family." In all forms of the Eskimo-Aleut languages, one's relatives are called *ilait* (singular *ila*), "parts [of something]." The word *ila* is almost always followed by a possessive ending, as in *ila*nga or *ila*a ("his/her/its part"). This possessive refers to the composite object, concept, or group made up of a number of *ilait*, rather than to an external possessor who would own one or several parts of a whole:

*aulautiup ila*ngit	"of a motor, *its* parts" (motor parts)
*puijiit ila*ngat	"of sea mammals, *their* part" (a species of sea mammals)
*ila*tit	"*your* [co-]parts" (the members of a group you belong to)
*ila*ga	"*my* [co-]part" (one member of a group I belong to)

To qualify as an *ila*, each separate part must possess some degree of individuality, as in *aulautiup ilangit* ("motor parts") above. An *aulauti* ("means for making something move [motor]") consists of the sum of its individual parts (carburetor, pistons, starter, etc.), each of which may have its own name. When something considered homogeneous is portioned out, its parts are not *ilait*. For example, a piece of cake cannot be called **kiikiup ilanga* ("of a cake, its part"). It is rather termed *aviullataq* ("that has been separated from [a cake]"). However, a cake may be said to have *ilait* when spoken about as the result of a culinary process, as in "*Kiikiup* ila*tsangit: sanaugaq, imiq, pujjusiuti amma pitatsaq*"—"The parts [*ilait*] used for [baking] a cake [are]: flour, water, baking powder, and sugar." In such a context, *ila* can even become a verbal base ("to add a component"), as in "*Kiik* ila*vaa*"—"She/he adds something [flour, icing, etc.] to the cake," or "*Uliga* ila*vara*"—"I add a piece to my dress [in order to lengthen or adorn it]."

Basically, then, the word *ila* can be defined as one individual part of a composite whole. This meaning is so general that its pragmatic use varies greatly according to context. For instance, *ilangit* ("its/their parts") is often translatable as "some of it/them," as in "*Qimmiit ilangit qakurtaujut ilangillu qirnitautillugit*"—"Some dogs are white, while some others are black" (literally, "Part of the dogs are white, while part [of the dogs] are black"). In the case of human beings, the wholes consist in any group they may belong to, temporarily or permanently, such as a team of workers, people travelling together, a family, and so on. Thus, *ilait* ("your part"),[5] *ilakka* ("my parts"), or *ilavut* ("our part[s]") generally denote one or several fellow member(s) of a group to which you, I, or we belong as component parts. According to context, these words can be translated as "your/my/our workmate(s), companion(s), relative(s)," and so on.

By definition, all components (*ilait*) of a whole must have something in common. If not, there would be no whole. As concerns humans (*inuit*), this means that the groups to which they are said to belong should be made out of other *inuit*. I realized this many years ago, when David Niviaxie, an elder from western Nunavik, explained that if you invite someone to join a team of fellow travellers, you should not ask him or her, as some speakers do, "*Maligumavit?*"—"Do you want to follow [us]?" The proper form of invitation is "*Ilaugumavit?*"—"Do you want to be [our] *ila*?" A dog may follow human travellers, but another *inuk* will normally become a full component part of the travelling team.

As far as kinship is concerned, the fact that a person's relatives are called *ilait*, the component parts of his or her (family) group, has important semantic consequences. It means that for Inuit, both immediate and extended family are primarily understood as composite wholes divided into individual components. Each of these components, Ego and his or her relatives, belong to a human community within which they are inextricably linked to one another through consanguinity (or adoption) and marriage. Of course, speakers of Inuktitut are not always conscious that when they call someone *ilaga*, "my relative," it really means "my co-part," or "a part of my collective self." Nevertheless, the semantics of *ila* shows that kinship stands at the very basis of Inuit society and social identity.

While relatives (*ilait*) are considered as parts of a whole, this whole is itself defined as a conglomerate of its parts: families are called *ilagiit*, "those who are component parts [*ilait*] for each other." Like the two sides of a coin, relatives are understood as parts of a family whole that is itself referred to as the mutual grouping of its component parts. Kin groups and their members are thus inseparable from each other.

Consanguine Kinship: Primary Relatives

The strength of kinship ties varies according to their proximity and nature. Generally speaking, the individuals Inuit call their *ilait* are related to them by blood, whether on their father's or mother's side. When Ego says of someone, "*Ilagijara*"—"I have him/her as my *ila*," or "*Ilagiittuguk*"—"Both of us are *ila*," it is because they share genes, although one's *ilagiit* may also include adopted individuals (see below). More distant blood relatives are called *ilagalait* ("lesser *ilait*"), deceased family members *ilaviniit* ("former *ilait*"), and relatives by marriage *ilapasiit* ("almost *ilait*").

As might be expected from a Euro-American as well as an Inuit stand-point, Ego's closest consanguine relatives are those directly related in an ascending and descending line (father, mother, sons, daughters), or within his or her own generation (brothers and sisters). As far as ascending or descending relatives are concerned, the terminology is fairly simple: in most Inuit dialects, everyone calls his or her father *ataata* and mother *anaana*, and Ego's son and daughter are called *irniq* and *panik*, respectively. As with the word *ila*, kinship terms are almost always followed by a possessive ending: *ataata*ga ("my father"), *anaana*it ("your mother"), *irni*nga ("his/her son"), *panin*git ("his/her/their daughters"). When used as terms of address, these words do not need a possessive, but their final vowel is lengthened: *Anaanaa!* ("Mommy!"); *Irniiq!* ("Son!").

According to the *Comparative Eskimo Dictionary* (Fortescue et al. 2010, 54, 28), the literal signification of *ataata* is "older male relative," and that of *anaana* is "older female relative." In Nunavik Inuktitut, the latter word is a cognate—probably a doubling—of *aana(q)*, "paternal grandmother," while in the Yupik languages *a(a)ta* means: "father." In Greenlandic Kalaallisut, *aatak/aataq* translates as "grandfather."

The word for son, *irniq*, is related to the verbal base *irni-*, "to give birth [to a boy or a girl]." In a culture where, according to classical ethnography, male children were preferred to females, it is conceivable that the basic meaning of *irniq* could be "the begotten one," a son being considered the prototypical offspring. As concerns the term *panik* (daughter), I have very tentatively suggested (2016, 69) that it might mean something like "who supplies [or is provided with] heat."[6] This etymology could allude to the fact that when she becomes an adult, Ego's daughter will tend the oil lamp (*qulliq*) in the igloo.[7]

Words for parents and their children thus function in a way quite similar to the way they do in English. By contrast, the terminology of primary family links within Ego's generation may look unfamiliar at first. The terms by which brothers and sisters address each other vary according to Ego's gender and relative age. Note that there is no word for "gender" in Inuktitut. This concept is usually translated as *arnauniq angutauniq* ("the fact of being a female, of being a male"). "Age" is *ukiuqarniq* ("the fact of havinq winters [i.e., years]").

If Ego is a male, he calls his older brother *angajuk* and his younger male sibling *nukaq*, while his sister is addressed as *naja*, whatever her age. In a parallel fashion, a female Ego calls her older sister *angajuk* and her younger one *nukaq*, but her brother of any age is called *ani*. *Angajuk* and *nukaq* therefore mean "elder sibling" and "younger sibling," respectively, or more properly, "elder or younger individual," since the words angajut*siq* and nukar*siq* (where -*siq* stands for "more so") currently apply to any person older or younger than another one, related or not. The older spouse in a married couple is the other's angaju*attanga* ("elder person attached to him/her"). According to Fortescue et al. (2010, 35), *angajuk* might be linked to the PE verbal base *angǝ-* ("to be big") and mean "who wants or tends [-*juk*] to be big." It would thus be related to *angijuq*, "he/she/it is big," but not to *angakkuq* ("shaman"). We saw in the preceding chapter that the latter word's PE etymology rather points at the idea of moving and getting free, without perhaps preventing modern speakers of Inuktitut from perceiving a meaningful relationship between bigness (*angi-*), eldership (*angajuk-*), and having access to shamanic light (*angakkuq*). As for the word *nukaq*, it might be related to *nuaq* (Fortescue et al. 2010, 265), a type of nephew or niece (see below).

The gender-bound usage of the appellations *angajuk* and *nukaq* shows that among siblings of the same sex, what matters most is their relative age, probably because age entails a sort of hierarchy between senior and junior brothers or sisters. With siblings of the opposite sex, age does not matter so much, although some Inuit dialects (but not Nunavik Inuktitut) distinguish between a man's older and younger sisters, and vice versa. In a society traditionally characterized by a clear division between male and female occupations, it is important to mark the fact that two siblings do not belong to the same gender. Hence the appellations *naja* and *ani*—rather than *angajuk* and *nukaq*—for a sister or brother whose sex differs from Ego's.

We might guess that the term *naja* reflects the PE verbal base *najə-*, "to bend head, to nod, to tremble." I have suggested (2016, 71) that together with *arnait* ("women") and *paniit* ("daughters"), sisters could arouse males sexually—by their alleged trembling, in this case. But this remains highly speculative. We are on firmer ground with the word *ani*, which is related to the base *ani-*, "to come out" (Fortescue et al. 2010, 29). Like Ego's son (etymologically, "the begotten one"), the brother of a woman would be defined as a prototypical offspring ("one who comes out [is born]"). This underlying synonymy might be linked to the fact that both brother and son are a woman's closest male relatives within her own generation and the following one.

A person's parents (father and mother) are his or her *angajurqaak* (in the dual grammatical number), or "antecedent elders." In Nunavik, the word *angajurqaaq* also means "leader of a traditional seasonal camp," as well as "institutional chief." The latter meaning appeared during the nineteenth century, with the advent of fur trading companies—the Hudson's Bay Company, for instance—whose chief traders were seemingly equated with parents because they provided Inuit with food items (in exchange for the products of their subsistence activities, of course). An assistant trader was called *angajurqaasuk* ("lesser parent/chief").

Ego's children (sons and daughters) are his or her *qiturngait* (singular *qiturngaq*); a twin is a *marruliaq* ("who has been made two") and a pair of twins are *qarisariik* ("two who are brains for each other"). The underlying signification of *qiturngaq* is "one who was recently soft and pliable" (Fortescue et al. 2010, 327), perhaps an allusion to a newborn's malleability, including its ability to change sex at birth, as we shall see later on. As will also be seen, when one of Ego's parents comes back to life because the parent's name soul (*atiq*) has been bestowed on a newborn baby, Ego's *angajurqaaviniq* ("deceased

parent") becomes his or her *qiturngaq*. And conversely, as Miaji, my late adoptive mother from Quaqtaq used to say, playing on the homonymy between
"parent" and "chief," *"Qiturngavut angajurqaatuinnavut"*—"Our children
[are] our real chiefs/parents." Among Inuit as with other peoples, caring for
young children monopolizes most of the time and attention of mothers and
fathers, making babies the rulers of the household.

In the same way that there is a generic term for both parents, one also
exists for brothers and sisters: *qatangutiit* ("siblings"). This word might be
related to PE *qatəg*, "chest" (Fortescue et al. 2010, 316) and mean "something
used for getting a chest," maybe a metaphorical comment on the genetic
proximity of siblings. More plausibly from a semantic standpoint, although
etymologically unproved, the word-base *qata-* might also be a cognate of the
affix *-qati* ("companion at doing or sharing something"). *Qatanguti* ("a means
for getting companions") would therefore refer to the collaboration among
siblings. Whatever the case may be, both full and half brothers and sisters are
called *qatangutiit*, whether they share both parents, just their father (*ataataqati*, "co-sharer of a father"), or only their mother (*anaanaqati*, "co-sharer
of a mother").

Dyadic relations among relatives—terms for kinship pairings (*tursurau-
tiit*, "means for addressing someone through kinship") used in mutual address
(e.g., father-son, sister-brother)—are expressed by the affix *-giik/-riik* (dual
number), "two individuals belonging to a pair, one term of which is . . . ," as
shown in the following examples:

irniriik	"two, one of whom is a son" (a son and his father or mother)
nukariik	"two, one of whom is a younger sibling" (a younger and an older sibling of the same gender)
najagiik	"two, one of whom is a sister" (a sister and her brother)

In the plural number (*-giit/-riit*), the same affix denotes groups of relatives
whose members may be part of more than one dyad:

panigiit	"a group including daughters" (two or more daughters with their father, mother, or both parents)

qiturngariit	"a group including offspring" (son[s] and/or daughter[s] with their father, mother, or both)
qatangutigiit	"a group of siblings" (brothers and/or sisters)

In each occurrence of *-giik/-giit* words for dyads and groupings (except for the last example above), the noun base designates the younger element of the dyad or group (*nukaq* vs. *angajuk*; *qiturngait* vs. *ataata* or *anaana*) or its female component (*naja* vs. *ani*), in other words, the relative considered "inferior," according to Saladin d'Anglure (2013, 141). Incidentally, the word *qiturngariit* is used for denoting a nuclear family (parents and their children), in contrast to extended family (*ilagiit*) or relatives in general (*ilait*).

Consanguine Kinship: Other Relatives

Beyond primary relatives, those closest to Ego, there exist secondary and more distant blood kin. Secondary consanguine relatives are those related to Ego through one intermediate individual, either directly (grandparents, grandchildren) or collaterally (uncles, aunts, nephews, nieces).

In Nunavik Inuktitut and several other dialects, grandparents are defined as smoother versions of one's parents (who were often quite strict, traditionally). Ego calls his or her paternal or maternal grandfather *ataatatsiaq* ("good father") and his or her maternal grandmother *anaanatsiaq* ("good mother"). As mentioned above, the paternal grandmother is called *aana(q)*, probably a morphologically more archaic version of the word *anaana* ("mother"). This designation might be linked to the fact that in traditional hunting camps, generally patrilocal—comprising an older man, his sons, and their families— the most senior woman, who acted as the camp's matriarch, was the paternal grandmother. Nowadays, in settled villages, paternal grandmothers are most often addressed as *anaanatsiaq*, like their maternal counterparts.

The terminology for great-uncles and great-aunts is similar to that for grandparents.[8] On my more recent visits to Quaqtaq, I stayed with my adoptive sister, Tiisi, the daughter of Saali and Miaji Tarqiapik. I remember her asking her grandchildren to greet me, their great-uncle, by saying: *"Ataatatsiangai!"*—"Hi, Grandddad!" Being quite young, they were generally too shy to do as she said.

All grandchildren (and great-nephews/-nieces), whether male or female, are called *irngutait* (singular *irngutaq*). According to Fortescue et al. (2010,

146), this word might have come from Proto-Inuit *inəq-* ("to finish something") + *-rutaq* ("a means for"). A plausible definition for grandchildren would thus be "means for completing Ego's family." Following the same logic, a great-grandchild is called *irngutalirqiuti*, "a means for being a means to complete Ego's family once again," or more simply, "a means for being a grandchild once again [i.e., in the following generation]." Today, when people live much longer than before, it is not unusual for Inuit to have great-great-grandchildren. These are called *irngutalirqitait*, "those who have been made grandchildren once more."

In a parallel fashion, one's great-grandfather and great-grandmother are respectively called *ataatatsialirqiuti* and *anaanatsialirqiuti* ("a means for being a grandfather/grandmother once again"). And great-great-grandparents are designated as *ataata-/anaanatsialirqitait* ("those who have been made grandfathers/grandmothers once more").

Great-grandparents and great-grandchildren are tertiary relatives (linked to Ego through two intermediaries, like cousins are). Let us now turn back to secondary kin, avuncular in this case. In Inuktitut, the terminology for consanguine uncles, aunts, nephews, and nieces is more complex than it is in English. As far as uncles and aunts are concerned, the names by which Ego addresses them depend on their gender as well as on their line of relation to Ego, whether paternal or maternal. This gives us four terms:

akka	Ego's father's brother (paternal uncle)
atsa	Ego's father's sister (paternal aunt)
angak	Ego's mother's brother (maternal uncle)
ajakuluk	Ego's mother's sister (maternal aunt)

I do not know of possible etymologies for *akka* and *atsa*. *Angak* may be related to *angajuk* ("older sibling, older person") and *angijuq* ("is big"): the maternal uncle would represent the senior or predominant person on Ego's mother's side of the family. As for *ajakuluk*, its base (*ajak-*) might perhaps be the same as that of the word *ajappaa* ("pushes it back with the hand") and, more pointedly, *ajappatuq* ("leans upon someone with his/her hand"), but this remains a guess. If it makes sense, the maternal aunt could possibly be seen by her nephews and nieces as a kind of family support, a reliable person on whom one can count. This appreciative view would be confirmed by the affix *-kuluk* ("nice little"), which would make the *ajakuluk* into a "nice little support."

Appellations for nephews and nieces do not take their gender into account but rather that of their uncles and aunts, as well as their paternal or maternal line. Here again, there exist four different kinship terms:

qangiaq	for a man, the son or daughter of his brother
anngaq	for a woman, the son or daughter of her brother
ujuruk	for a man, the son or daughter of his sister
nuakuluk	for a woman, the son or daughter of her sister

The only morphosemantic link I can guess for *qangiaq* is a possible relation with *qaa-* or *qanga-* ("upper part, top of something"). For a male Ego, his brother's son or daughter would be "one getting, or brought, to the top," but admittedly, this does not make much sense. As for *anngaq*, it might be related to the word *ani* ("brother of a woman"), through an older PE form (*anəngar*) meaning "older brother," plus the PE affix *-ar*, "thing that resembles" (Fortescue et al. 2010, 30). The paternal aunt addresses *anngaq*'s father as *ani*. It is therefore logical that her nephew—and by extension, niece—be called "one who is similar to an older brother."

The term *ujuruk* is cognate to *ujuraq*, a word found in the Yupik languages, where it means "younger sibling" or "younger brother." As with *anngaq*, morphosemantics might disclose a semantic proximity here between, in this case, a nephew or niece (*ujuruk*) and their maternal uncle, who is their mother's brother (*ujuraq* in Yupik). Finally, the word-base *nua-* in *nuakuluk* seems related to *nukaq* ("younger sibling"), followed by the same affix of affection, *-kuluk* ("nice little"), found in the name a *nuakuluk* gives to his or her maternal aunt (*ajakuluk*).

To sum up, here are the four *-giik/-riik* dyadic pairs involving uncles, aunts, and nephews/nieces:

akka (paternal uncle) ↔ *qangiaq* (a man's nephew/niece by his brother)

atsa (paternal aunt) ↔ *anngaq* (a woman's nephew/niece by her brother)

angak (maternal uncle) ↔ *ujuruk* (a man's nephew/niece by his sister) *ajakuluk* (maternal aunt) ↔ *nuakuluk* (a woman's nephew/niece by her sister)

It is noteworthy that three of the four terms for "nephew/niece" seem related in one way or another to words meaning "brother" or "sibling." This is not surprising, since the children of brothers and sisters extend into a new generation the kinship relations linking their parents. Indeed, in Nunavik, these offspring, who are first cousins, use mutual appellations identifying them as quasi-siblings:[9]

qatangutitsaq	"substitute sibling" (cousin of the same gender as Ego)
anitsaq	"substitute brother" (male cousin of female Ego)
najatsaq	"substitute sister" (female cousin of male Ego)

Children call their parents' first cousins as if they were their uncles and aunts, and are addressed by them as nephews and nieces. The affix *-tsaq* ("substitute, one made for"; plural *-tsait*) that is appended to the proper kinship term is also used for referring to one's stepparents, stepchildren, and stepsiblings. This suggests that cousins (*qatanguti*tsait) may be (or have been) perceived as prototypical stepsiblings, their uncles and aunts being at the head of the line to adopt them in case of death or other misfortune befalling their parents.

Matrimony

In traditional Inuit society, marrying was a simple affair without ceremonial formalities. When a boy and a girl from two acquainted families had reached puberty and acquired the knowledge, skills, and implements necessary to perform the activities expected from adults, their parents might tell them that they now were husband and wife. Most of the time, the girl went to live with the boy's family, although it often happened that the bridegroom stayed with his new in-laws for about two years before the couple moved to the camp of the boy's parents. These unions could easily dissolve during their first year of existence (*avittuuk*, "the two of them break up"), but as soon as a viable baby was born the relationship was usually permanent.

Christianity added to this pattern a church ceremony (*katititauniq*, "the fact of being put together"), performed when a missionary happened to travel to a hunting camp or when a couple visited a mission, but this was not considered essential. Modernity (from the 1960s on in Nunavik) introduced the right to select one's partner—with the parents' approval whenever possible—but even now, matrimony remains largely customary: any man and woman who live together with their children are acknowledged as *aippariik*, "two halves of a pair," or husband and wife (Dorais 2018a).

Male and female spouses are called *ui* ("husband") and *nuliaq* ("wife"). Elsewhere, I have proposed (2016, 68) that the term for "husband" might be related to the word-bases *uigu-* ("lengthen") and *uivar-* ("to go round by swerving from a straight direction") and mean "swerving, protuberance," an allusion to the erect penis. This may be erroneous from a strictly etymological standpoint because present-day *ui* derives from PE *ugi*, while *uigu-* and related forms come from *uyi-* (Fortescue et al. 2010, 393, 421). Once again, however, historical Inuit speakers may well hypothesize a semantic link between *ui*, "husband," and the first syllable of words evoking swerving or protruding.

I have also previously suggested (Dorais 2016) that *nuliaq* might be understood as "little female in heat,"[10] thus nicely complementing the sexual rendition I proposed for *ui*. This would also concur with the PE etymology of *nuliaq* found in Fortescue et al. (2010, 261): "one who—or with whom—one copulates," or "one who produces offspring" (cf. modern Inuktitut *nuliarpuq*, "he [man or male animal] copulates"; literally, "he gets at [-ar-] a *nuli* [female in heat?]"). Another derivation, suggested to me by the northern historian Kenn Harper, defines the word *nuliaq* in a completely different way. In North Baffin Inuktitut (but not in Nunavik), *nulik* is the kinship term used by Ego to refer to the parents of his or her son- or daughter-in-law. If *-aq* ("small, lesser") is affixed to *nuli(k)*, it yields *nuliaq*, "small or lesser in-law."

If my tentative but unproved morphosemantic interpretation of the words *arnaq* ("woman"), *anguti* ("man"; see preceding chapter), *ui* ("husband"), and *nuliaq* ("wife") makes any sense, it discloses an interesting semantic quartet explaining sexual relations (Dorais 2016, 70–71). *Arnaq* ("one who agitates something") sets *anguti* ("means for catching") in motion. Once agitated, *anguti*, in his role of *ui* ("one with something protruding"),[11] catches *nuliaq* ("little female in heat," or "with whom one copulates"), who in her capacity as an *arnaq* agitates *anguti* anew, thus perpetuating the reproductive cycle of humanity:

ARNAQ (woman) →→ *ANGUTI* (man)

NULIAQ (wife) ←←← *UI* (husband)

The words *ui* and *nuliaq* are rarely used for mutual address. Spouses rather call each other *aippaq* ("one in a pair"). In casual conversation, they mention their mate as aippa*ra* ("my half of a pair"), each spouse being referred to, for instance, as "*Pitaup* aippa*nga*"—"of Peter, his half of a pair [Peter's wife]." As with the already discussed concepts of "kinship" and "family," for which there does not exist any specific Inuit appellation (a relative is an *ila*, a "part of a whole"; family an *ilagiit*, "mutual parts"), a couple living in matrimony is most often referred to as "two halves of a pair" (*aippariik*). There exists a more formal term, *nuliariik* ("two people, one of whom is the other's wife"), but it is rarely heard, in Nunavik at least. Matrimonial couples are thus considered as prototypical pairs of a sort, a semantic image that outlines their social importance. This brings us back to the quotation by Louisa Kululaaq with which this chapter opened: "Forming a couple is not a game at all. Having a husband, having a wife should be done in a proper way."

Like *ila* ("part of a whole"), the word *aippaq* ("one in a pair") belongs to a very basic stratum of the Inuktitut lexicon.[12] It expresses a logical position: one of two members within a dyadic relation. *Aippaq* is generally followed by the affix *-giik/-riik* that expresses reciprocity between the two halves of the pair (as in *aippariik*), or by a possessive affix that refers to the other element in the relation. For instance, *aippanga* ("its half of a pair") is often translatable as "one of two" (or "the second one"), as in "*Illu aippanga angijuq aippanga mikijuutillugu*"—"One house is big, while the other is small" (literally, "One house, its [the other house's] half of the pair, is big, while its [of the first house's] half of the pair is small"). In the case of human beings, the pairs they form may be any grouping of two, temporary or permanent, such as hunting partners, two people travelling together, or a married couple.

The concept of *aippaq* and its extension to pairs of humans reflect the importance Inuit minds attach to the difference between "two" and "many," considered as radically diverging levels of plurality. This importance is embodied in the language, where two—or double (e.g., a pair of pants)—units are always in the dual grammatical number, while three or more are in the plural, as in *inuk* ("one person"), *inuuk* ("two persons"), *inuit* ("three or more persons"). In the Quaqtaq of my youth, when a boy suggested to a girl (or vice versa), "*Nuvulialaurluk*"—"Let's both of us [-*luk*] walk to Nuvuk" (a weather station about five kilometres north of the village), it had a very different emotional connotation than saying, "*Nuvulialaurta*"— "Let's all of us [-*ta*] walk to Nuvuk." In Nunavik, southern Baffin Island, and Labrador, the notions of "the two of them" and "all [three or more] of them" are expressed through two completely different words: *tamarmik* ("the two of them") and *iluunnatik* ("all of them").[13] This stresses once again the importance of dualism.

The *-giik/-riik* dyads, which denote the way two relatives address each other—the prototype of which is *aippariik*—offer a good example of the logics of duality. Kinship dyads can be considered pairs of a sort, albeit often combining dissimilar halves. In the word *anngariik* ("a nephew or niece and their paternal aunt [*atsa*]"), for instance, the two halves of the pair do not belong to the same generation. Heterogeneous dyads of this type are indicative of the binary logic that underlies the Inuit kinship system. Structurally speaking, the mere fact of positioning relatives into dyadic pairs is more important than bringing out the potential dissimilarities between the two halves of each pair. In view of this primacy of binary structure over contents, the progressive disappearance of the dual number in Greenlandic Kalaallisut (since the late nineteenth century), and more recently, among some young speakers of Inuktitut, reflects a profound transformation of the logics of the language, induced by schooling and pervasive bilingualism.[14]

As will be seen below, strict duality can be overcome by the ability of kinship positions to transform themselves—as when Ego's parents become his or her children through the attribution of their *atiq* to a newborn baby— or when a dyadic relation is extended to additional individuals. A good example of the latter situation is polygamy—or more precisely, polygyny (a man with two or more wives). In traditional Inuit society, a man could live simultaneously with several spouses, provided he was able to feed and clothe them. A bigamist was called *marruralik* ("one who got two of them") and his wives *aviliak* ("made to be shared"). In Nunavik, a few bigamous households—comprising a husband, his two wives (acknowledged as such by the community), and their children—were in existence until the early 1970s. In 1968, I met an elder in Salluit who had had three wives (because he was a very skillful hunter, he said), but had been forced by the Royal Canadian Mounted Police to repudiate two of them a decade or so earlier, on the grounds that polygamy was illegal in Canada.

Linguistically, bigamy poses a challenge to the expression of dyadic relations. We saw that "standard" (monogamous) couples are called *aippariik* ("two halves of a pair"). But what should the term be for a marital union involving three (when bigamous) or even four (in the case of the Salluit elder) partners? I never thought to ask the few bigamists I met. Since a pair cannot have more than two components, the plural form *aippariit* can only apply to several different couples ("many pairs of two halves [spouses] each"). A possible solution for polygamists is to affix *-riit* to the word-base *nulia(q)-* ("female spouse, wife"), thus yielding *nuliariit*, "a group including at least three persons, some of whom are wives." This term implies the presence of an *ui* ("husband"), but without specifying if there is only one or several of them. Therefore, *nuliariit* can be translated as "wives with their husband" (a polygynous union) or "wives with their husbands" (many couples). It might also translate as "a wife with her husbands [at least two of them]," to speak about the rare cases of polyandry (a woman with more than one husband) mentioned in the Inuit world (see Rasmussen 1931).

Without being bigamists, in earlier times many men entered into a wife-exchanging partnership with a friend. From time to time, they would "borrow" their friend's spouse for a few days or weeks, often because their own wife was sick or pregnant and could not go with them on a trip during which they would need help. Of course, they then returned the favour to their partner whenever needed (Saladin d'Anglure 2013, 165). The men and women involved in such partnerships were said to be *kiputtut* ("who change position one with another"), and couples of that type were called *aippaajugiik* ("pair of little spouses"). This custom has given rise to the legend of Inuit husbands lending their wife or daughter to any male visitor. It is true that this happened occasionally, but only with well-known, appreciated guests, and generally with the wife's or daughter's agreement.

Sexual freedom (barring incestuous relations)[15] was widespread and still is, with both genders initiating love affairs. A male lover is an *uisuk* ("lesser husband") and a female one a *nuliasuk* ("lesser wife"). In several dialects, though, lovers are respectively called *ittusuk* ("lesser old man") and *ningiusuk* ("lesser old woman") in colloquial speech. These names stem from the fact that up to the early 1960s (Saladin d'Anglure 2013, 143), spouses would refer to their partner as *ittura* ("my old man") and *ningiura* ("my old woman"). Nowadays, in casual conversation, a man may call his wife *arnara* ("my woman"), while she mentions him as *angutiga* ("my man"), both spouses together being known as *arnariik* ("two, one of whom is a woman"). In Nunavik, the question *"Kinamik arnaqarqit?"*—"Whom do you have as [your] woman?" is understood as "Who is your wife?" But in western Inuit dialects, such a question might be thought to mean "Who is your mother?" because one's mother and father are often referred to as *arnanga* ("his/her woman") and *angutinga* ("his/her man").

Kinship by Marriage

Inuktitut possesses a number of terms for in-laws, who are Ego's *ilapasiit* ("almost kin"), related through his or her own or a relative's matrimonial union. The necessity of naming one's various in-laws reflects the fact that through marriage, Ego and kin are endowed with a whole new set of quasi-relatives who must be distinguished from each other. Kinship by marriage falls into three categories of in-laws: 1) the spouses of Ego's relatives; 2) the relatives of Ego's spouse; and 3) the spouses of some primary relatives of Ego's spouse.[16]

In Nunavik Inuktitut, the first category includes the following words:

ningauk	husband of Ego's daughter, niece, or granddaughter
	husband of a male Ego's sister or cousin
ukuaq	wife of Ego's son, nephew, or grandson
	wife of a female Ego's brother or cousin
angutiarjuk	husband of Ego's paternal or maternal aunt
arnaajuk	wife of Ego's paternal or maternal uncle

The second category includes the following:

saki	father or mother of Ego's spouse
sakilirqiuti	grandfather or grandmother of Ego's spouse

sakiaq	brother or male cousin of Ego's wife
	sister or female cousin of Ego's husband
irniajuk	nephew of Ego's husband or wife
paniarjuk	niece of Ego's husband or wife

One term belongs to both these categories:

| *aikuluk* | for a male Ego: his brother's wife or his wife's sister |
| | for a female Ego: her sister's husband or her husband's brother |

The third category includes only two terms:

angajuurnguq	for a male Ego: husband of his wife's older sister
	for a female Ego: wife of her husband's older brother
nukaurnguq	for a male Ego: husband of his wife's younger sister
	for a female Ego: wife of her husband's younger brother

The terminology for kinship by marriage may look confusing at first, but it is organized around four basic principles:

1. Terms for brothers- and sisters-in-law are only used among persons of the same gender (e.g., *ningauk* ↔ *sakiaq* among men; *ukuaq* ↔ *sakiaq* among women), with the exception of *aikuluk*, the sole cross-gender appellation for same-generation in-laws.

2. *Saki* and, generally, its derivative *sakiaq* ("little *saki*") denote a primary consanguine relative of Ego's spouse, in the ascending (*saki* = "parent-in-law") or same (*sakiaq* = "brother-/sister-in-law [brother or sister of spouse]") generation.[17]

3. *Ningauk* and *ukuaq* denote the male and female spouse of a primary consanguine relative of Ego, respectively, in the descending (*ningauk* = "son-in-law"; *ukuaq* = "daughter-in-law") or same (*ningauk* = "brother-in-law [sister's husband]"; *ukuaq* = "sister-in-law [brother's wife]")

generation. By extension, these terms also apply to the spouse of Ego's grandchild, nephew/niece, and cousin.

4. All other names for in-laws are derivatives of consanguine kinship terms.

The central dyads of in-laws, those involving *saki, sakiaq, ningauk,* and *ukuaq,* can be summarized as follows:

ningaugiik	*ningauk* (son-in-law) ↔ *saki* (father-/mother-in-law)
ukuariik	*ukuaq* (daughter-in-law) ↔ *saki* (father-/mother-in-law)
sakiariik	*sakiaq* (wife's brother) ↔ *ningauk* (sister's husband)
sakiariik	*sakiaq* (husband's sister) ↔ *ukuaq* (brother's wife)

The word *saki* might be connected to *sakiat* ("rib cage"), maybe a metaphorical rendition of the part played by close in-laws in structuring kinship, but this is just a guess. *Ningauk* (PE *nəngaruk*) is etymologically close to *ninnga(r)-* (PE *nəngar-*), "to be angry," although I do not see any semantic connection between the two. As for *ukuaq,* it could be related to the verbal base *uku-* ("to bend forward") and mean "the one who bends or is made to bend." It might allude to the fact that in traditional patrilocal Inuit camps, the imported wife of a local man was expected to be submissive toward her mother-in-law and her husband's sisters, who consequently called her *ukuaq,* "the bending one." However, this is still a guess.

The term *aikuluk* is peculiar. It is the unique appellation available to persons of the same generation for addressing or mentioning an in-law of the opposite gender. For a man, it refers to his wife's sister as well as to his brother's wife, while for a woman, it denotes her husband's brother or sister's husband. The word sounds a little risqué because it applies the affix *-kuluk* ("nice little") to a social link (in-laws of opposite sex) that, up to the 1980s in certain places, was the object of much ritual avoidance. For example, two *aikuluuk* were obligated to speak to each other in the third person—or never at all in some regions—and marriage between them was prohibited (Saladin d'Anglure 2013, 144). Fortescue et al. (2010, 8) mention a connection between PE *agi,* the etymon of *ai-* in *aikuluk,* and Aleut words meaning "another one" and "guest." The term *aikuluk* would thus add an endearing affix to the modern reflex of a Proto-Eskimo-Aleut word-base denoting an alien guest. If this combination makes any sense, *aikuluk* might mean something like "nice little foreign guest."

The remaining appellations for in-laws derive from consanguine kinship terms, of which they constitute semantic extensions. If we follow Fortescue et al. (2010, 260), *angajuurnguq* and *nukaurnguq*, the terms by which the spouse of a younger sibling addresses the same-sex-as-Ego spouse of this sibling's older brother or sister, and vice versa, respectively mean "who is more of an older sibling [*angaju(k)*]" and "who is more of a younger sibling [*nuka(q)*]."[18] If *-rngu(ju)q* is taken in its modern, rather than etymological meaning, the pair of words may also be interpreted as "one who is dissatisfied with being an *angajuk* or a *nukaq*." In the first case, the siblings' spouses would call each other "older or younger sibling once more," meaning that both of them are an extension of their spouse's genealogical—and, thus, hierarchical—status of senior or junior sibling. In the second instance, which I deem less plausible semantically, the spouses would perhaps be said to be disappointed (or jealous?) of not being fully fledged older or younger siblings within the family to which they belong by marriage. In any case, the terms *angajuurnguq* and *nukaurnguq* appear to reinforce the age hierarchy among siblings of the same gender by extending it to their spouse.

The last set of appellations for in-laws concerns nephews/nieces and uncles/aunts by marriage. It denotes the relationships between the children of the siblings of a person's spouse, on the one hand, and the spouses of one's parents' siblings, on the other. In contrast with the avuncular terminology for consanguine relatives, no lexical distinction is made between the sides of the family to which uncles and aunts—and, by correlation, their nephews and nieces—belong, but the gender of nephews and nieces is denoted. The set of terms for avuncular in-laws includes two double dyads:

irniajugiik	*irniajuk* (nephew-in-law) ↔ *angutiarjuk* (uncle-in-law)
	irniajuk (nephew-in-law) ↔ *arnaajuk* (aunt-in-law)
paniarjugiik	*paniarjuk* (niece-in-law) ↔ *angutiarjuk* (uncle-in-law)
	paniarjuk (niece-in-law) ↔ *arnaajuk* (aunt-in-law)

The affix *-a(r)juk*, present in all four terms, means "small:"

irniajuk	"small son"
paniarjuk	"small daughter"
angutiarjuk	"small male man"
arnaajuk	"small woman"

These words sound intriguing. The affix *-a(r)juk* may be understood as referring to a lesser level of importance rather than to actual size. *Irniajuk* would thus mean "lesser son," and so forth. Moreover, the word-bases *anguti-* and *arna(q)-* are most probably used here with the meaning "father" and "mother," as they currently are in some Inuit dialects (see above). But why call uncles and nephews by marriage as if they were parents and their children?

It is conceivable that in former times, the preferred form of marriage might have been between cousins (as it is in several societies around the world), the uncles and aunts of Ego thus being seen as potential "lesser" (i.e., in-law) parents, with Ego becoming their "lesser" son or daughter. Since consanguine uncles, aunts, and nephews/nieces would have already used kinship terms denoting their respective family positions, only avuncular in-laws and their nephews and nieces would have needed to call each other by way of their virtual parent-child relationship.

If the second part of this proposition makes sense—in an avuncular relation perceived as virtually parental by marriage, consanguine relatives do not need new appellations—the basic assertion concerning preferred marital unions is not justified by ethnography. In Nunavik, for instance, marriage with first cousins was, and still is, discouraged, an attitude reinforced by the fact that cousins are considered as "substitute brothers (*anitsait*) and sisters (*najatsait*)." Another, related explanation would be that through adoption, which frequently involves siblings as givers or takers of children—see the interpretation of the word *qatangutitsait* proposed above—uncles and aunts can become parents for their biological and in-law nephews and nieces.

Alternatively, uncles and aunts often act as guides and advisors to their siblings' children, thus playing a parental role,[19] especially in the old days when several married siblings would reside in the same camp. Or, as seen above, since in most cases nephews and nieces are designated with terms pointing to a reproduction of the sibling relationship that unites their uncles, aunts, and parents, might it not be possible that they and their avuncular in-laws refer to each other as parents and children, thus reinforcing the symbolic reproduction of their genitors' original family group? Finally, a simpler explanation could be that if uncles and aunts by marriage are called "parents," while addressing their nephews and nieces as "children," this bars these non-consanguineous in-laws from mutual sexual unions because terminology draws them within the boundary of incestuous relations.[20]

Adoption

Besides consanguine kinship and kinship by marriage, there exists another form of kin relationship: adoption. Adopting children has always played a crucial part in the life of Inuit families. It has been estimated that in most Canadian Inuit communities, around 30 percent of the population are individuals who have been adopted, generally at birth (Dorais 1997, 66n9). Adoption frequently involves residents of the same community, often relatives (e.g., adopting a child from one's sibling), but nowadays the practice can extend to neighbouring villages. One of the motivations in offering a child for adoption is to provide a childless couple with someone who will continue their family. A home without children is not desirable. This is why older people whose offspring are growing up, widows in particular, may adopt young boys or girls, in order to enliven their days and help them with domestic tasks.

At a deeper level, though, adoption reflects the perception Inuit have that children, like game animals and nature in general, are a collective good that should be shared by all. The exchange of children—giving and receiving adoptees—is a means for creating and strengthening social ties with other members of the community. Within the family, it reinforces intergenerational relations when grandparents adopt a grandchild. It frequently happens that young women, who often beget at a very early age, donate their first child (*qiturngingauti*, "a means for giving birth for the first time") to their mother, perhaps as a replacement for their own future departure from home.

Adoption is called *tigusiniq* ("the fact of taking something or somebody with the hands"), the adoptee being a *tiguaq* ("one who has been taken with the hands"). Babies adopted at birth or soon after become full members of their new family, to the point that a girl who gives her child in adoption to her mother often addresses her own biological son or daughter as if she was their older sister. Adoptees can be referred to by affixing the morpheme -*taq* ("something added") to a relevant kinship term (e.g., *panittaq*, "adopted *panik* [daughter]"), but they are addressed as non-adoptees would be and address their adoptive parents as if these were their biological genitors.

In order to prevent consanguine marriages, and because in small communities family relations are common knowledge, adopted children know who their biological parents and siblings are. Moreover, they consider them their relatives. As was the case with polygamy, this challenges the binary nature of dyadic kinship relations. For an adopted girl, for instance, the *panigiik* ("two, one of whom is a daughter") dyad to which she belongs involves herself together with her two mothers and two fathers, adopted as well as biological. When asked, "*Kinauva anaanait?*"—"Who is your mom?" the girl will usually give the name of her adoptive mother, but she may add that her biological parent is so-and-so. For her, the dyadic mother-child relationship has thus become triadic. In northeastern Nunavik, one's biological mother is often called *puukuluk* ("nice little pouch"), an allusion to her gestatory role.

Being adopted increases the number of one's kindred, because an adoptee possesses two sets of relatives, adoptive and biological. This is often an asset for social relations, since the fabric of Inuit society is largely based on family links. By contrast, an orphan without parents and close relatives (*iliarjuk*) is socially isolated. The PE etymology of *iliarjuk* (Fortescue et al. 2010, 118) might be glossed as "a little one who has been put in a certain position," a possible allusion to the orphan's lack of agency, but in contemporary Inuktitut, *iliarjuk* can also be understood as "lesser partner [*ili(k)*-]." Traditionally, orphans were taken in by strangers or distant relatives, in whose home they often became a *kipaluk* ("servant"), a word whose PE etymon (*kəvgar*) is the same as that of *kiggaq* ("messenger, helper"). The myth of Kaujjaa(r)juk as I heard it in 1966, told by Jiimi Kuuttuq Koneak from Kuujjuaq (Nunavik), tells of an orphan boy who was forced by his evil caretakers to sleep in the porch of their snow house and eat with the dogs. One night, three polar bears visited him and made him grow magically in height and strength (*nulavuq*, "he/she grows thanks to magic") until he was able to kill everyone in the hunting camp except for his sister, who had brought him food from time to time. This myth teaches that those who abuse orphans will be punished.

Symbolic Kinship

Adoption may be considered a form of symbolic kinship, that is, a family tie not based on consanguinity or marriage. However, it remains grounded in parent-child relations, as well as in practices similar to those found in consanguine families. Inuktitut also possesses a few terms of quasi-kinship, the foundations of which have nothing to do with consanguinity or adoption. It must be made clear that when the relationships denoted by these terms are called "symbolic," this betrays a *Qallunaat* perspective. Since such relationships forge kinship ties as genuine as those stemming from biology or adoption, they are very real to Inuit.

The preceding chapter mentioned one such type of relation: that between a human being and his *nuliarsaq* ("spirit wife") or her *uirsaq* ("spirit husband"). The children produced by these marriages (*qiturngasait?*) are often invisible, but some of them are not, or they can be seen occasionally. It is said that the offspring of *uirsait* and *nuliarsait* are recognizable because they have no navel (*qalasiq*).

A more common type of symbolic kinship is the relation between a boy or girl and the midwife who delivered them. In northeastern Nunavik, up to the mid-1960s, childbirths occurred at home with the assistance of a self-taught local midwife (*ikajurti*, "habitual helper") and other women. It was only in 1967, with the opening of a small hospital in Kuujjuaq, that giving birth became systematically medicalized.

A boy calls his midwife *arnaquti* ("woman in [my] possession") and she calls him *angusiaq* ("the male [I have] made"). A girl's midwife is her *sanaji* ("who fashions something") while she is her *arnaliaq* ("the female [I have] made"). There exists a strong dyadic relation (*angusiariik, arnaliariik*) between midwives and the children they have helped being born. Traditionally, among other rituals (see Saladin d'Anglure 2000), a boy would give his *arnaquti* his first-caught animal of each species, or a share of it in the case of larger beasts. Similarly, a girl would bring to her *sanaji* a piece of each type of clothing she had sewed for the first time. This kind of gift was called a *qillaquti* ("tie [on the umbilical cord] belonging to someone"), an allusion to the part played by the midwife in tying up the navel string of the newborn.

When a boy had caught his very first "game," usually a snow bunting (*qupanuaq*), his *arnaquti* and other women would join in a circle around the young hunter to show him their pubis. In the same way, when a girl had completed her first stitching, her *sanaji* would gather a few men who would show their bellies to the girl (Saladin d'Anglure 2000, 101–2). These actions seemingly foreshadowed the sexuality of children, who were now starting to learn to be adults. In the case of boys, the word *arnaquti* ("woman one possesses") might have implied the midwife was their metaphorical spouse. Midwives thus supervised symbolically the social development of the future hunters and seamstresses they had contributed to "make." According to Schneider (1985, 221), a man and a woman who had the same midwife at birth called each other *nuliatsiaq* ("good or nice wife") and *uitsiaq* ("good or nice husband"). This may mean that individuals whose initiation into adult tasks and sexuality had been overseen by the same person were considered as belonging to a virtual pool of potential spouses.

With the generalization of medicalized pregnancies and births from the late 1960s on, *arnaqutiit/sanajiit* stopped presiding over deliveries. Some say that *Qallunaat* obstetricians and nurses were astonished when boys they had brought into the world a few years before sent them their first-caught *qupanuaq* or eider duck because they considered them to be their *arnaquti*. But as time went by, hospitals accepted the presence at delivery time of a woman who had been invited by the parturient to cut the newborn's umbilical cord (*mitsiaq/mik&iaq*, "that is shortened"). The *angusiariik/arnaliariik* relation and the traditional gifts it entailed thus remained customary, although the *arnaquti* or *sanaji* now became a sort of honorary godmother.

Last but not least, a very important symbolic kinship dyad is termed *sauniriik* ("two who have each other as a bone") in Nunavik, *atitsiagiik* ("who have each other as a nice name") in Labrador, and *atiriik* ("who have each other as a name") or *avvariik* ("who have each other as a half") in eastern Nunavut. These words denote the relationship that exists between two individuals who bear the same name (*atiq*), either because one of them is named after the other or because they share the same eponym (a person whose name is given to someone else). Two namesakes who share their name by chance (without reference to a common eponym) call each other *atitsiaq* ("nice name") in Nunavik. As we shall now see, the strong referential content of these terms— the sharers of a name are like a "bone" or a "half" to each other—expresses the crucial importance of this type of relation.

The Naming System

In the preceding chapter, we saw that *atiq* ("name") is one of the three souls present in any *inuk* ("human being"), and that etymologically, this word might be linked to the PE verbal base *atə(ði)-*, "to be the same" (Fortescue et al. 2010, 55). If this stands true, etymology would reflect the principal characteristic of name souls, given that eponyms are reincarnated (*inurur-tuq*, "he/she becomes an *inuk* [again]")—or co-incarnated if still alive—in those who receive their *atiq*, most generally at birth.[21] Indeed, the eponym (*sauniviniq*, "former *sauniq*" in Nunavik) and the person(s) bearing his or her name often share a number of personal characteristics. These are mentioned on occasion. In the camp of Airartuuq, for instance, a young girl named Charlotte once screamed when seeing a bumblebee near her face. This prompted her mother to say, "*Saalitiviniq taimatituutuinnalaurtuq igutsanik irsigami*"—"The late Charlotte [the girl's eponym] just behaved like that because she was afraid of bees." Stories are also told about children bearing the name of a person who was drowned and who consequently are afraid to go near water.

The spiritual and intimate nature of *atiq* explains why names must not be pronounced carelessly. Things are changing now, but for those who came of age before 1980, calling people by their given name was to be avoided by all means, except for parents addressing some of their young children.[22] Using kinship terms, nicknames (e.g., *qataak*, "pal"; from *qatanguti*, "sibling, cousin"),[23] and diminutives (e.g., *Suu* for *Suusi*, "Susie") was preferable. In Quaqtaq, when my adoptive mother asked for her *panik* ("daughter") and my adoptive father for his *anaana* ("mother"), I knew they were seeking after their eldest daughter, *Tiisi* (Daisy). Qualifying affixes added to personal names (e.g., *Ivakallak*, "little plump Eva," or *Mitiarjuk*, "small Mitiq") are another way to lessen the rudeness of direct naming. This also helps to distinguish numerous individuals who bear the same name.

Elders still consider it rude to ask someone, "*Kinauvit?*"—"Who are you [i.e., What is your name]?" When I visited Tasiujaq (Nunavik) for the first time, the patriarch of the community, Willie Cain, suddenly said to me: "*Iliranartualummik apirigumagakkit, qailaurit!*"—"I have something very embarassing to ask you, so please, come!" We left his tent and walked up to a rock on which he invited me to sit before asking me, "*Kinaugaluarqit?*"—"Who are you anyway?" It would have been much more polite for him to ask someone else, even in my presence, "*Kina una?*"—"Who is this one?" But since nobody around knew me, Willie had to resort to a direct question, the rudeness of which he tried to attenuate somewhat with the affix *-galuar-* ("however, anyway").

Because *atiq* souls revive in children, when a birth occurs in a community or when a newborn child is back from hospital with his mother, everyone shakes hands with the baby in order to welcome the deceased individual back home. Soul revival also explains, at least in part, why Inuit children are rarely if ever scolded and should never be hit. Such an action would be offensive to the reincarnated ancestor.[24]

The most complete narration of the reincarnation of a name soul has been published by Saladin d'Anglure (1977; see also Saladin d'Anglure 2018, Chapter 1). It is the transcription of an oral interview in which a late elder from Igloolik, Rose Iqallijuq, recounts her intrauterine memories. She remembers being her maternal grandfather Savviuqtalik (one of the names she had received at birth), lying in his grave. The old man's *tarniq* soul ("human-like shadow") rises up and after some time sees his own daughter coming out of her snow house to urinate. Being thirsty and cold despite his winter clothing, he enters his daughter and finds himself inside her uterus (*igliaq/illiaq*, "little platform"), nude on the sleeping platform (*igliq/illiq*) of a small igloo. Savviuqtalik's *tarniq* and *atiq* souls have parted company, the former going to the abode of the dead and the latter becoming a fetus (*inuksaq/inutsaq*, "future person") in his daughter's womb. From time to time, the head of a dog appears at the door of the igloo-shaped uterus, vomiting food. Iqallijuq explains that it is the penis of her father, whose sperm (*ittaaq*, "little ooozing liquid") helps nourish the fetus. After several months, Savviuqtalik has grown so big that he must get out of the uterus. Instinctively, he seizes the masculine implements (harpoon, *savik* knife) at the left of the door but then realizes he does not want to be cold again hunting on the ice, and perhaps drowning like his father will in the near future, as he already knows. The fetus thus takes hold of the feminine utensils (oil lamp, *ulu* knife) at the right of the door and exits the uterus. His penis then shrinks, his perineum splits, and Savviuqtalik is born a girl.

Iqallijuq's narrative has much to say about the *atiq* soul. When it reincarnates as a fetus, the soul remembers its previous life. These recollections disappear at birth, but some people like Iqallijuq retain the memory of their intrauterine existence. In Quaqtaq, I once heard a man saying he remembered being in his mother's womb. When I reported this to other people

I was visiting, expressing doubts about the man's sincerity, my host, Susie Aloupa, replied with some astonishment, *"Ilitsili qallunaat aulajiqattangillasi piaratsauvitsinik?"* —"But you *Qallunaat*, don't you remember the time you were a fetus?" She then explained that some individuals do have such memories. For example, Susie said, the man I had mentioned used to recount that he did not want to exit his mother's uterus because hearing voices outside made him feel shy (*ilirasuttuq*). It was only after some time that he finally decided to be born.

Like spirits and shamans, fetuses have some knowledge of the future. According to Iqallijuq, Savviuqtalik knew that his [Iqallijuq's] father would drown the following fall when hunting on the sea ice, and this prompted him not to live a hunter's existence once again. *Atiq* souls can thus decide to change sex at birth. In the case of males becoming females, as Savviuqtalik did, this phenomenon is called *sipiniq* ("the action of splitting"). It is—or was, before the advent of hospitals—commonly attested by Inuit, in Igloolik as well as in Nunavik and elsewhere in the Arctic.

Newborns may receive several names—and conversely, a name can be transmitted to more than one person. Iqallijuq tells how an old woman present at her birth asked that the new baby be called Iqallijuq. She thus became, at the same time, Savviuqtalik and Iqallijuq, hosting two *atiq* souls: that of her maternal grandfather and another one she shared with the old woman. For Iqallijuq's mother, her daughter was above all Savviuqtalik. This is why she considered the child as her own father, calling her "dad" and making her wear masculine clothing, up to the time Iqallijuq had her first periods (*aunaartuq*, "she bleeds profusely") and became fit for marriage.

Addressing and disguising children as if they were their own eponyms introduces us to a crucial dimension of Inuit kinship: the reincarnation of *atiq* souls entails the reproduction of family relationships and of the -*giik*/ -*riik* dyads that express them. Disguise may be disappearing—although in the early 1990s, a number of North Baffin boys and girls were still being clothed and identified according to the gender of their *atiq*—but addressing people with kinship terms that reflect the way their eponyms addressed each other is still prevalent all across the Inuit world, except perhaps in West Greenland.

I first became aware of eponymous kinship during my 1965 stay in Airartuuq. I did not yet speak Inuktitut then, but I had brought with me a list of Inuit kinship terms and wanted to check my knowledge of local family relations. So I asked Simeonie, a ten-year-old boy who had learned some English at school, questions of the following type: "Is Jaiku [Simeonie's father] your *ataata?*" or "Is Susie [his little sister] your *naja?*" I was somewhat baffled by his answers, which were to the effect of "No, Jaiku is my *angajuk* [older brother]," and "Susie is my *anaanatsiaq* [grandmother]." At the time, I concluded that due to the influence of school, Inuit children had become completely ignorant of their own kinship system.

I was completely wrong, of course. Simeonie's answers reflected how he actually addressed his father, sister, and other relatives, through eponymy rather than consanguinity. He had likely been given the name of Jaiku's younger brother, and Susie may have hosted the *atiq* soul of her own (and Simeonie's) grandmother. The grandmother in question was probably on their maternal side because otherwise Simeonie would have called his sister *anaana* ("mother"), being himself the reincarnation of his father's younger brother, who had the same mother as Jaiku (see Figure 1). As far as Jaiku was concerned, he probably called his son Simeonie *nukaq* ("younger brother") and his daughter *saki* ("mother-in-law"), while Susie would have addressed him as *ningauk* ("son-in-law") and her brother Simeonie as *irng-utaq* ("grandchild").

This way of expressing kinship relations with reference to one's *sauni-viniq* ("former *sauniq,*" or eponym) challenges once more the strict binary nature of the *-giik/-riik* dyadic pairs. Simeonie is at the same time Jaiku's son and younger brother, sharing with him two dyadic relations: *irniriik* ("son-father") and *nukariik* ("younger-older sibling"). But there is more. Let us suppose that Simeonie's eponym (Jaiku's younger brother) had received his *atiq* from his mother's paternal uncle, while Jaiku himself, through another of his names, revived his mother's sister, Napa (traditional Inuit names are genderless). The two brothers would thus have shared a *qangiariik* ("niece-paternal uncle") dyadic relation, Jaiku calling his younger sibling Simeonie *akka* ("paternal uncle"), while being called by him *qangiaq* ("niece/nephew"). Now, Jaiku might well have decided to reproduce this *qangiariik* relation with his son Simeonie who, after all, hosted the *atiq* soul of Jaiku's mother's paternal uncle by way of his own (Simeonie's) eponym, Jaiku's younger brother. Therefore, the ten-year-old Simeonie I knew could have been simultaneously the son, younger sibling, and uncle of his biological father, Jaiku, thanks to a rearrangement of kinship relations induced by eponymy, as illustrated in Figure 1.

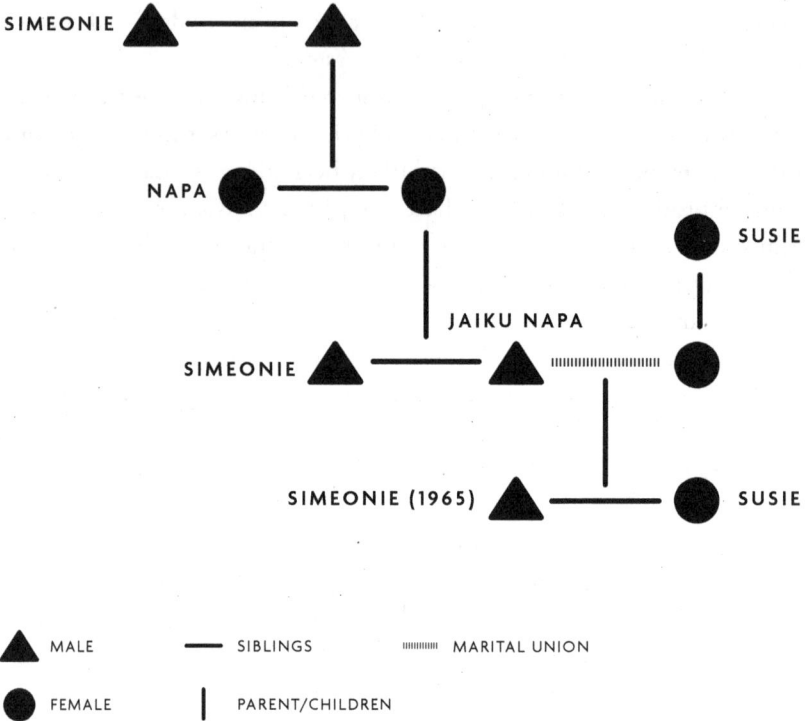

Figure 1. Kinship Relations and Eponymy.

Such a rearrangement is complicated by the fact that any individual may have several names (up to ten in northeastern Nunavik), each of which can be shared by several persons. This multiplies the number of kinship dyads into which one can enter, as well as the number of individuals sharing the same dyad, because through eponymy, each name and its bearers are likely to be linked by kinship to the bearers of many other names (as with Jaiku Napa, linked to the relatives of his *sauniviniik* [eponyms] Jaiku and Napa), and maintain *sauniq* relationships with those who share a common *atiq* with them.

How do Inuit manage to navigate such an apparently inextricable jungle of family relationships? As a general rule, only some of all available kinship ties are activated. A person may even ignore several of the names he or she received at birth. In practice, when addressing a child, senior interlocutors take the initiative in using this or that kinship appellation with the younger individual—thus activating a specific dyadic relation—according to the significance the appellation has for them. For example, Iqallijuq's mother probably called her daughter *ataata*, with reference to Savviuqtalik, the name of her own father, while other people referred to the child as Iqallijuq, or even Rose after her family became Catholic. Very early in their life, children are taught to react properly to kinship appellations addressed to them, responding for instance with *"Aningai!"*—"Hi, brother!" when hearing someone saying *"Najangai!"*—"Hi, sister!" They thus gradually develop their own mental repertory of the appellations they are expected to use with those around them.

As mentioned, in northeastern Nunavik children are generally given up to ten names or so. This is also the case in several other regions, although in western Nunavik, during the 1970s at least, most people had only two first names: a traditional Inuit one and a Christian name. Formerly, Inuit did not use family names (*atirusiq*, "lesser name"). In seasonal camps and among regional bands, everybody knew or had heard of everyone else, and individuals bearing the same name could be distinguished by referring to their immediate relatives or the place they lived, or through the use of qualifying affixes. In Quaqtaq, for instance, *Putulialuk Aalupaup nukanga* ("Big Putulik, Aloupa's younger brother") was not the same person as *Putulik Matiusiup irninga* ("Putulik, Matucey's son").

When Inuit became sedentary residents of larger villages, *Qallunaat* administrators who did not speak the language insisted on the necessity of identifying the families to which people belonged. In Canada, from the 1960s on—after a period during which all Inuit had received from the Canadian government a plastic medal (*ujamik*, "that is on the upper torso") engraved with a personal identification number—it was decided that Inuit needed family names (Alia 1994). An Inuk civil servant visited all communities in order to advise families on the surname suggested for each of them. Most of the time, these surnames were patronyms, that is, the given name under which the older male in an extended family, or his deceased father or grandfather, was or had been usually known. This resulted in some elders receiving their own name as family name (e.g., *Jusipi Jusipi*, "Joseph Joseph"). Some individuals refused to adopt such patronyms, instead choosing one of their own traditional names as their surname (e.g., Peter [Christian name] Aupaluk [traditional first name, chosen as family name]), though in most cases, the transmission of patronyms to younger generations introduced into the Inuit naming system a patrilineal bias unknown until then.

Nowadays, family names are commonplace among Inuit. They are transmitted by male Egos to their wife and children. Many first names, however, have retained their function of reviving *atiq* souls. A minority of them are traditional—that is, pre-Christian—but names inspired by Christianity, often taken from the Bible, were readily adopted as acceptable vehicles for reincarnating *atiit*. Their only difference with traditional appellations is that they are gender-bound and tend to be transmitted to individuals of the same sex as their *sauniviniq*, at least in the case of "public" names (see below).[25] Other, secondary names, though, do not always agree with the biological gender of their bearer.

Traditional names are drawn from the general lexicon of Inuktitut. They often have surprising meanings, but these are not taken into consideration when used as names. Here are a few examples:

Putulik	One with a hole
Qulliq	Soapstone seal-oil lamp
Usuarjuk	Little penis
Atiittuq	One without a name
Nasaq	Hat
Inugaluaq	Extremely small person

Jaakkak	Two persons or things to which I have done something
Qupanuaq	Snow bunting, small bird

Christian names introduced by missionaries have been adapted to the pronunciation of Inuktitut, although bilingual individuals may now prefer to pronounce them as in English:

Miaji	Mary
Saali	Charlie
Jupi	Job
Siaja	Sarah
Paasa	Bertha
Papi	Bobbie
Taiviti	David
Ulipika	Rebecca

In Quaqtaq, a village comparable to many other small communities in Nunavik and eastern Nunavut, children are usually given three names at a minimum. These names generally cover three categories (Dorais 1997, 63):

"Public" name: a name used with those who do not have a personal relationship with the name-bearer, especially in the public sphere (school, administration); it is generally chosen by the parents because they like it; oftentimes, its use is new to the community.

"Memorial" name(s): the name(s) of recently deceased resident(s) of the village, or of individual(s), deceased or still alive, particularly cherished by the child's parents; such names imply the transmission of *atiq* souls.

Sauniq names: the names of relatives or, more rarely, friends of the child's family, generally but not always deceased, whose *atiq* the parents or grandparents want to revive; this category is the most likely to include pre-Christian names.

By way of example, a male child born in 1993 in Quaqtaq was named as follows (Dorais 1997, 63):

Norman: public name

Aqiggialuk: memorial name (a man from Quaqtaq who had died in 1990)

Saali: *sauniq* name (maternal grandfather; still alive in 1993)[26]

Miaji: *sauniq* name (maternal grandmother; deceased)

Maasiu: *sauniq* name (maternal uncle; deceased)

Uili: *sauniq* name (paternal grandfather; deceased)

Jaji: *sauniq* name (paternal great-uncle; still alive in 1993)

Putulialuk: *sauniq* name (a non-kin whose relatives asked that he be revived)

Not all Inuit children are given so many names, and the number of *sauniit* and "memorial" appellations may vary according to family ties and circumstances (e.g., the number of recent deaths in a community), but the example of Norman shows that the transmission of souls through eponymy is still alive and well in the Arctic.

Conclusion

Our stroll through the vocabulary of kin relationships has disclosed several interesting semantic links among kinship terms, as well as between these and some fundamental concepts of Inuit thinking. As far as such concepts are concerned, we observed that there do not exist any specific terms for "family" and "kindred." In Inuktitut, a group of relatives is an *ilagiit*, "those who are component parts for each other," and any relative is an *ila*, a part of a structured whole. In a parallel way, the two members of a matrimonial couple are *aippariik*, "two halves of a pair," each of them being an *aippaq*, one of a pair, for the other. Families and couples are thus considered as social embodiments of the general concepts of plurality and duality, the linguistic expression of which is strongly marked in the Inuit language, notably through the existence of two non-singular grammatical numbers: plural and dual.

As far as kinship is concerned, relations between kin are also marked by binary terms expressing reciprocal family ties. By adding the affixes *-giik* or *-riik* after a kinship term (most generally the one that applies to the junior or female component of a pair of relatives), any type of relationship between two family members can be expressed as a dyad, as in *iririik* ("a son and his father or mother"), *najagiik* ("a sister and her brother") or *nuliariik* ("a wife and her husband").

The morphosemantics of kinship terms is revealing in several ways. By way of example, some words expressing avuncular links (uncles, aunts, and their nephews/nieces) seemingly aim at reconstructing among nephews and nieces the brother and sister relationships of their parents' generation. This applies to consanguine ties. Uncles and aunts by marriage are rather considered as potential parents, and they address their nephews- and nieces-in-law as if they belonged to a lesser category of sons and daughters. Likewise, according to a tentative but etymologically unproved reconstruction, the underlying semantic links between the words for "woman," "man," "husband," and "wife" might point to a metonymic description of sexual intercourse and reproduction.

Beyond kinship terms in the strictest sense—consanguine or by marriage—kin relations extend in various directions. Adoption is a major institution among Inuit, applying to about 30 percent of the population. Adopted children are considered to be full members of their adoptive family, but they continue to be related to their biological parents and siblings. This challenges the strict duality of binary family relationships since, for instance, an adoptee's *iririik* ("son-parent") dyad comprises two fathers and two mothers. Other extensions of kinship include the ties between a person and the midwife who presided at his or her birth, and above all, eponymic kinship. In the latter case, when a baby is given the name of a deceased (or more rarely, living) individual—who becomes the baby's eponym, its *sauniq* ("bone") in Nunavik—the child's body starts to host or to transit through the *atiq* ("name") soul of that person, who revives in the newborn. Kinship relations involving the eponym in his or her former life are perpetuated by the new baby, who for example will call its father *irniq* ("son") and be called *anaana* ("mother") in return, if it was given the name of its paternal grandmother. Eponymic relationships may entail an often complex rearrangement of kinship terminology.

Words for kinship and naming stress the crucial importance of family ties in Inuit society. Before the advent of sedentary villages and wage-earning jobs, families formed the very basis of social relationships and economic activities. I remember a middle-aged hunter from Quaqtaq whose two brothers had moved to another community. He complained about having problems finding suitable hunting and trapping partners because, he said, "*Qatangutaujut kisiani qulanngivigijausuut*"—"Siblings are the only ones you can trust on a permanent basis." Besides your *ilait* ("relatives"), you may have *inuuqatiit* ("those who share [one's] life [i.e., companions]") and *piqatiit* ("those who do something with someone [i.e., friends]"), but they cannot replace your family.

Because traditional Inuit society was based on family ties, when people travelled to another camp or another region, they tried to find out if they would be related to residents of that place through consanguinity, marriage, or eponymy. This was particularly important for males, who had to be accepted as hunting partners by local men. Seasonal camps were informally ruled by the patriarch of the principal extended family (*angajurqaaq*, "antecedent elder [i.e., parent]"), provided he was physically fit and possessed a collective boat (*umiaq*), thus becoming an *umialittaaq* ("boat owner"). However, no ruling positions existed beyond that. Shamans had some influence, but did not rule camps unless they were themselves patriarchs. However, an *angajurqaaq* could strengthen his leadership by enlisting the support of a local shaman (Saladin d'Anglure 2013, 209).

I have often heard Inuit claim that formal chiefs are an invention of *Qallunaat* that was unknown to them, thus implying that they had enough *isuma* ("reason") to govern themselves correctly without needing to be given orders by someone else. And unlike Yupiit from Siberia and Alaska, as well as several North American First Nations, Inuit of the eastern Arctic did not wage war—*unatartuq*, "he/she tries to kill human beings," related to PE *unaðmi-*, "to challenge" (Fortescue et al. 2010, 404). On occasion, however, individuals would murder other people (*inuartuq*, "gets at [i.e. kills] a human being"), non-Inuit considered dangerous, for instance, or someone whose wife they wanted to steal. The latter deed entailed family feuds (*akiniartuq*, "he/she deals with somebody facing him/her [i.e., takes revenge]").

Despite such outbursts of violence, family ties and eponymy generally succeeded in maintaining social peace among Inuit groups (*saimmautijut*, "they are in a state of mutual ease or consolation"). Names in particular played an important part in this process. In his doctoral dissertation, the anthropologist Christopher G. Trott (1989) has shown that in northern Baffin Island—and this also applies to other regions—*atiit* were often linked to specific *nunait* ("lands, places"). When a name disappeared from one location after a death or outmigration, it was soon replaced, thanks to eponymy or to the immigration of someone known under that name—and thus, particularly welcome—in that location. Trott has also shown that *atiit* are intimately related to the human bodies that transit through them, endowing these with personal traits that have endured and will endure over the past and future generations. I would add that the social identity of a human being can therefore be defined along two dimensions. Synchronically, it consists in the presence, here and now, of a name soul within a body (or vice versa), or in the confluence of a number of *atiit* in this same body. Diachronically, identity also consists in the totality of each name soul's reincarnations over time in different bodies; or put another way, in all the successive bodies that have transited and will transit through a name soul.

CHAPTER FIVE

Words for Speaking about the Human Body

Taakkuningalu inuuqativinirminik irqaigivuq. Naulaup naanga alitsimajuq irqaivaa. Irravingit nuitajut nanuup kukinginnut naanga alittaunirami. Ammalu nanurmut tuqungajumut aigivuq. Qaujivurlu taanna nanuq qinirialaurtanga tuqummat niungagut kingulliingagut ikiqarmat ataatangata ikililaurmagu unaarminut. Akunili takunnariiramiuk savinnit tigusiluni nanuq pilasivaa.

He remembers them, his late companions. He remembers Naulaq's ripped-up belly. His bowels were visible because his belly had been ripped open by the claws of the polar bear. And he walks toward the dead bear. He realizes that this bear he had searched for died with an injury in his hind legs because his father had wounded it with his harpoon. When he has looked at it for a long time, he seizes one of the knives and starts cutting the bear up.

MARKOOSIE (2011, 148)

As shown in this quotation from Markoosie's novel *Angunasuttiup naukkut-inga*, Inuit have no difficulties speaking about anatomy because their language possesses a rich vocabulary for describing human and animal bodies.[1] The preceding chapter described some kinship terms that have anatomical connotations, like *saki* ("parent-in-law")—which might perhaps be connected to *sakiat* ("rib cage")—or in Nunavik, like *sauniq* ("bone")—the term by which two persons sharing the same name through eponymy call each other. It may be surmised that kinship relations and the names that embody them form the structural backbone of *ilagiit* ("those who are component parts for each other," i.e., families and kindred), and thus of traditional Inuit society, in the same metaphorical way as the skeleton (*sauniit*, "the bones") structures the physical *timi* ("body").

We also saw in Chapter 3 that *inuit* ("humans") and *uumajuit* ("animals") alike possess a *timi* that provides them with all the skills necessary to procure their livelihood and reproduce themselves within *sila* ("the environment"). In contradistinction to most animals, however, *inuit* are also fully endowed with *isuma* ("thought, reason"), a mental faculty enabling them to understand how to behave optimally.

The etymology of the word *timi* is unclear, but it is noteworthy that in some Inuit dialects (including Nunavik), *timaani* ("in its *timi*") refers to a higher location nearby, such as the *nuna* ("landward") area of a small island (Spalding 1998, 159), or the position of a stranded object that the rising tide cannot reach (Qumaq 1991, 219). Nowadays, this meaning has apparently become nearly obsolete, although it survives in the noun phrase *kamiup timinga*, "the *timi* of a boot," in other words, its leg.[2] Nevertheless, the existence of such a signification means that semantically, the relation between, say, the main portion of a *nuna* and its neighbouring peripheral parts (coastal inlets and islands, for instance) is or was seen as analogous to the link between a human body and its periphery: limbs and head. Indeed, the head, *niaquq*, whose possible PE etymology is "an attached part that is bending" (Fortescue et al. 2010, 243), as well as the limbs, *avatit* ("that surround something") are not considered by Inuit as belonging to *timi*, properly speaking.

In this chapter, we will explore the vocabulary pertaining to *timi* and its attachments: *niaquq* and *avatit*. The description will be limited to a number of terms denoting important parts of external and internal anatomy because Inuit words for speaking about the human body are too detailed and too numerous to be dealt with exhaustively—they include very specific appellations such as *pirta(r)niq* ("back of the knee") or *arsaqurnaq* ("*triceps brachii* muscle").[3] Besides anatomy, properly speaking, the chapter will also discuss words that express various bodily aspects of human nature, as well as terms dealing with physical sensations and health.

Body Parts

To start with, the human body comprises six basic elements common to *timi* and to its attachments: *sauniit* ("bones, skeleton"), *qisik* ("skin"), *uvinik* ("skin-covered flesh"), *auk* ("blood"), *taqait* ("veins and arteries"), *nukiit* ("nerves, muscles").

The word *sauniit* (singular *sauniq*) denotes all the bones of the body— several of which have their own specific names (e.g., *qimirluk*, "bad ridge" [i.e., backbone, spine; also called *qujaq*];[4] *tulimaaq*, "small rib" [i.e., human or smaller animal's rib])—including the skull (*niaquviniq*, "former head"). *Sauniq* refers to animal bones too, including fish bones, and also to the shell of eggs (but apparently, not that of shellfish). The stone or pip of a fruit is called *saunaaq* ("small *sauniq*"). Bones are filled with *patiq* ("marrow"). A tentative underlying signification of the word *sauniq* might be "the fact of [-*niq*] being buried [*sau*-]," a possible allusion to the invisibility of bones lying under flesh and skin. *Qisik* denotes the uppermost layer of human (and seal) skin. It is covered with *mirquit* (singular *mirquq*), "human and animal hair." *Uvinik* designates human flesh together with its skin. Open flesh is *niqi* ("meat").

Blood is called *auk*. It runs through the *taqait* (singular *taqaq*), veins and arteries. In all Inuit dialects (but not in the Yupik languages), the noun *auk* is connected to the verbal bases *auk*-, "to melt, to thaw" (cf. *auttuq*, "it melts") and *au*-, "to rot" (cf. *aujuq*, "it rots").[5] Tellingly, the verb *auttuq* also means "he/she bleeds from the nose," and its derivative *aunaartuq* (with affix -*naar*-, "to make one be like that," according to Schneider 1979, 278) signifies "he/she makes him-/herself bleed" (i.e., "he/she bleeds profusely [as from a wound]"). When ice or snow thaws, it is as if *nuna* ("the land") were bleeding. And conversely, blood is equated with flowing water produced by thawing.

The latter metaphor makes sense with reference to the shamanic language. According to Rasmussen (quoted in Dorais 2010, 168), in the central Canadian Arctic, the shamans' word for "child" was *quatsiaq* ("who is frozen hard"). The development of the young may well have been considered as a symbolic process of progressive thawing, whereby blood ran more and more freely in the children's veins, up to the time when, at puberty, girls started to bleed (*aunaartuq*, "she has her periods"). This might bring us back to *nuna*, a female domain according to Inuit symbolism (Saladin d'Anglure 1986, 39) that bleeds like a menstruating woman when ice and snow start to thaw.

As a final reference to blood, and on a much lighter side, chocolate is called *aukuluk* ("nice little blood") in northeastern Nunavik and *aunnguaq* ("imitation of blood") in the western part of that region.

A last word denoting an anatomical component shared by *timi* and its attachments is *nukiit* ("nerves, sinews, muscles"; singular *nuki*). Since nerves and muscles generate motion and bodily activity, *nuki* also translates as "strength"—physical and, metonymically, moral. A very strong person is said to be *nukilialuk*, "one who has much *nuki*."

In addition to these general terms, the vocabulary of body parts can be subdivided into four sections. Two of these relate to *timi*, properly speaking, and two more to its attachments.

Qatigaak or Kiati (Upper Trunk)

The word *qatigaak* ("upper trunk [especially the thorax]") is in the dual number (singular *qatigaq*) because Inuit speakers have an anatomical concept of the upper section of the trunk (from the neck to the waist) with its two breasts, lungs, and sets of ribs. *Qatigaak* might relate to the affix *-qati* ("companion at doing something") and mean "two that do something together," the twinned parts of the trunk acting as functional pairs. But this is just a guess. Fortescue et al. (2010, 316) rather suggest a possible link with PE *qatǝ* ("deep or loud voice"). Another word for the upper trunk is *kiati* (etymologically, "area lying just outside something else"). It is quasi-homophonous with *kiasik* ("shoulder blade"; etymologically, "almost situated just outside"). This reference to externality might perhaps mean that when viewed by others, a person's upper trunk constitutes the outer surface of a container holding several important inner elements, one of which, *kiasik*, is "almost outside," since its shape shows under the skin. Another, simpler explanation for *kiati* could be that because of its often-protruding bust and abdomen, the upper section of the body is visually prominent in comparison with the pelvis and limbs area.

The trunk extends into the neck (*qungasiq* or *qungisiq*), which connects it with *niaquq*, the head (see below). The front of the neck is the throat, *iggiaq*, whose PE etymology is "the place where one swallows" or "the action of swallowing" (Fortescue et al. 2010, 134).[6] Among other components, *iggiaq* includes the larynx (*nijjaavik*, "where continuous sounds are produced," and *turqujaaq*, "that is associated with choking on food repeatedly") and in its lower section, the trachea or windpipe (*tursuk*).[7] The latter term has generated a number of metaphorical derivatives, including the following:

tursuuk	entrance tunnel of a snow house, porch of a modern house ("double windpipe" [in the dual number because igloo tunnels were made of two adjoining sections])
tursuaq	tube ("small windpipe")
tursutaq	stovepipe, chimney ("added windpipe")
tursurartuq	he/she addresses someone by a kinship term ("calls someone out [using his/her windpipe] repeatedly")
tursurauti	kinship term, nickname ("a means for addressing someone")

The most prominent external parts of the upper trunk are these:

savvik/sagvik	chest (possibly related to *saa*, "front part," and to *sakiat*, "rib cage," although this is unproved)
amaamak	woman's or man's breast (dual *amaamaak*; cf. *amaama*, "breastmilk" in baby talk [see Chapter 3]); from PE *ama(C)-*, "to suckle" (cf. *amaamattuq*, "a baby suckles")
iviangiq	woman's breast (dual *iviangiik*; probably related to the verbal base *iva-*, "to incubate;" in western Nunavik, a woman's breast is called *ivaniq*, "the fact of incubating")[8]
tunu	back (cf. *tunuani*, "in his/her back," i.e., "behind him/her"; cf. also *tunusuk*, "lesser *tunu*," i.e., "nape of the neck")
naaq	belly, abdomen (cf. *naaraji*, "a big-bellied individual")
qalasiq	navel; related to *qala(aq)* ("bubbles in boiling water, swirl made by an animal plunging into water"); metaphorically, the navel might be a hollow swirl (Therrien 1987, 41)
tui	shoulder (dual *tuik*)

The internal organs (*irraviit*, "viscera") include the following:

puvak	lung (dual *puvaak*); related to the verbal base *puvi-* ("to swell, be inflated")
uummati	heart ("what gives life"; cf. *uumajuq*, "one that is alive," i.e., "an animal" [see Chapter 2])
kanivauti	diaphragm (possible guess: "a means for being usually ahead"); cf. *kani(r)-* ("be ahead") + *-va(k)-* ("usually") + *-uti* ("means for"); maybe an allusion to the diaphragm's uppermost position over the viscera [?]
aqiaruq	stomach ("associated with the lower belly [*aqiaq*]"); it might be thought that *aqiaq* is related to the verbal base *aqit-* ("to be soft"), but their PE etymons are different: *aq(ə)yar* ("lower belly") vs. *aqit-* ("be soft") (Fortescue et al. 2010, 43–44)
inaluat	intestines (singular *inaluaq*); cf. *inaluujaq* ("that looks like intestines," i.e., "spaghetti" [northeastern Nunavik] or "coiled bannock bread" [western Nunavik])
tartuq	kidney (dual *tartuuk*); possibly related to *taaq-* ("to be dark") because of its dark colour and the fact it was considered one of the seats of *tarniq*, the shadow soul (Bordin 2003, 285)
tinguk	liver

With its protruding bust and belly, and because it hosts life-regulating organs (heart, lungs, stomach), *qatigaak* or *kiati* ("upper trunk") is, indeed, the most prominent part of *timi* ("body"), together with its upper attachment, *niaquq* ("head"). However, below *qatigaak*, *timi* includes another section, *kuutsinaaq* ("pelvis and hips"). The junction of both parts of the trunk, called *qitiq* ("the middle [i.e., the waist]"), marks the anatomical centre of the body.

Kuutsinaaq (Pelvis and Hips)

The word *kuutsinaaq* (*kuuttinaaq* in some Nunavut dialects) might be glossed as "that can be made to be [*-naaq*] iliac bones [*kuutsiik*]." It denotes the bony belt located in the lower part of the trunk, that is, the pelvis (Bordin 2003, 193). From the outside of the body, this is the area of the hips (cf. *makitiq* [hip], "that gets up repeatedly").

The lower rear part of the pelvis includes the buttocks, which have two appellations (usually heard in the dual number):

up-/ukpatiik	buttocks and upper part of thighs (singular *uppat/ukpat*); possibly related to *uku-*, "to bend forward" (Fortescue et al. 2010, 397), it might mean "that are used for bending (*uku-*) repeatedly (*-pa[k]-*)";[9] the word can apply to humans but it usually designates the hindquarters of animals
nuluuk	fleshy part of the buttocks (singular *nuluq*)

Itiq ("anus") exits between the buttocks. This word, whose PE form is *ətə-*, could be related to *ətə-* ("to be deep"; Inuktitut *iti-*) (Fortescue et al. 2010, 129). It is homophonous with the PE verbal base *ətər-*, but the latter's meaning, "to wake up," does not have anything to do with the anus. According to Bordin (2003, 276), the word *itiq* is probably linked to *itirtuq* ("he/she enters, comes in") because the anus was formerly considered as an entrance of the soul into the body (see the story of Savviuqtalik in the preceding chapter). Bordin's suggestion might stand true for speakers of Nunavik Inuktitut and a few other dialects (e.g., Aivilik and Labrador), but in most forms of the Inuit language, the verbal base for "entering" is *isir-* rather than *itir-*. On a lighter note, what we call "heart" in a deck of cards is dubbed *itiq* in northeastern Nunavik. In Quaqtaq, an urban legend tells how many years ago, a pious *Qallunaaq* teacher had brought with him a large white flag with a red heart in the middle, symbolizing Christ's love for humanity. When he invited people to pray in front of the opened flag, everybody wondered why they should worship an anus.

The PE root for the sexual organs is the same for both genders: *ucug* (Fortescue et al. 2010, 391). Modern Inuktitut, however, distinguishes between male and female organs: the penis is called *usuk* and the vagina or vulva, *utsuk* (or *uttu[u]k*). What does this slight phonemic difference underlie? Bordin (2003, 210) quotes the Danish linguist Louis Hammerich, according to whom it would express a dual or binary relationship: container (*utsuk*) versus contents (*usuk*). In my opinion, Hammerich is right when mentioning duality, but I do not agree with his interpretation of a container. The word *utsuk* might rather be an old dual form of *usuk*, now lexicalized. In the morphologically conservative Alaskan and western Canadian Inuit dialects, the dual number can indeed be marked by doubling the initial consonant of the last syllable of the word (Dorais 2010, 64), as in *iqaluk* ("one fish")/ *iqalluk* ("two fish") or *tasiq* ("one lake")/*tatsik* [or *tatchik*] ("two lakes"). *Utsuk* could thus mean "double organ." In the Yupik languages, the term designating the female sexual organ is actually in the dual. According to Spalding (1998, 193), in North Baffin Inuktitut, where the consonant grouping *ts* has become *tt*, the cognate of *utsuk* is *uttuuk*, with both an archaic (*tt* derived from *ts*) and a modern (*-uk*) dual marker. In Kalaallisut (West Greenlandic), the female sexual organ is called *utsuut* with a plural marker (*-ut*) because in that dialect, the dual number is not in use anymore.

But why would the female organ be "double?" In their definition of the word *uttuuk* (North Baffin dialect), Ootoova et al. (2000, 142) provide a very concise explanation: "*Uttuuk* [dual]: *Arnaup angmaningit*"—"Vagina: A woman's apertures." While the male *usuk* lets both urine and sperm come out through the same orifice, the female *utsuk* has two separate openings (Bordin 2003, plate VIIC): the urinary meatus (*nakasuup sullua*, "bladder's tube") and the vagina (*ammaniq/angmaniq*, "aperture"). Hence the dual nature of *utsuk*. This duality is rendered more intricate by the fact that the *ammaniq* shelters an organ seen as male-like in some parts of Nunavik: *usuapik* ("small penis"), the clitoris. It can thus be conjectured that the dual nature of *utsuk* also stems from the fact it consists of both an opening (*ammaniq*) and an internal "small penis," or "one looking like a penis" (*usuužaq*) in northern Alaska (Bordin 2003, 177, 179). Elsewhere, though, the clitoris is known as *utsuup nuvua* ("tip of the *utsuk*") or *uviuq* ("that swells or tilts for long [?]").

Testicles are called *ijjuuk/igjuuk*. This word in the dual number might be etymologically related to PE *igður-* ("to coagulate, get stiff"). In Nunavik, the ovary is sometimes called *ijjuujaq* ("that looks like a testicle") because both organs are perceived as sharing the same reproductive function, according to Therrien (1987, 97). In the northeastern part of that region, dried beans are known as *ijjuujait* ("that look like testicles"), and sausages (or carrots) as *usuujait* ("that look like a penis"; singular *usuujaq*). It has already been mentioned (Chapter 2) that the pointed prow of a kayak is an *usuujaq*, too.

We also saw that the uterus is called *illiaq/igliaq* ("little sleeping platform [in an igloo]"). Other internal items related to the pelvic area include the following:

irsuq/ir&uq	large intestine, colon ("thing for shrinking or contracting"; probably an allusion to the contractions that accompany the act of defecating)
anaq	excrement (related to *ani-*, "to come out"); cf. *anartuq*, "he/she defecates"
nakasuk	bladder (possible guess: "lesser [-*suk*] stalk or stem [*naka(q)-*]"; the allusion is unclear); cf. *nakasunnaq* ("that resembles a bladder," i.e., "calf of leg") and *nakasuujaq* ("that looks like a bladder," i.e., "light bulb" in North Baffin)
itiruq	urine ("something associated with the anus")

Niaquq (Head)

The head, *niaquq*, is an attachment of *timi*, the uppermost one, as hinted by an already mentioned possible etymology: "an attached part that is bending." According to Taamusi Qumaq (1991, 352), *niaquq* is the seat of *isuma* ("thought, reason"):

Niaqura—Uvanga niaqura nangminira isumaqautiga, niaquqanngikuma isumaqarajanngitunga.

My head—My head, of myself, my own possession, my container of thoughts. If I had no head, I would not have thoughts.

Niaquq hosts one prominent internal organ, *qaritaq/qarisaq/qarasaq* ("brain"). The PE form of the word is *qaqətar* or *qaqitar* (Fortescue et al. 2010, 312). At first glance, *qaritaq* thus appears related to modern Inuktitut terms such as *qaqilirtuq* ("tries to get an object or animal out from under something"), *qaqiartuq* ("he/she feels humble, meek"), or *qaqivittuq* ("it gets up a little, rises itself a bit"), where the verbal base *qaqi(t)-* seems to mean "to be in a hidden position." This could allude to the fact that the brain is hidden inside *niaquq*. However, this is just a guess, since the PE etymon of modern *qaqi-* is *qaqu(r)-* (Fortescue et al. 2010, 313). According to Bordin (2003, 296), *qaritaq* derives from the stem *qari-* ("cavity"), although he does not elaborate on this assumption. The idea of "cavity" could possibly be based on a semantic link between *qaritaq* and *qariaq* ("secondary snow house opening on a main one"; see Chapter 6) postulated by Bordin.

No definition of *qaritaq* is found in Qumaq's dictionary, but in Ootoova et al.'s *Uqausiit tukingit* (2000, 628), the cognate North Baffin term *qarasaq* is defined as follows: "It is inside the head of all living beings [*uumajuit*], its [the head's] container of thoughts, it is soft when cut into pieces, this is the brain." Such a definition seems to apply primarily to the brains of game animals ("it is soft when cut into pieces"), but it includes the idea of a "container of thoughts" (*isumaqauti*, the very same word used by Qumaq when he defines *niaquq*) that mostly concerns humans—although Ootoova et al. may attribute some sort of thinking to animals. This idea that the brain is a "container of thoughts" may explain why the Inuktitut word for "computer" is *qaritau-jaq/qarasaujaq* ("that looks like a brain").[10]

Unlike *timi*, *niaquq* harbours on a small surface a relatively large number of external parts, several of which are apertures. Most of these parts are on the face, called *kiinaq*. This word also means "edge of a knife." Etymologically, it would be related to PE *kəgə-* (modern Inuktitut *kii-*), "to bite," and could be glossed as "that is able to bite" (Fortescue et al. 2010, 180). It is quite possible that the cutting edge of a knife and a face hosting a toothed mouth were both considered as biting instruments, but Inuit speakers may have also perceived a semantic link between *kiinaq* and *kina?* ("who [is he/she]?"), a person's face being the best means to identify him or her visually. Because of the fact that in Canada, as in many countries, the face of the reigning sovereign appears on coins as well as on postage stamps, money is called *kiinaujaq* ("that looks like a face") in Inuktitut and, in Nunavik at least, a stamp is a *kiinannguaq* ("imitation of a face").

The upper section of the face, the forehead, is called *qauq*. One might guess this word relates to the stem *qa(a)-* ("top or surface of something"), but it is also quasi-homophonous with the stem *qau-* ("light" and its derivatives expressing the notion of "knowledge"). According to Fortescue et al. (2010,

302), however, the PE etymon of *qauq* is *qagur*, rather than *qaru-*, the etymon of *qau-*. It may be surmised, though, that for historical speakers of Inuktitut, since the forehead hosts *qaritaq*, it is perceived as the seat of thinking and knowledge and, for this reason, *qauq* might be considered a *bona fide* derivative of *qau-*, as assumed by Saladin d'Anglure (2018, 52).

Other prominent anatomical elements of the head include the following:

nujait	head hair (singular *nujaq*); a white hair is a *qiiq* (cf. *qiilik*, "who has [-*lik*] white hair"); a bald person is said to be *nujaittuq* ("who has no head hair") and one without any hair is a *mirqui(t)tuq* ("who is deprived of body hair")
iji	eye (dual *ijiik*); cf. *ijautiik* ("used for the eyes," i.e., "glasses"), *iggaak* ("that look like eyes," i.e., "snow goggles, sunglasses") and *ijiirtuq* ("suppresses someone's eyes [sight]," i.e., "he/she hides")
qallu/qablu	eyebrow ("position for being [PE -*lu(r)*] inside [PE *qav-*]" [i.e., below the supraorbital arch?]); cf. *qallunaaq*, "prominent eyebrow," i.e., "European person" (see Chapter 3)
qimiriaq	eyelash (etymologically, "place for examining something")
siut(i)	ear (dual *siutiik*)
qingaq	nose and (metaphorically) vent hole at the top of a snow house (dual *qingaak*, "the two nostrils"); cf. *surluuk* (singular *surluk*), the cavities of the nostrils (might be related to *sulluk*, "something for blowing," i.e., "tube, elongated hole" [Fortescue et al. 2010, 104]); cf. also *surlulirijuq* ("deals with nostrils," i.e., "rubs his/her nose")
umik	beard (plural *umiit*, "facial hair"); seemingly related to PE *uməg-* ("to cover something"); cf. *umilik* ("who has a beard," i.e., "bearded man") and *unngijartuq* (derived from *umiijartuq*, "he removes his facial hair," i.e., "shaves his face")

| *tallu/tablu* | chin |
| *alliruq* | lower jaw ("small lower object") |

The mouth is called *qanəq* in the Yupik languages and *qaniq* in all Inuit dialects. This word also functions as a verbal base (*qanər-/qanir-*) in a majority of language areas, with meanings reflecting the general idea of speaking: "to speak, to talk idly, to quarrel, to argue." According to Fortescue et al. (2010, 309), it might be related to PE *qalər-* ("to utter a characteristic cry [animal]") and *qatə* ("deep or loud voice"). This means that the mouth seems primarily perceived as an organ for uttering sounds.

Within the lips (*qaniusinaa*, "edge of the mouth")[11] stand the teeth (*kigutiit* [singular *kiguti*], "means for biting"; cf. *kigutinnguat*, "imitations of teeth," i.e., denture). The roof of the mouth is its *qilak*, the very same term that also designates the sky and the vault of the snow house. This homonymy illustrates an important tendency of Inuit symbolism: to play upon scale changes. At a micro level, the roof of the mouth is analogous to the vault of the igloo that is itself analogous, in a macro dimension, to the vault of the sky, all three entities sharing the same appellation, *qilak*. Another example of this process was mentioned in Chapter 2: in the shamanic language, the caribou were dubbed *nunaup kumangit* ("lice of the earth"). Far from being just a metaphor, this phrase expressed the idea that at a micro level, lice are equivalent to caribou (*kumaruat*, "giant lice"), the latter being edible walking animals that proliferate at the surface of *nuna* just as lice do on human hair and animal fur. To a shaman in celestial flight (*ilimmarturniq*, "learning continuously and repeatedly" [Fortescue et al. 2010, 115]),[12] caribou would appear as if they were as small as lice (Saladin d'Anglure 2018, 263–64).[13]

The most conspicuous internal organ of the mouth is the tongue. In all Inuit dialects, it is called *uqaq*, and as a verbal base *uqar-* means "to speak, to say." The tongue is thus defined as "the speaking one." This concurs with Qumaq's definition of *uqara* ("my tongue") in his *Inuit uqausillaringit* (1991, 102): "My own thing, my tongue, it is inside my mouth; it has no bone; my tongue [is] my means for being able to say [*uqar-*] something that makes sense." Interestingly enough, in the Yupik languages, the word for "tongue" is *ulu(q)*, while the verbal base for "saying something, speaking" is *apər-*, a cognate of Inuktitut *apiri-* ("to ask a question"). What is noteworthy here is that in the Inuit dialects, *ulu* refers to a woman's rounded half-moon knife. I became aware of this difference when I briefly visited the

Alaskan town of Nome in 1987. With my host Vera Metcalf, a distinguished Yupik intellectual and cultural activist, I was discussing some lexical differences between Inuktitut and her native Central Siberian Yupik language.[14] When I mentioned that in Inuktitut, a woman's knife was called *ulu*, she started laughing. "In Siberian Yupik, *ulu* means 'tongue,'" she said, adding that the name of the woman's knife was *ulaaq*, "lesser tongue," or conjecturally, "looking like a tongue," probably because of its shape, rounded like the tip of a tongue.

It may therefore be considered that the term *ulu* is a PE word that survived in the Inuit dialects with the restricted meaning of "rounded knife." A new word for "tongue," *uqaq*, was probably derived at some point from the Inuit verbal base *uqar-* ("to speak"). Fortescue et al. (2010, 400) suggest implicitly that *uqar-* and *ulu(q)* might share the same root *u-*, followed in the latter word by the PE affix *–lu(r)* ("place or thing for performing an action"). But it does not elaborate on the potential meaning of *u-*, nor on that of *-qar*. Interestingly, the current Inuit word for "cheek" is *uluaq*. It is homophonous with some dialectal forms of the Yupik term for "woman's knife," but etymologically, it stems from a PE root, *u&ugag*, that has nothing to do with *ulu(q)*, whether it be a tongue or a knife.

Avatit (Limbs)

The body parts attached to the upper trunk (arms) and to the pelvis (legs) are called *avatit* ("which surround something"). Etymologically, this term derives from the word-base *av(a)-* ("around") + *-tə* ("area in such a direction") and can be glossed as "area around" (cf. *avativut*, "the area around us," i.e., "our environment"). It is related to *avaluq* ("thing for surrounding," i.e., "fence") and *avataq* ("a surrounding one," i.e., "inflated sealskin used as a buoy in sea mammal hunting"). As shall be seen in the next chapter, Inuit numerals are largely patterned on the human body, and the word *avatit* also denotes number twenty.

The appellation for the upper limbs, *taliik* (singular *taliq*), "two arms," is related etymologically to *tatə-* ("to shove in [hands]") and *tatyur-* ("to lead by the hand") (Fortescue et al. 2010, 357). The right side of someone or something is *talirpik* ("the very best arm"), and the left side *saumik* (possibly, "that makes something veer to the side"). A left-handed person is also called *saumik*. The elbow is *ikusik*, related to the PE verbal base *ikug-*, "to hack at" (an allusion to nudging?).

The word for "hand" is *aggak*. In Nunavik, though, it is always used in the plural (*aggait*). As was the case with the term *qatigaak* ("upper trunk")— usually in the dual number because the trunk hosts two sets of ribs—*aggait* reflects an anatomical concept of the body: the hand is perceived as five separate sets of finger bones rather than as a single unit. On the outside, however, these skin-covered bones form one palm, *itimak*, a word related to the verbal base *iti-* ("to be deep").

Fingers (*aggait*) have nails, *kukiit* (singular *kukik*; this word also means "claw, hoof"). Each finger has its own appellation:

kullu/kublu	thumb
tikiq	forefinger, index ("that points at something"); the word also denotes a thimble
qitirsiq/qitir&iq	middle finger ("the middlemost one")
mikiliraq	ring finger ("that becomes smaller [than *qitirsiq*]")
iqirquq	little finger; according to Fortescue et al. (2010, 156), the PE etymon of this word, *iqəlqur*, could be glossed as "something associated with width"; such a meaning is obscure and it seems plausible, albeit unproved, that historical speakers glossed *iqirquq* as "that reaches the corner of the mouth" (cf. *iqi[q]-* ["corner of the mouth"] + *-rquq* ["to reach a body part"]), in a probable allusion to the Inuit game where two opponents pull at each other's *iqiq* with their little finger until one of them gives up

As with *aggait* and for the same reason, the term for "foot," *itigak/isigak*, is only heard in the plural (*itigait*) in Nunavik. Etymologically, it could mean "that resembles a toe-cap" (Fortescue et al. 2010, 160), a gloss that seems strange (why would a body part be named according to the garment that covers it?). The foot has a sole (*aluq*, "that is in a low position"; the word also applies to the sole of a shoe), a heel (*kimmik*) and toes (*itigait/isigait*), of which only the big toe has a name, *putuguq*, that can be conjecturally glossed as "that becomes [-*guq*] a hole [*putu*-]," although this does not seem to make much sense. Feet belong to the lower attachment of the body, the two legs (dual *niuk*, singular *niu*). The upper section of a leg is its *qurturaq* ("thigh"), its middle joint the *siirquq* ("knee"), and its lower part the *qanaaq* ("shin").

Bodily Actions and Physical Characteristics

Human bodies are constantly involved in various activities, and they possess physical characteristics that differentiate them from one another.

Bodily Actions

The basic, all-encompassing word denoting human activity is *pijuq* ("he/she does something"). The stem *pi-* is semantically "empty." As a verbal base ("to do") it can express any kind of action (e.g., *nakit* pi*vit?* "wherefrom are you doing [i.e., coming]?"), and as a noun base ("thing"), any type of entity (e.g., pi*kka*, "my things"). It allows some affixes, which must otherwise attach to specific bases, to form generic verbs or, more rarely, nouns:

pijumajunga	I want to (-*juma*-) do (i.e., "I want")
pirqajartugut	we are able to (-*rqajar*-) do (i.e., "we can")
pigiaqartut	they have to (-*giaqar*-) do[15] (i.e., "they must")
piirpaa	he/she suppresses (-*ir*-) something (i.e., "he/she takes it away")
pigijara	I have it as (-*gi*-) something (i.e., "I own it")
piquti	possessed (-*quti*) thing (i.e., "someone's possession")

In Nunavik, older Inuit often used verbal *pi-* in a very elegant way, now seemingly forgotten. Instead of describing their (or someone else's) deeds as an enumeration of successive actions ("I did this, and that, and that . . ."), they rather reported them as a coordinated series of activities contributing to one all-encompassing operation, mentioned in conclusion by way of *pi-*:

Tupatsungalu, annuraarsungalu, niritsungalu, aullasungalu, pijunga.

Waking up, putting my clothes on, eating, and leaving, [this is what] I *did*.

Nominal and verbal *pi-* have contributed to the formation of a number of lexicalized words. Here are a few examples (some of them previously mentioned):

piujuq	that which is good ("that or who is something")
piaraq	young animal [child in northeastern Nunavik] ("young thing")
pirurtuq	he/she/it grows ("he/she/it becomes something")
pivalliajuq	it develops ("it does something more and more")
pisuttuq	he/she/it walks ("he/she/it needs to do something")
pinasuttuq	he/she works [Nunavik] ("he/she strives to do something")

To do or to be something is a serious matter. The base *pi-* implies that what is done is useful, and what is defined as a "thing" is for real. Otherwise, *pi-* must be affixed with the morpheme *-nnguaq-* ("pretending, imitating"), as in *pinngua(r)tuq*, "he/she pretends to do something" ("he/she plays or fakes") and *pinnguaq*, "something imitated" ("toy, copy, or imitation of an object").

Inuktitut words expressing what human bodies tend to do are too numerous to be listed exhaustively. As was the case with body parts, only a few prominent bodily activities will be discussed here. Some of them have already been mentioned, such as *nirijuq* ("he/she eats"), related to *niqi* ("meat"), the prototypical Inuit item of food, and *imirtuq* ("he/she drinks"), derived from *imiq* ("water"). We also saw that the term expressing the action of defecating, *anartuq* ("he/she defecates"), is based on *anaq* ("excrement"), itself related to *ani-* ("to come out"). Urine is called *itiruq* ("associated with the anus"), and "he/she urinates" translates as *quijuq*, a word that might be metonymically (if not etymologically) linked to *quik* ("thighbone, femur"), probably because urine is liable to flow down the thigh (cf. *quingilitaq*, "protection for the thighbone," the name given to diapers in northeastern Nunavik). "He/she farts" is *nilirtuq* (guessed to be related to *nilli(r)tuq*, "emits a sound"; cf.

niliq, "a fart"), and in at least one Nunavik village, beans are called *nilarnait* ("those that produce farts").

The verbal base *sinik-* renders the notion of sleeping (*sinittuq/sinik-tuq*, "he/she sleeps"). One who feels sleepy is said to be *uirnga(r)tuq* ("who opens his/her eyes [*uit-*] for the first time [as if he/she had just woken up]"). Sleepiness can result from tiredness (*taqajuq*, "he/she is tired"; from PE *taqa-*, "to stop or give up"). Something or someone tiring is *taqanartuq* ("that makes one feel tired"). *Tupattuq/tupaktuq* means "he/she wakes up." It derivates from the PE base *tupag-* ("to be startled"). Once awakened, one may want to wash. In Nunavik, a semantic distinction exists between "he/she washes his/her face" (*irmituq*; etymologically, "makes it [filth] fade from a part of his/her body" [Fortescue et al. 2010, 126]) and "he/she washes his/her whole body or something else [clothes, dishes, etc.]" (*uvvatuq*; cf. *uvvauti*, "that is used for washing," i.e., "soap, detergent"). Outside Nunavik (and Labrador), the verbal bases *irmik-* and/or *uasar-* (borrowed from the English "[to] wash") are used for speaking about washing in general. Someone or something *saluma-juq* (etymologically, "swept or cleaned away") is clean, while a *salumaittuq* ("that is not *saluma-*") person or object is dirty or filthy.

Several words denote the physical manifestations of emotions. According to Taamusi Qumaq (1991, 569), smiling (*qungattuq*, "he/she smiles") allows people to express their inner feelings for themselves, unless asked by others to share the reason of their smile and thus add a social dimension to their emotion:

A person remembers something that makes him/her smile without uttering a sound, although when asked: "What are you doing?" he/she will tell [why he/she smiles]. Surprisingly, such an individual can behave in a way that generates a lot of smiles, and this without being seen, even by one person.

Here are a few other terms for physical manifestations of feelings:

ijurtuq   he/she laughs (cf. *ijurna[r]tuq*, "that is laughable or funny [makes one laugh]")

qiajuq	he/she cries (cf. *quvvik*, "tear," perhaps related to Proto-Yupik *qunik*, "matter in eye" [Fortescue et al. 2010, 344])
paajuq	he/she fights, struggles (may be related to *patittuq/ patiktuq*, "slaps someone or something"); cf. *saala* ("a loser") and *saalaqartuq* ("has a loser," i.e., "he/ she wins")
kunik-/kunittuq	he/she kisses someone (with the nose or mouth)
kujak-/kujattuq	he/she has sexual intercourse ("uses his/her lumbar vertebrae")

It is worth mentioning that the word *saalaqartuq* (under *paajuq*, above) betrays a preference of Inuktitut for using indirect language when direct speech would sound too aggressive, bragging, or intrusive. Instead of saying "he/she wins," one must speak in a more subdued tone: "he/she has a loser." In Chapter 3, we already witnessed two instances of this process, with *ajunngi(t)tuq*, "he/she is not without power [i.e., is competent, efficient]," and *quviasugunnaiqit?* "are you not happy anymore?" (instead of "are you sad?"). In a similar way, a deceased person is often said to be *inuugunnaituq* ("not living anymore") rather than *tuqungajuq* ("in the situation of having died [i.e., being dead]").

Another series of words denotes various movements of the body. We have already mentioned one such term, *pisuttuq/pisuktuq* ("he/she walks"). Here are further examples:

ingittuq	he/she sits (related to *illiq/igliq*, "sitting and sleeping platform in an igloo"); cf. *itsivajuq/iksivajuq* ("is seated") and *itsivautaq* ("means for being seated," i.e., "seat, chair")[16]
nalajuq	he/she is lying down
makittuq	he/she rises up (cf. *Makivvia*, "his [Jesus's] time for rising up [resurrecting]," i.e., "Easter")
aijuq	he/she goes somewhere (cf. *aivaa*, "fetches it")

qaijuq	he/she comes (related to PE *qaru*, "dawn" [cf. modern *qauq*, "daylight"] because dawn "comes" when night ends? [Fortescue et al. 2010, 314]); cf. *qaippaa* ("brings it")
aulajuq	he/she/it moves (cf. *aulla[r]tuq*, "starts to move," i.e., "departs, goes away").
anijuq	he/she exits, goes, or comes out (cf. *anna[k]tuq*, "it starts to go out," i.e., "it [game] escapes")
itirtuq/isirtuq	he/she enters (cf. *itaartuq*, "enters repeatedly, forcibly," i.e., "breaks into a house or tent")
tikittuq	he/she arrives (cf. *tikippaa*, "comes to it, reaches it")

Physical Characteristics

Human bodies possess various characteristics as to their size, physical capabilities, appearance, and so on. In Inuktitut, such characteristics—whether belonging to humans, animals, or inanimate objects—are usually expressed by words with a verbal-nominal ending (see Appendix) and can be listed in opposite pairs, as in the following examples:

angijuq	is big (related to *anga-*, as in *angajuk*, "elder sibling")
mikijuq	is small
takijuq	is tall, long
naittuq	is short
quinijuq	is fat (perhaps related to *quinattuq*, "is ticklish [trembles?]")[17]
sallu	a thin one (related to *saattuq*, "it is thin, flat")
sungujuq	is strong (Nunavik)
sanngijuq	is strong (Nunavut, Labrador)
sanngii(t)tuq	is weak ("is not strong"; Nunavik, Nunavut, Labrador)
sukattuq	is fast (*sukkajuq* in North Baffin)
sukkai(t)tuq	is slow ("is not fast")

iniqunartuq   is pretty ("provokes cooing [as to a baby]")

iniqunaittuq   is ugly ("is not pretty")

All the above terms can be made into comparatives and superlatives. In order to understand how these are derived, it should be noted that qualifying bases with a verbal-nominal ending (*-juq/-tuq*) are actually verbal (e.g., *taki-*, "to be tall, long").[18] By way of example, in order to derive a comparative or superlative out of *takijuq* ("he/she/it is tall" or "one who/that is tall"), its base must first be nominalized:

taki- + *-niq* (nominalizer) = *takiniq* ("the fact of being tall," i.e., "tall stature")

From here, we have two choices. For deriving a comparative, the nominal affix *-(t)saq* ("likely to be") is added to *takiniq*, and for a superlative, *-paaq* ("utmost") is affixed:

takiniq + *-(t)saq* = *takinirsaq* (likely to be a stature that is tall, i.e., taller)

takiniq + *-paaq* = *takinirpaaq* (utmost in tall stature, i.e., the tallest)

This may sound confusing at first, but the semantic logic of this process becomes apparent when *takinirsaq* and *takinirpaaq* function within actual sentences:

*Ilin*nit *takinirsa*u*junga*

Starting from (*-nit*) you, I am (*-u-*) likely to be of a tall stature

I am taller than you

*Uvatti*nit *takinirpaa*ngu*junga*

Starting from (*-nit*) us, I am (*-ngu-*) the utmost in tall stature

I am the tallest among us

The underlying meaning of these sentences is that starting from you or us as a point of comparison, (1) my stature is tall compared to your stature and

I am thus taller than you are (otherwise, my stature would not need be mentioned), or (2) I am the utmost (highest) in tall stature and thus the tallest by comparison with us all. If the comparison is to be reversed, the negative *-nngi(t)-* is inserted in proper position: *takinnginirsaujunga* ("I am likely to be of a non-tall stature," i.e., "I am shorter") and *takinnginirpaanguvunga* ("I am the utmost in non-tall stature," i.e., "I am the shortest").

Physical Sensations and Health

One major characteristic of human and animal bodies is their ability to experience various types of sensations, some of which are symptomatic of ill health, that is, physiological dysfunction. We saw in Chapter 3 that in Inuktitut, the verbal base *ippi-* or *ikpi-* expresses the notion of "feeling," whether it be emotions or bodily sensations (cf. *ippigusuttuq*, "feels something"; and *ippigivaa*, "feels it"). *Ippi-/ikpi-* can also mean "to take notice or be aware of something," as in "*Ippiginnginakku atsunainngitunga*" — "Because I didn't notice him/her, I did not say goodbye." For Inuit, then, physical and emotional feelings as well as mental perceptions belong to a single conceptual category, that of total awareness (physiological, intellectual, and emotive) of one's surroundings.

Physical Sensations

Basically, the physical sensations are those that are *ippigijait* ("felt") through the four senses of the body: sight (*takuniq*, "the fact of seeing"), hearing (*tusarniq*, "the fact of hearing"), smell-taste (*naimaniq*, "the fact of smelling-tasting"), and touch (*attuiniq*, "the fact of touching something").

The general notion of seeing is expressed by the verbal base *taku-* (cf. *takujuq*, "he/she sees"; *takuvaa*, "sees him/her/it"), which has generated a number of derivatives:

tap-/takpi(k)tuq	he/she sees very well (contraction of *takuviktuq*, "sees a lot"); cf. *tappii(t)tuq* ("does not [-it-] see well, is short-sighted")
takunna(r)tuq	he/she looks at something ("makes oneself seeing")

takunnati	pupil of the eye ("a means for making oneself seeing")
takurngatuq	he/she is scared by someone ("sees for the first time")

In Alaskan Inupiaq, the word-base for "seeing" is *tautuk-*, and *taku-* has a restricted meaning of "to go and see how she/he is faring . . . to check on it" (MacLean 2014, 332). In all non-Alaskan Inuit dialects, though, it is *tautuk-* that has a limited signification: "to look at something with some attention." A blind person is said to be *tautunngi(t)tuq* ("one who does not look"). Examining something (e.g., pictures in a photo album) very attentively is *qimirruar-* ("having a propensity to look at things").

A nominal derivative of *tautuk-*, *tauttu* denotes someone's or something's look or appearance. It is generally followed by a possessive affix, as in *tauttu*a ("his/her/its look"). Like *tautuk-*, *taku-* can be converted into a noun by doubling its middle consonant and affixing a possessive. *Takku*a ("his/her/its *takku-*"), for instance, means "the gaze of," as in "*Guutiup takkuani*"— "Of God, in His gaze (i.e., under the gaze of God)."

Nowadays, *tauttu* is often used for rendering the word "colour."[19] In Nunavik Inuktitut—some terms may slightly vary in other dialects—the colour spectrum (including black and white) is divided into six principal categories, plus a seventh one that only applies to animal fur or hide. Each category has a specific name (two for the seventh one) that most often ends with *-taq* ("that belongs, is added to," or "that has been made so"). Morphologically, colour terms are nouns (e.g., *qirnitaq*, "something black"). Here are these words, translated by English adjectives for practical purposes:

qirnitaq	black, of a dark colour ("added dark surface [*qirniq*]")
qakurtaq	white, of a pale colour ("that has been bleached [*qakirtuq*]")[20]
aupartuq	red, pink,[21] orange (related to *auk*, "blood"); cf. *aupaluktuq* ("that makes blood visible"), another word for "red" (e.g., in the western Hudson Bay dialects)

tungujurtaq	blue, green, purple (etymologically, "added element that looks like the dark sky or a ripe berry [*tungu-*]"; [Fortescue et al. 2010, 384])
qursutaq	yellow (etymologically, "added element that looks like urine [PE *qurə-*]")
kajuq	brown, reddish fur (cf. *tiriganniaq kajuq*, "red fox"), blond hair
sinarnaq	grey fur
isurtaq	grey whale hide ("added murky element")

Note that Inuit colour terms do not correspond exactly to their English equivalents. In Nunavik Inuktitut, for instance, "red," "pink," and "orange" are subsumed under the same word, *aupartuq*, while "blue," "green," and "purple" are called *tungujurtaq*. Does this mean that Inuit are colour-blind? No, of course not. The colour spectrum forms a seamless continuum that any language must subdivide more or less arbitrarily into separate categories, to which names are given. These semantic divisions are not exactly the same in each language. In Inuktitut, for example, as in Vietnamese and many other tongues, the section of the spectrum that English speakers consider as comprising two separate colours called "blue" and "green" is viewed as an undivided category, named *tungujurtaq* in Inuktitut and *xanh* in Vietnamese. In the former language, intermediary shades are denoted thanks to affixes, as in *tungujuangajuq* ("partly *tungujurtaq*," i.e., "bluish, greenish").

Other words having to do with sight include the following:

nasittuq	he/she looks all around, surveys his/her surroundings from a height
nuijuq	he/she/it appears, becomes visible (possibly related to the verbal base *nuut-/nuuk-*, "to move, to change place [thus being seen]")

ajji	image, similitude (*ajjigiik*, "pair of images," i.e., "two that are similar"); cf. *ajji(n)nguaq* ("imitation of an image," i.e., "photo, picture"), *ajjiliurtuq* ("makes an image," i.e., "takes a photo"), and *ajjiliuruti* ("means for making an image," i.e., "camera")
minguartuq	he/she paints a surface ("smears frequently")

Hearing is expressed by the verbal base *tusar-*, as in *tusartuq* ("he/she/it hears") and *tusarpaa* ("he/she/it hears it"). Adding the affix *-a-* gives *tusaajuq* ("hears continually"), which also means "he/she understands what is said."[22] An interpreter or translator is a *tusaaji*, "one who understands what is said [in another language]." Metonymically, *tusar-* can also mean "to have heard about something," as in "*Kanataup angajurqaanga qaujimanagu,* tusar*sima-vigijarali*"—"Without knowing [by experience] Canada's prime minister, I have heard about him, though."

Like *tusar-*, *naalak-* ("to listen to") has both an immediate and an extended meaning. *Naalattuq/naalaktuq* can be understood as "hears attentively," as well as "obeys what is asked of him/her." The derivative *naalauti* ("a means for listening," i.e., "radio set") stems from the first meaning, while the second sense shows up in the name *Naalagaq* ("who is listened to," i.e., "the Lord [and any master]"). The interjection *ata!* (*ala!* in Nunavik) means "Listen! Be quiet!"

The word *nipi* ("human voice, sound") might be related to Proto-Inuit *nəmaaq-*, "to cry out in pain" (Fortescue et al. 2010, 250). A voice recording machine is a *nipiliuruti* ("means for fabricating a voice"). "He/she/it emits a sound" is either *nilli(r)tuq* ("provides with sound," from *nipilirtuq*) or *nijja(r)-tuq* ("receives a sound," from *nipijja[r]tuq*). As we already saw, "to speak" is *uqar-* (cf. *uqausiq*, "used for speaking," i.e., "word"). The verbal phrase "he/she asks a question" can be rendered by *apirijuq* or, for a more substantial interrogation, *apirsu(k)tuq* (etymologically, "asks in a deliberate way"). In Nunavik, anthropologists are sometimes called *apirquit* ("those who ask many questions"). "He/she answers" is *kiujuq*.

In Inuktitut, words linked to the expression of smell and taste are often the same, these two senses being considered as one. *Naimavaa* means "he/she/it smells it."[23] In some dialects west of Hudson Bay, it is also understood as "tastes it" (Spalding 1998, 60), but in Nunavik and North Baffin, both

Qumaq and Ootoova et al. assert that *naima-* is experienced *qingarmigut*, "through one's own nose."

Naima- may be restricted to smell in Inuktitut, but in that group of dialects, there is no specific word for "tasting." "He/she tastes it" is rendered by *uuttu(r)paa* ("has a try at it, measures it"; literally, "tries it repeatedly"). The verbal base *uuttur-/uuktur-* refers to any form of testing or measuring, whether material goods (food, clothing, etc.) or abstract notions (e.g., a task to attempt) are concerned. In the present-day language, *uuttuuti* ("that is used for testing or measuring something") translates the word "example" (as well as any measuring tool), as *uuttuutigilugu*, "for example" (literally, "having it as a means for testing [i.e., as a measure for comparison]"). It may therefore be inferred that the notion of "tasting" is so weak semantically that no dedicated term is needed for expressing it.

The word *tipi* ("odour, flavour") applies to both smell and taste, as do the affixes *-arniq* and *-sunniq*, both of which mean "there is a smell or flavour of" (e.g., *uaniuja*arniq, "it smells or tastes onions"). Something *mamartuq* smells/ tastes good, but if it is *mamaittuq* ("not *mamartuq*"), its odour or flavour are bad. Both *mamar-* and PE *ama(C)-* ("to suckle"; cf. Inuktitut *amaama-*) might derive from the same proto-form (Fortescue et al. 2010, 205). The word *mamartuq* is often used for denoting any sweet flavour, while something sour is *siirna(r)tuq* (etymologically, "that provokes oozing out [like fermented meat]"). In western Nunavik, the term for "sugar" is *mamarsauti* ("means for making something taste or smell good"), but in the northeastern part of that region, the very same word means "perfume."

Interestingly enough, someone said to be *mamartuq*, whether male or female, is deemed to give sexual pleasure. Indeed, sexuality is often expressed via food metaphors. *Angutiturtuq* ("eats a man") means "she has sexual intercourse," while *arna(r)turtuq* ("eats a woman") conveys the opposite meaning. The first time I visited Kuujjuaq as a married man, Kuuttuq, a blind elder famous for his storytelling (cf. the myth of Kaujjaajuk, summarized in Chapter 4), traditional singing, and skill at teasing people (*mitanngua[r]- tuq*, "pretends to mock"; cf. *mitattuq/mitaktuq*, "mocks someone"), asked me: "*Kaappit?*"—"Are you hungry?" When I inquired why I should be hungry, he said: "*Qaninngitualummiimat arnait tutirqajanngitait*"—"Because your wife is in a place far away, you cannot sleep with her [*tutittuq/tutiktuq*, "sleeps with someone under the same blanket"]."

The fourth sense, touch, is usually expressed by the verbal base *attur-/ aktur-* (cf. *attu[r]paa*, "touches it," and *attuijuq*, "touches something"). Here are a few examples, chosen among the numerous words linked in one way or another to physical feelings experienced at the surface of the body (when touching or being touched) or within it:

maittuq	[skin] is sensitive, hurts when touched (possible underlying signification, "that is without skin" [Fortescue et al. 2010, 202])
kijja(k)tuq	that is rough to the touch
qairartuq	that is smooth ("is continually without anything on top of it")
manirartuq	that is smooth-surfaced ("that is continually flat [object or ground]"); cf. *maniittuq*, "that is uneven" ("that is not *manik-*")
iqartuq	he/she is stiff, benumbed (e.g., by cold); cf. *iqartik* ("that makes one benumbed," i.e., "outer layer of skin")
apurtuq	he/she/it knocks up against something
imirusuttuq	he/she feels thirsty ("needs to drink")
kaattuq/kaaktuq	he/she feels hungry

Health

When bodily sensations become abnormal or provoke pain, it may mean that one's health is affected. In Inuktitut, no dedicated word translates as "being in good health." This notion must be expressed by way of more general terms such as *naammasiartuq*, "he/she is really (-[t]siar-) OK" (cf. *naamma[k]tuq*, "it is correct, sufficient") or, more frequently, *qanuinngi(t)-tuq*, "he/she has (or, there is) no problem" (often with the connotation "it doesn't matter"). The Euro-American salutations "How are you?" and "How do you do?" are now commonly heard in the Canadian Arctic, where they have been translated as *Qanuippit?* ("Do you have a problem?").

Qanuippit? is a contraction of Proto-Inuit *qanuq* ("how?") + *itpit* ("are you?"). The non-contracted form is still in use in Alaskan Inupiaq (MacLean 2014, 125, 254) as well as in Greenlandic. In modern Inuktitut, *Qanu(q)-ippit?* seems to have taken the connotation of "Is there something problematic or questionable with you?" This question is normally answered with "*Qanuinngi(t)tunga*"—"I don't have any problem." This way of avoiding the presumption that one's interlocutors are in good shape—thus possibly embarrassing them if they are not—constitutes another instance of the already mentioned Inuit preference for indirect language.

Someone who feels pain is said to be *aanni(r)tuq* ("he/she is in pain"). A sick person is *aanniajuq* ("one who endures pain continually"). Pain and illness are understood as alien elements that enter the body, travel through one or another of its organs (Therrien 1995), and exit when the patient heals (*aarqi[k]tuq*, "he/she/it is repaired"). This notion of "moving through" explains why the translative noun ending *-kkut* ("through something"; see Appendix) is used when speaking about *aanniat* ("continuous pains [diseases, illness]"):

Naukkut aanniqit?—[Through] where do you feel pain?

Niukkut aannitunga—I feel pain through the leg

Naukkut aanniavit?—[Through] where are you sick?

Tingukkut aanniajunga—I am sick through the liver [I have a liver disease]

In Nunavik, a nurse is an *aannia*siurti, a "disease hunter" ("one who goes after disease"). The affix *-siur-* ("to look for, to go after") is the one used for speaking about hunting animals (see Chapter 2), as in *tuttu*siurtuq ("hunts caribou"). Pain and illnesses, which travel though the body (*timikkut*), can seemingly be sought after and caught, like game travelling through the land (*nunakkut*) or in water (*imarmi*). Disease hunting was formerly the task of shamans, but it is now undertaken by doctors (*aanniasiurtimariit*, "complete disease hunters") and nurses. The word *aanniasiurti* should not be confused with *aanniasiuti* ("something useful for illness"), which designates any medicine or drug (e.g., a pill, *iigatsaq*, "that is to be swallowed"). The affix *-siuti* ("useful for") may be added to most names of body parts, with the meaning: "[medicine] useful for that organ" (e.g., *niaqursiuti*, "useful for the head," i.e., "Aspirin"). A nursing station or hospital is called *aanniavik* ("the place where people are sick").

The affixes *-lu(k)tuq* ("has a bad") and *-ngujuq* ("endures pain in") attached to the name of any body part express the fact that one feels discomfort or is ill through that organ, as in *puval*lu(k)tuq ("has bad lungs," i.e., "suffers from tuberculosis") or *niaqu*ngujuq ("endures pain in the head," i.e., "has a headache"). A few diseases have their own name. This is the case with measles (*aupallaajuq*, "is red in many places"). Cancer used to be called *aarqiqajanngituq* ("[the disease from which] one cannot heal"), but with the progress of medicine, this discouraging appellation was rejected and Inuit now call cancer *kaggutiq* ("that makes one drop progressively").

Inuit elders assert that before the arrival of *Qallunaat* in the North, infectious diseases like flu and colds were unknown. Nowadays, however, they have become commonplace. *Nuvattuq/nuvaktuq* means "he/she has a cold or flu," from *nuvak* ("spittle, mucus" and, by metonymy, "cold, flu"), a word that might be related to *nigguq*, "fish slime" (PE *nəvgur*, from *nəvə-*, "to cling to"; Fortescue et al. 2010, 266, 254–55). "He/she coughs" is *quirtu(r)tuq* (with the frequentative affix *-tu[r]-*, implying that coughing occurs repeatedly). Someone with fever is said to be *uunartuq* ("who is hot").

Skin problems already existed before contact with *Qallunaat*. They include *ajuat* (singular *ajuaq*, "abscess, boil"), which may generate *marniq* ("pus"). The former word might be guessed to mean "that break loose [*aju-*] frequently" (an allusion to boils popping up at random?), while the latter is a contraction of *maqiniq* ("the fact of oozing [*maqi-*]"). A pimple is a *pinguq*; interestingly, an isolated hill in the middle of a flat area is also called *pinguq*. This is an example of the already mentioned propensity of Inuit symbolism to play with scale changes. Another skin problem, *kalait* ("scabies," singular *kalak*) was frequent among children (*kalattut/kalaktut*, "they are scabby, covered with scabs") before Inuit had access to decent sanitary facilities.

Finally, some health problems are caused by one's own behaviour. A person who drinks *imialuk* ("big water," i.e., "alcohol") can become *aangajaattuq*, "drunk" (literally, "who is in a state of being frequently dizzy or fainting"). Drunkenness (*aangajaanniq*, "the fact of being drunk") can make someone *miriar-* ("to vomit, throw up"). Taking illicit drugs also causes *aangajaanniq* and consequently, such substances are called *aangajaanna(r)tut* ("that make one become *aangajaattuq*").

Conclusion

This incomplete description of the lexicon pertaining to the human body started with two assertions: (1) Inuit have a very detailed knowledge of external and internal anatomy, even using anatomical terms without any English equivalent (e.g., *sangujiniq*, "root of the big toe"; literally, "the fact of changing direction"); and (2) for them, the body (*timi*, "main portion") is limited to the trunk and pelvis, with the head (*niaquq*; etymologically, "attached bending part") and limbs (*avatit*, "surroundings") being considered as peripheral, albeit important organs.[24]

As far as anatomy is concerned, it is a mystery to me how Inuit, who never opened human bodies nor, until recently, had any close contact with *Qallunaat* medicine, acquired such detailed anatomical knowledge. Their experience with flensing animals, especially mammals, surely allowed them to extrapolate to humans what they knew about flesh, bones, and some internal organs, but they also probably learned about bodies by observing "bowels [made] visible because [a] belly has been ripped open by the claws of [a] polar bear," as in Markoosie's quotation at the beginning of this chapter. Inuit were also competent at curing burns and open wounds (often by placing seal blubber on them), as well as mending broken bones, two skills that would have contributed to their knowledge of anatomy.

Many words designating body parts describe their appearance or their functioning. The lungs, for instance, are called *puvaak*, a term related to the verbal base *puvi-* ("to swell"). *Iggiaq* ("throat") can be glossed etymologically as "the place where one swallows" or "the action of swallowing," while *uummati* ("heart") means "what gives life." The word for "brain," *qaritaq*, might possibly be "something hidden [inside the head]," but it is also defined by Ootoova et al. as a "container for thoughts."

Some anatomical terms have generated a number of derivatives. The word *tursuk* ("windpipe"), for instance, has been the source of various appellations: *tursuuk* ("porch of a house, entrance tunnel of an igloo"), *tursurauti* ("kinship term, nickname"), and so on. Using the names of body parts (bones in particular) for speaking about kinship and naming suggests that kin relations form the structural backbone of families and kindred, and consequently of traditional Inuit society, in the same metaphorical way as the skeleton (*sauniit*, "bones") structures the physical body.

Besides anatomical terms, this chapter has discussed several words denoting actions, physical characteristics, and sensations that have to do with the human body. We saw in particular that for Inuit, the classic "fives senses" are actually four, smell and taste being considered a single tool for experiencing one's physical surroundings. We also saw that like other languages, Inuktitut divides the colour spectrum into semantic categories that are not necessarily equivalent to those of English. For example, "blue," "green," and "purple" are considered to be the same colour (*tungujurtaq*), and "red," "pink," and "orange" (*aupartuq*) are deemed similar to each other.

We also discovered that Inuktitut does not possess a specific word for "health." A healthy person is said to be "really correct" (*naammasiartuq*) or "without problems" (*qanuinngi[t]tuq*). Because Inuit do not want to look too aggressive or intrusive when speaking, they often prefer to use indirect speech, as when asking, "Do you have problems?" (*Qanuippit?*), meaning "How are you?" Speaking about pain and illness (*aanniaq*)—understood as alien elements travelling through various organs of the body, where they are hunted (*-siur-*) by nurses and doctors (*aaniasiurtiit*) who search for them as hunters do with game animals—is not considered aggressive, though. Asking someone: "In what way are you sick?" (*Naukkut aanniavit?*) is perfectly polite.

Last but not least, bodies are gendered. The relationships their owners maintain with nature, as well as with their fellow humans, are highly influenced by the fact that people are considered as being either men or women. This is not reflected directly in the language. Inuktitut and the other Inuit dialects have no grammatical gender—they do not distinguish between "he," "she," "it," "him," or "her"—nor do they possess any affix that would "genderize" an otherwise neutral noun base. Let us remember, too, that pre-Christian personal names were—and remain—genderless. Moreover, the language does not have any word for "gender" or "sex." Humans (and animals) are said to be either male (*anguti*) or female (*arnaq*)—though a male fetus can become female at birth (cf. Chapter 4)—with terms for sex-specific body parts,[25] but without a word denoting the general notion of biological or social sexuality. As we saw in the preceding chapters, gender distinctions are often implied in the very meaning of appellations for age categories (e.g., *surusiq*, "boy" vs. *niviarsiaq*, "girl") and kinship positions (the words used when addressing siblings, for instance). In the next pages, it will be shown that in the present-day world, gender can also come up in conversations that facilitate socializing.

CHAPTER SIX

Words for Socializing in the Contemporary World

Ai—Inuk inuuqatiminik nilliujijuq takujaminik taanna uqausiq tungasukkaigutik angirtisigutik.

Hi!—A person orally addresses a companion that he/she sees; this word [is] a means for making [people] comfortable and responsive.

TAAMUSI QUMAQ (1991, 105)

In the summer of 1694, the French Canadian explorer Louis Jolliet was sailing along the north shore of the Gulf of St. Lawrence. Near the southwestern entrance to the Strait of Belle Isle, he met a small group of Inuit whose leader, as he recorded in his diary, greeted him as follows: "*Ahé, ahé, thou tcharacou!*" According to Jolliet, this meant "Hail! Hail! Lay down arms! [*Salut, salut, bas les armes!*]," an utterance that can be reconstructed as "*Ai! Ai! Tutsiarakku*"—"Hi! Hi! I beg it" (Dorais 1980). What was the Inuit family chief—whom Jolliet called their *Capitaine*— begging for? His greeting was probably a way of showing his peaceful intentions, coupled with a request for trading with the French.

The exclamation *Ai!* still constitutes the common form of greeting in Inuktitut. Even *Qallunaat* living in the North know that upon passing or meeting someone you know, you must say "*Ai!*" or better yet, "[So-and-so] *ai!*" as in "*Miajing*ai" ("Hi Mary!") or "*Maasiung*ai" ("Hi Matthew").[1] Northern residents also learn that whenever greeted, they should acknowledge the salutation by answering "*Aa!*" (Nunavik and Labrador) or "*Ii!*" (elsewhere), in other words, "Yes!" In the opening quotation, Taamusi Qumaq nicely summarizes the social function of the word *Ai!* According to him, this exclamation is "a means for making people comfortable," used for establishing a pleasant relationship with somebody one sees—or hears on the telephone (*uqalauti*, "a means to talk for a long time"), where "*Ai!*" takes the place of the English "Hello!" In order to be activated, the social bond it establishes must be acknowledged by the person who is greeted. So *Ai!* is also "a means for making people respond [i.e., acquiesce, say yes]."

In this last semantic stroll, we will look at some words Inuit use for socializing with each other. Because this socialization now takes place in a modern North American setting, we shall also examine how contemporary residents of the Arctic talk about the communities where they live.

Words for Socializing

Words for socializing include all particles and other types of utterances (question words, phrases, etc.) that people use when contacting each other and/or inquiring about their mutual conditions, circumstances, and activities. These are too numerous to allow for any attempt at an exhaustive survey. Accordingly, I shall limit my description to two types of social expressions: greetings and question words dealing with identity, place, and time.

Greetings

We just saw that over 300 years ago, the greeting *Ai!* was already in use in the Strait of Belle Isle area. As centuries passed, however, Inuit became acquainted with Euro-American ways and gradually added to their *Ai!* new greetings inspired by *Qallunaat*. Nowadays, people meeting each other or speaking on the phone are also expected to ask, "*Qanuippit?*"—"How are you?" As shown at the end of the preceding chapter, the literal meaning of this perfunctory question is "Do you have a problem?" Most of the time, it is answered with "*Qanuinngi(t)tunga*" or "*Qanuinngilanga*"—"I do not have a problem," but some people, elders in particular, may consider it a genuine inquiry and answer, for instance, "*Qanuilluananga nuvakkalualirpunga*"—"Even though I do not have much of a problem, I am suffering from a cold."

This type of indirect or allusive verbal exchange can be refined by resorting to negative questioning. If, for example, I suspect that my companion might actually be suffering from something, I may ask him or her, "*Qanuinngilatit?*"—"Don't you have a problem?" I will be relieved if the answer is "*Aa/Ii, qanuinngilanga*"—"Yes, I do not have any problem," although my initial guess would have been corroborated by an answer such as "*Auka/Aakka qanuigalattunga*"—"No, I have some problems." In the same way, if I would like someone to go somewhere with me but am quite sure that he or she will not, I would ask, "*Qainngilatit?*"—"Are you not coming?" and expect my interlocutor to answer positively, "*Aa/Ii qainngilanga*"—"Yes, I am not coming." When used judiciously, negative questioning has the advantage of generating positive answers, thus preventing responders from embarrassing the questioner (and themselves) with a rude "No!"

As shown in the preceding examples, answering negative questions is not done the same way in English as it is in Inuktitut. In the former language, these questions are answered by "No!" if the person who is questioned agrees with his or her interlocutor in negating something, as in "Don't you understand?"—"No, I don't understand." In Inuktitut, however, as in many other languages (e.g., Japanese and Vietnamese), one answers "Yes!" when agreeing with the core of the question and "No!" otherwise:

Tukisinngilatit? Aa/Ii tukisinngilanga; Auka/Aakka tukisivunga

Don't you understand? Yes, I don't understand; No, I understand

In Nunavik and Labrador, the words for "yes" and "no" are *aa* and *auka*, respectively.[2] Elsewhere, "yes" is generally *ii* (*aap* in West Greenlandic), but "no" takes several different forms according to dialect: *irqi* (East Greenlandic), *naagga* (West Greenlandic, Alaskan Inupiaq, Inuvialuktun, Kivalliq), *imannaq* (Inuinnaqtun), *iiq* (Nattilingmiutut), *aakka* (North Baffin, Aivilik), *aggaq* (South Baffin). It seems to have been harder for the Inuit language to find a way to deny something than to make an affirmation, hence the dialectal diversity of the words for "no."

Many speakers, especially women, who feel shy or are afraid to sound too assertive will raise their eyebrows briefly (*qallunittut*) instead of saying "Yes!" or wrinkle their nose (*narsi[t]tut*; related to PE *narə-*, "to smell" and Proto-Inuit *narru-*, "is disgusted by something") in place of "No!" Sometimes, a question cannot be answered by "Yes!" or "No!" either because one does not know about what is asked or because there is a good reason (e.g., politeness, prudence, timidity, lack of time) not to answer. In such cases, one may reply, "*Imma(r)qa*"—"Maybe" (*imma-*, "thus, there" + *-[r]qa*, "perhaps" ["it is perhaps thus or there"]). However, the best way not to commit oneself is to answer, "*Aatsuk!*" (Nunavik) or "*Aamai!*" (Baffin Island and western Hudson Bay)—"I don't know!" *Aatsuk!* is related to *Asu!* ("Indeed!"), generally heard in the derivatives *Asuguuq!* ("You're right! [indeed it is said]") and *Asuilaak!* ("Finally! There it is! [indeed, that is to say]"). If the responder is really ignorant about the subject of the question, he or she would answer, "*Qaujimanngilanga*"—"I do not know," or, less abruptly, "*Qaujimannginama*"—"Because I do not know [I cannot answer you]."

Some decades ago, Inuit wage earners noticed that their *Qallunaat* co-workers greeted them with "Good morning!" when arriving at their workplace. This was soon transposed into Inuktitut, with a slightly different meaning: "*Ullaa(k)kut!*"—"During the morning!" Variants also appeared: "*Unnu(k)sakkut!*"—"During the incoming evening [i.e., afternoon]! [Good afternoon!]" and "*Unnu(k)kut!*"—"During the evening! [Good night!]." As with *Ai!* and *Qanuippit? Ullaa(k)kut!* is one of the very few local words that most *Qallunaat* living in the North have mastered and use when addressing Inuit.

Many *Qallunaat* have also learned to say "Thank you!" The Inuit translation of this word phrase varies according to dialects, but in most areas, it derives from the verbal base *quja(t)-* ("to be thankful")—which *Qallunaat* generally mispronounce as *kuja(k)-* ("to have sexual intercourse")—with the addition of exclamative affixes:

Qujanaq!	"How thankful!" (Inupiaq, Nattilingmiutut,[3] Greenlandic)
Qujanainni!	"How thankful it makes [me]!" (Inuvialuktun)
Quana!	"How thankful!" [*quja-* > *qua-*] (Inuinnaqtun)
Qujannamiik!	"How thankful indeed!" (Aivilik, Baffin Island)

In the western Hudson Bay area, "Thank you!" translates as "*Matna!*" (possibly, "This [is it]!"). In Nunavik and Labrador, the expression of thankfulness derives from the base *nakur-* ("to deserve gratitude"):

Nakurmiik!	"Worthy of gratitude indeed!" (Nunavik)
Nakummiik!	"Worthy of gratitude indeed!" (Labrador)
Nakurami!	"Because it deserves gratitude!" (Kangiqsujuaq [Nunavik])

In all Inuktitut dialects, *Qujana!* means "Never mind! Don't bother!" Conjecturally, this could be a shortened form of *Qujanak!* ("Don't be thankful! [because it is not worth it]") or an ironical rendition of *Qujanaq!* ("How thankful!") above.

The fact that there exist several different ways to translate "Thank you!" hints at the possibility that before the arrival of *Qallunaat*, Inuktitut had no equivalent for this English exclamation. Indeed, Nunavik elders say that formerly, the common way for thanking someone was to utter a rather high-pitched "*iiiiih*" sound (*sirijuq*, "he/she makes a cry of thanks"; from PE *ciri-*, "to be eager"). Nowadays, this sound is still occasionally heard from very old people.

Thanking someone in the *Qallunaat* way—with words—also entailed the adoption of an expression acknowledging a person's thanks, the equivalent of the English "You're welcome!" In Inuktitut, after having been graced with a *qujannammiik* or *nakurmiik*, one is expected to answer, "*Ilaali!*"—"But [*-li*] that is to say!" Note that *Ilai?* (the contraction of *ilaa* and *ai*) means "Is it not so?"

Besides imported greetings such as "How are you?" "Good morning!" "Thank you!" and "You're welcome!" Inuit have long used another practice of *Qallunaat*: shaking hands. In most areas, "Let's shake hands!" has been translated as "*Tigulaurluk!*"—"Let's both of us hold each other's hand!" But in eastern and, increasingly, western Nunavik, the common way of inviting someone to shake hands is to say, "*Saimuurluk!*" Since the base *saimuur-* ("to shake hands") is apparently unknown anywhere else, it may be interesting to look into its origin.

The English version of Schneider's Nunavik dictionary (1985, 335) has an entry for *saimu*, rendered as "Hi! Goodbye! Peace be with you!"[4] Another entry, *saimuurpaa*, is translated as "He says 'peace!' to him" (in the French version: "*Il lui dit: 'salut!' il le salue ainsi*"). A third entry, *saimuurtut*, translates as "They shake hands (on arrival or departure)."[5] In his Inuktitut-French dictionary (1970a, 309), Schneider mentions that the terms *saimu* and *saimuurpaa* are mostly used around Kuujjuaq and that the former name of this community, Fort Chimo, might come from *saimu*.[6]

I think otherwise. In view of the fact that *saimu(ur)-* was practically unknown outside the Kuujjuaq and Ungava Bay area when Schneider was working on his dictionary (in the 1950s and early '60s), this base had plausibly developed locally as a phonological adaptation of the name "Chimo" (rather than the other way around). The literal meaning of *saimuurtut* ("they [many] shake hands") and *Saimuurluk!* ("Let's both of us shake hands!") would thus be "They/Let's do as in Chimo." In 1830, the Hudson's Bay Company (HBC) trading post at Fort Chimo was the very first *Qallunaat* establishment in Canadian Inuit territory outside of Labrador, and it was probably there that the northeastern Nunavik people became acquainted with shaking hands. Hence the meaning I propose for the verbal base *saimuur-* is "to do as in Chimo." As for the name "Chimo," I am quite sure it is a shortened version of the ethnonyms *Iischiimeu* (in Eastern Cree) and *Iischimaaw* (in Naskapi)—that is, "Eskimo"—used by the Indigenous guides of the HBC explorers and traders who travelled from James Bay to Inuit country at the bottom of Ungava Bay in the early 1800s (Morantz 2016, 26–28). Ballantyne (1858, 146) mentions that the HBC employees in Ungava referred to Inuit as "Chimos." This was undoubtedly a corrupt rendering of the Cree and/or Naskapi terms.

Visits to relatives, friends, and neighbours are natural occasions for using greetings. Before the advent of television, the internet, regular working hours, and meetings of all kinds, visiting other households was the principal leisure activity in Inuit camps and early villages. People were expected to visit each other every few days. One time in Quaqtaq, when I entered a tent, the housewife told me, "*Ninngagalappunga*"—"I am somewhat mad at you." "*Sumut?*"—"Why?" I asked. "*Ullunik pingasunik pulaarunnairavit*," she answered: "Because you have not visited us over the last three days."

Nowadays, even though Inuit complain that they do not have time to see each other anymore, visiting relatives and friends remains an important social activity, albeit on a less frequent basis. The literal meaning of *pulaar-tuq* ("he/she goes on a visit") is "he/she enters somewhere frequently or for a long time." When somebody is at home, the door is not locked (*atsungirtuq*, "he/she fastens, locks") and visitors enter without knocking. A knock at the door (*survatartuq*, "he/she makes noise repeatedly") indicates that the visitor is a *Qallunaaq*. Formerly, most visits were individual. Men visited their male acquaintances, women (with their babies) their female friends, and children their peers of the same gender and age. While men mostly discussed subsistence activities, women spoke about their domestic tasks, including the care of children. These days, visitors are often couples with their youngest kids, and conversations deal with family life and community affairs.

If the visitor is not a familiar figure, he or she will be welcomed with "*Tungasugit!*" — "Feel comfortable!" In Nunavik, another common greeting is "*Tujurminak!*" — "Don't [-*nak*] feel bored or homesick!" Once again, this is an instance of negative discourse. The verbal base *tujurmi-* ("to feel bored") is linked to the terms *tujurmiaq* ("guest"; literally, "one who has been sent away once again") and *tujurmiuvik* ("host"; literally, "a place to be sent away again"), two words that derive from *tujur-* ("to send something to someone who is away"). It is as if guests were presents sent to hosts, who expect the "gifts" they receive to enjoy their stay with them ("Be comfortable! Don't feel bored!").

Unfamiliar visitors or those who are back from a trip are urged to recount any experience that might be of interest to their hosts: "*Unikkalaurit!*" — "Please tell about something!" They are also invited to drink tea or, less frequently, coffee, with bannock or bread: "*Tiitulaurit! Kaapitulaurit! Panirtitalik, niaquujalik*" — "Please take some tea, some coffee! There is bannock, there is bread." If fresh meat or fish are available, or if the family is eating, visitors are expected to partake of the food or meal: "*Kaanngilatit? Nirilaurit! Uujulik, iqalulik*" — "Are you not hungry? Please eat! There is boiled meat, there is fish." As we saw earlier, sharing one's catch (*ningirtut*, "they share game") and, nowadays, being generous with food and other goods procured with one's monetary income are considered of primary importance by contemporary Inuit, men as well as women.

Visitors may decline an invitation to eat: "*Nakurmiingai! Kaagunnailirtungali nirikainnarama*" — "Thank you, hey! But I am not hungry anymore because I have just eaten." If they eat with their hosts, visitors can signal that they have had enough by saying: "*Aqiattutunga*" — "I have much of a belly" ("I am full"). When leaving a house they have been visiting, occasional or one-time guests — as well as anyone departing for a long journey — may bid goodbye to those who stay. In Nunavik and Labrador, this is expressed by the exclamation "*Atsunai!*" — "Go ahead, hey! Fare well, hey!" [*atsut/aksut*: "Go for it! Fare well!" + *ai*], echoed by the hosts.[7] In most parts of Nunavut, the departing party would say, "*Tagvauvusi!*" — "You people are right here!" while those remaining would answer, "*Taavauvusi!*" — "You people are out far away!" (Spalding 1998, 147–48). Nowadays, however, the most common way of parting company is to say, "*Bai!*"—"Bye!" or "*Siiju!*"—"See you!"

Question Words

Just before I left for my first summer of fieldwork in Quaqtaq, my research supervisor, anthropologist Bernard Saladin d'Anglure, told me that if I wanted to learn Inuktitut and know about those among whom I was to live, there were two questions I should ask as often as possible. Both dealt with the identity of things and persons: "*Suna una?*"—"What [is] this?" and "*Kina una?*"—"Who [is] this one?"

In the word *suna?* the ending -*na*, which seems to refer to the concept of being located somewhere (all demonstratives in the singular basic case end with -*na*, as in *una*, "this here"), is added to the base *su(k)-* ("what?"). The literal meaning of *suna?* could thus be "what is here or there?" The ending -*na* is deleted in a few lexicalized forms, such as *sumut?* ("because of what?" i.e., "why?"). *Su(k)-* can also act as a verbal base, as in *suvit?* ("what are you doing?") or *suva?* ("what is he/she doing? what is going on?"). With a lengthened -*va* and a tone of astonishment, *suvaa?* ("what is going on indeed?") means "is it not surprising?" Surprise can also be expressed by way of the composite lexeme *sunauvva* (*suna* ["what?"] + *uvva* ["or, else"]): "surprisingly."

The word *kina?* ("who?") links the base *ki-* ("who?") to the ending -*na* and can be understood as "who is here or there?" In most dialects (but not in Nunavik), -*na* is sometimes deleted, as in *kikkut?* ("who [plural]?") and *kia?* ("whose?"). Generally speaking, though, the derivatives of *kina?* are based on the full form of the word:

kinakkut?	who [plural]? [Nunavik] (*kina-* + -*kkut* ["a group of people"]; literally, "the group of who?"); cf. *kinakkut ukua?* ("who [are] these ones?")
kinagivait?	you have him/her as who? (i.e., "what is your kinship relation with him/her?")[8]
kinauvit?	who are you? (i.e., "what is your name?")

Interestingly, in the North Baffin dialect, the word for "what?" is *kisuk?* rather than *suna?* It seems as if both *ki-* ("who?") and *-suk* ("what?") were amalgamated into one term: "who-what?" (although in North Baffin, *kina* still means "who?"). I do not know if *kisuk?* actually stems from such an amalgam, as the base *ki-* may not be the same one found in *kina?* A guess might be that it has a broader signification, encompassing the notion of "who?" in a more general concept: anything, human or not, whose identity is investigated. *Kisuk?* ("what?") could then be parsed into *ki-* + *-suk* [lesser]: "what lesser [because it is not human?] entity?"

Besides the "what?" and "who?" question words, there exist other, more specialized interrogatives. We already mentioned two of them: *qanuq?* ("how?") and *sumut?* ("why?"). The former term was discussed in the preceding chapter, in relation to the verbal phrase *Qanuippit?* ("How are you?"). The latter (*sumut?*) is a lexicalized word comprising *su(k)-* ("what?") and *-mut* (singular allative), the literal meaning of which is "for what? because of what?" (see above).

Four interrogatives deal with one's relation to space. Each of them ends with a case of the nominal declension (slightly modified in two instances) that has to do with motion (see Appendix). Three of these question words start with *na-*, the already mentioned morpheme—generally used as an ending—that expresses localization and might conjecturally be found in the term *nuna* (see Chapter 1). The fourth one derives from *nauk?* ("where [near the speaker]? what?"). As suggested by Fortescue et al. (2010, 223), *nauk?* could be parsed as *na-* + *-uk* ("it," as in *takuvi*uk? "do you [-*vi(t)*-] see [*taku-*] it [*-uk*]?") and would literally mean "where it [is]?"

nani?	where? wherein? (locative case ending)
namut?	whereto? (allative case ending)
nakit?	wherefrom? (ablative case ending)
naukkut?	whereby? through where? (translative case ending)

Words answering these interrogatives, whether nouns or localizers, must bear the same case ending as the question. For instance, "*Naniippa?*" ("Where is he/she?") is answered by "*Illu*mi" ("In the house") or "*Maani*" ("Here") (locative case ending).

As far as I know, there is no Inuit word expressing the general and rather abstract concept of "space."[9] A possible rendition could be *naniinniq*, "the fact of being [some]where." The more restricted notion of "place, room for someone or something," however, is rendered by a word of its own, *ini*, as in *iniqarunnai(r)tuq*, "there is no room left" (e.g., on a fully booked flight).

In a similar way, Inuktitut does not have a word for "time." In his *Dictionnaire français-esquimau* (1970b, 385), Schneider proposes *maannaugunnaituq* ("what is no longer now"), but this term refers exclusively to the past. The expression of time (and space) is generally related to specific events, thanks to the affix *-vik* ("time or place for"), as in *quviasuvvik*, "time for rejoicing" (e.g., Christmas) or "place for rejoicing" (e.g., a banquet hall). The semantic link between time and space also shows up in the word *maanna* ("now"), etymologically linked to *manna* ("this one here"). According to Fortescue et al. (2010, 202), the ancestral form of *maanna*, PE *maðətən* ("now"), would have been a cognate of modern Inuktitut *matsutun(aq)*, "like this one here." Note that in western Nunavik, *maanna* means "later on," and "now" is rendered by *taga-taga*, a word phrase related to *tagga* ("there it is!").

Besides specific question phrases such as "*Qatsinik ukiuqalirqit?*"—"How many winters do you have [how old are you]?" or "*Qatsi(n)ngurqa?*"—"How much is it becoming [what time is it]?" most dialects have two general interrogatives linked to time: *qanga?* ("when in the past?") and *qakugu(q)?* ("when in the future?"). In southern Baffin, Nunavik, and Labrador, however, only one word for "when?" is in use: *qanga?* For Fortescue et al. (2010, 310), this lexical distinction between past and future reflects the morphological difference between the causative (or perfective) and conditional (or imperfective) verbal moods (see Appendix). Like the causative, *qanga?* refers to an event that has actually happened, since it is positioned in the past. By contrast, *qakugu(q)?* inquires about something that has not happened yet, in the same way the conditional mood expresses the eventuality that an event might occur. Indeed, the second syllable of both interrogatives corresponds to the etymological forms of the causative (*-nga-*) and conditional (*-ku-*) endings, respectively.[10]

Answers to *qanga?* and *qakugu[q]?*—and to other questions as well—may include verbs marked for tense, as in "*Qanga tikippit?*"—"When [did] you arrive?" *Tikikainna(r)qunga*"—"I just arrived." The period of time when an event occurred or might occur is usually expressed by way of affixes.[11] These allow speakers to distinguish between near and distant past and future:

nirikainna(r)tunga	I ate a moment ago (*-kainnar-*)
nirirqaujunga	I ate today (*-rqau-*)
nirilaurtunga	I ate earlier than today (*-laur-*)
nirilangajunga	I shall eat in a moment (*-langa-*)
niriniartunga	I shall eat today (*-niar-*)
nirilaartunga	I shall eat later than today (*-laar-*)

More general terms dealing with the relativity of time—some of which are actually position words or demonstratives—include the following:

akuni	for/since a long time (literally, "its own middle space" or "in middle spaces"; i.e., between then and now [?])
taitsumani	formerly, in the past (literally, "in that one [period of time] positioned far away")
(uvat)siaruq	later on

When the affix *-tuinnaq* ("genuine") is added to a question word, it endows it with a meaning corresponding to English "any" or "ever," as in *kinatuinnaq* ("anyone"), *qanutuinnaq* ("anyhow"), *nanituinnaq* ("anywhere, wherever"), *qangatuinnaq* ("whenever"), and so on. A "genuine" *kina?* or *qanga?* is one that is not yet connected to a specific person, event, or circumstance, and can therefore refer to anything.

Whether they are greetings, interrogatives, or something else, words for socializing are expected to convey a sense of respect for those one is addressing. Some topics of conversation must be avoided between men and women, particularly those about sex and intimate activities, even though verbal exchanges between genders are quite easygoing and may include playful teasing.[12] When I was conducting my doctoral research on words designating objects introduced by *Qallunaat* (Dorais 1983), I remember asking a man what sanitary napkins were called. He answered that he did not know. Women, he said, probably had a term for that, but he had never heard it because menses and intimate hygiene were not topics to be discussed between genders. In another vein, children must not hear their parents' and other adults' opinions on people. Like all human beings, Inuit love to gossip, but in order to preserve social harmony, what is said about neighbours must remain confidential. This is why gossiping should be avoided in the presence of the young, who are likely to repeat without discretion what they hear.[13]

Social harmony and consideration for others also explain why swearing is not highly developed in Inuktitut. A woman who is angry at another woman may say, *sotto voce*, "*Utsukallaaluit!*"—"Your little fat vagina!" In her dictionary of the Labrador dialect, Rose Jeddore (1976, 5) translates the word *Aahaakkik!* ("Your two vaginas!")[14] as "Darn you!" As for Nunavik men, they may utter *Irq!* or *Irqaaluk!* ("Big bottom!") when irritated with something, such as barely missing a target, according to Qumaq (1991, 1). But as far as I know, this is about the extent of genuinely Inuit swear words, at least in Nunavik, although bilingual individuals now have access to a large repertoire of English oaths and French Canadian *sacres* (e.g., *Tapirnak!* "*Tabernacle!*").

From a more strictly linguistic perspective, there are affixes that attenuate the directness and possibly intrusive nature of a question, order, or invitation. Readers may remember old Willie Cain, who wanted to know my name—an inquiry he found very intrusive—and finally asked me, "*Kinaugaluarqit?*"—"Who are you anyway?" (Chapter 4). The morpheme *-galuar-/-raluar-* can be translated, according to context, as "anyway, however, despite, even." It expresses the fact that speakers realize that while their question is too direct or their assertion apparently conflicts with another statement, they cannot avoid uttering it. See for instance: "*Tukisi*galuar*qit?*"—"However, do you understand?" (even though it is not really deferential to believe you do not), the answer to which could be: "*Qallunaangu*galuar*sunga inuttituusuungu-junga*"—"Even though I am a *Qallunaaq*, I am used to speaking Inuktitut" (despite the fact that *Qallunaat* are expected to ignore the language).

Giving orders to other people or inciting them to do something is generally considered un-Inuit. All adult individuals are supposed to know how they should behave and consequently, people try to keep a low profile, refraining from bragging about their feats and bossing others. This explains why the direct use of the imperative mood is very restricted. For instance, the order *Qaigit!* ("Come!") is only given to young children or when in a hurry. Otherwise, there are three ways to mitigate an order: displacing it to the near future; relegating it to a relatively distant past; or transforming it into a possible approaching event. Here are some examples:

Using the affix *-lir-* ("to be about to"):

qailirit!	"be about to come!"
tusalirit!	"be about to hear!"
tiitulirit!	"be about to take some tea!"

Using the affix *-laur-* (relatively distant past):

qailaurit!	"may you have come!"
tusalaurit!	"may you have heard!"
tiitulaurit!	"may you have taken some tea!"

Using the imperfective appositional mood (see Appendix) in place of the imperative:

qailutit!	"while coming [you will do that]!"
tusarlutit!	"while hearing [you will do that]!"
tiiturlutit!	"while taking some tea [you will do that]!"

Inuit have no word for "politeness," but they practise and express it in various ways. As we just saw, downplaying orders and requests by playing upon tenses and verbal moods constitutes an effective equivalent to using "Please!" unknown in Inuktitut, as are formal salutations like "Madam" or "Sir."[15] As for the ubiquitous Euro-American phrases "Excuse me!" and "I am sorry!" they have been translated as *"Ilaaniunngi(t)tuq!"*—"It is not intentional!" The literal meaning of the word for "intentional," *ilaanit*, is "from a part of him/her." Therefore, something done voluntarily is like an active fragment extracted from the person who exercises his or her will.

Words for Talking About Contemporary Inuit Communities

Nowadays, socializing generally occurs within *nunaliit* ("those having a *nuna* [land]"), the permanent villages that display, as we shall see, most of

the architectural, economic, dietary, administrative, and social characteristics of other North American communities. Because modern villages are
much more populous than traditional camps, sociability is often restricted
to one's extended family, workmates, and friends. But on the whole, Inuit
words and rules for socializing remain essentially similar to what they have
always been, even though people frequently complain that these rules are
not as respected as they should be.

Buildings and Infrastructure

The physical look of contemporary Inuit communities, even the smaller
ones, is quite different from the clusters of winter snow houses (*illuvigait*,
"little big residences") or summer tents (*tupiit*) that were typical in the eastern Canadian Arctic (except for Labrador) until the mid-1950s. Modern
communities also differ from the agglomerations of self-built cabins and
one- to three-room prefabricated houses issued by the federal gouvernment
(*illujuat*, "super-residences"), commonly used during the 1960s and early
'70s. The economic and social development of the 1970s through the '80s,
induced by the territorial and political agreements Inuit signed with governments all over the Arctic, has transformed their habitat into villages that
are generally well-built, although chronically short of a sufficient number of
available residences.

Speakers of Inuktitut had to find words to give names to these new structures. Since this was done on a completely informal basis, the appellations
given were not always the same from one region to another, with the result
that similar elements are often designated by a variety of words. So, as was
the case in the preceding chapters, most terms mentioned in the following
pages will be those from one area: northeastern Nunavik.

In contrast to former times, northern communities are now built along
streets, *arqutiit*. This word can apply to any type of road, route, or trail,
whether marked or not—for instance, the coastal itinerary of a boat going
from point A to point B. Its PE etymon, *aprun*, is possibly linked to *apərə-*,
"to ask" (Fortescue et al. 2010, 41). An *aprun* or *arquti* would thus be a
"means for asking," plausibly a structured way for interrogating the landscape about the route to follow, for the most part using place names (see
Chapter 1). It is noteworthy that in the Arctic, including Greenland and
most of Inuit Alaska, there are no built *arqutiit* outside villages and their

surrounding territory. In Canada, only Inuvik (with a road linking it to the Yukon) and Tuktoyaktuk (linked to Inuvik) in the Mackenzie Delta have a land-based route to the outside.

Nunakkuujuut, "those that go by land [motor vehicles],"[16] travel village streets, along which *illuit* ("houses") are arranged in a more or less regular pattern. The word *illu* (*iglu* in the North Baffin and western Canadian dialects) means "residence" (cf. *angirraq*, "home"; literally, "[place for] coming back") and denotes any type of rigid structure built or erected to shelter people: a house (made of snow,[17] wood, or other materials), an apartment, the cabin of a boat, and even one's room in a hospital. Inuit houses, whether snow or wood, are entered through a *tursuuk* ("double porch"), a word that, as we saw in the last chapter, also means "windpipe." The parts of a house include the following:

natiq	floor; cf. *nataaq* ("small *natiq*"), the bottom of a container
akinnaq	wall (etymologically, "that looks like a means for facing something")
ukkuaq	door (related to PE *uməg-*, "to close off or cover" [Fortescue et al. 2010, 403])
igalaaq	window (PE *əgalər*, "smokehole"; from *əga-*, "to cook" + -&ər, nominalizer: "the action of cooking" [Fortescue et al. 2010, 108])
qulaaq	ceiling ("that reaches the upper side")

Unlike snow igloos, which were circular (cf. *ammalukitaq*, "circle, sphere"; literally, "that opens frequently and repeatedly [in the image of a hole]"), modern houses have walls that form right angles (cf. *sikkitaq*, "square, rectangle, cube"; etymologically, "made to be steep"). Houses are divided into a number of rooms, *qariat* (singular *qariaq*, "secondary snow house opening on a main one"); etymologically, "places for coming up [when entering traditional houses?]" (Fortescue et al. 2010, 314). The different rooms are usually designated by a verbal base describing their function, followed by the affix -*vik* ("place where"):

sinivvik	bedroom ("place for sleeping"); this word also means "bed" in western Nunavik
quijartuvik	bathroom, toilet ("place where one goes to urinate"); also *anariartuvik* ("place where one goes to defecate")
igavik	kitchen ("place for cooking")
pulaarvik	drawing-room, parlour ("place for visiting")

Furniture and appliances now found in Inuit homes include the following items:

illiq/igliq	bed ("sleeping and sitting platform in a snow igloo"; related to PE *ingət-*, "to sit")
uvvavik	wash basin, sink ("place for washing")
iluunnaniarvik	bathtub ("place for looking after the whole [body]")
tarratuuti	mirror ("means for looking at one's own reflection")
qurvik	toilet bowl, chamber pot ("place for watering something with urine"); also *anarvik* ("place for defecating")
kiatsauti	stove, cooking range ("means for getting some warmth")
quaqauti	freezer ("container for frozen things")
nillinartuqauti	refrigerator ("container for cooled things")
saa	table ("what is in front of one")
itsivautaq	chair, seat ("means for being seated"); cf. *itsivautaaluk* ("big *itsivautaq*"), a couch
tiivi	television set (from the English "TV")

As can be seen, most of the words listed above are easily decipherable because their literal meanings constitute explicit descriptions of how or why the objects or places they denote are used. However, a few terms (e.g., *ukkuaq, igalaaq, illiq, qurvik*) belong to the lexicon of traditional material culture and derive from ancient etymons that can only be retrieved thanks to linguistic analysis.

This predominance of descriptive appellations also shows up in the names given to the various types of buildings usually found in Inuit villages, as well as to those who work in these buildings:[18]

ilinniavik	school ("place for studying"); cf. *ilinniatuq* ("seeks to learn"), he/she studies; *ilinniati* ("one who studies"), a student; and *ilinniatitsiji* or *ilisaiji* ("one who makes people study"), a teacher
aanniavik	nursing station, hospital ("place where people are sick"); cf. *aanniasiurti* ("one who goes after disease"), a nurse, a doctor
niuvirvik	store, trading post ("place for selling and buying"); cf. *niuvirti* ("one who buys and/or sells"), a trader, a storekeeper
tutsiavik	church ("place for praying"); cf. *tutsiatitsiji* ("one who makes [people] pray"), a lay preacher
allavik	office ("place for writing"); cf. *allati* ("one who writes"), an office worker, a secretary
puliisikkut	police station ("group of policemen"); cf. *puliisi* (from the English "police"), a police officer
sinittavik	hotel, guest house ("place for sleeping repeatedly")
nirivik	restaurant, dining room ("place for eating"); cf. *igaji* ("one who cooks"), a cook, a chef (from *igajuq*, "he/she cooks," itself a derivative of *iga*, "hearth for cooking")
ikumaliurvik	power plant ("place for making electricity")
mivvik	airport, landing strip ("place for landing")

It should be noted that the word for "electricity," *ikuma*, actually means "fire" (literally, "burning"). As for *mivvik*, it derives from the base *mit-* ("to land"), drawn from the vocabulary of ornithology. If something can land, it can fly, too, and accordingly, in most Inuit dialects the word for "airplane" derives from *timmi-* or *tingi-*, "to fly [like a bird]." In western Nunavik, for instance, an aircraft is called *timmijuuq* ("that is in the habit of flying"). In northeastern Nunavik, however, a plane is a *qangattajuuq* ("that is in the habit of ascending") and a pilot, a *qangattajuurti* ("one who operates a *qangattajuuq*").

The "ascending (or flying) ones" are semantically opposed to "those that go by land" (*nunakkuujuut*, "motor vehicles"). A third means of conveyance is the *umiaq* ("boat"), which travels by water. We saw in Chapter 2 that formerly, the word *umiaq* denoted the large collective skin-covered craft that transported women, children, and their belongings (while men followed in their kayaks). It was owned by an *umialittaaq* ("a given one who has an *umiaq*"). After contact with *Qallunaat*, all types of boats were called *umiat* (traditional skin boats thence being referred to as *umiatuinnait*, "genuine *umiat*"), and the word *umialittaaq* was applied to a ship's master or captain. Sailors were dubbed *kipaluit* ("servants"). Nowadays, five principal categories of watercraft are known in Nunavik communities: *umiarjuaq* ("super-*umiaq*," i.e., "ship"), *umiaraaluk* ("big *umiaq*," i.e., "motorized schooner"), *nilirtu(r)tuq* ("that farts repeatedly," i.e., "speedboat"), *umiaraaq* ("very small *umiaq*," i.e., "rowboat"), and *qajariaq* ("that is like a kayak," i.e., "canoe" [with an outboard motor: *qianngujuuq*, "that sounds like crying"]). A marine propeller is homonymous with the dorsal fin of a whale: *anguuti* ("a means to make it move on in water"). The inboard engine of a boat, as well as the motor of an aircraft or of a land vehicle, are generally called *aulauti* ("a means for making something move"). All types of engines are fed with *ursualuk* ("big blubber"), one or another variety of refined petroleum.

Numerals and the Economy

Since the advent of *Qallunaat* traders, over two centuries ago in some areas of the Arctic, Inuit have become familiar with commercial exchanges. These progressively complemented and then superseded the barter of goods (*taursiturniq*, "the fact of providing frequently a replacement [for something]") that had always existed among Inuit. One important effect of trading and, later on, wage work, was to force the speakers of Inuktitut to expand their numerical system.

Traditional Inuit numerals (*kisitsigutiit*, "means for dealing with them one by one"; or in some dialects, *naasautiit*, "means for completing multiple tasks") are anthropomorphic, that is, patterned on the human body and more specifically on the limbs, with their ten fingers and ten toes for a total of twenty units. The language reflects this anthropomorphy. For example, the number twenty can be expressed as follows: *avatit* ("the limbs") in several dialects, including Nunavik; *iñuiññaq* ("a total person") in Alaskan Inupiaq; and *ii naattungu* ("completing a person") in East Greenlandic.

Barring some slight phonological differences, numbers one to five are the same in all Inuit dialects. Note that for Inuit, counting usually starts from the little finger of the left hand:

atausiq	one ("means for [-*usiq*] being in one piece [*ata-*; cf. *atajuq*, "he/she/it adheres, is attached to"]")
marruuk	two; etymologically, *malrug-* (related to *malig-*, "to follow") + -*uk*, dual number
pingasut	three; etymologically related to *pingna*, "this one up there" (Fortescue et al. 2010, 287), an allusion to the third, longest finger
sitamat	four; possibly related to PE *citə(g)-*, "to be hard" (Fortescue et al. 2010, 93); maybe an allusion to the fact that the fourth (index) finger is the only one usually able to stand erect steadily
tallimat	five; etymologically, "they [numbers] make an arm [*taliq*]"

For numbers six to nine, the Nunavik dialect has adopted an arithmetical pattern of numeration:

pingasuujurtut	six ("they are three more than once")
sitamaujunngigartut	seven ("they are not quite four more than once")
sitamaujurtut	eight ("they are four more than once")
quliunngigartut	nine ("they are not quite ten [*qulit*]")

In most other dialects (e.g., North Baffin), the number six is called *arviniliit* or *arvinilik* ("they have, or there is, a crossing"), an allusion to the fact that in finger-counting, one has to cross over from the left to the right hand. The next three numerals, however, resort to arithmetic (examples below are in North Baffin):

arviniliit marruungnik	seven ("they have crossings, two of them")
arviniliit pingasunik	eight ("they have crossings, three of them")
quliqanngituinnartut	nine ("they do not really have ten units")

The word for "ten" is *qulit* everywhere, although in western Nunavik *tallimaujurtut* ("they are five more than once") is also heard. *Qulit* means "upper parts," in this case the upper limbs, now complete since the ten fingers have been counted. Beyond that point, speakers carry on with arithmetic, in Nunavik (below) and several other dialects (e.g., North Baffin):

qulillu atausirlu	eleven ("and ten and one")
qulillu marruulu	twelve ("and ten and two")
qulillu quliunngigartulu	nineteen ("and ten and nine")

In Greenland, however, "eleven" is *aqqanillit*, "they have a downward motion," a clear allusion to the fact that speakers now have to use their toes for counting. In the Cape Dorset (southwest Baffin Island) speech of the early twentieth century, the allusion was clearer yet: the word for "eleven" was *itikkanuurtut*, "they are moving toward the feet."

Beyond number twenty (*avatit*, "limbs"), computing consists of *avatit*-based additions and multiplications:

avatillu atausirlu	twenty-one ("and twenty and one")
avatillu qulillu	thirty ("and twenty and ten")
avatillu qulillu marruulu	thirty-two ("and twenty and ten and two")
avatit marruuk	forty ("two [times] twenty")
avatit marruuk tallimallu	forty-five ("two [times] twenty and five")

avatit pingasut qulillu	seventy ("three [times] twenty and ten")
avatit tallimat	100 ("five [times] twenty")
avatit tallimat atausirlu	101 ("five [times] twenty and one")
avatit qulillu pingasullu	260 ("thirteen [times] twenty")

The culmination of this system is 400, *avatit avatit* ("twenty [times] twenty") or *avatimmarik* ("a complete twenty"). It is theoretically possible to go further, as the Catholic missionary in Quaqtaq once tried, preaching about the 5,000 people Jesus fed by the multiplication of loaves (Luke 9:14). However, everyone in the congregation answered negatively when the missionary asked if they had understood how many people were present: *avatit avatit qulillu marruulu qulillu*, "twenty [times] twenty [times] ten-and-two plus ten," i.e., 20 x ([20 x (10 + 2)] + 10) = 5,000.

Like most hunter-gatherers, Inuit did not need high numbers. Their arithmetic was limited by the concrete context of its usage (Denny 1981). The late Tuumasikallak, an elder from Kangirsuk (Nunavik), reported that during his youth at the beginning of the twentieth century, men sometimes held competitions whose winners were those who could reach the highest number in counting. The most skillful competitors were not able to exceed the figure sixty (Baillargeon et al. 1977, 101). In former times, beyond a certain number, objects needing to be counted were simply said to be *amisut* ("numerous").

People were not expected to own many possessions. In Nunavik, the word for "he/she is rich" is *atsuituq* (*ak&uittuq* in North Baffin and western Nunavut), "is not poor." *Atsuituq* is the negation of *atsujuq/ak&ujuq*, "he/she is poor," as if poverty was the usual lot of Inuit. Of course, these terms are one more instance of indirect or negative language, whereby individuals try not to look too assertive when speaking. In an egalitarian society, being "not poor" sounds less boastful and provocative than being "rich." The word *iluittuq* ("that is entire, a whole quantity") offers another example of negative—and metaphoric—language, since its literal meaning is "that has no inside" (i.e., "that does not hold any hollowed cavity [and thus forms one solid block]"). It might be surmised that *iluittuq* and *iluunnatik* ("all of them") share a common word-base, but this is not the case. According to Fortescue et al. (2010, 117, 140), the PE etymon of the latter term is *əlu(r)-* ("all, whole," maybe related to *əlur*, "width"), while that of the former is *ilu-* ("inside"). It should be recalled from Chapter 4 that in Nunavik, southern Baffin Island,

and Labrador, *iluunnatik* means "all of them" and *tamarmik*, "both of them," while everywhere else, it is *tamarmik* that means "all." Note that the base *tama(r)-* in *tamarmik* also seems to occur as an affixed enclitic (see Appendix), *-tamaat* ("all, each of them"), as in *ullu*tamaat ("every day"); *-tamaat* is distinct from *-limaaq*, "all of it" (cf. *ullu*limaaq, "all day [long]").

As the preceding paragraphs suggest, the traditional numerical system was not really fit to handle large numbers. When *Qallunaat* traders started buying the furs, skins, ivory, whale oil, and other commodities produced by Inuit, they assigned a monetary value to each item they bought, as well as to the goods they sold in exchange. People thus became acquainted with *kiinaujaq* ("that looks like a face"), "money," in the form of tokens issued by the Hudson's Bay Company and other trading concerns at first, before regular coins and banknotes started circulating in the Arctic. Quite rapidly, it seems, Inuit adopted English numerals—Danish ones in Greenland[19]—at least for figures exceeding *qulit* ("ten") or *avatit* ("twenty"). During my first stays in Nunavik in the mid-1960s, monolingual speakers, including most elders, were able to count in English. Nowadays, Inuktitut numbers from one to five as well as the terms for "ten," and sometimes "twenty," are still heard, but English is generally preferred for counting.

Trade thus transformed the mode of numeration of Inuit, in the same way that Christianity modified their relation to time, as discussed in Chapter 3. The notion of "exchange value," *aki* ("that is opposite to something [i.e., that can take the place of a barterable good]"), took a monetary connotation. The most common meaning of *aki* became "price," as in "*Qaritaujarma* aki*nga, taalait turi untirit vivti nain*"—"The price of my computer [is] $359 [cf. *taala*, "dollar"]." Current derivatives of *aki* include the following:

akilirpaa	he/she pays it ("provides it with an opposite")
akilitsaq	debt ("that is to have a price [i.e., to be paid back]")
akitujuq	costly, expensive ("that has a big price")
akikittuq	cheap, inexpensive ("that has a small price")

The difference between simple barter and commercial trade is best illustrated in the way the word *aki* is used. If, for instance, a hunter wants to exchange something against one of his dogs, he would ask, "*Sunamik akiqarpa?*"—"What is its [dog's] *aki*?" The answer might be, "*Qukiutimik akiqartuq"*—"Its *aki* [exchange value] is a gun." But if the hunter wants to sell his dog, it would rather be the potential buyer who would ask, *"Akinga qatsit?"*—"Its *aki* [is] how much [*qatsit*]?"[20] The seller might answer, *"Nainiti taalanik akiqartuq"*—"Its *aki* [price] is ninety dollars"; or to make it short, *"Nainiti taalarartuq"*—"It gets [*-rar-*] ninety dollars"; or shorter yet, *"Nainititurtuq"*—"It eats [*-tur-*] ninety."

In Inuktitut, the notions of selling and buying are subsumed under a single verbal base, *niuvir-* ("to participate in an exchange of goods, to barter, to trade"), possibly related to Proto-Yupik *navər(ar)-* ("to borrow or exchange"; Fortescue et al. 2010, 242). Both seller and buyer are *niuvirtuuk* ("two who exchange goods"), but a professional trader or storekeeper is a *niuvirti* (see above). Something offered for sale is a *niuviatsaq* ("that is to be sold/bought").

Another important semantic consequence of the arrival of *Qallunaat* in the Arctic was the introduction of the concept of "work." Pre-contact Inuit had words for various specific tasks linked to the production or transformation of goods, but apparently no general term for "working." One could, for instance, be hunting (*uumajursiutuq*, "searches for animals"), fishing (*iqalunniatuq*, "deals with fish"), erecting a snow house (*illuliurtuq*, "builds a house"), making or repairing a tool or another object (*sanajuq*, "fashions something"), or sewing (*mirsu[r]tuq*, "sews"), but these occupations were not considered as belonging to a special category of activities. They were just ways of doing something (*pijuq*, "does"; *sunngi[t]tuq*, "is not doing anything").

Things changed with the introduction of money and wage work. Some activities, such as trapping for trade or doing something in exchange for payment, became seen as different from other daily tasks, especially since missionaries taught that these occupations were strictly forbidden on Sundays. For instance, carving stone, ivory, or bone figurines in order to sell them was dubbed *sananngua(r)niq* ("the fact of pretending to fashion something"). A new notion corresponding more or less to the European concept of "work" thus appeared. This concept was progressively extended to all subsistence activities, as these became increasingly likely to generate some money—and were forbidden on Sundays, even when done without any idea of financial gain. During the 1960s, I often heard indefatigable hunters or seamstresses being referred to as "people who work a lot" (*pinasuttualuit*).

The new notion had to be given a name. Because such names were coined separately in various areas of the Arctic, the current words for "working" often vary from one Inuit dialect to another:

savaktuq	Alaskan Inupiaq, Inuvialuktun, Inuinnaqtun ("works on something")
pilirijuq	Kivalliq ("is occupied with something")
irqanaijartuq	North and South Baffin, Kivalliq ("is completing a task")
pinasuttuq	Nunavik ("strives to do something")
suliatsaqavuk	Labrador ("has something to be done")
sulivuq	Greenlandic ("is occupied at making something")

Now that employment, whether salaried or for oneself, has become ubiquitous among Inuit, words like *irqanaijartuq* and *pinasuttuq* are heard very frequently. In Nunavik, any steady worker is a *pinasutti* ("one who works on a regular basis")—and also a *sanaji* ("one who fashions things") if an artisan—but there exist specific terms, which often include the composite affix *-liriji* ("one who deals with something") for different types of jobs: *illuliriji* ("who deals with houses [carpenter]"), *aulautiliriji* ("who deals with motors [mechanic]"), *ikumaliriji* ("who deals with electricity [electrician]"), *inuusiliriji* ("who deals with the life of people [social worker]"), *ilinnianiliriji* ("who deals with education [curriculum designer]"), and so on.

Work, dollars, and commerce can thus be considered as fully fledged Inuit realities. Along with schools and the English language, they belong to what Saali, my adoptive father from Quaqtaq, called the *kiinaujaliurutiit* ("means for fabricating money"), contrasting them, without denying their usefulness, to the already discussed *maqainniq* ("travelling on the land") (see Chapter 2).

Food

In modern Inuit communities, diet generally consists of a mix of local ("country") and imported ("southern") victuals (*niqi*, "food"). The former (*Inuit niqitsangit*, "food items of Inuit"), usually laid out on a cardboard on the floor of the kitchen or living room, are eaten with the hands and a knife (*savik* for men, *ulu* for women), while the latter (*Qallunaat niqitsangit*, "food items of *Qallunaat*") are served at the table (*saa*) and handled with a fork (*kapurqauti*, "means for thrusting in") and a spoon (*urviujaq*, "that looks like an *urviq* [traditional metal ornament]"; or *alutsauti*, "means for licking"). In Inuit homes, it is not infrequent at mealtime to see teenagers and adults eating country food on the floor, while children sit at a table displaying southern dishes such as spaghetti (*inaluujait*, "that look like intestines") or pork ribs (*kuukkusiviniq*, "former [i.e., dead] pig") with potatoes (*patiitasi*, from the English "potatoes").

We saw in Chapter 2 that the traditional diet consisted essentially of game meat such as *tuttuviniq* ("dead caribou") and *natsiviniq* ("dead ringed seal"). Nowadays, these are still eaten, whether raw, cooked, or as *qajuq* ("meat or fish broth"), but in larger communities, game is not always available. Southern food, bought in local stores or ordered on the internet (*qaritaujakkut*, "by way of what looks like a brain [i.e., a computer]") or by phone (*uqalautikkut*, "by way of what is used to talk for a long time"), thus accounts for an important and often prevalent part of the modern diet.

Several *Qallunaat* food items, some of them mentioned in the preceding chapters, have been known for over 100 years,[21] such as the following (in northeastern Nunavik):

sanaugaq	flour ("manufactured [food] item")
tii, kaapi	tea, coffee (from the English "tea," "coffee")
pitatsaq	sugar ("something fit for being added [to food]")
qatsiugaq	oatmeal, porridge ("that has been made into a soup")
tariuq	salt ("[the] salty [one]," i.e., saltwater)
qarqujaq	biscuit ("piece of cooked and dried meat")

To these early imported culinary staples should be added *tupaaki* ("tobacco," a word borrowed from the English), used at first for chewing (*uqummiasajaq*, "stuff fit for being kept in the mouth")—chewing gum is *kutsuq* ("chewable tree resin")—and then for smoking the pipe (*supuurutituinnaq*, "genuine *supuuruti*") or cigarettes (*supuurutiit*, "means for blowing a long time"), lighted with *matsisiit* (from the English "matches").

Among other, more recently imported items, the following can be mentioned:

pata	butter (from the English)
papa	pepper (from the English)

uaniujaq	onion (probably from the English, with affix *-ujaq*, "that looks like")
usuujaq	carrot, sausage ("that looks like a penis")
pattaujaq	orange ("that looks like a ball")
qupirruajuit	rice ("little bugs")
suitisi	candy (from the English "sweets")
jama	jam (from the English)
imiraq	soft drink, juice ("little water"; as distinguished from *imialuk*, "big water [i.e., alcohol]")
immuk	milk ("human or animal milk")

We already saw in Chapter 5 that several *Qallunaat* food items were named according to their alleged similarity to body parts (e.g., *usuujaq* above). It is also noteworthy that in the field of nutrition, the proportion of words borrowed from English is higher than in other semantic domains. This is probably due to the fact that items such as tea (*tii*) or butter (*pata*) were so different from pre-contact foodstuffs that they could not be likened to any element of traditional Inuit culture. As a consequence, they were borrowed together with their English appellation, the pronunciation of which was adapted to the phonology of Inuktitut. Because of generalized bilingualism, this is not the case anymore. Imported food items are often designated by their English name, and modern culinary borrowings such as pizza or sushi have never received an Inuit appellation.

Government and Administration

At the end of Chapter 4, we saw that traditional Inuit groups did not have formal chiefs. As long as they were physically fit, male family heads played a leading part in organizing hunting expeditions, moving camps, and overseeing the sharing of meat after the hunt. In Nunavik, these leaders were called *angajurqaat* ("parents") and/or *ataniit* (singular *ataniq*, "the fact of being attached [to each other]"). Being united like a family and living in harmony was the primary social ideal of pre-contact Inuit.

The advent of commercial trade introduced another form of leadership. *Qallunaat* chief traders, who provided hunters and trappers with imported goods, became known as *angajurqaat*, while their assistants were *angajurqaasuit* ("lesser parents, lesser chiefs"). Canadian Inuit were told by the traders and missionaries (*ajuqirtuijiit*, "teachers") that they should obey the supreme overseer of their land, the British *ataniq* ("king/queen").

After the Second World War, a new ruling entity became predominant in Canada's Arctic: *kavama* or *gavama* ("government"). From its federal seat in Ottawa, this anonymous body of *angajurqaat* started exercising a quasi-parental authority over Inuit, deciding what was good or bad for them. To implement its policies, *kavama* dispatched various representatives to the North: policemen (*puliisiit*),[22] teachers (*ilisaijiit*), nurses (*aanniasiurtiit*), and, above all, *inulirijiit* ("those who deal with people")—the administrators responsible for developing permanent communities, as well as distributing family and old age allowances (*piarait/ittuit kiinaujangit*, "children's/old people's money") and other financial aids. Together with traders and missionaries, these people belonged to an all-powerful caste of *Qallunaaraaluit* ("Big *Qallunaat*").

In Nunavik, from the 1960s on, another *kavama* started deploying its own policemen, teachers, and administrators: the Quebec provincial government. The local Inuit at this point established a distinction between the federal *kavamaaluk* or *kavamatuqaq* ("big" or "old government") and provincial *kavamaapik* or *kavama nutaaq* ("little" or "new government") administrations. Both ruling bodies encouraged Inuit to vote (*niruartuq*, "he/she chooses someone or something") in elections, even though their tiny demographic size deprived Inuit of any influence on legislation making.

The situation changed in the next decade (1970s), when the progressive settlement of Aboriginal claims endowed Inuit with new, semi-autonomous legislative and administrative bodies (*timiit*). In Canada, as seen in Chapter 1, these changes gave the word *nuna* ("land") a new dimension: that of a territory partly or totally owned and administered by its Indigenous occupants (e.g., Nunavut, Nunavik, Nunatsiavut). Nowadays for instance, besides *Kanataup kavamanga* ("the government of Canada"), there exists a *Nunavut kavamanga* ("the government of Nunavut"), whose prerogatives are similar to those of a provincial legislature, with members of the legislative assembly (*maligaliurtiit*, "those who make laws"), a premier (*sivulirti Nunavummi*, "the one who leads in Nunavut"), and government ministers (*ministait*, singular *minista*).

In Nunavik, the James Bay and Northern Quebec Agreement of 1975 has instituted a regional administration, the *Kativik nunalilimaat kavamangat* ("Kativik [place for uniting] government of all villages"). Each village (*nunalik*, "that has land") possesses its own municipal administration (*kavamaapik*, "little government"), with an elected mayor (*sivulirti*, "the one who leads")[23] and councillors (*katimajiit*, "those who meet or join together"; this word also applies to the members of any committee or assembly).

All over the contemporary North, there now exist codified laws (*maligait*, "which are followed") and rules (*piqujait*, "which are ordered"). Public justice (*maligaliriniq*, "the fact of dealing with laws") is administered by judges (*irqatuijiit*, "those whose task is to remember [one's deeds]") sitting in a tribunal (*irqatuivik*, "place for remembering frequently"). Individuals who are found guilty (*saasimatsijuq*, "he/she faces [his/her crime]") may be sent to jail (*parnanairsivik*, "place where one is not anymore made ready [to leave]"), even though modern Inuit, like their predecessors, favour measures for restoring social harmony (*saimmautigutiit*, "means for making people at peace") rather than punishment (*akigiarniq*, "the fact of getting a retribution [for one's misdeeds]").[24]

Social Organizations and Leisure Activities

Besides federal, territorial (or provincial), regional, and municipal governing bodies, the Canadian Arctic is also home to a number of non-governmental organizations. The most important among them, economically and socially, is probably the co-operative movement, present in the North since the early 1960s. In Inuktitut, it is generally known as *kuapakkut* ("*kuapa* [from the English abbreviation "co-op"] people") or *katujjiqatigiit* ("the group of those who team together"). Almost all Inuit villages have their co-op store, and the word *kuapalialaurta!* ("let's go to the co-op!") is commonly heard when people want to go shopping.

In Nunavik, there also exist regional organizations established under the James Bay and Northern Quebec Agreement. These include the Makivik Corporation (*Makivvik*, "Place for raising up"), whose mandate (*tilijausimaguti*, "means for doing something that has been commanded") is to work at the general development (*pivallianiq*, "the fact of doing something more and more"; or *pirurpalianiq*, "progressive growth") of Quebec Inuit. In the field of education, the Kativik School Board (*Kativik ilisarniliriniq*, "Kativik, the fact of dealing with teaching") administers Nunavik schools and trains its own teachers of Inuktitut. As far as health and social services are concerned, a dedicated board (*ilusilirinirmut katimajiit*, "those who meet concerning the fact of dealing with the state of health") oversees the operation of the regional hospitals and nursing stations.

Even though Inuit work hard and, with the proliferation of Indigenous and other (e.g., church) organizations, have many occasions to attend meetings and participate in committees, they can still find time to indulge in leisure activities (*pinngua[r]tuq*, "he/she pretends to do something [i.e., plays]"), which have become increasingly diversified with the introduction of imported toys (*pinnguat*, "imitations of things") and games. In modern communities, traditional pastimes such as visiting and telling tales have declined—but not disappeared—over the last decades (see the first section of this chapter), replaced as they were by television and the internet. Some older games are still played, though: *qijugait* ("little [pieces of] wood"), checkers or cards; and *ataniirtut* ("they take each other's king"), chess, also called *inugait* ("little persons") in some places after a traditional game played with seal knuckle-bones. Among other ancient games mentioned by Saladin d'Anglure (2013, 199–200), such as *ajagaq* ("that is shoved away [cup-and-ball]") and *ajaraaq* ("string figures"; possible etymology, "that is barely shoved away" [Fortescue et al. 2010, 64]), only *katajjaniq* ("throat singing"; literally, "falling repeatedly," maybe an allusion to the drumstick beating the *qilauti* [traditional drum])[25] seems to have survived. *Illukitaarniq* ("juggling"; literally, "using both of them [hands] repeatedly") is occasionally performed, but the traditional juggling songs are only known to elders—although some children may now learn them in Inuit language classes.

Sports commonly practised include *ajuttaq* ("soccer, football"), *pattak* ("ball"; related to *patit-/patik-*, "to slap or clap")—a baseball bat is an *anaullauti* ("means for striking something with a stick")—racing (*ullautigiaq*, "running together"), *haki* ("hockey"), ice skating (*siarrijariaq*, "slipping continuously"), downhill tobogganing or skiing (*siturariaq*, "sliding repeatedly"), and swimming (*puijjurariaq*, "swimming repeatedly"). Recreation also includes communal dancing (*tanasiq*, from the English "dance") and playing musical instruments. Instruments currently heard in Inuit communities are:

kukittapauti	guitar ("means for using one's fingernails repeatedly")
agiaruti	violin ("means for acting as if one was filing")

nijjauti	accordion ("means for emitting a sound")
niinigaq	piano or organ (mostly electronic) ("that which one has pressed with his/her hands")
anaullagaq	drum ("that is struck with a stick")

Finally, besides computers (*qaritaujait*, "those that look like brains"), leisure activities involving some measure of technology include photography (*ajjiliuriaq*, "making an image [i.e., photographing something]") and cinema (*tarralijaariaq*, "making a reflection [i.e., projecting a movie]").

Conclusion

Inuit are an eminently social people, expected to utter greetings upon passing someone else and to exchange a few words if time allows. The most common salutation, *Ai!* is usually preceded by the name of the greeted person (e.g., "*Miajingai!*" — "Hi, Mary!") in order to make this person comfortable. Greeting also implies the establishment of a bond between both interlocutors, since the greeted individual should acknowledge the greeter by answering, "*Aa!*" or "*Ii!*" — "Yes!" and normally return the salutation.

People expect to live in harmony, and one way to achieve this is to use words and phrases that do not risk sounding aggressive or intrusive. Indirect speech and negative utterances enable speakers to minimize the impact of assertions that their interlocutor might find uncomfortable. For example, instead of asking, "How are you?" Inuit prefer to say, "*Qanuippit?*" — "Is there something problematic with you?" and in Nunavik, visitors may be greeted with "*Tujurminak!*" — "Don't feel bored or homesick!" Direct questions can be softened thanks to the affix *-galuar/-raluar* ("however"), as in "*Aullalangagaluarqit?*" — "However, will you be leaving soon?" This is less intrusive than "*Aullalangavit?*" — "Are you about to leave?" Linguistic attenuation also works with imperatives. Instead of giving a direct order such as "*Itsivagit!*" — "Sit down!" social interaction is smoother with "*Itsivalirit!*" — "Be about to sit!" or "*Itsivalaurit!*" — "May you have sat down!" In former times, these means for enhancing sociability through the linguistic expression of politeness undoubtedly contributed to allowing Inuit families and semi-nomadic bands to preserve their unity, avoid violence, and remain socially functional.

With the establishment of larger settled communities, endowed with all the trappings of contemporary North American culture, traditional sociability has been partially undermined. However, many of its supporting values and practices were preserved,[26] and recently achieved political, social, and cultural autonomy has endowed Inuit with educational and other tools enabling them to work efficiently at developing their identity (*inuuniq*, "being Inuit") in the midst of the modern world. As we shall now see, there is no doubt that the words of their language can play a major part in this process.

Words for the Future

Ammalu uqausiup aippanganik ilinniaramik amisunillu
asinginnik uqausirnik inuttitut, makkuagalait asingit
ilinniatangit ajjigiinngituillu, tamakkuangummata
uqumaittuuqattasimajupaaluk nurqainarpatullu
ajjigiinngitunik pijjutiqarsutik.

They [students] are taught in a second language, while
having to learn many new words in Inuktitut and
studying several different subjects. In view of all that,
the situation is always very heavy for them and they
just drop out of school, even though they would have
various opportunities [if they graduated].

EVA DEER (2015, 72)

As we conclude our stroll through the language of Inuit, it is time to summarize some salient aspects of the semantic materials described and discussed in
the preceding chapters. We must also reflect upon the part semantics might
play in supporting the identity and cultural future of those who speak the Inuit language. As suggested in the quotation above, uttered by an experienced
educator, such a reflection should be of particular importance to the young
because they live in a context that is "always very heavy" (*uqumaittuuqattasimajupaaluk*). Besides being taught their Indigenous tongue, students have
to learn to behave functionally in a predominantly English-speaking world
that extends far beyond their native communities.

Words, Etymologies, and Microsystems
The lexical materials gleaned during our strolls belong almost entirely to
Inuktitut, the group of Inuit dialects in use in western Hudson Bay, Baffin

Island, Nunavik (Arctic Quebec), and Labrador. More specifically, the words
we discussed were generally drawn from the subdialect spoken in northeastern Nunavik, for the simple reason it is the one I am most familiar with.

In Inuktitut, an effect of polysynthesis[1] is that when words are parsed into
their constituent parts, they often yield an underlying signification differing
from although related to their current meaning. Sometimes, this signification
is easily decipherable by speakers of the language, as with the term *qaritaujaq*, "computer"—which literally means, "one looking like [*-ujaq*] a brain
[*qarita(q)-*]"—even though a majority of bases and affixes resist immediately
achievable parsing. However, by resorting to etymology—whether based on
reconstructed Proto-Eskimo and Proto-Inuit roots, or on a semantic comparison between current morphemes—it becomes possible to elicit tentative
hidden significations useful for digging deeper into Inuit thought, as demon-
strated by the word *siqiniq*, "sun": "splashing, sprinkling [of light]."

Our strolls through six different semantic domains—environment and
land; animals and subsistence activities; humans and spirits; family, kinship,
and naming; the human body; socializing in the contemporary world—have
disclosed a number of words, over 1,400 of them, expressing various aspects
of Inuit culture. In many cases, the analysis proposed for these words yielded
explicit or metaphorical descriptions of the function, behaviour, or appearance of the notions, persons, or objects they denote. Here are a few examples:

atausiq	number one ("means for being in one piece")
inuusuttuq	youth, young adult ("one who strives to be a person")
qarqaq	hill, mountain ("high area")
tasiq	lake ("that stretches out")
natsiq	ringed seal ("nodding head")
uummati	heart ("what gives life")

Some words offer a direct entry into traditional symbolism. For instance,
the term *silatujuq*, "who has much *sila*" (i.e., "is wise, intelligent") refers to the
fact that all human beings possess within themselves an encapsulated bubble
of *sila* ("outdoor, weather," and by extension, the whole world), the air they
breathed when uttering their first cry at birth. Similarly, the word *arsa(r)-
niit* ("games of ball") designates the northern lights because this natural

phenomenon was understood to be a reflection of the souls of the dead who played soccer in the sky. Another seemingly symbolic appellation is *kivgaluk* or *kivvaluk* ("muskrat"), whose literal meaning is "the little messenger."

In several cases, morphosemantics (deciphering the underlying significations of words through the semantic analysis of their morphemes) has allowed us to elicit microsystems of meaning, in other words, lexical groupings whose combined components generate a significant discourse. In the field of the environment (Chapter 1), the names of the seasons exemplify one such system.

In northeastern Nunavik—and elsewhere too, with a few minor differences—the terms denoting the seasons start with the word-bases *uki-* or *upi-*. The *uki-* seasons are those during which the land and water are freezing or frozen. These are, in reverse chronological order, *ukiuq*, "winter" (of unknown etymology), *ukiaq*, "fall" ("lesser *ukiuq*"), and *ukiatsaq*, "early fall" ("incoming *ukiaq*"). As for the *upi-* months, they comprise (again in reverse order) *upirngaaq*, "summer" (possibly, "that is surprised or suprising at first"),[2] *upirngaalaaq*, "early summer" ("very small *upirngaaq*"), and *upirngasa(a)q*, "springtime" ("incoming *upirngaaq*"). These six words thus tell us about an opposition between the glacial and warmer periods of the year, and the progression that can be observed within each, from an incipient ("surprising" in the case of thaw) to a full manifestation of freezing or thawing.

Another semantic system concerns the classes or genera of animal species (*uumajuit*, "those who are alive"). There are six of them in Nunavik (Chapter 2), designated according to their respective habitats. Three groups of species are defined as occupying specific portions of *sila* ("the outside"): *iqaluit* ("fish") dwell in salt or fresh water (*imaq, imiq*); *pisuttiit* ("the walkers," i.e., land mammals) roam the land (*nuna*); and *timmiat* ("those that fly," i.e., birds) spend a large part of their time soaring across the air (*sila* in a restricted sense). The three remaining groups are defined as overlapping different habitats: *puijiit* ("those appearing out of water," i.e., sea mammals) intersect the boundary between water and the air they must breathe; *tininnimiutait* ("inhabitants of beach areas uncovered at low tide," i.e., shellfish) live in water at high tide and on land (the beach) the rest of the time, thus overlapping *imaq* and *nuna*; and finally, *qupirruit* ("those that are split [between various habitats?]," i.e., bugs) are found in all three zones—water, land, and air. The names of the genera thus teach a crash course in animal ecology.

In the combined fields of human behaviour (Chapter 3) and kinship relations (Chapter 4), the morphosemantic analysis of the words for "woman" (*arnaq*), "male man" (*anguti*), "husband" (*ui*), and "wife" (*nuliaq*) might reveal how sexual relations operate. According to a tentative, etymologically unproved interpretation, *arnaq* ("one who agitates something") would set *anguti* ("means for catching") in motion. Once agitated, *anguti*, in his role of *ui* ("one with a protuberance"), would catch *nuliaq* ("little female in heat" or "one who undergoes copulation"),[3] who, in her capacity as *arnaq*, would agitate *anguti* anew, thus perpetuating the reproductive cycle of humanity.

Rather than having a tale to tell, the terms denoting the principal parts of the human body (Chapter 5) offer a description of the relative importance and position of the trunk, head, and limbs. In Inuktitut, the word usually translated as "body," *timi*, applies primarily to the trunk. Semantically, it refers to a central and higher location (*timaani*, "in its *timi*") in relation to a periphery. Indeed, many speakers do not consider that the trunk's peripherals, the head and limbs, belong to *timi*, properly speaking. Accordingly, a possible gloss of the term for "head," *niaquq*, is "an attached part that is bending," while the limbs, *avatit*, are "those that surround something."

With their ten fingers and ten toes, the limbs have always been used by Inuit as a means for counting. This is why several words pertaining to the traditional numerical system consist of metaphors inspired by anatomy (Chapter 6):

pingasut	three; etymologically related to *pingna*, "this one up there" (an allusion to the third, longest finger)
tallimat	five; "they [numbers] make an arm" (with its five fingers)
arvinilik	six; "there is a crossing" (from one hand to the other)
qulit	ten; "upper parts" (the upper limbs)
aqqanillit	eleven (in Greenlandic Kalaallisut); "they have a downward motion" (from the fingers to the toes)
avatit	twenty; "the limbs" (ten fingers and ten toes)

The preceding paragraphs exemplify the semantic possibilities of a polysynthetic language like Inuktitut. By constructing words whose underlying meaning suggests a definition of their surface signification, and by grouping these words into microsystems of meaning, Inuktitut provides its speakers with fragments of discourse that help to explain various aspects of the surrounding universe.

A Morphosemantic Model

Even if the meaningful microsystems elicited in the preceding chapters concern a variety of semantic fields, they are far from including a majority, or even a large minority of the words gleaned during our strolls. Therefore, this book cannot claim to offer an exhaustive and totally structured image of traditional Inuit thinking as expressed through language. More research is needed in order to elicit other systems of meaning and relate them to each other.[4] However, by outlining the semantic relationships among some of the key terms pertaining to each field examined in this book, it is still possible to propose a tentative model of the underlying world view revealed through morphosemantic analysis.

Top and centre of this model (Figure 2) stands the word *sila*. We saw that this term has several interrelated meanings: "the outside, weather, air, intelligence." In its broadest signification, *sila* refers to the fundamental principle that regulates the seasons, the movements of the heavenly bodies and those of the animals, as well as human *isuma* ("reason, thought"). Inuit lexicographer Taamusi Qumaq (1991) describes *sila* as void and ethereal, contrasting it with *nuna* ("land, solid ground, earth") that is solid and firm.

Nuna is encompassed within *sila*, as is *qilak* ("that weaves a net over *nuna* [?]"), the sky, with its luminaries: *siqiniq* ("splashing, sprinkling"), the sun; *tarqiq* ("light, beautiful obscurity"), the moon; and *ulluriat* ("emissions of daylight"), the stars and planets. In Inuit cosmology, the importance of *nuna* comes right after that of *sila* because *nuna* supports life, providing humans (and animals) with all they need to survive and reproduce. Etymologically, the second syllable of the word *nuna* might refer to the fact of being located somewhere, and indeed, a genuine *nuna* is a location inhabited by humans, any unoccupied space being deemed *nunagijaunngi(t)tuq* ("not held as a *nuna*").

Broadly speaking, *nuna* ("land, territory") includes two major elements: *nuna* proper ("solid ground, earth") and *imaq* ("water, especially the sea"). Both elements harbour life, human and animal, as well as plants (*pirurtuit*, "the growing ones"), whether *nunajait* ("pieces of *nuna*," i.e., lichens, moss, and berries) or seaweed. *Uumajuit* ("the living ones"), animals, are

Figure 2. A Morphosemantic Model of Some Inuit Keywords.

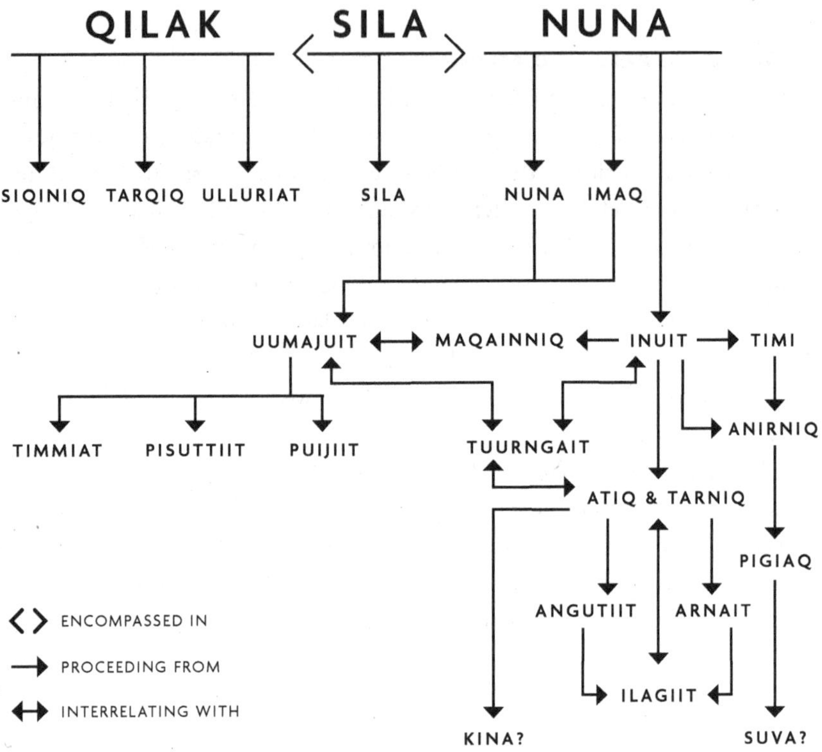

subdivided, as seen above, into a number of genera and species whose principal habitat is terrestrial (e.g., *pisuttiit*, land mammals), marine (e.g., *puijiit*, sea mammals), or connected to *sila*—here with the restricted meaning of "air" (e.g., *timmiat*, birds).

In contrast to animals, which are related to only one element or overlap the boundary between two of them (water and air in the case of *puijiit*), *inuit*, humans, proceed directly from *nuna*, because they are able to live on both land and water (in the latter case, thanks to boats or snow houses built on the sea ice).[5] Many of them fly in airplanes, and some even reach *qilak*, the sky: the shamans of yore visiting the moon spirit, as well as modern astronauts. The double etymology of the word *inuk* ("living body" and "owner/animator") defines humans as animated beings who are able to decide how to manage their surroundings, thus reflecting their agency in relation to land and sea.

In order to feed and (formerly) clothe themselves, *inuit* must catch animals (*uumajuit*). This is done by way of *maqainniq* (possibly, "not to carry a kayak on one's own shoulders," i.e., using hunting gear the way it should be), travelling and living on the land in search of game. *Maqainniq* aims at provoking encounters between men and their prey. These contacts (expressed by the affix -*si*-, "to encounter") include several stages and must show respect toward animals. *Uumajuit* are sentient creatures who know how generous those who hunt them are. Thus, far from being just a kill, *uumajursiu(r)niq* ("searching for animals, hunting") is a highly moral activity.

Both men and animals have a *timi* ("central position"), a body that is kept alive thanks to *anirniq* ("vital breath"), a type of soul that allows bodies to involve themselves in action (*pigiaq*, "doing") but disappears at death. Humans possess two other personal souls, while animals seemingly share in their species's collective soul. One of the personal souls is *tarniq* ("being dark"), a human-like shadow that survives death and should, ideally, reach *qilak*, the sky (and heaven). The other soul is *atiq*, the name. When a baby is named after a deceased or elderly person, this individual is revived in a new body (that thus transits through an old name), and his or her identity is at least partly transmitted to the child. Hence the etymology of the word *atiq*: "being the same."

Inuit can be either male (*angutiit*, "means for being big or [?] for catching") or female (*arnait*, "who agitate [?]"). As mentioned earlier, these words possibly refer to the respective roles of men and women in the reproductive cycle (and sexual act), men being attracted by women in order to be able to catch them. This process generates *ilagiit* ("those who are component parts for each other"), families. Each family member is an *ila* ("part"), an element of the whole group they form together. There thus exists a necessary relationship between individuals (*ilait*) and their families (*ilagiit*) because by definition, all "parts" must belong to a whole, and all groups of "components" must be made out of individual parts.

Inuit families include relatives by blood, marriage, or adoption. Moreover, through the interrelation of *ilagiit* with *atiq*, the name soul, family members reincarnate the individuals whose names they bear, and the reincarnation of these names revives the kinship relations that once linked their former bearers. For instance, if my daughter is named after my mother, I would call her *anaana* ("mummy") rather than *panik* ("daughter").

Together with *inuit* and *uumajuit*, *atiq* is interrelated with *tuurngait*, "spirits." These suprahuman beings are invisible to most people, but shamans (*angakkuit*; possible etymology, "skilled at moving and getting free") could see them thanks to their enlightening power (*qaumaniq*, "diffusing light"). More importantly, *angakkuit* enlisted *tuurngait* as their familiar spirits, in order to heal people or bring animals and good weather back. Some of these helpers were *uumajuit* with special powers. Other spirits were the souls of deceased shamans who offered their help to someone reincarnating them by bearing their name. This may explain the etymology of the word *tuurngait*: "those who have been secured," that is, those whom *angakkuit* have bound into a lifelong intimate relationship.

As a final note, this morphosemantic model generates two questions. One, *kina?* ("who is he/she?") proceeds from *atiq*, and the other, *suva?* ("what happens?"), from *pigiaq* ("action"). Both interrogations are primarily related to *inuit*, as they seek to inquire about human identity and doings, although *suva?* can also refer to any type of occurrence. But since *inuit* proceed from *nuna*, itself encompassed within *sila*, *kina?* and *suva?* bring us back to the top of the model, inviting us to consider Inuit words as a possible source of reflection on the place of human beings within the larger world.

Words for the Future

The words discussed in the preceding chapters and schematized in the model above leave us with a thesaurus or repertoire of semantic images that open a door on Inuit thought. As I mentioned at the start of our strolls, modern speakers of Inuktitut and other Inuit dialects do not always have access to these images, which either consist of hidden—and often tentative—significations elicited through an etymological or comparative analysis of bases and affixes, or, when decipherable in current morphology, are superseded by their more immediate meanings. The word *ajagutaq* ("rainbow") exemplifies the latter situation. Its underlying signification of "sky-splitter" can be easily inferred by speakers, but it fades behind its surface meaning, exactly as the English term "rainbow" is not usually thought of as a bow that has to do with rain.

Despite the apparent difficulty in accessing many or most semantic images elicited throughout this book, I am convinced that the analyses at the source of the lexical materials discussed during our strolls are not useless. Our thesaurus introduces us to some of the basic cognitive signs and symbols undergirding the language and the culture it translates.[6] Because the contemporary linguistic expressions of these symbols, the Yupik languages and Inuit dialects, have remained very close to their Proto-Eskimo ancestor as far as word-bases, affixes, and grammar are concerned, we have every reason to believe that the semantic images they convey have preserved at least some of their significance. Consequently, we may suppose that if Inuit gain access to the underlying significations of their words, their language can help them reconnect with their deepest identity. Such a reconnection should be particularly useful to younger people who, as mentioned in the opening quotation, have a very heavy load to bear in this changing and expanding world.

The concepts of *sila* and *nuna* have the potential to play an important part in reinforcing personal and collective identity. In traditional Inuit thinking, *sila* is conceived as a kind of matrix that shelters and regulates everyone and everything. Those who behave *sila*-wise—who show respect and generosity toward people, animals, and the environment in general—can be confident that they act properly. Their behaviour will result in harmony with their family and community, and they will live at peace with themselves. If everyone behaves *sila*-wise, the whole world will experience moral reassurance (*saimmainiq*, "being consoled, at peace"). This way of thinking is reminiscent of Chinese Taoism, according to which everything in the universe is regulated by a supreme, non-personal principle, *qi*,[7] although in a modern Christian context, God might be considered as *sila*'s mover. This is what an Inuk teacher implicitly meant when I asked her, many years ago, who or what the grammatical subject to which the ending -*puq* ("he, she, it") was referring in the word *surujup*puq ("it rains"). Her answer was, "*Guutiunngilaq?*"— "Is it not God?"

Human beings are connected to *sila* through *nuna*, the land. In contrast to the all-encompassing void of *sila*, *nuna* is a grounded location, as possibly expressed by its second syllable, -*na* ("there"). It is important for contemporary Inuit to remember that their *nuna*, the land they inhabit, is a source of moral comfort that has always provided them with everything needed for making a living. Nowadays, on top of its natural resources, *inuit nunangat*, the land of Inuit, has become a provider of economic, social, political, and cultural power. By relying upon their rights of *nunaqarqaa(r)tuit* ("first owners of the [arctic] land"), Inuit are able to negotiate with the outside world all they need for developing a modern society, while preserving their own values and identity.

Like human beings, animals too are grounded in *nuna*, although their habitat is often limited to either solid land or water. Their appellation of *uumajuit* ("living beings") can be extended to humans because like them, they posses an *uummati* ("what gives life to a creature"), a heart. Humans and animals may thus be considered as belonging to the same family of animated sentient beings and for this reason, they should maintain an intimate relationship with each other. *Uumajuit* are not human, but they have their own ways of knowing and behaving, and, above all, willingness to offer themselves as prey.

As mentioned earlier, the very word designating humans, *inuit*, refers to their nature as animated beings, as well as to their status as "owners/animators"—individuals capable of deciding how they should deal with their surroundings. Being an *inuk*—or an ethnic Inuk—means that far from being powerless in the face of difficulties, one possesses agency over one's environment and life projects, whether as a "big guy" or "catcher" (*anguti*, male) or "agitator" (*arnaq*, female). This agency is grounded in *isuma*, reasonable thinking, an essentially human mental faculty that enables *inuit* to remember, to know, and to become aware of what is good or bad. *Isuma* is acquired progressively. Only *inummariit* ("complete persons") or *innait* ("completeness")— adults—and *inutuqait* ("long-standing persons")—elders—are fully endowed with it. No wonder, then, that adolescents and young adults, *inuusuttuit* ("those who are striving to be persons"), often appear to act in a slightly *isumaittuq* ("without *isuma*") way, which should be considered normal at their age: they have not yet become completely reasonable individuals. This might explain why a possible etymology of the word *isuma* could be "having reached the end [of acquiring reasonable thinking?]."

Knowledge acquired through *isuma* is called *qaujimaniq* ("the fact of having become aware"). This term starts with the word-base *qau-* ("light"). To know about something is to be enlightened. Therefore, it is the mental light generated by knowledge that entails awareness, which enables *inuit* to discriminate between what is good (*piujuq*, "that is something") or bad (*piunngi[t]tuq*, "that is not something"), convenient (*i&u-/isuartuq*) or inconvenient (*i&u-/isuittuq*), useful (*sunatsaujuq*, "that is fit for being or doing something") or useless (*aturatsau[n]ngittuq*, "that is unfit for being used"). Knowledge comes through learning. Traditionally, young Inuit learned by listening to their parents, watching adults, and trying to understand their surroundings, but nowadays school education and the electronic media must be added to this list.

Human beings belong to families, *ilagiit*, groups of closely interlinked "component parts." This means that as long as *inuit* are in contact with their *ilait*, the other "parts" of their family groups, they are not alone: there exist people on whom they can count. Kinship links extend beyond blood and adopted relatives. *Atiit*, names, transmit the identity and parental relations of their former bearers (the eponyms) to those who are given these names at birth. Individuals who have the same eponym share in a common identity. In Nunavik, they call each other *saunira*, "my bone," as if they were part of one body. This identity is also shared with their deceased eponym, their *sauniviniq* ("former bone"). In this way, Inuit are intimately linked, thanks to their *atiit*, to the generations of their ancestors whose identity they carry on in the contemporary world, and also their future descendants who will bear their names. For the young in particular, knowing who they formerly were and who they will be as persons tends to increase their self-awareness and their sense of continuity between past, present, and future.

The Inuit transmission of names parallels the reflections of psychologist Carl G. Jung (who proposed the concept of the collective unsconscious) on the perenniality of a person's identity. According to Jung, "Each woman extends back into her mother and forward into her daughter" because she transmits to the next generation the psychic part of the collective unconscious received from her mother. In this way, "a 'reconstruction' . . . of the life of the ancestors occurs and, by means of the bridge constituted by the present life of the isolated being, it is prolonged in future generations" (Jung and Kerényi 1968, 223). This is reminiscent of Inuit views about the *atiq* soul. Women or men who bear the name of one of their grandparents and have given the name of their own mother or father to their child *are*, at the same time, their parent's mother or father and their child's daughter or son, thus "[finding their] reasonable place in the life of the generations" (Jung and Kerényi 1968, 223).

The preceding paragraphs offer but a few examples of how inquiring about the underlying significations embedded in Inuit words can provide modern Indigenous residents of the Arctic with semantic tools useful for envisioning the full wealth of their culture and world view and, ideally, endow them with an enriched knowledge of who they are. Inuit speakers have long been interested in eliciting the hidden meanings of their words, and it is my hope that this will develop into a genuine tradition of etymological research. As an added bonus, learning about the morphosemantics of Inuktitut should give *Qallunaat*, non-Inuit, an opportunity to delve deeper into the intellect of a North American Aboriginal people that greatly deserves to be better understood.

Our semantic strolls have also outlined the intrinsic value and importance of the Inuit language. Its speakers have a very rich vocabulary at their disposal, words that can easily be used as bases for deriving neologisms. More importantly, these terms often allow Inuit to express ideas and describe their surroundings in a way that would not be possible in most other languages. This is the case, for instance, with localizers, adverbs and demonstratives that enable speakers to point out between ten and twenty different portions of space, with a specific word for each. Similarly, current Inuktitut has several hundred words pertaining to human anatomy, including very precise terms that are only known to medical doctors in *Qallunaat* languages. The importance of duality should also be mentioned. It finds its expression in a grammatical dual number and a propensity to classify entities into dyadic pairs. In view of these and previous examples elicited through semantic analysis, it is obvious that preserving the Inuit language must be a priority, exposed as it is to the potentially corrosive ubiquitous presence of English.

In 1985, the politicians and cultural activists preparing for what would become the Territory of Nunavut established a post-secondary training program for young Inuit. The objective of this curriculum was to provide Nunavut with Indigenous upper-level staff competent in *Qallunaat*-style administrative, business, and other professional practices, but also cognizant of Inuit culture, language, history, and values. Some thirty years later, a similar program aiming to "explore modern global issues from an Inuit perspective," according to its website (sivunitsavut.ca), was set up in Nunavik. Both curricula were given the same name, Sivuniksavut (or Sivunitsavut): "What will become our vanguard or future [*sivuniq*]," that is, our future leaders.

The word-base *sivuni(q)-* can be translated as "the forepart of something." But it also expresses anteriority in time, meaning "a period before now." Sivuniksavut graduates are expected to be the incoming leaders of Nunavut and Nunavik, while being simultaneously appointed to renew the Inuit past in their role of "future anteriority." This double definition seems particularly suitable for those who will replace and revive in a metaphorical way the former family and band leaders, whose power was also based on knowledge. But there will be a difference. Besides *inuit qaujimajatuqangit* ("the things that Inuit have known for long," traditional knowledge), the *sivuniksait* ("incoming vanguard") will have acquired all of the learning needed to lead their people into a global future, neither forgetting nor forfeiting who they have always been and shall continue to be: the *nunalituqait*, "long-standing landholders," of the North American Arctic.

Polysynthesis: A Big Word for Something Fairly Simple

Inuit piusirminik uqausirminillu aturmata
tukisiutigunnasiarsutik pijumajaminik
pijumanngitaminillu uqaqattautigunnasutik
qanutuinnalimaaq.

Inuit use their own customs and their own words, thus
being able to understand each other well and to discuss
what they want and what they do not want, and this on
absolutely any topic.

TAAMUSI QUMAQ (1988, 3)

As mentioned in the Introduction, Inuktitut and all other members of
the Eskimo-Aleut linguistic family are polysynthetic languages. The word
"polysynthetic" may look somewhat forbidding at first, but its meaning
is relatively simple. We saw that polysynthesis—"plural association" in
Greek—is the combination within a single word of a number of concepts
(conveyed by different morphemes, or word-internal significant units) that
many other languages would express by way of a whole sentence or, at least,
with more than one word. Most North American Aboriginal languages are
polysynthetic (Mithun 2017), as are a number of other tongues—Turkish,
for instance or, in a lesser way, Hungarian and Japanese.

As far as word formation is concerned, there exist two principal types of polysynthetic languages (Mattissen 2017, 74): affixal, where only one lexical root per
word is allowed, and compositional, allowing more than one root. Eskimo-Aleut
belongs to the first type (with only one word-base; see Introduction), while
Algonquian (e.g., Cree and Ojibwe) and Iroquoian (e.g., Mohawk) languages are
examples of the second (for an Iroquoian example, see Steckley 2007). Because

this book deals with the forms and meanings of polysynthetic Inuit words, it may be useful to give a brief description of the lexical and grammatical structure of Inuktitut. In order to do so, I adopt a distributive methodology; that is, an analysis of the combinative properties of Inuit words and morphemes. Examining the way these combine, or refuse to combine, with each other should enable us to elicit the four basic parts of speech of Inuktitut: verbs, nouns, localizers, and particles.[1] As with the other chapters of the book, most examples are drawn from the northeastern variety of the Nunavik dialect.

Words

Let us suppose we are observing two Inuit speakers from northeastern Nunavik addressing each other. We might note the following exchange from their conversation:

Inuinamisuuvut

Aiguuq tikittuqartungavanngat

Upon further observation, we would discover that our speakers sometimes change the order of some sequences in their utterances. For instance, they could say:

Amisuuvuninuit

Aiguuq avanngat tikittuqartuq

We could thus identify five speech units that seem to enjoy a degree of mobility, but whose constitutive parts cannot be handled independently:

(1) *inuit* (2) *amisuuvut* (3) *aiguuq* (4) *tikittuqartuq* (5) *avanngat*

By asking our speakers about the signification of these units, we would discover that each has its own meaning and that some of them express a complete statement, translatable as a sentence in English:

(1) "people" (2) "they are numerous" (3) "well!" (4) "there are arrivals" (5) "from there away"

Moreover, we would find that each unit enters into a specific syntactic relationship with the other units:

(1) subject (2) qualifying event (3) conjunction (4) event + object (5) spatial circumstance

These partly mobile speech units, each with their own meaning and grammatical function, may be defined as *words*. In the present example, they combine to form two sentences, uttered in turn by our two virtual speakers:

Inuit amisuuvut; or *Amisuuvut inuit*.

"There are many people."

Aiguuq tikittuqartuq avanngat; or *Aiguuq avanngat tikittuqartuq*.

"Well! There are [people] arriving from there away."

Word-Bases

Inuit words can be subdivided into smaller significant units, morphemes. Some morphemes (shown below in italics) always occur in word-initial position:

Inu(k)-it *amisu*-uvut *aiguuq tikit*-tuqartuq *av*-anngat

These are the basic units of the word, those that its total meaning rests upon. In our example, these units mean:

"human person" "many units" "well!" "to arrive" "there away"

These non-mobile (always in initial position) significant units that rule, so to speak, the semantics of the word are called *word-bases* (or stems, or radicals). Each word must contain one—and only one—word-base.

In the Nunavik dialect of Inuktitut, the word-base is often deleted in colloquial speech if it has previously occurred in the conversation and is implied by the speaker. In the following quotation—drawn from the autobiographical narrative of Eva Deer, an elder I recorded in Quaqtaq in 2013—missing bases are marked by a dash in Inuktitut and appear between square brackets in English:

*Ilinnialilaursimajunga -qataulaursimajunga. Taima
-juviniugaluarsunga...*

I have started to study, I have been a [school]-mate. So, after I had [done] that... (Deer 2015, 69).

Affixes

There is a second type of morpheme: units that always occur in the middle or at the end of a word. One word may include two or more of these units, whereas there is only one word-base—and the same unit may occur several times:

inu-*it*(1) amisu-*u*(2)-*vut*(3) tikit-*tu(q)*(4)-*qar*(5)-*tuq*(6) av-*anngat*(7)

These morphemes qualify, specify, or transform the initial meaning expressed in the word-base:

plural(1) "to be"(2) third-person(3) "one who"(4) "to have"(5) third-person(6) "from"(7)

These mobile (their position may vary) significant units added to a word-base—directly or after another mobile unit—are called *affixes*.

Categories of Affixes

According to their position within words and their semantic and/or grammatical functions, affixes may be classified into three broad categories: grammatical endings, derivational (or lexical) affixes, and enclitics.

Grammatical Endings

Grammatical endings (or endings, for short) generally occur in word-final position. All words—except for one limited category, that of particles—must end with an affix of that type and include only one of them, as in our example:

inu-*it* amisu-u-*vut* tikit-tu-qar-*tuq* av-*anngat*

Endings mark the syntactic function of the word (i.e., its relationship with other words) within a sentence:

-*it*: subject of an event (in the plural form)

-*vut*: person and mood of an event (third-person plural assertive)

-*tuq*: person and mood of an event (third-person singular indicative)

-*anngat*: spatial circumstance (in the ablative form ["from"])

Note that in this Appendix, the term "event" applies to anything that can happen, whether it be an action (e.g., walking), an attribution (e.g., having), the assertion that something exists (e.g., being), or something else. In English, events are usually expressed by verbs.

Grammatical endings thus act as compulsory markers of a word's function within the sentence. For this reason, they rule, so to speak, the morphosyntax of the word; in other words, the way its form and, secondarily, its position in the sentence express the nature of its relationship with neighbouring words.

Derivational Affixes

Derivational affixes generally occur between the word-base and the grammatical ending. Their presence is not compulsory. Their function consists in modifying or transforming the meaning of the word-base:

-*u*- (in amisu-*u*-vut): to be something or someone

-*tu*(*q*)- (in tikit-*tu*-qar-tuq): one who does—or that does—something[2]

-*qar*- (in tikit-tu-*qar*-tuq): to have—or there is—something
or someone

Enclitics

Enclitics always occur at the very end of words, even after the grammatical ending. Any type of word can include a final enclitic. These affixes do not really fall under morphosyntax. They rather consist of non-compulsory semantic addenda expressing a kind of afterthought that follows an otherwise complete word, or they act as conjunctive affixes linking two words or two parts of a sentence. For instance, the word *aiguuq* in our example is a lexicalization of the word-base *ai-* ("hey!") and the enclitic -*guuq* ("it is said"). It translates as "well!" used as a conjunction introducing the response to an assertion that has just been uttered. Other enclitics include -*kiaq* ("don't know!"), -*lu* ("and"), -*li* ("but"), among others.

Events, Entities, and Positions

To summarize so far, Inuit words are structured as follows:

word-base +/– derivational affix(es) + grammatical ending
+/– enclitic(s)

The first three types of morphemes can be subdivided into classes based on their semantic relationships with events that happen (verbal), entities that are named (nominal), or positions that are pointed out (spatial localization). I will now discuss these classes, starting with grammatical endings.

Verbal Endings

Verbal endings always occur in word-final position (unless followed by an enclitic). They convey simultaneously the following notions:

The person (first, second, third) of the subject of an event

In some endings, the person of the first (direct) object of an event

The singularity, duality, or plurality of the subject (and, eventually, object)

The mood of the event[3]

For instance, the endings below, which are in the indicative mood, can attach to the word-base *taku-* ("to see"); some of these endings express the person of the subject alone ("the seer" in the present example), while others (transitive endings) also mention the person of the direct object ("what is seen"). The difference between transitive and non-transitive endings is that with the transitive, emphasis is placed on the object rather than the subject of an event. For instance, *illu* ["house"] *takujara* should be properly translated as "the house, I see it." Note that the following list of transitive endings is far from exhaustive:

TAKU-	Singular	Dual	Plural	Transitive
first-person subject	*-junga* "I see"	*-juguk* "we (two) see"	*-jugut* "we see"	*-jara/-javut -jagit* "I/we see it; I see you (1)"
second-person subject	*-jutit* "you (1) see"	*-jutik* "you (2) see"	*-jusi* "you see"	*-jait/-jatit/-jarma* "you (1) see it/them/me"
third-person subject	*-juq* "he/she sees"	*-juuk* "they (2) see"	*-jut* "they see"	*-jaanga/-jaatit/-jangit* "he/she sees me/you (1)/them"

There are sets of endings for each of the nine grammatical moods currently used in Nunavik Inuktitut, and this for all subject and object persons. The following examples show these moods in the second person singular, non-transitive:

Mood	Examples	(word-base *taku-* "to see")
Assertive	*-vutit*	"you see" (in a strong assertion)
Indicative	*-jutit*	"you see"
Interrogative	*-vit?*	"do you see?"

Imperative-optative	*-git!*	"see! may you see!"
Causative (perfective)	*-gavit*	"because you see; when you saw"
Conditional (imperfective)	*-guvit*	"if you see; when you will see"
Dubitative	*-mmangaarpit*	"(wondering) if you see"
Perfective appositional	*-tsutit*	"while you saw, are seeing"
Imperfective appositional	*-lutit*	"while you will be seeing"

The assertive mood is only heard when the speaker makes an assertion that stands by itself, opens a longer statement, or brings a statement to its definitive conclusion. Otherwise, the indicative must be used. See, for instance, the opening sentence from Deer's narrative (2015, 65, 23):

Iva Deer-ngu*vunga [assertive] *Quartamiuq nipiliurtaulanga*junga [indicative].

My name is Eva Deer from Quaqtaq [and] I am about to be recorded.

In Inuktitut, the indicative is the default mood.[4] This is why all verbs quoted in the preceding chapters—with a very few exceptions—bear an indicative ending, generally in the third-person singular (*-juq* after a vowel; *-tuq* after a [sometimes implicit] consonant, "he/she/it").

It is interesting that the causative mood (sometimes called perfective) expresses the fact that to the best of the speaker's knowledge an event has actually happened. Hence its English translation as "when, in the past" (by definition, a past event has already occurred) or "because" (the fact that an event has had an effect offers a proof of its occurrence). By contrast, the conditional (or imperfective) mood expresses the eventuality that if something occurs, something else might happen. Hence its use for expressing the English notions of "if" and "when, in the future." Since no one can be sure about the future, "if you see" and "when you'll see" (*takuguvit*) are synonymous.

Nominal Endings

Nominal endings express the semantic and grammatical relationships that a word can have with the other words in a sentence, when used for naming one, two, or several entities—an object, person, animal, natural phenomenon, concept, or anything else known by a word that generally corresponds to a noun in English. There are eight of these endings, which play more or less the same role as noun cases in Latin, German, Russian, and other languages. Here is a list, with examples in the singular:

Endings	Examples (word-base *ilisaiji-*, "teacher")	
Basic	ilisaiji-Ø[5]	takujuq ("*the* teacher sees")
		takujara ("*the* teacher, I see her/him")
Relative	ilisaiji-*up*	takujanga ("*the* teacher sees it")
		illunga ("*of* the teacher, his/her house [the teacher's house]")
Instrumental	ilisaiji-*mik*	takujuq ("he/she sees *a* teacher")
		tujurtanga ("he/she sends him/her *a* teacher")
Locative	ilisaiji-*mi*	nirijuq ("*at* the teacher['s place], he/she eats")
Allative	ilisaiji-*mut*	pisuttuq ("*toward* the teacher, he/she walks")
		ninngatuq ("*because of* the teacher, he/she is angry")
Ablative	ilisaiji-*mit*	qaijuq ("*from* the teacher['s place], he/she comes")
		nainnisaq ("shorter *than* the teacher")
Translative	ilisaiji-*kkut*	aijuq ("*through* the teacher['s place], he/she goes")
Simulative	ilisaiji-*tut*	uqartuq ("*like* the teacher, he/she speaks")

Besides semantic and grammatical relationships, nominal endings can also express the grammatical person of the actual or rhetorical owner(s) of the entity that is named. In such a case, they take special (possessive) forms that vary according to that person. Here are a few examples where endings attached to the word-base *nuna-* ("land") express different grammatical persons and types of relationships:

nuna-*nga*	"his/her land" (basic)
nuna-*ganut*	"toward my land" (allative)
nuna-*nnit*	"from your (one of you) land" (ablative)
nuna-*tti(n)ni*	"in our land(s)" (locative)
nuna-*ngit*	"his/her/their lands" (basic)

Verbal-Nominal Endings

We have seen above that the verbal endings of the third-person indicative are *-juq* (singular), *-juuk* (dual), and *-jut* (plural)—or *-tuq, -tuuk, -tut* after a consonant-final base or affix. These endings are ambiguous: they can stand for the subject of a verb, as in *taku*juq ("he/she sees"), *tikit*tuuk ("both of them arrive"), or *tusar*tut ("they hear"); but they may also act as nominal endings in the basic form. In that case, their respective meanings are "one who sees," "two persons who arrive," and "people who hear." This means that these endings can transform an event into an entity (e.g., "he/she sees" becomes "a seer").

The affixes denoting passive objects, *-jaq(-taq)/-jaak(-taak)/-jait(-tait)*, behave in a similar but more restricted way. With a possessive ending, they can be understood as designating either the object of a transitive event or a possessed entity (cf. *taku*jara, "I see it," and "my seen entity" [the entity I see]). Without a possessive, however, they can only be nominal (cf. *taku*jaak, "two entitities that are seen").

Like other nominal endings, *-juq/-juuk/-jut* and their alternate forms *-tuq/-tuuk/-tut* can occur under all eight forms of the nominal declension, as in *taku*juup ("a seer's"), *tikit*tuu(n)nut ("toward two persons who arrive"), or *tusar*tutitut ("like hearers"), but possessive forms cannot attach to them. They may enter into lexicalized word-bases, as in the initial example of this Appendix, where the base *tikittu(q)-* in *tikittu-qar-tuq* ("there are arrivals") results from the lexicalization of *tikit-* ("to arrive") and *-tuq* ("one who").

A large number of words expressing a quality or property attributed to someone or something—the adjectives of English—include this *-juq/-tuq* verbal-nominal ending. As we saw in the Introduction, this is the case with *piujuq* ("he/she/it is good" or "someone or something good"). Other examples include *naittuq* ("he/she/it is short," "someone or something short"), and *aupartuq* ("it is red," "something red").

Localization Endings

There are four *localization endings*. Like some nominal endings—namely the locative, allative, ablative, and translative—they mark spatial relations. However, their forms are special and, as will be seen later on, they can only attach to a closed set of word-bases (localization bases). These endings are not tied to grammatical number (singular, dual, plural) or grammatical possession (my, your, etc.):

Locative	*-ani* ("in, at")
Allative	*-unga* ("toward")
Ablative	*-anngat* ("from")
Translative	*-una* ("through")

One of the words from the hypothetical conversation shown at the beginning of this Appendix may be taken as an example: *avanngat* ("from there away"). The ablative ending *-anngat* marks the fact that someone or something is coming or has come from a specific localization in space (from "there away" in this case).

The Classes of Word-Bases

Let us now turn our attention to word-bases. Like endings, they play a crucial part in defining the semantic and grammatical relations of words within sentences. As with endings, bases can be verbal, nominal, or related to localization. However, there also exists a fourth class of word-bases, that of particles.

Verbal Bases

Verbal word-bases are word-initial morphemes that must always be followed by a verbal ending when there is no affix between base and ending. These bases express the occurrence of an event, as in the following examples:

tikip-puq	to arrive – third-person singular assertive ("he/she arrives")
taku-junga	to see – first-person singular indicative ("I see")
tusaa-guvigit	to listen – second-person singular/third-person plural transitive conditional ("if you [one] listen to them")
qanni(r)-tuq	to snow – third-person singular indicative ("it snows")
aannia-vitik?	to be sick – second-person dual interrogative ("are both of you sick?")

Nominal Bases

Nominal word-bases are word-initial morphemes that must be followed by a nominal ending when there is no affix between base and ending. They denote an entity (object, quality, concept, person, etc.), as in the following:

inu(k)-it	human person – plural basic ("many people")
illu-mi	house – singular locative ("in the house")
tuqu-nganut	death – third-person singular possessive allative ("until his/her death")
qimmi(q)-ma	dog – first-person singular possessive relative ("my dog's")
allauti-ittitut	pencil – dual simulative ("like two pencils")

A small number of nominal word-bases accept both nominal and verbal endings. They mostly denote animals:

natsi(q)-up	ringed seal – singular relative ("the ringed seal's")

natsi(q)-tunga   ringed seal – first-person singular indicative ("I caught a ringed seal")

Localization Bases

Localization word-bases are word-initial morphemes that must be followed by an ending of localization. Unlike verbal and nominal bases, they do not admit the presence of an affix between the word-base and its ending. They form a very small set; there are only ten of them in Nunavik Inuktitut. Localization bases express spatial positioning per se, as in the following examples:

av-anngat   a position far away from the speaker – ablative ("from far away")

ma-unga   a position near the speaker – allative ("toward here close by")

pa-una   a position far from and higher than the speaker – translative ("through up there")

qam-ani   a position from inside the speaker – locative ("here inside")

Particles

Particles constitute a special type of word-base. They cannot be followed by an ending and thus are not really ruled by the morphosyntax of Inuktitut. The only reason they may be considered as bases is that enclitics can be attached to them. Like enclitics, they act as interjections or conjunctions, or they replace complete words:

aiguu(q)-lajuq   well! – he/she says ("well! says he/she")

niangar-li!   how wonderful! – but ("but how wonderful it is")

qanur-lu?   how? – and ("and how?")

The Classes of Derivational Affixes

Derivational affixes occur between the base and the ending of words. According to the type of word-base to which they attach, they can be divided into two broad categories: verbal-based and nominal-based affixes.[6]

Verbal-Based Affixes

Some derivational affixes always attach to a verbal word-base (or word-base plus affix[es]). According to the class of endings that may be affixed to them, they can be subdivided into two categories: verbal transformers and verbal non-transformers.

Verbal transformers (VN affixes) must be followed by a nominal ending. This means that the words within which they occur undergo a semantic and grammatical transformation. Because the base is verbal, they would require a verbal ending if it were not for the VN affix that transforms them into a noun. These affixes can denote several concepts:

A means whose end is the event expressed in the word-base:

tusaa-*guti*　　　　　to listen – means for ("something used for listening")

The passive object of the event expressed in the word-base:

taku-*jaq*　　　　　to see – passive object ("something that is seen")

The nominalization of the event expressed in the word-base:

ilinnia(r)-*niq*　　　　　to study – nominalizer ("the fact of studying, schooling")

Verbal non-transformers (VV affixes) must be followed by a verbal ending. Thus, they do not transform the basic semantic and grammatical nature of the words within which they occur. Here are some concepts they denote:

The temporality of the event expressed in the word-base:

tusa(r)-*laur*-tunga	to hear – distant past – I ("I have heard; I heard")
taku-*kainna(r)*-tutit	to see – immediate past – you one ("you just saw")
niri-*niar*-tut	to eat – close future – they ("they will eat later today")

A modality of the event expressed in the word-base:

pisu(k)-*rqajar*-tugut	to walk – to be able to – we ("we can walk")
aulla(r)-*ruma*-gutta	to leave – to want – if we ("if we want to leave")
piu-*nngi(t)*-tuq	to be good – negative – he/she/it ("he/she/it is bad")

An aspect of the event expressed in the word-base:

qia-*si*-juq	to cry – starting to – he/she ("he/she starts crying")
pi-*giir*-qita?	to do – stopping to – do we? ("do we stop doing it?")
tiki(t)-*sima*-junga	to arrive – already done – I ("I am arrived")

Nominal-Based Affixes

In contrast to the preceding affixes, these always attach to a nominal word-base (or word-base plus affix[es]). They subdivide into two categories—nominal transformers and nominal non-transformers—according to the class of endings that may be affixed to them.

Nominal transformers (NV affixes) must be followed by a verbal ending. This means that the words within which they occur undergo a semantic and grammatical transformation. Because their base is nominal, they would require a nominal ending if it were not for the NV affix that transforms them into a verb. These affixes can express several concepts, such as the following:

An event whose object is the entity denoted by the word-base:[7]

illu-*liur*-tuq	house – to build – he/she ("he/she builds a house")
ui-*qar*-qit?	husband – to have – do you? ("do you have a husband?")
nulia(q)-*ri*-jara	wife – to have as – I . . . her ("I have her as [my] wife")

The existence of the entity denoted by the word-base:

Aani-*u*-junga	Annie – to be – I ("I am Annie, my name is Annie")
amisu-*u*-jusi	many of them – to be – you ("there are many of you")
piuju(q)-*u*-jutit[8]	someone who is good – to be – you one ("you are good")

A small number of N V affixes attach to nominal endings. They express the occurrence of an event whose meaning is directly related to that of the ending:

illu-mi-*it*-tut	house – singular locative ending – to be in/ at – they ("they are in the house")
illu-mi(t)-*nnga(r)*-tut	house – singular ablative ending – to come from – they ("they come from the house")
illu-ganu(t)-*ur*-tut	house – first-person singular possessive allative ending – to do – they ("they do [i.e., go] toward my house")
illu-(k)ku(t)-*ur*-tut	house – singular translative ending – to do – they ("they do [i.e., go] through the house")
illu-titu(t)-*ur*-tut	house – plural simulative ending – to do – they ("they do [i.e., look] like houses")

Verbal transformations of this type, triggered by a derivational affix, also occur with endings of localization. In such cases, however, it is sometimes the whole ending that is modified, as in *av*unga ("toward a position far away"), which becomes *av*unnga(r)*tut* ("they go toward a position far away from them") when made into a verb.

Nominal non-transformers (NN affixes) must be followed by a nominal ending. They do not transform the basic semantic and grammatical nature of the words within which they occur. Here are some concepts they express:

A quality or property attributed to the entity denoted by the word-base:

inu(k)-*tsiaq*	person – good, beautiful ("a good person")
tupi(q)-*alu(k)*-it	tent – big – plural ("big tents")
ulu-*tsaq*	*ulu* [woman's knife] – material for ("material for an *ulu*")

Someone or something owning the entity denoted by the word-base:

illu-*lik*	house – who/what owns something ("owner of a house")[9]

Finally, a few derivational affixes may attach to both types of word-bases, verbal as well as nominal, as in these examples:

taku-*mmarik*-kunga	see – completely, really – I ("I really see")
inu(k)-*mmarik*	person – complete ("a complete person" [an adult])

The Classes of Words

Now that we have reached the end of this typological analysis of all categories of morphemes, it is possible to identify the parts of speech (or classes of words) found in Inuktitut. There are four of them: verbs, nouns, localizers, and particles. Each class is defined by the combination of its constitutive elements: word-base, derivational affixes, and ending.

Verbs

Words belonging to the class of *verbs* often form a complete sentence by themselves (e.g., *tusalaartaka*, "I will hear them"). They are generated along two basic patterns (where V = verbal and N = nominal):

V word-base +/− v v affix(es) + V ending (+/− enclitic[s])

taku-rqau-jara-(guuq)

"[it is said that] I saw him/her/it today"

N word-base + n v affix +/− v v affix(es) + V ending (+/− enclitic[s])

illu-liur-nia(r)-tunga-(guuq)

"[it is said that] I will build a house"

Nouns

Words belonging to the class of *nouns* do not generally form a complete sentence by themselves (e.g., *tupialugani*, "in my big tent"). They are generated along two basic patterns (where N = nominal and V = verbal):

N word-base +/− n n affix(es) + N ending (+/− enclitic[s])

illu–apim-mi-(lu)

"[and] in the little house"

V word-base + v n affix +/− n n affix(es) + N ending (+/− enclitic[s])

tusaa-guti-tsia(q)-mul-(lu)

"[and] because of a good instrument for listening"

There exist other words that can be counted as nouns, in view of the fact that (1) they denote one, two, or many entities; and (2) all eight endings of the nominal declension may attach to their base, though never in the possessive form. Among these broadly defined nouns are the adjectives, which represent entities rather than free-standing qualifiers (e.g., *qakurtaq*, "something white," as in *atigiqartunga* qakurtamik, "I have a parka, [I have] something white" [i.e., I have a white parka]). As mentioned above, many adjectives end with the verbal-nominal ending *-juq/-tuq* and thus can behave as either nouns or verbs in the third-person indicative (e.g., *angijuq*, "something big" or "he/she/it is big").

Numerals, too, belong to the class of nouns. What translates in English as "one, two, three . . ." literally means "one entity (*atausiq*), two entities (*marruuk*), three entities (*pingasut*) . . ." (e.g., *inunnut* pingasunut *pisuttunga*, "toward people, toward three entities, I walk" [i.e., I walk toward three persons]). Finally, personal pronouns in the first and second person of the singular, dual, and plural may be considered as entities ("me, you, us") and can take the eight endings of the nominal declension (e.g., uvannut *pisuttutit*, "toward me, you walk"). They thus qualify as nouns. In the third person, however, words belonging to the subclass of nominal localizers (see below) are used in lieu of personal pronouns.

Localizers

Words belonging to the class of *localizers* are generated along the following pattern (where L = localization):

L word-base + L ending (+/− enclitic[s])

av-unga-(li) ("[but] toward there far away")

Particles

Words belonging to the class of *particles* are generated along the following pattern (where P = particle):

P word-base (+/− enclitic[s])

aiguuq-(lajuq) ("well! [says he/she]")

An Intermediate Subclass:
Nominal Localizers (Demonstratives)

Localization word-bases can be followed by a set of special endings marking all eight forms of the nominal declension in the singular and dual-plural (these two numbers having merged together). These transform the words into nominal localizers, that is, terms pointing to an entity positioned in a specific portion of space, much like the English demonstrative pronouns. Here are a few examples:

an-na	a position far away from the speaker[10] – singular basic ("that one far away")
pa-kkunuuna	a position far from and higher than the speaker – plural translative ("through those up there")
u-minga	a position very close to the speaker – singular instrumental ("this one very near [direct object]")
ma-tsuma	a position near the speaker – singular relative ("this one's")

This combination generates a subclass of words that stand midway between nouns and localizers. These words denote entities that can relate to other elements in a sentence the same way nouns do—thanks to the eight singular and dual-plural forms of the nominal declension—but such entities are entirely defined by their position in space.

Internal and External Morphosyntax

The word patterns just elicited belong to the internal morphosyntax of Inuktitut—the relationships among morphemes within words. These patterns are highly schematic. In actual speech, one word may include several derivational affixes, as well as more than one ending, as happens when a nominal or localization ending is transformed into a verbal morpheme. For instance, the following words can be currently heard:

kiinauja(q)-li(k)-alu(k)-u-guma-nngi(t)-tuguk

N word-base – NN – NN – NV – VV – VV – V ending

money – who has – big – to be – to want – negative – first-person dual indicative

"The two of us do not want to be big owners of money" [i.e., very rich]."

pinasu(k)-qati-tsia(q)-ri-ja(q)-u-laur-tu(q)-li

V word-base – V N – N N – N V – V N – N V – V V – V ending – enclitic

to work – mate – good – to have as – passive object – to be – past – third-person singular indicative – but

"But he/she was had [i.e., was considered] as a good workmate."

illu-mi-i(t)-rquu(r)-tut

N word-base – N ending – N V – V V – V ending

house – singular locative – to be in – probably – third-person plural indicative

"They are probably in the house."

For practical reasons, the number of affixes is limited. A word that would be too long might become unintelligible. Thus, the total number of morphemes per word rarely exceeds nine or ten units, although elders are renowned for their skill in using very long lexical items. In her autobiographical narrative, for instance, Eva Deer often utters words with more than ten morphemes, as in this sentence, whose last element comprises a word-base followed by twelve affixes (Deer 2015, 66):

Taima ilinniavik *sanajaulaursimajuviniujutsaulirmat*

sana-ja-u-laur-sima-ju-vini-u-ju-tsa-u-lir-mat

So it is with the school *because it now reaches the point* [in the narrative] *of having already been built.*

It should be noted that within a word, the order in which morphemes occur plays an essential part because the meaning of an affix always influences the overall signification of the preceding elements. For example, the meaning of *taku*-sima-rqau-*jara* ("I had seen it then") differs from that of *taku*-rqau-sima-*jara* ("I have already seen it") due to the alternate position of the two middle morphemes.

By contrast, as far as external morphosyntax (i.e., relationships between words) is concerned, the order of words has only a stylistic importance because endings clearly indicate the morphosyntactic behaviour of each word. For instance, if someone says *Jaani takujuq illumik* ("John sees a house"), he or she is understood as well as when using the preferred construction

Jaani illumik takujuq. In at least one case, however, the order of words has a semantic function: when there is series of two or more nouns with possessive relative endings. For instance, the series *Pitaup ataatangata aippangata umianga* ("Peter's father's partner's boat") does not mean the same thing as *Pitaup aippangata ataatangata umianga* ("Peter's partner's father's boat"). In this type of construction, words with a possessive ending are always semantically determined by the noun immediately preceding them.

To conclude, we can see that as with other polysynthetic languages, speakers of Inuktitut create their own words as they need them. Of course, in order to do so, they must draw from the corpus of word-bases, endings, derivational affixes, and morphosyntactic rules in use in their speech community. Even though these rules and morphemes are limited in number,[11] they allow speakers to generate an almost boundless quantity of words and sentences. Due to the limited number of available morphemes, however, the precise meaning of a word is often linked to its context of use. This is the case, for instance, with *illusaq* ("material for a house"), a word that can denote a type of snow fit for erecting an igloo, as well as plywood, planks, bricks, and other materials when discussing modern building activities.[12] This does not prevent the Inuit language from displaying a truly tremendous creative power, which our stroll through the cultural semantics of Inuktitut has allowed us to witness.

Notes

Introduction: Words from the Past

1   All translations from Inuktitut and French are the author's.

2   For a pictorial description of daily life in Quaqtaq from the 1960s to the early 1990s, see Dorais (2017c).

3   Information on the dialectology and pronunciation of the Inuit language is found at the end of this Introduction.

4   Letters in parentheses are omitted when the word-part to which they belong is followed or, more rarely, preceded by another part.

5   More precisely, these terms mean "he/she/it is good/bad" or "someone who/something that is good/bad."

6   Interestingly enough, for the thirteenth-century Italian philosopher and theologian Thomas Aquinas, all that exists is essentially good. In the words of Aquinas's modern exegetist Jacques Maritain (quoted in Le Goff 2003, 109), "All that is, is good to the very extent that it is: being and the good are convertible terms." This shows that when human beings ponder the meaning of existence, Arctic hunter-gatherers and a medieval Catholic philosopher can share similar ideas. In a short essay, Willem Rasing (2012) outlines similar convergences between certain Inuit words pertaining to ethics and the philosophical concepts discussed by Aristotle in his *Nicomachean Ethics*.

7   It is interesting to note that in one Inuit dialect, East Greenlandic, a large number of words belonging to the pre-contact lexicon have two levels of meaning (Robbe and Dorais 1986). Due to a local taboo forbidding people to speak the name of a deceased person, and because traditional names were drawn from ordinary language, many words current in other Inuit dialects were progressively replaced with new descriptive terms, as individuals bearing these words as names passed away. For example, when Natsiq ("Ringed Seal") died at some point in the past, the animal was renamed *miigattak* ("the very small one"), a term still in current use.

8   In some restricted cases (see Appendix), a word may be exempted from showing an ending. Note that a third, marginal type of affixes (enclitics) is discussed in the Appendix.

9   In linguistic usage, reconstructed etymological roots are usually preceded by an asterisk (*aku[r]*). In this book, however, except in the Glossary where they have another function, asterisks are only used to signal the fact that a word or phrase given as an example is considered incorrect or unintelligible by Inuit speakers.

10 According to online data from Statistics Canada (statcan.gc.ca) and Statistics Greenland (stat.gl).

11 In 2016, the Nunavut and pan-Canadian Inuit authorities decided to coin the word "Inuktut" to refer to the Indigenous language of Nunavut that includes both Inuktitut and Inuktun dialects.

Chapter One: Words for Speaking about the Environment and the Land

1 The Aleut cognate of *cila* is *sla-*. It also means "wind" and "compass point."

2 In this book, "supranatural" is preferred to "supernatural," because of the possible Christian connotation of the latter word.

3 In Aleut, "land" translates to *tanax̂* (where *x̂* sounds like Spanish *j*), a distant cognate of *nuna*.

4 A barometer is called *silasiuti* ("that is used in connection with *sila*").

5 For Saladin d'Anglure (2018, 303–4), *sila* as a cosmological regulator has several points in common with the Chinese concept of *qi* and might be related to a northeastern Asian form of proto-Taoism.

6 For a discussion of how Inuit perceive their personal relation to the environment, see Stairs and Wenzel (1992).

7 Letters in parentheses or, less frequently, square brackets belong to variants of the word, in the same or in other dialects. In northeastern Nunavik, the word for "springtime" may thus either be *upirngasaq* or *upirngasaaq*.

8 In western Nunavik, as in most Inuit dialects, the word *upirngaaq* applies to springtime, and summer is called *aujaq*, probably a cognate of the word-bases *au-*, "to rot," and *auk-*, "to thaw."

9 As in "*Upinnarani!*"—"No wonder!" (literally, "not being surprising").

10 In many languages, this natural phenomenon receives a descriptive name (e.g., in English, rainbow; French, *arc-en-ciel* [bow in the sky]; and Vietnamese, *cầu vòng* [curved bridge]).

11 Derived from Proto-Eskimo, Proto-Inuit is the language spoken in northwestern Alaska by the direct ancestors of present-day Inuit, before some of them started migrating to the Canadian Arctic and Greenland about 800 years ago.

12 The word *sirmiq* also denotes the ice and earth coating put on sled runners. In Greenland, it means "ice," and more specifically, "glacier."

13 *Kinirtaq* also means "bannock" (bread whose dough has become compact after cooking) in western Nunavik.

14 Ethnographic and linguistic data on the perceptions of the land-water (including ice) interface in Nunavik can be found in Scott Heyes's 2007 doctoral dissertation ("Inuit Knowledge").

15 A stove is called *kiatsauti* ("means for getting some warmth").

16 *Urqu* is generally affixed with a possessive morpheme (cf. *urqu*ani, "*on its* lee-side"). Its opposite is *aggu* ("windward side"; etymologically, "going against wind" [Fortescue et al. 5]).

17 The shamanic aura may be understood as a manifestation of the para-human light shamans shed on *sila*, a light that enables them to perceive beings and occurrences invisible to ordinary people.

18 According to Fortescue et al. (317), the immediate PE etymon of *qauji-* is *qa(C)u(ði)-* ("to become conscious"), which is itself related to *qaru*, the etymon of *qau*.

19 In North Baffin, the winter days during which the sun does not rise and when light is almost completely absent are called *ulluit taujut* ("days that are dark"). Conversely, when the sun shines for twenty-four hours during summer days, night is called *unnuattak* ("another [kind of] night," or "absence of night") (Ootoova et al. 2000, 374, 153).

20 For a thorough study of traditional Inuit astronomy, see John Macdonald, *The Arctic Sky* (1998).

21 According to Michael Fortescue (personal communication), comparison between the various meanings of *nuna* in all Eskimo-Aleut languages and dialects shows that originally, this word applied to the largely uninhabited tundra. Its current preferred use for denoting inhabited lands would have appeared after Eskimo-Aleut speakers settled in semi-permanent seasonal camps and in sedentary villages.

22 Our research was funded by the Geographical Commission of Quebec. In the early 1970s, the information we gathered was used by the Northern Quebec Inuit Association during their negotiations with the provincial government, in the context of the James Bay and Northern Quebec Agreement of 1975. It proved that many Inuit still alive at that time, as well as their forebears, had inhabited and/or travelled through the entire area of Quebec north of the 55th parallel.

23 This concurs in a way with the biblical image of "wilderness," *inuqanngi[t]tuq* ("that has no humans"). It was in such a wilderness, a *nunagijaunngituq*, that Jesus met with the devil during his forty-day fast in the desert (Luke 4:1–13).

24 In a way, *imaq* ("water") is semantically opposed to *nuna* ("dry land"), but from a wider perspective, *imaq* is part of *nuna* because it constitutes the most important resource for sustaining human, animal, and plant life (Qumaq 1991, 29).

25 "Down there" because on most maps, the areas of North America inhabited by *Qallunaat* lie below Inuit Nunangat. The Inuktitut phrase *taunani qallunaani* has been modelled on the English idioms "down South" and "up North."

26 In Nunavik, all areas collectively owned by Inuit under the James Bay and Northern Quebec Agreement are administered by Landholding Corporations, the *nunamik tigumiartiit* ("those who hold the land in their hands").

27 In his dictionary, Taamusi Qumaq (1991, 396) uses the word *nunarjuaq* ("super-*nuna*") for rendering the concept of "country."

28 In Greenlandic Kalaallisut and, more rarely, in other Inuit dialects, the consonant *v* may elide before the vowel *u*.

29 *Kangir&uk* in most dialects other than Nunavik. The etymology proposed here is a guess.

30 Schneider (1970b, 259) also mentions the words *imarpik*, *imavik*, and *imavialuk* (all three meaning "huge water") for ocean.

31 Although no bull caribou has been seen in Pangnirtuuq in living memory (Christopher Trott, personal communication).

32 For speakers of Vietnamese, a language where the past is also said to stand in front of us, and the future at our back, this viewpoint is perfectly logical. Because our mind can see (i.e., recall) what has already happened, the past stands before us, while the unseen future is behind us.

Chapter Two: Words for Speaking about Animals and Subsistence Activities

1 In 1978 near Igloolik, children—or dogs, according to another version—broke a *silaaksaq*. As a consequence, the village was covered with fog for much of the summer.

2 But conversely, the verb base *inuulir-* ("to start being an *inuk*" [i.e., to be born]) applies to both humans and animals.

3 Selling game to *Qallunaat* may be acceptable, provided it is done on a small scale. Similarly, making surplus meat and fish available free of charge to anyone in need, against money issued to hunters by local authorities, is approved because it is considered an extension of communal sharing (Gombay 2010; Searles 2016).

4 For a thorough description of animal taxonomy and symbolism among Inuit, see Vladimir Randa's PhD dissertation (1994), as well as his article "Qui se ressemble s'assemble" (2002). In a more recent book, Laugrand and Oosten (2015) propose an exhaustive analysis of how Inuit perceive various types of animals.

5 The classification of animals may vary slightly according to dialects. For an East Greenlandic example, see Dorais (1984).

6 In Greenland, for instance, this word in both West and East Greenlandic only applies to the different species of seals.

7 On the natural environment and fauna of Nunavik, see Saladin d'Anglure (2013, chap. 1), from which I borrow the Latin names of species.

8 According to Saladin d'Anglure (2013, 42), in Kangirsujuaq, on the Nunavik (southern) shore of the Hudson Strait, the word *tikaagulliq* (note the final *-q*) refers to the common porpoise (*Phocaena phocaena*). This might be a regional usage of the term. In the neighbouring village of Quaqtaq, I had several occasions to spot *tikaagulliit* and indeed, in terms of size, they looked more like porpoises or dolphins than killer whales.

9 The situation was somewhat different in the west. In Alaskan waters, the stock of whales diminished noticeably due to whalers, but the *arviq* did not disappear. Up until today, whale hunting in *umiat* (skin boats, now powered by an outboard motor) has remained an essential element of northern Alaska's Iñupiaq culture.

10 Or *qilalugaq qirnitaq* ("black *qilalugaq*").

11 One might be tempted to suppose that *qilalugaq* starts with the base *qilak-* ("sky" or "to tie"), but if this were the case, the word should have ended up being pronounced **qilallugaq* or **qilaglugaq*, rather than *qilalugaq*.

12 On 12 July 1966, near the Airartuuq hunting camp, I saw in the distance what appeared to be two black dots on the sea's horizon, one following the other. My Inuit companions told me that this might be *Lumaajuq* being dragged along by the harpooned whale to which she was attached (*Lumaartalik*, "the one with *Lumaa[juq]*"). However, I did not hear her shouting "*Lumaa*."

13 The common denominator between a young caribou and a nephew or niece seems linked to the fact that each is younger than something (an adult animal) or someone (one's aunt) else.

14 The lemming (*Lemmus trimucronatus*) is a field-mouse-sized arctic rodent that constitutes the principal source of food for fox and snowy owl.

15 In areas where it is abundant (the Mackenzie Delta, for instance), muskrat is also eaten.

16 Nowadays, though, because of global warming, the habitat of the Atlantic salmon is said to have extended to some northern Nunavik and possibly Baffin waters (Watt-Cloutier 2016, chap. 6).

17 I have not found any evidence of the the presence of whitefish (*kavisilik/kapisilik*) in Labrador and Greenland. Its name was thus seemingly ready to fill an empty niche: that of a region's most important non-*iqaluk* species of fish, whether *Coregonus clupeiformis* in the eastern and central Canadian Arctic, or *Salmo salar* in Labrador and Greenland.

18 This conjectured gloss is explainable by the fact that clams extend a long protuberance that goes upward, from the sand-buried shell to the surface. So, *ammuumajuit* appear to beachcombers as being seen from above, looking down (cf. *ammuu-*, "looks at it downward"). In Arctic Bay (northern Baffin Island), a small boy's scrotum is dubbed *ammuumajuq*, and in Pangnirtuuq (southeastern Baffin), a clam is often called *usuk*, "penis" (Christopher Trott, personal communication).

19 As we just saw, the habitat of shellfish oscillates between water and relatively solid ground, but *tininnimiutait* cannot move between land, properly speaking, and the open sea, as polar bears do.

20 This English version was later translated into French, German, and Danish. All quotations found here are from a more recent (2011) version of the novel, published in Inuktitut and French (in a new translation from the English).

21 In the latter command *r* is apical (pronounced with the tip of the tongue). This sound is absent from current Inuktitut, where *r* is uvular (articulated at the back of the mouth).

22 *Tuttuvaq* also means "moose."

23 PE *maqəg-*; etymological *ə* is realized as *a* before a vowel; hence *maqainniq*, not **maqiinniq*.

24 Of course, this only concerns those animal species that are actually hunted, fished, or trapped.

25 The gun has become so adapted by Inuit culture that the word-base *qukir-*, which originally meant "to be deafened by a loud noise" (Fortescue et al., 341), is now understood by Inuktitut speakers as "to shoot with a gun."

26 As mentioned in a previous endnote, skin *umiat* provided with an outboard motor are still in current use in Alaska.

27 I have observed a related phenomenon among Vietnamese elders, who feel hungry after two or three days without rice.

28 From *iva-*, "to swing while moving" (cf. ivakka[r]tuq, "makes oneself [-kka[r]tuq] swing while moving") + PE *-lu*, "thing for."

Chapter Three: Words for Speaking about Humans and Spirits

1   The ethnonym "Eskimo" is still heard in Alaska, where it refers to people of either Inuit or Yupik descent.

2   Interestingly, Qumaq's conception of a "receptacle for thoughts" is not that far from the Greek word Aristotle uses for defining the intellect: νοήτικον (*noëtikon*), "that makes one think."

3   In the Mackenzie region and among Alaskan Inuit, white Europeans are called *Tanngit* (singular *Tanik*). This word, whose origin is unknown, might I think have been borrowed from Hawaiian *Piritanik*, "Britannic" ("British"), by way of Hawaiian men who sailed on late nineteenth-century American whaling vessels. Among speakers of the Yupik languages, a white European is called a *Kassak*, from Russian *Kazak* ("Cossack").

4   Written in syllabic characters by an unschooled woman from Kangiqsujuaq (Nunavik), Mitiarjuk Nappaaluk's novel tells about the daily life of a young widow (Sanaaq), at the period of incipient contacts with *Qallunaat* in northernmost Nunavik. First published in Inuktitut in 1984 and in a French translation (by Bernard Saladin d'Anglure) in 2002, it finally appeared in English in 2014 under the title *Sanaaq: An Inuit Novel.*

5   In Dorais, *The Language of the Inuit* (2010, 89), the last sentence was erroneously translated as "Inuit are really astonished that these people have lost their faculty of speech."

6   In Greenland, for perhaps the last century, the appellation *Qallunaat* has only applied to Danes. Other nationalities are known under separate names, either idiosyncratically Greenlandic (e.g., *Tulut*, "English," from "[How] do you do?") or borrowed from Danish (e.g., *Franskit*, "French").

7   In southern Baffin Island, black people are called *Puutukiit* ("Portuguese"), because at the turn of the twentieth century, American whalers operating in that region were in the habit of hiring black Portuguese-speaking sailors from the Cape Verde islands.

8   Indigenous Greenlanders have long called themselves *Kalaallit* (*Kalaattit* in eastern Greenland), a phonetic adaptation of the Old Norse ethnonym (*Skræling*) given them by medieval Vikings.

9   According to the linguist Anna Berge (2018), many Aleut-Eskimo cognates could stem from a relatively recent process of borrowing rather than from a common ancestral language. These loan forms, though, would mostly concern traditional technology, so that cognate words expressing very basic concepts such as "human being" could still belong to an older substratum.

10 In the case of animals, the word-bases *angu(ti)-* and *arna(q)-* may be followed by specifying affixes, such as *-viaq* ("big but not much so") in anguti*viaq* and arna*viaq*, "male/female bird."

11 As in the verbal base *arpa-* ("to move or run continually"), that may be analyzed as *ar-* ("to move, run") + *-pa-* ("frequently, in a larger way").

12 On the acquisition of Inuktitut by Nunavik children, see Allen (1996).

13 The apostrophe stands for a glottal stop: a sharp and brief interruption of the airflow between the *a*s.

14 On the relationship between intelligence and *sila*, see Chapter 1. The connection between *isuma* and nature is expressed quite graphically in the Inuinnaqtun dialect, where an intelligent person who understands well is said to be *qapuittuq*, "without foam [in the mind]."

15 The word-bases *isuar-* and *isuit-* are specific to the Nunavik and South Baffin dialects of Inuktitut. They are the local forms of *i&uar-/i&uit-*, found in other Inuit dialects. For this reason, these bases cannot be related to the words *isuma* and *isuk*.

16 In several Inuit dialects, the word-base *alia-* has an opposite meaning: "being unhappy, lonely, or sad."

17 The verbal base *kappia-* ("to be afraid of") expresses fear engendered by any type of situation, while *irsi-* only refers to extreme fear caused by a living being, human or animal.

18 The importance of sharing and mutual aid characterizes many Indigenous groups. For example, in November 2015, I was invited to participate in a pig feast on the Aboriginal Atayal lands of Fuxing, in northwestern Taiwan. Upon arrival, I was almost immediately told that for the Atayal, sharing food with many people and, more generally, helping each other were primary values which differentiated them from the majority Chinese society.

19 Human name souls can also be reborn in animal forms, according to a myth from the eastern Canadian Arctic. The myth tells about a battered wife who changes into a dog when her husband tries killing her, and whose *atiq* soul then enters various animal bodies in succession, before finally being born again as a human male baby (Saladin d'Anglure 2018, Chapter 8).

20 *Tau* derives from *taru*. It is noteworthy that in some forms of Yupik, the word *taru* was used until relatively recently as the current term for "human being" (Fortescue et al., 364). In Aleut, the cognate word *tayaĝu-x̂* (where *ĝ* sounds like French *R*—pronounced back in the throat—and *x̂* like Spanish *j*) also means "person, male man" (Bergsland 1994, 395).

21 Spirits do not cast a shadow, but this does not mean they do not possess a *tarniq*. According to Harriet Kiliutaq (personal communication), an Inuk educator from Nunavik, *tarniq* might be connected to *taaq* ("darkness") because the soul is invisible.

22 For northern Baffin Inuit, the first humans were immortal, becoming young again when they reached old age. It was overpopulation that incited an old woman to shout, "*Tuqu! tuqu! Unataq! unataq!*"—"Death! Death! War! War!" (Rasmussen 1929, 92). The alternation between life and death then appeared.

23 Animal spirits could appear under various guises: a bear or a wolf, but also a *qupanuaq* ("small bird") or an *auvvik* ("caterpillar"). In the early twentieth century, a shaman from western Hudson Bay even had a biblical lion as his *tuurngaq*.

24 In pre-Christian Nunavik and Labrador, *Tuurngaaluk* was the master spirit of the caribou. According to Turner (1894, 200–201), *Tuurngaaluk* lived in a cave near Cape Chidley, at the northeastern tip of Ungava Bay, in the guise of a polar bear.

25 The word is sometimes interpreted as "the action of tying something." However, if this were the case, the combination of *qilak-* ("to tie") + *-niq* ("action of") would have given *qilangniq* rather than *qilaniq*.

26 On the shamanic language, see Dorais (2010, 133–34 and 167–68).

27 In Nunavik Inuktitut, the verb "to give" can be translated as three different words: *tunivaa* ("he/she gives it"); *aittupaa* ("he/she gives him/her [something]"; literally, "fetches him/ her repeatedly"); *tujurpaa* ("he/she sends him/her [a gift]").

28 The literal meaning of *itsirarjuat* is not completely clear, but it seems based on the pre-1960s Catholic ritual, when the priest said mass with his back to the congregation, bowing for a long moment before starting prayers. The word might also be related to

the verbal base *iksigar-* ("to write"), in use in at least one dialect of the western coast of Hudson Bay (Schneider 1970a, 85).

29 In its basic, pre-Christian meaning, the verbal base *uppi(r)-/ukpir-* ("to believe") refers to one's appreciation (based on common sense) of the credibility of what is said, as in *uppinanngituq* ("it does not make one believe [i.e., it does not make sense]") or *uppingilla-git* ("I don't believe you").

30 This need for a radical change of orientation explains why overzealous missionaries transformed *tuurngait* into devils and forbade Inuit from practising leisure activities that had nothing to do with shamanism: throat singing, for instance, or telling traditional stories.

31 Or *Anirnialuk* ("Great Spirit") among some Catholics.

32 Outside the eastern Canadian Arctic (as well as in Labrador), Inuit use the current European alphabet.

33 On the relationship between literacy and orality among modern Inuit, see Hot (2009) and Dorais (2018b). On the expansion of the Eskimo-Aleut vocabulary in order to translate some of the concepts related to Christianity, see Berge and Kaplan (2016).

Chapter Four: Words for Speaking about Family, Kinship, and Naming

1 The opposite situation (an absent mother) is not mentioned by Louisa Kululaaq, probably because it is almost nonexistent.

2 Closed groupings based on patrilineal kinship are found among speakers of the Siberian Yupik language, however.

3 In English, Italian, and Vietnamese (but not in Inuktitut, as we shall see), the children of the siblings of Ego's spouse, and potentially the grandchildren of his/her spouse by remarriage are called by the same terms as his/her nephews/nieces/grandchildren by blood, although with a qualifying phrase: "nephew/niece/grandchild by marriage"; "*nipote acquisito* [acquired *nipote*]"; "*cháu theo hôn nhân* [*cháu* according to marriage]."

4 For a complete description of kinship terminology in northeastern Nunavik, see Saladin d'Anglure (2013, 139–54). Nelson Graburn (1964) proposes an analysis of kinship terms among the Nunavik Inuit, linking them with basic societal and family attitudes. On kinship and naming in eastern Nunavut, see Otak and Pitsiulak-Stevens (2014).

5 *Ilait* ("your part") is homophonous with *ilait* ("many parts"), because in the eastern Inuit dialects, the grammatical endings *-in* ("your") and *-it* (plural) have merged together, which is not the case in Western Canadian Inuktun and Alaskan Inupiaq.

6 Cf. the word-base *pa-*, "heat" (as in par*qaar-*, "to emit heat"), + *-nik*, "to be provided with" (as in *u*inik-, "to get a husband").

7 Or less plausibly, because she is a woman (*arnaq*) who "agitates" men (see preceding chapter), a daughter would "heat" males sexually (Dorais 2016, 71).

8 This is also the case in Vietnamese and several other languages.

9 But there remains a lexical distinction between cousins and siblings, however slight, thus fulfilling one of Morgan's definitional criteria for "Eskimo-type" kinship systems. In Nunavut, there exist more specific terms for cousins, such as *illuarjuk* ("little partner") in South Baffin (Spalding 1998, 23).

10 Cf. the word-base *nuli-*, "female in heat" (as in nuli*ujuq*, "it [dog] is [-*u*-] an animal in heat"), plus -*aq*, "small" (Dorais 2016, 68).

11 According to Schneider (1985, 199), in Labrador, the penis was formerly called *naulik*, "the harpooning one." Saladin d'Anglure (personal communication) remembers the Nunavik author Salome Mitiarjuk once telling him that when she was young, women jokingly asked each other if their husband had "harpooned" them the preceding night.

12 This is so in Inuktitut. In Yupik and some Inuit dialects, it is the word-base *al(r)ar-* that conveys the basic meaning of "one of a pair," while *aippaq* means "mate, spouse."

13 Such a distinction is absent from other regions of the Canadian Arctic, where *tamarmik* means "all of them," and *iluunnatik* is not used (see also Chapter 6).

14 In the eastern Canadian Arctic, it is often said of young and not-so-young speakers: "Their Inuktitut is a direct translation from the English, because they think like *Qallunaat.*"

15 Nowadays, Inuit organizations such as Nunavik's Avataq Cultural Institute consider it crucially important to record the genealogies of the population they serve, in order to avoid potential unions between individuals who are unaware that they are related.

16 The North Baffin term *nulik*, "parent of the spouse of Ego's child" (see above), unheard in Nunavik, is the only word I know that denotes a relative of the spouse of a relative of Ego.

17 The word *sakiaq* also applies to the cousin—and, according to Schneider (1985, 335), to the uncle and aunt—of Ego's spouse. Another derivative of *saki*, *sakilirqiuti* ("means for being a *saki* once again"), denotes a grandparent-in-law (Ego's spouse's grandfather or grandmother).

18 This etymology postulates that the affix -*rnguq* is a reflex of PE -*nər* ("more of").

19 Cf. *ajakuluk* ("mother's sister"), whose conjectured meaning might be "nice little support."

20 I do not know of any Inuktitut word for "incest." According to Saladin d'Anglure (2013, 162), an incestuous individual is said to be *silaittuq* ("without *sila* [intelligence]").

21 The terms "reincarnation" and "co-incarnation" may not be totally adequate to describe the transmission of names. Inuit rather conceive names as permanent entities through which human bodies transit—one or several at the same time—from generation to generation.

22 See Kublu and Oosten (1999) for a detailed description of how one Inuk from Igloolik addresses the members of her family and is addressed by them.

23 Before Inuit became familiar with European first names and patronyms, traders, missionaries, and other *Qallunaat* residents in the North were often called by descriptive nicknames: *Tunusuittuq* ("one without a nape"), *Ijautialuuk* ("big spectacles"), *Nipiluk* ("bad voice"), etc.

24 Interestingly enough, a similar attitude of avoiding an offence to ancestors also exists in Vietnamese culture, but it works in an inverted way. In Vietnam, children *are* scolded and hit, often very harshly, but it is forbidden to name them after their parents' ancestors, so as to avoid any offence against these.

25 Some years ago, I told my adoptive sister in Quaqtaq that I was now old and would like, if possible, to co-live in her family by transmitting my name as a secondary appellation to one of her future grandchildren. She answered this was a great idea, but that I would have to wait till a daughter or daughter-in-law became pregnant with a boy and, of course, agree

to give him my name. This occurred a few years later, even though I would not have had any problem with a female *sauniq*.

26 A year before, Saali had almost drowned when on a hunting expedition. This accident, added to his age (he turned 68 in 1993), may explain why his life was linked to that of his newborn grandchild through eponymy. This action allowed him to share in the baby's vitality.

Chapter Five: Words for Speaking about the Human Body

1 The names of animal body parts, those of mammals in particular, are generally similar to the terms dealing with human anatomy, sometimes with a slight morphological difference, as with *niaquq*, "human or middle-sized animal head," vs. *niaquaq*, "head of a walrus or whale" (literally, "big head").

2 In modern Inuktitut, the word *timi* also translates as "public organization." This is a semantic calque of English: "[public] body."

3 For an exhaustive overview of Inuit anatomical terms, see Guy Bordin's illustrated analytical lexicon of anatomy (2003). Michèle Therrien's *Le corps inuit* (1987) offers a semiotic analysis of how the human body is envisioned by the Nunavik Inuit.

4 The word *qimirluk* also denotes the stem of a leaf or plant.

5 According to Fortescue et al. (48), the PE roots for "to rot" (*aru-*) and "blood" (*aðug*) are different, but they have "contaminated" each other (i.e., become homophonous) in the Inuit language, thus entailing the perception of a semantic proximity between the two notions.

6 Cf. PE *igə-*, the etymon of modern Inuktitut *ii-* ("to swallow"), as in *iivaa* ("swallows it").

7 *Tur&cuk* in most dialects other than Nunavik.

8 The semantic link between breastfeeding and incubating eggs might mean that both processes are perceived as sharing the same function: to stimulate the early growth of young humans and animals. In the case of mammals, this is done by feeding them with milk, but as far as birds are concerned, the initial development of the chick is achieved through incubation.

9 If this is actually the case, the buttocks (*uppatiik*, "a means for bending") would be inversely analogous to the hips (*makitiq*, "that gets up repeatedly"), both parts of the pelvic area being designated by their respective contribution to the flexion of the waist.

10 This word might be calqued on the English phrases "artificial brain" and "electronic brain."

11 *Qaniusinaa* is one of the very few Inuktitut terms made out of two separate words joined together into a single lexical unit. It can be parsed as *qaniu(p)* ("of the mouth") *sinaa* ("its edge").

12 On the relationship between "flying" and "learning," see the definition of *ilimmarturtuq* in Ootoova et al. (2000, 84): "He [shaman] flies when, resorting to this shamanic way, he ascends in the air thanks to his *tuurngaq*, being able to see the things he wants to know, which are not related to his terrestrial [knowledge]."

13 The marine equivalents of *nunaup kumangit* are *imaup kumangit*, the *puijiit* that congregate in the long hair of Sedna, the mistress of sea mammals, when she feels offended by humans (Saladin d'Anglure 2018, 263–64).

14 Vera Metcalf is from St. Lawrence Island, an Alaskan isle off the northeasternmost coast of Russia, where Siberian Yupik is spoken.

15 Literally, "they (-*tut*) have (-*qar*-) the action of (-*gia[q]*-) doing (*pi*-)." This is the exact semantic equivalent of English: "they have to do," except that because Inuktitut has no infinitive mode, "to do" is rendered by a verbal base (*pi*-) followed by a nominalizing affix (-*gia[q]*-).

16 In modern parlance, *itsivautaq* also means "the president of an assembly," a semantic calque from the English: "the chair(person) of a meeting."

17 *Quinattuq* might be related to the Proto-Inuit base *quiliqta*-, "to tremble" (Fortescue et al., 341).

18 Even though these bases are verbal, the words they generate translate as either verbs or noun phrases, according to the semantic context of the clause where they appear (see Appendix). In order to become comparatives or superlatives, non-verbal qualifying bases such as *sallu*- ("one who is thin") must first be verbalized with the affix -*u*- ("to be"), as in *salluu*- ("to be a thin one," i.e., "to be thin").

19 On the etymological and environmental sources of colour words in Eskimo-Aleut, see Fortescue (2016).

20 *Qakirtuq*, "bleached (by sun and air)" can be guessed at as "that has wasted itself."

21 According to Schneider (1970b, 355), the newly coined word *kutsuujaq* ("that looks like bubble gum") was used in Kuujjuaq (Nunavik) during the 1960s to denote the colour pink.

22 As seen in Chapter 3, the general verbal base for "understanding" is *tukisi*- ("to encounter a lengthwise axis").

23 In Siberian Yupik, two cognates of *nai(ma)*-, *narə*-, and *naar*-, also mean "to kiss with the nose."

24 Note that in my *Cassell's New French-English Dictionary* a large part of the translation of the word "*corps*" ("body") could apply to Inuktitut *timi*: "body trunk as opposed to limbs etc. . . . main portion, chief part."

25 Although, as was discussed, the names of the male and female sexual organs are almost identical: *usuk* ("single organ," i.e., "penis") and *utsuk* ("double organ," i.e., "vagina").

Chapter Six: Words for Socializing in the Contemporary World

1 When *ai* is attached to a name, the euphonic consonant *ng* usually appears at the end of that name in order to avoid the occurrence of three or four consecutive vowels that *Miaji*-ai or *Maasiu*-ai would generate.

2 In Labrador, under the influence of the Moravian missionaries who came originally from Germany, "yes" and "no" were formerly also expressed by the borrowed words *jaa* (German *Ja*) and *niija* (German *Nein*).

3 According to Spalding (1998, 62), "Thank you!" also translates as "*Saturnak!*" ("Don't take it back!") in Nattilingmiutut.

4 The last meaning ("Peace. . .") is a tentative English translation of the word *Salut!* ("Hail! Greetings!") found in the original (French) version of Schneider's dictionary.

5   During my first stay in Quaqtaq, when inquiring about shaking hands, I was told that I should shake hands with local people (adults, children, and babies alike) who had spent at least one night outside the village, as well as with travellers newly arrived from somewhere else. This rule applied in reverse to my own absences and arrivals.

6   This explanation seems to have originated in a novel published in 1858 by a former Hudson's Bay Company employee, R.M. Ballantyne, in which he asserts, "Chimo ... is an Esquimaux word of salutation, and is used by the natives when they meet with strangers" (Ballantyne 1858, 146).

7   Wishing departing people to "fare well" (*Atsut!/Aksut!*) could be a calque of the old English greeting "Farewell!" The fact that Labrador and Nunavik Inuit were the first to entertain sustained contacts with *Qallunaat* might explain why they would have coined this calque, generally unknown in Baffin Island and western Hudson Bay.

8   "Who" refers here to the kinship term used by Ego for addressing a person, as in "*Kinagivait?—Anaanagijara*" ("Who have you her for?—I have her as 'mother' [i.e., I call her 'mom']").

9   Space as defined by astrophysicians is part of *silarjuaq* ("super-*sila*"), the all-embracing externality (see Chapter 1).

10   The first syllable of both interrogatives, *qa-*, might have the same etymon as *qa-* in *qanuq?* "how?" and, perhaps, *qatsit?* "how many?" (Fortescue et al., 310).

11   Although in Alaskan Inupiaq, some verbal endings have an intrinsically past or present connotation. According to Hayashi (2011), in Inuktitut, the affixes for tense also express verbal aspects.

12   Except, of course, among relatives who are (or rather were) ritually prohibited from addressing each other (see Chapter 4).

13   It remains to be seen if, and up to what point, such precautionary habits have been transferred to Facebook and other social networks; I would guess they have.

14   The dual number in *aahaakkik* seems to confirm my supposition (Chapter 5) that in comparison with men, women are considered to have a double sexual organ.

15   When speaking Inuktitut, everyone is called by his or her first name, irrespective of their age, social condition, political or professional status.

16   A train is a *nunakkuujuukutaaq* ("long one that goes by land").

17   According to Taamusi Qumaq (1991, 54), an igloo or snow house is called *illuvigaq* when empty, but *illu* when referred to as a lived-in place.

18   The names of occupations generally start with a verbal base describing what the occupation is about, followed by the affix *-ti/-ji* ("one who does this on a regular basis").

19   And German numbers in the Moravian missions of Labrador.

20   *Qatsit?* also means "how many?" "How much is it?" can be translated by "*Qatsirarpa?*"—"How much does it get?" and "*Qatsiturpa?*"—"How much does it eat?" In the second case, money is assimilated to the concept of a consumable, quasi-edible good.

21   Most of these items already appear in a handwritten Inuktitut word-list compiled in 1887 at Fort Chimo (Kuujjuaq, Nunavik) by the naturalist and ethnologist Lucien Turner (mss deposited at the Smithsonian Institution, Washington, DC).

22 The Royal Canadian Mounted Police had actually been present in the Arctic since the early twentieth century, but with only a handful of detachments scattered over two million square kilometres.

23 Interestingly, the word *sivulirti* also designates the head animal in a dog team.

24 The base *aki-* in *akigiarniq* is the already discussed morpheme *aki*, meaning "exchange value."

25 According to Schneider (1970a, 109), the base *katajja-* derives from "*katakpoq* [*katap-puq*], to fall, they say, it is as if one were letting him-/herself fall oftentimes."

26 For a Nunavik-based description of Inuit values, see Annahatak (2014).

Conclusion: Words for the Future

1 Recall that in the polysynthetic Inuit language, words are built according to the speaker's needs, out of a finite number of verbal, nominal, or other bases, plus affixes and endings.

2 In most Inuit dialects, the word *upirngaaq* means "springtime," summer being called *aujaq* (related to the base *auk-*, "to thaw"). The "early surprise" signification of *upirngaaq*'s possible etymon might thus allude to the sudden outburst of vernal thawing conditions after eight or nine *uki-* months.

3 When women talk about sexual intercourse, they often express themselves in the passive, e.g., being "harpooned" by their husband, or (Christopher Trott, personal communication) being *kujaktaq* ("the object of copulation"). This supports the semantic image of men catching women.

4 Further research should also examine how the parsing and etymological analysis of affixes, a process that has not been duly considered in the present book, can contribute to morphosemantics.

5 As noted in Chapter 2, two animals are at ease on both land and water: *nanuq*, the polar bear; and *qimmiq* ("that is shy and respectful"), the dog that follows its human master. This is one of the reasons why these species cannot be easily classified into a particular genus.

6 This infra-semantic system of underlying significant symbols is that of semiotics.

7 Not unlike popular Taoism, where the regulating system of the universe may be given a human form (the Jade Emperor), traditional Inuit cosmology often personalized *sila*, for instance under the guise of the giant baby *Naarjuk*, "Big Belly."

Appendix: Polysynthesis: A Big Word for Something Fairly Simple

1 The present Appendix is inspired by an article I published many years ago in French (Dorais 1974). Excerpts from that paper are used here with the permission of the original publisher. For a more complete overview of the grammar of Nunavik Inuktitut, readers may consult Dorais (1988; 2010, chap. 3; 2017a, chap. 8), as well as Schneider (1972–76).

2 Actually, this affix *-tu(q)-* is the same morpheme as the ending in *tikittuqar*tuq. According to its position within the word and the semantic context of the sentence in which it appears, it can act either as a grammatical ending or a derivational affix.

3 A mood is a way to talk about an event. For instance, is the narration of the event presented as an assertion, a question, an order, something that might happen?

4 In this, Inuktitut differs from Greenlandic Kalaallisut, where the assertive is the default mode and the indicative has a participial meaning (e.g., *tusartunga*: "I hear" in Inuktitut, and "I, hearing" in Greenlandic). It should be noted that in the Greenlandic and some other linguistic traditions, what I call "assertive" is often designated as "indicative," while my "indicative" is called "participial."

5 'Ø' stands for a "zero-ending," the significant absence of any audible or visible (in writing) marker. When speakers hear or see the word *ilisaiji* without any ending, they know that it cannot express anything else than the basic nominal relationship in the singular number.

6 For an exhaustive study of affixes in the Inuit language, readers may consult Fortescue (1983). A categorization of derivational affixes (based on Fortescue's) with Nunavik Inuktitut examples can be found in Dorais (2010, 289–91).

7 This process is often called "noun incorporation" (Mithun 2009).

8 The word-base *piuju(q)* stems from the lexicalization of *piu-* ("to be good") and *-juq* ("someone or something who" in the present context). As was discussed in the Introduction, *piu-* could itself be a lexicalization of *pi-* ("something") and *-u-* ("to be"). Thus, the literal meaning of *piujuujutit* might be "you are someone who is something."

9 This suffix can also refer to a rhetorical owner; *illulik* would then mean "there is a house."

10 Due to morphophonemic considerations (i.e., a change in the pronunciation of a morpheme triggered by its phonological environment), the final *v* in the localization base *av-* has become *n* with the addition of the ending *-na*.

11 A count of the number of morphemes in use in Nunavik Inuktitut yields an approximate total of 760 word-bases, 950 grammatical endings, and 490 derivational affixes and enclitics (Dorais 2017b, 155).

12 For a reflection on the fact that some semantic classifications that appear obvious to speakers of English (e.g., the difference between snow and planks) are not necessarily marked or even significant in other languages, see Clément (2017, 552).

Glossary of Inuit Words

This glossary lists in alphabetical order the Inuit words discussed in the book, except for those used as grammatical examples in the Introduction and the Appendix. Each entry includes the current English meaning of the word, its possible underlying signification or etymological link, when decipherable, and the page where the word is first analyzed. Letters enclosed in brackets [ ] are variants or are not heard in the Nunavik dialect. Significations preceded by an asterisk (*) result from informed guesswork rather than solid etymological analysis (see Introduction, "Some Epistemology"). Abbreviations: D = dual number; PL = plural number; Nvik = Nunavik; Nvut = Nunavut; N = North; NE = northeastern; W = western.

AA!/II!
Yes!
/168

A'ALUK
something dangerous (baby talk)
/82

AANA[Q]
paternal grandmother
[linked to] *anaana* (mother)
/106

AANGAJAANNA[R]TUT (PL)
illicit drugs
that make one become *aangajaattuq*
(drunk)
/165

AANGAJAANNIQ
drunkenness
the fact of being *aangajaattuq* (drunk)
/165

AANGAJAAATTUQ
he/she is drunk
is in a state of frequent dizziness or
fainting
/165

AANNIAJUQ
he/she is sick
endures pain continually
/164

AANNIAQ
disease, illness
continuous pain
/164

AANNIASIURTI
nurse
one who goes after disease (disease
hunter)
/164

AANNIASIURTIMARIK
doctor, physician
a complete *aanniasiurti* (disease hunter)
/164

AANNIASIUTI
medicine, drug
something useful for illness
/164

AANNIAVIK
hospital, nursing station
place where people are sick
/165

AANNI[R]TUQ
he/she is in pain
/164

AARLUK
orca, killer whale
/44

AARQI[K]TUQ
he/she heals, mends
he/she/it is repaired
/164

AARQIQAJANNGITUQ
cancer (former name)
(the disease from which) one cannot heal
/165

AASIVAK
spider
*large crawler
/55

AATSUK!/AAMAI!
I don't know!
(*Aatsuk!* linked to) *Asu!* Indeed!
/171

AGGAIT (PL)
hand (Nvik), fingers
/151

AGGAK
hand (Nvut)
/151

AGGU
windward side
going against wind
/236

AGIARUTI
violin
means for acting as if one was filing
/196

AI!
Hi! Hello! Hail!
/168

AIJUQ
he/she goes somewhere
/155

AIKULUK
sibling-in-law of the opposite gender
nice little foreign guest
/118

AIPPAAJUGIIK (D)
traditional swinger couple
pair of little spouses
/116

AIPPANGA
the other one (of two)
its half of a pair
/114

AIPPANGAT
Tuesday
their second one (day)
/98

AIPPAQ
spouse, partner
one in a pair
/114

AIPPARIIK (D)
marital couple
the two halves of a pair
/113

AITTUPAA
gives him/her something
fetches him/her repeatedly
/241

AIVAA
he/she fetches it/him/her
/155

AIVIQ
walrus
(linked to) *ayag-*, to thrust/push with a
pole
/44

AJAGAQ
cup-and-ball game
that is shoved away
/196

AJAGUTAQ
rainbow (Nvik)
means for separating two parallel objects
/22

AJAJA
man's personal song
/95

AJAKULUK
maternal aunt
*nice little support
/110

AJARAAQ
string figures
that is barely shoved away
/196

AJJI
image, similitude
/161

AJJIGIIK
two that are similar
a pair of images
/161

AJJILIURIAQ
photography
making an image (photographing
something)
/197

AJJILIURTUQ
he/she takes a photo
makes an image
/161

AJJILIURUTI
camera
means for making an image
/161

AJJI[N]NGUAQ
photo, picture
imitation of an image
/161

AJUARNAQ
barnacle
that looks like an abscess
/54

AJUAT (PL)
abscesses, boils
*that break loose frequently
/165

AJUNNGI[T]TUQ
is competent, efficient
is not without power
/85

AJUQIRTUIJI
Anglican minister
who teaches for a long time
/95

AJURNA[R]MAT
nothing can be done
because it makes one powerless
/84

AJURNA[R]TUQ
it is out of one's power
it makes *ajur-* (being powerless)
/84

AJURTUQ
is powerless, impotent
he/she cannot do anything more
/84

AJUTTAQ/AJUKTAQ
soccer, football
/196

AKI
exchange value, price
that is opposite to something
/189

AKIANI
across
in a portion of space opposing him/her/it
/36

AKIGIARNIQ
punishment
the fact of getting a retribution (for misdeeds)
/195

AKIKITTUQ
cheap, inexpensive
that has a small price
/189

AKILIRPAA
he/she pays it
provides it with an opposite
/189

AKILITSAQ
debt
that is to have a price
/189

AKINIARTUQ
takes revenge, has a feud
deals with someone facing him/her
/136

AKINNAQ
wall
that looks like a means for facing something
/182

AKITUJUQ
it is costly, expensive
that has a big price
/189

AKKA
paternal uncle
/110

AKUNI
for a long time
its own middle space, in middle spaces
/178

ALAASIKA
Alaska
(from the English Aleut loan word "Alaska")
/30

ALIANARTUQ
provokes joy (Nvik)
makes someone *alia-* (rejoice)
/86

ALIASUTTUQ
is happy, rejoices (Nvik; opposite meaning elsewhere)
/86

ALIQ
harpoon line
/65

ALIRTIIK (D)
pair of stockings
lower area
/68

ALLA
First Nation person (Nvik)
stranger
/ 75

ALLAIT/AGLAIT (PL)
letters, written material
decorative patterns, ornamental spots
/97

ALLAIT IJJUJUT (PL)
the Bible
the thick writings
/97

ALLANGUAQ
narwhal (Nvik)
imitation of ornamental spots
/45

ALLANIARTUQ
he/she reads
deals with *allait* (letters)
/97

ALLATI
office worker, secretary
one who writes
/184

ALLATUQ/AGLARTUQ
he/she writes
draws or sews decorative patterns
/97

ALLAUTI
pencil, pen
that is used for writing
/97

ALLAVIK
office
place for writing
/184

ALLIAQ
mattress
the one under
/47

ALLINGISUNGARVIK
Saturday
not observing a taboo for the last time
/98

ALLIQ
nether world of the dead
the lower one (underground)
/91

ALLIRIIRTUT (PL)
Monday
they have finished observing a taboo
/98

ALLIRUQ
lower jaw
small lower object
/149

ALLIRUTI
taboo
means for being forbidden from doing so
/94

ALLITUQARTUQ
Sunday
there are people respecting a taboo
/98

ALLITUT (PL)
Sunday
they respect a taboo
/98

ALLU/AGLU
seal's breathing hole
place for getting out
/65

ALUQ
sole of foot or shoe
that is in a lower position
/151

ALUTSAUTI
spoon
means for licking
/191

AMAAMA
breastmilk (baby talk)
(linked to) *amaamak*, breast
/82

AMAAMAK
breast (woman/man)
(linked to) *ama(C)-*, to suckle
/142

AMAAMATTUQ
a baby suckles
(linked to) *amaama*, breastmilk
/142

AMARUQ
wolf
associated with carrying something on
the back
/48

AMAUTI
parka for carrying a baby
means for carrying someone on one's back
/69

AMAUTILIALUK
ogre
the big one with a parka for carrying
babies
/93

AMIQ
skin, hide (land mammal)
/68

AMIRIKA
United States
(from the English "America")
/30

AMISUT (PL)
numerous
/188

AMMALUKITAQ
circle, sphere
that opens frequently and repeatedly
/182

AMMANIQ
vagina
aperture
/145

AMMUUMAJUQ
Arctic clam
*that is looked down at from above
/54

ANAANA
mother, mommy
older female relative
/105

ANAANAQATI
half-sibling by mother
co-sharer of a mother
/108

ANAANATSIALIRQITAQ
great-great-grandmother
who has been made a grandmother once
more
/110

ANAANATSIALIRQIUTI
great-grandmother
means for being a grandmother once
again
/110

ANAANATSIAQ
(maternal) grandmother
good *anaana* (mother)
/109

ANAQ
excrement
(linked to) *ani-*, to come out
/146

ANARIARTUVIK
bathroom, toilet
place where one goes to defecate
/183

ANARTUQ
defecates
(linked to) *anaq*, excrement
/146

ANARVIK
toilet bowl
place for defecating
/183

ANAULLAGAQ
drum
that is struck with a stick
/197

ANAULLAUTI
baseball bat
means for striking something with a stick
/196

ANGAJUATTANGA
older spouse in a couple
the older person attached to him/her
/106

ANGAJUK
elder sibling
who wants or tends to be big
/106

ANGAJURQAAK (D)
parents (father and mother)
antecedent elders
/107

ANGAJURQAAQ
camp leader, chief parent
/107

ANGAJURQAASUK
assistant trader
lesser *angajurqaaq* (chief trader)
/107

ANGAJURQAAVINIQ
deceased parent
former *angajurqaaq* (parent)
/107

ANGAJUTSIQ
older than
more *angajuk* (elder) than
/106

ANGAJUURNGUQ
spouse of spouse's older sibling
older sibling once more
/118

ANGAK
maternal uncle
(linked to) *angajuk*, elder and *angijuq*, big
/110

ANGAKKUQ
shaman
who moves about, strains to get free,
sways
/94

ANGIJUQ
he/she/it is big
(linked to) *angajuk*, elder
/156

ANGIRRANIQ
ghost
the fact of returning back home
/91

ANGIRRAQ
home
(place for) coming back
/182

ANGIRTUQ
he/she says: "Yes"
/94

ANGUNASUTTI
hunter
one who usually hunts
/62

ANGUNASUTTUQ
one who hunts
strives to catch game
/62

ANGUSIAQ
boy delivered by midwife
the male who has been made (by midwife)
/124

ANGUTI
male person or animal
means for being big, *means for catching
/80

ANGUTIARJUK
Ego's aunt's husband
lesser male man (i.e., father)
/117

ANGUTITURTUQ
she eats a man
has sexual intercourse with a man
/162

ANGUTIVIAQ
male bird
smallish big male
/240

ANGUUTI
whale fin, boat propeller
means to make it move on in water
/45

ANGUVAA
he/she catches it
/81

ANGUVIGAQ
spear
small occasion or place for catching
something
/65

ANI
brother (for a woman)
one who comes out (is born)
/107

ANIJUQ
he/she exits, goes/comes out
/156

ANIRNIALUK
God (Roman Catholic)
Great Spirit (great vital breath)
/90

ANIRNIQ
vital breath, spirit
the fact of breathing out
/89

ANIRNIQ PIUJUQ
Holy Spirit (Catholic)
Good Spirit (good vital breath)
/90

ANIRTIRIJUQ
he/she respires
breathes out repeatedly
/89

ANITITSIGIAQ
exorcism (Christian)
the action of chasing (devils) away
/95

ANITSAQ
female Ego's male cousin
substitute brother
/112

ANIU
snow for making water
/23

ANNA
that one farther away
/34

ANNA[K]TUQ
it (game) escapes
it starts going out
/156

ANNGAQ
woman's brother's child
one who is similar to an older brother
/111

ANNURAAQ
piece of clothing
(linked to) *atə-*, to put on
/68

ANURI
wind
/22

APA
to urinate (baby talk)
/82

APAAPA
solid food (baby talk)
/82

APIRIJUQ
he/she asks a question
/161

APIRQUQ
anthropologist (Nvik)
one who asks many questions
/161

APIRQUTI
question
means for asking, interrogating
/94

APIRSU[K]TUQ
he/she asks, interrogates
asks in a deliberate way
/161

APPAK/AKPAK
murre
(linked to) alaᵹ-, wiping, sweeping
/50

APURTUQ
knocks up against something
/163

APUTI[K]
snow on the ground
a means to cover something with snow
/24

AQIAQ
lower belly
/143

AQIARUQ
stomach
that is associated with aqiaq (lower belly)
/143

AQIATTUTUNGA
I am full (after meal)
I have much of a belly
/174

AQIGGIQ
rock ptarmigan
/51

AQIGGIUJAQ
chicken (W Nvik)
that looks like a ptarmigan
/61

AQIGGIVIK
willow ptarmigan
big aqiggiq (ptarmigan)
/51

AQILLUQAAQ
drift of soft snow
very tender material
/23

AQQANILLIT (PL)
eleven (Greenland)
they have a downward motion
/187

ARNAAJUK
Ego's uncle's wife
lesser woman (i.e., mother)
/117

ARNALIAQ
girl delivered by midwife
the female who has been made (by midwife)
/124

ARNAQ
female person or animal
*who makes something move, who agitates
/81

ARNAQUTI
midwife delivering boy
woman owned by someone (the boy)
/124

ARNARIIK (D)
marital couple (convivial)
two persons, one of whom is a woman
/117

ARNA[R]TURTUQ
he eats a woman
he has sexual intercourse with a woman
/162

ARNAVIAQ
female bird
smallish big female
/240

ARNGUAQ
amulet
that looks like hanging something
/94

-ARNIQ/-SUNNIQ
there is a smell or flavour of
/162

ARPIK
Arctic raspberry
/32

ARQA[R]TUQ
dives, loses altitude
goes down repeatedly
/42

ARQUTI
road, street, route, trail
means for asking (one's way)
/181

ARSAQURNAQ
triceps brachii muscle
(linked to) *arsaquq*, humerus/upper arm
/139

ARSA[R]NIIT (PL)
northern lights
football games (of the dead)
/27

ARVIK/ARVIQ
bowhead whale
(linked to) *arvar-*, to go down, to dive
/45

ARVINILIIT/-LIK
six
they have/there is a crossing
/187

ARVINILIIT MARRUUNGNIK
seven (N Baffin)
they have crossings, two of them
/187

ARVINILIIT PINGASUNIK
eight (N Baffin)
they have crossings, three of them
/187

ASU!
Indeed!
/171

ASUGUUQ!
You're right!
indeed it is said
/171

ASUILAAK!
Finally! There it is!
indeed, that is to say
/171

ATA!/ALA!
Listen! Be quiet!
/161

ATAANI
under
in his/her/its underside
/36

ATAATA
father, daddy
older male relative
/105

ATAATAQATI
half-sibling by father
co-sharer of a father
/108

ATAATATSIALIRQITAQ
great-great-grandfather
who has been made a grandfather once more
/110

ATAATATSIALIRQIUTI
great-grandfather
means for being a grandfather once again
/110

ATAATATSIAQ
grandfather
good *ataata* (father)
/109

ATAJUQ
adheres, is attached to
/186

ATANIIRTUT (PL)
chess game
they take each other's king
/196

ATANIQ
camp leader, king, queen
the fact of being attached (to each other)
/193

ATATAA!
Ouch!
/25

ATAUSIQ
one
means for being in one piece
/186

ATIGI
hooded tunic, duffle parka
that is put on
/68

ATIQ
name, name soul
(linked to) *atə[ði]-*, to be the same
/90

ATIRIIK (D)
name-sharers (Nvut)
two who have each other as a name
/125

ATIRUSIQ
family name
lesser name
/131

ATITSIAGIIK (D)
name-sharers (Labrador)
two who have each other as a nice name
/125

ATITSIAQ
namesake (Nvik)
nice name
/125

ATSA
paternal aunt
/110

ATSAQ/AK&AQ
black bear
/48

ATSU-/AK&UNAAQ
leather thong
/43

ATSUITUQ/AK&UITTUQ
he/she is rich
he/she is not poor
/188

ATSUJUQ/AK&UJUQ
he/she is poor
/188

ATSUNAI!
Goodbye! (Nvik)
go ahead, hey; fare well, hey
/174

ATSUNGIRTUQ
fastens, locks (e.g., door)
/173

ATSUT!/AKSUT!
Go for it! Fare well!
/174

ATTU-/AKTUIJUQ
he/she touches something
/163

ATTU-/AKTU[R]PAA
he/she touches it
/163

ATTUINIQ
the sense of touch
the fact of touching something
/158

ATTUQ
adult seal
big thing
/44

ATUARNIQ
north wind (NE Nvik)
following a path
/22

ATUARTUQ
he/she reads
follows a visible track
/97

ATURATSAUNGITTUQ
it is useless
that is unfit for being used
/209

AUJAQ
summer
(linked to) *au-*, *auk-*, rotting, thawing
/236

AUJUQ
it rots
/140

AUK
blood
(linked to) *aut-*, to melt, and *au-*, to rot
/140

AUKA!/AAKKA!
No!
/170

AUKULUK
chocolate (NE Nvik)
nice little blood
/140

AULAJIVAA
he/she remembers it
(linked to) *aula-*, to move
/84

AULAJUITTUQ
it is immobile
it cannot move
/29

AULAJUQ
he/she/it moves
/156

AULASAUTI
fishing line and hook
used for trying to make it move
/65

AULAUTI
motor, engine
means for making something move
/185

AULAUTILIRIJI
mechanic
one who deals with motors
/191

AULLA[R]TUQ
he/she departs/goes away
starts to move
/156

AUNAARTUQ
bleeds profusely, has her periods
makes oneself bleed
/140

AUNNGUAQ
chocolate (W Nvik)
imitation of blood
/140

AUPAANGAJUQ
reddish
partly *aupartuq* (red)
/160

AUPALLAAJUQ
measles
it is red in many places
/165

AUPALUKTUQ
red (W Hudson Bay)
that makes blood visible
/159

AUPARTUQ
red, pink, orange
(linked to) *auk*, blood
/159

AUTTUQ
it melts, thaws, he/she bleeds from the nose
/140

AUVVIK
caterpillar
place for crawling
/55

AVALUQ
fence
thing for surrounding
/150

AVANI
far away
/34

AVATAQ
inflated sealskin buoy
a surrounding one
/150

AVATILLU ATAUSIRLU
twenty-one
and twenty and one
/187

AVATILLU QULILLU
thirty
and twenty and ten
/187

AVATILLU QULILLU MARRUULU
thirty-two
and twenty and ten and two
/187

AVATIMMARIK
four hundred
a complete twenty
/188

AVATIT (1) (PL)
limbs
area around, which surrounds something
/139

AVATIT (2) (PL)
twenty
the limbs (ten fingers and ten toes)
/186

AVATIT AVATIT
four hundred
twenty (times) twenty
/188

AVATIT MARRUUK
forty
two (times) twenty
/187

AVATIT PINGASUT QULILLU
seventy
three (times) twenty and ten
/188

AVATIT QULILLU PINGASULLU
two hundred and sixty
thirteen (times) twenty
/188

AVATIT TALLIMAT
one hundred
five (times) twenty
/188

AVATIVUT
natural environment
what surrounds us
/150

AVILIAK (D)
shared wives
two who are made to be shared
/115

AVINNGAQ
lemming
*one that starts to divide itself
/49

AVITTUUK (D)
the spouses separate/divorce
the two of them break up
/112

AVIULLATAQ
piece of something
that has been separated from something
/104

AVVARIIK (D)
name-sharers (Nvut)
two who have each other as a half
/125

BAI!
Bye!
(from the English "Bye!")
/175

GUUTI
God
(from the English "God")
/96

HAKI
hockey
(from the English "hockey")
/196

IGA
hearth for cooking
/184

IGAJI
cook, chef
one who cooks
/184

IGAJUQ
he/she cooks
(linked to) *iga*, cooking hearth
/184

IGALAAQ
window
smokehole (literally, the action of cooking)
/182

IGAVIK
kitchen
place for cooking
/183

IGGAAK (D)
snow goggles, sunglasses
that look like eyes
/148

IGGIAQ
throat
place or action of swallowing
/141

IGIMAQ
harpoon
that is thrown repeatedly
/64

IGUNAQ
gamey meat
the fact of extracting oil from blubber
/67

IGUTSAQ
bumblebee
that strives to sting
/55

IIGATSAQ
pill
that is to be swallowed
/164

II NAATTUNGU
twenty (East Greenlandic)
completing a person
/186

IJAUTIIK (D)
glasses
used for the eyes
/148

IJI
eye
/148

IJIIRTUQ
he/she hides
suppresses someone's eyes (i.e., sight)
/148

IJIRAIT
invisible human beings
who are made invisible
/93

IJJILIRTUQ
temperature is very cold
that gets coldness
/25

IJJUK/IBJUK
soil
sod
/31

IJJUUJAIT (PL)
dried beans (NE Nvik)
that look like testicles
/146

IJJUUJAQ
ovary (Nvik)
that looks like a testicle
/145

IJJUUK/IGJUUK (D)
testicles
(linked to) *igður-*, to coagulate, get stiff
/145

IJURNA[R]TUQ
is laughable, funny
he/she/it makes one laugh
/154

IJURTUQ
he/she laughs
/154

IJURU[JU]Q
ghost
/91

IKAJURTI
helper, midwife
one who helps habitually
/124

IKAJURTUQ
he/she helps someone
/88

IKANI
there
/34

IKAURNIQ
hour
going across something
/98

IKKARUQ
shoal
that becomes shallow
/33

IKKATUQ
it is shallow
/33

IKKII!
How cold!
/25

IKUMA
fire, electricity
burning
/184

IKUMALIRIJI
electrician
one who deals with *ikuma* (electricity)
/191

IKUMALIURVIK
power plant
place for making electricity
/184

IKURTUT (PL)
boats are hauled upriver
/61

IKUSIK
elbow
(linked to) *ikug-*, to hack at
/151

IKUUTAQ
bow drill, modern drill
means for hacking
/65

ILA
part of a whole, member of a group, relative
/103

ILAALI!
Welcome! (after thanks)
but that is to say
/172

ILAANIT
something intentional
from a of him/her
/180

ILAANIUNNGI[T]TUQ!
Excuse me! I am sorry!
it is not intentional
/180

ILAGALAIT (PL)
distant blood relatives
lesser *ilait* (relatives)
/105

ILAGIIT (PL)
family, kindred
those who are component parts for each
other
/105

ILAI?
Is it not so?
that is to say, hey?
/172

ILAIT (PL)
relatives, companions
parts of something
/103

ILANGIT (PL)
some of it/them
its parts, their parts
/104

ILAPASIIT (PL)
relatives by marriage
almost *ilait* (relatives)
/105

ILAVINIIT (PL)
deceased relatives
former *ilait* (relatives)
/105

ILIARJUK
orphan
little one put in some position, *lesser
partner
/123

ILIMMARTURNIQ
shamanic flight
learning continuously and repeatedly
/149

ILINNIANILIRIJI
curriculum designer
one who deals with education
/191

ILINNIATI
student
one who studies
/184

ILINNIATITSIJI
teacher
one who makes people study
/184

ILINNIATUQ
he/she studies
seeks to learn
/184

ILINNIAVIK
school
place for studying
/184

ILIPPAA
he/she learns it
*finds it to be familiar
/85

ILIRANARTUQ
is worthy of respect
is a source of *ilira-* (high respect)
/89

ILIRASUTTUQ
he/she feels high respect
wants to ask for something but does not
dare
/88

ILISAIJI
teacher
one who makes people study
/184

ILISIIRNIQ
casting a spell
putting oneself into place
/95

ILISIIRQUTI
spell, charm
means for casting a spell
/95

ILISIIRTUQ
spell caster, sorcerer
one who practises *ilisiirniq* (spell casting)
/95

ILITAQ
recognized, learned
someone/something found to be familiar
/85

ILITARSIJUQ
recognizes someone/something
enters in contact with something familiar
/85

ILLIAQ/IGLIAQ
uterus
little *illiq/igliq* (sleeping platform in an igloo)
/146

ILLIQ/IGLIQ
bed, sleeping platform
(linked to) *ingət-*, to sit
/183

ILLU/IGLU
house, inhabited structure, residence
/182

ILLUARJUK
cousin (South Baffin)
little partner
/242

ILLUJUAQ
wooden house
super-residence
/66

ILLUKITAARNIQ
juggling
using both of them (hands) repeatedly
/196

ILLULIRIJI
carpenter
one who deals with houses
/191

ILLUSAQ
snow for making an igloo
material for a house
/23

ILLUVIGAQ
snow house, igloo
little big residence
/66

ILU
the inside of
/188

ILUITTUQ
that is entire, whole
that has no *ilu* (inside)
/188

ILUMIUTAQ
fetus
dweller of the inside
/31

ILUPPIAQ
inner set of clothing
most inside
/68

ILUUNNANIARVIK
bathtub
place for looking after the whole (body)
/183

ILUUNNATIK (PL)
all of them (Nvik)
(linked to) *alur*, width
/188

ILUVIQ
tomb
(linked to) *a&u-*, to put in a certain way
/91

IMAALUK
sea
big water
/28

IMAQ
water (esp. saltwater)
contents of something (especially of sea)
/31

IMARPIK
ocean
huge water
/237

IMAVI[ALU]K
ocean
huge water
/237

IMIALUK
alcohol
big water
/165

IMIQ
(drinkable) water
freshwater
/31

IMIRAQ
soft drink, juice
little water
/193

IMIRTUQ
he/she drinks
uses *imiq* (water)
/66

IMIRUSUTTUQ
he/she feels thirsty
needs to drink
/163

IMMA[R]QA
maybe, perhaps
(it is) possibly thus or there
/171

IMMUK
store-bought milk
human or animal milk
/193

IMMULIURTI
cow (W Nvik)
milk maker
/61

INALUAT (PL)
intestines
/143

INALUUJAIT (PL)
spaghetti, coiled bannock
that look like intestines
/192

INGITTUQ
he/she sits
(linked to) *illiq/igliq*, platform in an igloo
/155

INGIULIIT (PL)
swells
to form ridges back and forth
/33

INI
place, room for something
/177

INIQUNAITTUQ
he/she is ugly
is not *iniqunar-* (pretty)
/157

INIQUNARTUQ
he/she is pretty
provokes cooing
/157

INNA
that one
/34

INNAQ
mature adult (Nvut)
completeness
/80

INNGI[R]TUQ
he/she sings a hymn
makes a loud sound
/96

INUARTI
murderer
one who gets at human beings
/87

INUARTUQ
commits murder
gets at (kills) a human being
/136

INUGAGULLI[GA]IT (PL)
dwarves
the small ones provided with fingers and
toes
/93

INUGAIT (PL)
chess, knuckle-bones game
little persons
/196

INUINNAIT (PL)
western Nunavut Inuit
the genuine people
/78

IÑUIÑÑAQ
twenty (Alaskan Inupiaq)
a total person
/186

INUIT NUNANGAT
the Inuit homeland
the land of Inuit
/27

INUK/INUIT
human person(s), Inuit
animated being who "owns" other beings
/78

INULIRIJI
government administrator
one who deals with people
/194

INULUK
a bad individual
bad person
/79

INUMMARIK
mature adult (Nvik)
complete person
/79

INUNGMARIIT (PL)
Nattilingmiut Inuit
the complete people
/78

INUNGMARIK
traditional Inuk (Nvut)
complete person
/80

INU-/IÑUPIAT (PL)
northern Alaskan Inuit
the real people
/78

INURQITUQ
is a good individual
is a good person
/79

INURURTUQ
he/she reincarnates
becomes a person (once again)
/79

INUT-/INUKTITUT
Inuit language/customs
(doing) like human beings
/79

INUTSAQ/INUKSAQ
human fetus
future person
/79

INUTSUK/INUKSUK
stone cairn
that resembles a person
/65

INUTUINNAIT (PL)
eastern Arctic Inuit
the only genuine people
/78

INUTUQAQ
elderly individual
long-standing person
/79

INUUGUNNAITUQ
he/she is deceased
is not living anymore
/155

INUUJARTUIT (PL)
East Asians
those who look like Inuit
/77

INUUJUQ
he/she is alive
he/she is a human person
/40

INUULIRTUQ
he/she is born
starts to be a person
/79

INUUNIQ
Inuit identity
the fact of being Inuit
/198

INUUQATI
companion
who shares the life of someone
/136

INUUSILIRIJI
social worker
one who deals with the life of people
/191

INUUSIQ
human life
the fact of being an *inuk* (person)
/82

INUUSUTTUQ
youth, young adult
who is striving to be a person
/79

INUVIALUIT (PL)
Mackenzie Inuit
the big real people
/78

INUVINIQ
deceased person, corpse
former person
/79

IPIRAQ
harpoon line
that is tied
/65

IPPA[K]SAQ
yesterday
that will be (considered as) some time ago
/26

IPPI-/IKPIGIJAIT (PL)
feelings, sensations
that are felt
/86

IPPI-/IKPIGIVAA
he/she feels it, notices it
/86

IPPI-/IKPIGUSUTTUQ
he/she feels something
/158

IQALUK
fish (properly, trout or char)
/52

IQALUNNIATI
fisher(man)
one who usually fishes
/62

IQALUNNIATUQ
he/she fishes
deals with fish
/62

IQALUPPIK
Arctic char
the very best *iqaluk* (fish)
/52

IQALUUNAPPAA
mermaid
half-part of a fish
/57

IQARTIK
outer layer of skin
that makes one benumbed
/163

IQARTUQ
he/she is stiff, benumbed
/163

IQIRQUQ
little finger
*that reaches *iqiq* (the corner of the mouth)
/151

IRINALIURUTI
magic song or formula
means for producing a scream
/95

IRMI[K]TUQ
washes face (Nvik), washes (Nvut)
makes it (filth) fade
/154

IRNGUTALIRQITAQ
great-great-grandchild
who has been made a grandchild once
more
/110

IRNGUTALIRQIUTI
great-grandchild
means for being a grandchild once again
/110

IRNGUTAQ
grandchild, grand-nephew
means for completing (one's family)
/109

IRNIAJUK
nephew by marriage
lesser son
/118

IRNIQ
son
the begotten one
/106

IRNIRIIK (D)
a son and his parent
two, one of whom is a son
/108

IRQ!/IRQAALUK!
Big bottom! (swear word)
/179

IRQANAIJARTUQ
works (N and South Baffin)
he/she is completing a task
/191

IRQAPAA
he/she remembers it
(linked to) *irqaq*, bottom of a body of
water
/84

IRQATUIJI
judge
whose task is to remember (one's deeds)
/195

IRQATUIVIK
tribunal
place for remembering frequently
/195

IRQILIK/ITQILIK
Dene person (W Arctic)
one with louse nits
/75

IRQIQ
louse nit
/55

IRRAVIIT (PL)
viscera
/143

IRSIJUQ
he/she is frightened
(linked to) *ira-*, to be horrified
/87

IRSINARTUQ
that is frightful
it provokes *irsi-* (fright)
/87

IRSUQ/IR&UQ
large intestine, colon
thing for shrinking or contracting
/146

ISARUQ
wing
something attached in order to extend
limbs
/51

ISIQ
smoke, steam
/53

ISIRITSIAQ
smoked meat or fish
that has been exposed to a lot of smoke
/67

ISIURALITTAAQ
grey trout
with some (colour of) smoke on it
/53

ISU-/I&UARTUQ
it is suitable, convenient
that is well
/73

ISU-/I&UITTUQ
unsuitable, inconvenient
that is not well
/86

ISUK
end, extremity
/83

ISUMA
thought, reason
anxious/annoyed, *having reached the
end
/83

ISUMAINNAQ
without limits, at will
a genuine *isuma* (thought)
/86

ISUMAITTUQ
he/she is stupid
is without *isuma* (reason)
/83

ISUMAJUQ
he/she thinks, reflects
uses his/her *isuma* (thought, reason)
/73

ISUMANNIK!
As you wish!
(you may follow) your *isuma* (thought)
/86

ISUMAQARVIK
intellect
receptacle for thoughts
/73

ISUMATUJUQ
he/she is wise, intelligent
has much *isuma* (reason)
/83

ISURTAQ
grey whale hide
added murky element
/160

ITAARTUQ
breaks into a house/tent
enters repeatedly, forcibly
/156

ITIGAIT (PL)
foot (Nvik), toes
those resembling toe-caps
/151

ITIGAK/ISIGAK
foot (Nvut)
that resembles a toe-cap
/151

ITIJUQ
it is deep
/33

ITIMAK
palm of the hand
(linked to) *iti-*, to be deep
/151

ITIQ
anus
(linked to) *iti-/ətə-*, to be deep
/144

ITIRTUQ/ISIRTUQ
he/she/it enters
/156

ITIRUQ
urine
something associated with the anus
/146

ITIVIANI
on the other side
on his/her/its other side
/36

ITSIRARJUAQ
Catholic priest
who bows forward, his back turned on
people
/95

ITSI-/IKSIVAJUQ
he/she is seated
/155

ITSIVAUTAALUK
couch
big *itsivautaq* (seat)
/183

ITSI-/IKSIVAUTAQ
seat, chair, chairman
means for being seated
/155

ITTAAQ
sperm
little oozing liquid
/127

ITTUIT KIINAUJANGIT (PL)
old age allowance
old people's money
/194

ITTUQ
old man
/81

ITTUSUK
male lover (convivial)
lesser old man
/116

IVAJUQ
it (bird) incubates
/52

IVALU
sinew, sewing thread
*something for swinging while moving
/68

IVANIQ
woman's breast (W Nvik)
the fact of incubating
/142

IVIANGIQ
woman's breast
(linked to) *iva-*, to incubate
/142

IVITAARUQ
red trout
little red earth
/53

JAMA
jam
(from the English "jam")
/193

JAMAIT (PL)
Germans
(from the English "German")
/77

JISUSI KIRISTUSI
Jesus Christ
(from the English "Jesus Christ")
/96

KAAPI
coffee
(from the English "coffee")
/192

KAAT-/KAAKTUQ
he/she feels hungry
/163

KAGGUTIQ
cancer
that makes one drop progressively
/165

KAIVALLAGUSIQ
hour
the fact of revolving
/98

KAJUQ
brown, reddish (fur), blond (hair)
/160

KAJUSIJUQ
perseveres, carries on
starts to be strong
/13

KAKIVAK
three-pronged fish spear
that has the habit of stinging
/65

KALAALIQ/KALAALLIT
Greenlander(s)
(from the Old Norse "Skræling")
/240

KALAALLIT NUNAAT
Greenland
the land of the *Kalaallit* (Greenlanders)
/27

KALAIT (PL)
scabs
/165

KALAT-/KALAKTUQ
he/she is scabby
has *kalait* (scabs)
/165

KALLU
thunder
/22

KAMIALUUK (D)
pair of shoes or boots
big *kamiik* (sealskin boots)
/69

KAMIIK (D)
pair of sealskin boots
/43

KANAJUQ
sculpin
/53

KANANI
down here
/34

KANATA
Canada
(from the English "Canada")
/30

KANGIRSIŽUQ
understands (Alaska)
enters a bay
/84

KANGIRSUK/ḴANGIR&UK
bay, cove
*that looks like a location nearer to land
/32

KANGUQ
snow goose
/50

KANIVAUTI
diaphragm
*means for being usually ahead
/143

KANNA
this one down here
/34

KANNGUSUTTUQ
he/she is ashamed
/89

KAPPIANARTUQ
it is fearful
it provokes *kappia-* (fear)
/87

KAPPIANARTUVIK
hell (Christian)
the huge terrifying one
/91

KAPPIASUTTUQ
he/she is afraid
feels anxious
/87

KAPURQAUTI
fork
means for thrusting in
/191

KATAJJANIQ
throat singing
falling repeatedly
/196

KATAUJAQ
rainbow (Nvut)
looks like the doorway of a snow house
/22

KATIMAJIIT (PL)
councillors, committee members
those who meet or join together
/195

KATITITAUNIQ
church marriage
the fact of being put together
/113

KATUJJIQATIGIIT (PL)
co-operative movement
the group of those who team together
/195

KAUK
walrus (or elephant) hide
/44

KAUTAQ
hammer
means for hammering
/65

KAVAMA/GAVAMA
government
(from the English "government")
/194

KAVAMAAPIK
municipal administration (Nvik)
little government
/195

KAVAMA NUTAAQ
government of Quebec (Nvik)
the new *Kavama* (government)
/194

KAVAMATUQAQ
government of Canada (Nvik)
the old *Kavama* (government)
/194

KAVARTUQ
he/she feels blue
/87

KAVI-/KAPISILIK
whitefish, salmon
that has scales
/52

KAVISIQ
fish scale
(linked to) *kapi-*, to sting
/52

KIANI
here outside
/35

KIAPPALUTTUQ
temperature is warm
generates a feeling of warmth
/25

KIASIK
shoulder blade
almost situated just outside
/141

KIATI
upper trunk
area lying just outside something else
/141

KIATSAUTI
stove, cooking range
means for getting some warmth
/183

KIGGAQ/KIVGAQ
messenger, helper
(linked to) *kavag-*, to lift (a load)
/49

KIGGAVIK
falcon
the big solitary (*and/or the big
messenger)
/51

KIGUTANGIRNAQ
Arctic blueberry
which makes one lose his/her teeth
/32

KIGUTIIT (PL)
teeth
means for biting
/149

KIGUTINNGUAT (PL)
denture, false teeth
imitation of teeth
/149

KIINANNGUAQ
postage stamp (Nvik)
imitation of a face
/147

KIINAQ
face, edge of a knife
that is able to bite
/147

KIINAUJAQ
money
that looks like a face
/189

KIJJA[K]TUQ
that is rough to the touch
/163

KIMMIK
heel
/151

KIMMINAQ
huckleberry
which makes one grit his/her teeth
/32

KINA?
who? (singular)
who is here/there?
/175

KINAGIVAIT?
what is your kin relation?
you have him/her as who?
/175

KI[NA]KKUT? (PL)
who? (plural)
the group of who?
/175

KINATUINNAQ
anyone
a genuine *kina* (who?)
/178

KINAUVIT?
what is your name?
who are you?
/175

KINGUANI
at the back, after
in his/her/its hind part
/36

KINGUK
small shrimp
*that moves backward
/54

KINIRTAQ
compact snow, bannock (W Nvik)
something compact
/23

KINNA
this one close outside
/35

KIPALUK
servant, sailor
(linked to) *kiggaq*, messenger, helper
/123

KIPUTTUT (PL)
wife-exchange partners
who change position one with another
/116

KISITSIGUTIIT (PL)
numerals
means for dealing with them one by one
/185

KISUK?
what? (N Baffin)
*what lesser entity?
/176

KITTU-/KIKTURIAQ
mosquito
that bites repeatedly
/55

KIUJUQ
he/she answers
/161

KIVVA-/KIVGALUK
muskrat
dear little messenger
/49

KUANNIQ
edible seaweed
/54

KUAPA
a co-operative
(from the English abbreviation "co-op")
/195

KUAPAKKUT (PL)
the co-operative movement
the *kuapa* (co-operative) people
/195

KUJAPIK
meat around the vertebrae of large sea
mammals
/67

KUJAT-/KUJAKTUQ
has sexual intercourse
uses his/her lumbar vertebrae
/155

KUKIK
nail, claw, hoof
/151

KUKITTAPAUTI
guitar
means for using one's fingernails
repeatedly
/196

KUKITUALIK
horse (W Nvik)
that has a single hoof
/61

KULLU/KUBLU
thumb
/151

KUMAK
louse
(linked to) *kuməg-*, to scratch
/55

KUMARUAT (PL)
caribou (shamanic language)
giant lice
/149

KUNIT-/KUNIKTUQ
he/she kisses someone
/155

KUPAIK
Quebec
(from the English "Quebec")
/30

KUTSUQ
chewing (bubble) gum
chewable tree resin
/192

KUTSUUJAQ
pink (NE Nvik)
that looks like bubble gum
/245

KUUK
river
that flows
/32

KUUKKUSI
pig (Nvik)
(from the Algonquian [cf. Innu *kukush*])
/61

KUUKKUSIVINIQ
pork ribs
former (dead) pig
/192

KUUTSIIK (D)
iliac bones
/144

KUUTSINAAQ
pelvis (with hips)
that can be made to be iliac bones
/144

KUUTSIUTI
mink
one concerned with rivers
/49

-LUTTUQ/-NGUJUQ
is ill through a body part
has a bad (organ), endures pain in (organ)
/165

MAANI
here, this one here
/34

MAANNA
now, later on (W Nvik)
like this one here (cf. *manna*, this one)
/177

MAANNAUGUNNAITUQ
time (past)
what is no longer now
/177

MAARALAJUQ
it (dog) moans
it says "*maa*"
/61

MAITTUQ
skin is sensitive, hurts
that is without skin
/163

MAKITIQ
hip
that gets up repeatedly
/144

MAKITTUQ
he/she rises up
/155

MAKIVVIA
Easter
his (Jesus's) time for rising up
/155

MAK&AK
bearded seal (shamanic language)
searching for waves
/43

MALIGAIT (PL)
laws
which are followed
/195

MALIGALIRINIQ
justice
the fact of dealing with laws
/195

MALIGALIURTIIT (PL)
members of legislature
those who make laws
/194

MALIIT (PL)
shattering waves
that press up against something
/33

MALITTUQ
follows someone or something
/73

MAMAITTUQ
it smells/tastes bad
it is not *mamartuq* (smelling/tasting
good)
/162

MAMARSAUTI (1)
sugar (W Nvik)
means for making something taste good
/162

MAMARSAUTI (2)
perfume (NE Nvik)
means for making someone smell good
/162

MAMARTUQ
it smells/tastes good
(linked to) *ama(C)-*, to suckle
/162

MANIITTUIT (PL)
broken ice heaped on land
those whose surface is uneven
/37

MANIITTUQ
that is uneven
is not *manik-* (flat)
/163

MANIRARTUQ
that is smooth-surfaced
is continually flat (object or ground)
/163

MANITUPA
Manitoba
(from the English "Manitoba")
/30

MANNA
this one
/34

MANNGUQ
melting snow
/23

MANNIK
egg
/50

MANNIK INULIK
egg with an embryo
an egg with someone in it
/79

MAQAINNIQ
travelling on the land
*the fact of not carrying a kayak
/62

MAQAIVVIK
hunting/fishing location
place where one *maqait-* (travels on land)
/30

MA[R]RAQ
clay, mud
(linked to) *maqə-/maqu-*, oozing/
suppurating
/31

MARNIQ
pus
(contraction of) *maqiniq*, the fact of
oozing
/165

MARRULIAQ
a twin
who has been made two
/107

MARRURALIK
bigamist
one who got two of them
/115

MARRUUK (D)
two
(linked to) PE *malig-*, to follow
/186

MASAK
wet falling snow
/23

MATSISIIT (PL)
matches
(from the English "matches")
/192

MATTAAQ/MAKTAAQ
beluga/narwhal skin
lesser *mattaq/maktaq* (whale skin)
/46

MATTAQ/MAKTAQ
skin of the bowhead whale
which is gnawed
/46

MAUJAQ
soft snow on the ground
soft ground
/23

MIKIGAQ
raw food (meat, etc.)
that is bitten off
/67

MIKIGIAQ
steel trap
tearing something away with the teeth
/65

MIKIGIARNIATI
trapper
one who usually traps
/62

MIKIGIARNIATUQ
he/she traps
deals with traps
/62

MIKIJUQ
he/she/it is small
/156

MIKILIRAQ
ring finger
that becomes smaller
/151

MILUGIAQ
black fly
one that goes sucking out
/55

MINGUARTUQ
he/she paints a surface
smears frequently
/161

MINISTA
government minister
(from the English "minister")
/194

MIRIARTUQ
he/she vomits, throws up
/165

MIRQUIT (PL)
human or animal hair
/140

MIRQUIT[T]UQ
is without any hair
who is deprived of body hair
/148

MIRQUTI
sewing needle
used for sewing
/68

MIRSU[R]TUQ
she/he sews
/68

MISIRAQ
rancid seal or beluga oil
repeated dips
/67

MITANNGUA[R]TUQ
he/she teases
pretends to mock
/162

MITAT-/MITAKTUQ
he/she mocks someone
/162

MITIQ
eider duck
/50

MITIVINIQ
eider duck meat
former (dead) eider duck
/67

MITSIAQ/MIK&IAQ
umbilical cord
that is shortened
/125

MIUGGUTUQ
it (dog) howls
it says "*miu*"
/61

-MIU[TA]Q/-MIUT
inhabitant(s) of
one who is/those who are there
/31

MIVVIK
airport, landing strip
place for landing
/184

NAALAGAQ
the Lord, a master
who is listened to
/161

NAALATTUQ
he/she listens to
/161

NAALAUTI
radio set
means for listening
/161

NAAMMA[K]TUQ
it is correct, sufficient
/163

NAAMMASIARTUQ
is in good health, is OK
who/that is really correct, sufficient
/163

NAAQ
belly, abdomen
/142

NAARAJI
big-bellied individual
(linked to) *naaq*, belly
/142

NAASAUTIIT (PL)
numerals
means for completing multiple tasks
/185

NAIMANIQ
smell and taste
the fact of smelling and tasting
/158

NAIMAVAA
he/she smells it
/161

NAITTUQ
he/she/it is short
/156

NAJA
sister (for a man)
*who bends her head, nods, trembles
/107

NAJAGIIK (D)
a sister and her brother
two, one of whom is a sister
/108

NAJATSAQ
male Ego's female cousin
substitute sister
/112

NAJJUK/NAGJUK
antler, muskox horn
(linked to) *nayət-*, to get caught or
snagged
/47

NAKASUK
bladder
*lesser stalk or stem
/146

NAKASUNNAQ
calf of leg
that resembles a bladder
/146

NAKASUUJAQ
light bulb (N Baffin)
that looks like a bladder
/146

NAKASUUP SULLUA
urinary meatus
the bladder's tube
/145

NAKIT?
wherefrom?
from which location?
/176

NAKURMIIK!
Thank you! (Nvik)
worthy of gratitude indeed
/172

NAKURSATUQ
he/she thanks
finds it worthy of praise because it is good
/88

NALAJUQ
he/she is lying down
/155

NALLIGUSUTTUQ
feels concerned, loves
(linked to) *nangət-*, to finish it up
/86

NALLUQ
caribou wading place
wading in water
/47

NALUNARTUQ
is difficult to understand
that makes one ignorant
/84

NALUVAA
he/she ignores it
(linked to) *nallir*, which one
/84

NAMMAUTI
pack saddle
used for carrying something on one's back
/61

NAMUT?
whereto?
to which location?
/176

NANI?
where? wherein?
in which location?
/176

NANITUINNAQ
anywhere, wherever
a genuine *nani* (where?)
/178

NANNUTUQ
he/she got a polar bear
he/she "polar bear-ed"
/63

NANUQ
polar bear
/58

NANURAQ
polar bear skin
that looks like a polar bear
/59

NANURSIUTUQ
goes looking for a bear
is in frequent contact with polar bears
/63

NAPAARTUQ
tree
one that stands up
/32

NARSI[T]TUQ
wrinkles his/her nose
(linked to) *narə-*, to smell, *narru-*, be
disgusted
/170

NASAQ
hood, hat
/ 69

NASITTUQ
looks around, surveys from a height
/160

NATAAQ
bottom of a container
small *natiq* (floor)
/182

NATARQUNAQ
hail
resembles cartilage
/22

NATIQ
floor
/182

NATSIAQ
baby ringed seal
small *natsiq*
/43

NATSIQ/NATTIQ
ringed seal
(linked to) *naj[ə]qur/najangar-*, nodding
head
/43

NATSISIURTUQ
goes looking for seals
is in frequent contact with ringed seals
/63

NATSITAQ
ringed seal that has been caught
one that has been "ringed seal-ed"
/63

NATSIVINIQ
ringed seal meat
former (dead) ringed seal
/67

NAUJAQ
seagull
/51

NAUJAVIK
glaucous gull
big *naujaq* (seagull)
/51

NAUK?
where? (close by), what?
where it (is)?
/176

NAUKKUT?
whereby?
through which (close) location?
/176

NAULAQ
harpoon head
(linked to) *naulik-*, to throw a harpoon
/65

NIAQUAQ
head (walrus or whale)
big head
/244

NIAQUNGUJUQ
he/she has a headache
endures pain in the head
/165

NIAQUQ
head
an attached part that is bending
/139

NIAQURSIUTI
Aspirin
(medicine) useful for the head
/164

NIAQUUJAQ
bread
that looks like a head
/66

NIAQUVINIQ
skull
former head
/140

NIGGUQ
fish slime
that clings to something
/165

NIGIIQ
east wind (NE Nvik)
/22

NIINIGAQ
piano, organ
that which one has pressed with his/her hands
/197

NIJJAAVIK
larynx
where continuous sounds are produced
/141

NIJJA[R]TUQ
he/she/it emits a sound
receives a sound
/161

NIJJAUTI
accordion
means for emitting a sound
/197

NIKKU/MIKKU
dried meat
/67

NILAK
freshwater ice
/24

NILARNAIT (PL)
beans (Nvik)
those that produce farts
/154

NILIQ
a fart
(linked to) *nilirtuq*, he/she farts
/154

NILIRTUQ
he/she farts
*(linked to) *nilli[r]tuq*, emits a sound
/153

NILIRTU[R]TUQ
speedboat
that farts repeatedly
/185

NILLATUQ/NILLIJUQ
he/she/it cools down
/25

NILLINARTUQ
temperature cools down
that makes one becoming colder
/25

NILLINARTUQAUTI
refrigerator
container for cooled things
/183

NILLI[R]TUQ
he/she/it emits a sound
provides with sound
/161

NIMIRIAQ
snake
one that winds itself round
/56

NINGAUK
son-in-law/brother-in-law
(linked to) *ninnga[r]-*, to be angry
/117

NINGIRTUQ
receives a share of the catch
/88

NINGIRTUT (PL)
they share their catch
/41

NINGIUQ
old woman
/81

NINGIUSUK
female lover (convivial)
lesser old woman
/116

NINNGATUQ
he/she is angry
/87

NIPI
human voice, sound
(linked to) *nəmaaq-*, to cry out in pain
/161

NIPILIURUTI
voice recording machine
means for fabricating a voice
/161

NIPIVIK
west
where the sun sets
/36

NIQI
food, flesh, meat
(linked to) *niri-*, to eat
/66

NIQITSAJAQ
flour (W Nvik)
meat-to-be
/66

NIQITUINNAQ
meat
genuine *niqi* (food)
/66

NIRITSIVIK
Friday
time for feeding (people)
/98

NIRIVIK
restaurant, dining room
place for eating
/184

NIRJUTI
large game animal
means for eating
/42

NIRLIQ
Canada goose
(linked to) *nirlur-*, to raise head
/50

NIRUARTUQ
he/she votes
chooses someone or something
/194

NIRUMITTUQ
tepid
is soft and warm
/25

NIU
leg
/152

NIUVIATSAQ
good offered for sale
that is to be sold and bought
/190

NIUVIRTI
trader, storekeeper
one who buys and/or sells
/184

NIUVIRTUUK (D)
they (two) barter, trade
(linked to) *navər[ar]*-, to borrow or
exchange
/190

NIUVIRVIK
store, trading post
place for selling and buying
/184

NIVIARSIAQ
girl
made to stay close, *knocked down
backward
/81

NIVIURTUQ
wants to be with loved one
clings repeatedly to something
/86

NUAKULUK
woman's sister's child
nice little younger sibling
/111

NUIJUQ
appears, becomes visible
(linked to) *nuut-/nuuk-*, to move/change
place
/160

NUILAQ
fur around parka hood
*(linked to) *nui-*, to appear
/61

NUIT
three-pronged bird dart
/65

NUJAIT (PL)
head hair
/148

NUJAITTUQ
bald (on head)
who has no head hair
/148

NUKAQ
younger sibling
(linked to) *nuaq*, nephew
/106

NUKARIIK (D)
two same-sex siblings
two, one of whom is a younger sibling
/108

NUKARSIQ
younger than
more *nukaq* (young) than
/106

NUKATUGAQ
caribou yearling
a younger one that is eaten
/47

NUKAURNGUQ
spouse of spouse's younger sibling
younger sibling once more
/118

NUKI
nerve, sinew, muscle, strength
/141

NUKILIALUK
is very strong
has much *nuki* (strength)
/141

NULAVUQ
he/she grows thanks to magic
/123

NULIAQ
wife
little female in heat with whom one
copulates
/113

NULIARIIK (D)
marital couple
two persons, one of whom is the other's
wife
/114

NULIARPUQ
he copulates (man/animal)
he gets at a female in heat
/113

NULIARSAQ
succubus spirit
would-be wife
/93

NULIASUK
female lover
lesser wife
/116

NULIATSIAQ
woman sharing man's midwife
good/nice wife (for the man)
/125

NULIK
for Ego, father/mother of his/her child's
spouse (N Baffin)
/113

NULUAT (PL)
fishing net
the laced ones
/65

NULUUK (D)
buttocks (fleshy part)
/144

NUNA
land, earth, solid ground
*positioned in space
/28

NUNAJAQ
lichen, plant, pebble
piece of *nuna*
/32

NUNAKKUUJUUKUTAAQ
train
a long one that goes by land
/246

NUNAKKUUJUUQ
motor vehicle
one that goes by land
/182

NUNALIK
village
which has a *nuna* (land), there is a *nuna*
/30

NUNALITUQAQ
Indigenous person
ancient holder of the land
/75

NUNANNGUAQ
map
imitation of the land
/30

NUNAQARQAATUQ
Indigenous person
one who held land before (first
inhabitant)
/75

NUNARJUAQ
country
super-*nuna* (land)
/237

NUNATSIAVUT
northern Labrador
our beautiful land
/27

NUNAVIK
Arctic Quebec
huge land
/27

NUNAVUT
Territory of Nunavut
our land
/27

NUNIVAKKAQ
long-tailed mouse
one that is picked up from the ground
/49

NUNIVATTUQ
gathers edible plants
prowls about the real, big *nuna* (land)
/32

NURRAQ
baby caribou
(linked to) *nurar[ar]*, nephew/niece
/47

NUTARAQ
infant, baby
new being
/79

NUTILLIQ
speckled trout
the oldest one
/53

NUVAK
spittle, mucus, cold, flu
(linked to) *nigguq*, fish slime
/165

NUVAT-/NUVAKTUQ
has a cold or flu
(linked to) *nuvak*, spittle, mucus
/165

NUVIUVAK
fly (insect)
one that hangs around very much
/55

NUVUJAQ
cloud
piece of thread, *part of a promontory
/22

NUVUK
cape, promontory
tip of a pointed object
/32

PAAJUQ
he/she/it fights, struggles
(linked to) *patittuq*, slaps someone/
something
/155

PAANI
up there
/34

PAARNGUSUUQ
reptile
one that usually crawls
/56

PAASIVUQ
understands (Greenland)
enters the mouth of a fjord
/84

PAINNGUTUQ
he/she feels homesick
is tired to stay alone
/87

PAKAAKUANI
chicken (NE Nvik)
(from the Algonquian [cf. Innu
pakakuan])
/61

PAMIURTUUQ
otter
one with a big tail
/49

PANA
snow knife for the igloo
spear, lance
/68

PANIARJUK
niece by marriage
lesser daughter
/118

PANIGIIK (D)
a daughter and her parent
two, one of whom is a daughter
/123

PANIGIIT (PL)
daughters and parent(s)
a group including daughters
/108

PANIK
daughter
*who supplies or is provided with heat
/106

PANIRTITAQ
bannock bread
that has been dried
/66

PANITTAQ
adopted daughter
a *panik* (daughter) who has been added
/123

PANNA
that one up there
/34

PANNIQ/PANGNIQ
adult male caribou
/47

PAPA
pepper
(from the English "pepper")
/192

PARNANAIRSIVIK
jail, prison
place where one is not anymore made
ready
/195

PATA
butter
(from the English "butter")
/192

PATIITASI
potatoes
(from the English "potatoes")
/192

PATIQ
marrow
/140

PATITTUQ/PATIKTUQ
he/she/it slaps, claps
/155

PATTAK
ball (for playing)
(linked to) *patit-/patik-*, to slap or clap
/196

PATTAUJAQ
orange
that looks like a ball
/193

PAUNGA
upward, landward
toward up there
/35

PAURNGAQ
berry
firstly fastened down
/32

PI
something
/152

PIARAIT KIINAUJANGIT (PL)
family allowance
children's money
/194

PIARAQ (1)
young animal
young thing
/44

PIARAQ (2)
child (NE Nvik)
young thing
/79

PIARATSAQ
human fetus (NE Nvik)
future *piaraq* (child)
/79

PIGIAQARTUQ
he/she must
he/she has to do
/152

PIGIVAA
he/she owns it
he/she has it as something
/152

PIIRPAA
he/she takes it away
he/she suppresses it
/152

PIIRSITUQ
there is a snow blizzard
it carries things away
/23

PIJUMAJUQ
he/she wants
he/she wants to do
/152

PIJUQ
he/she does something
/152

PIKANI
up here
/34

PIKIUTTUQ
he/she gathers eggs
(linked to) *pakyu*, egg
/52

PILIRIJUQ
works (W Hudson Bay)
he/she is occupied with something
/191

PILLITAJUUQ
flea, sand-hopper
that has the habit to hop repeatedly
/55

PINASUARUSIQ
week (workable)
the fact of working
/98

PINASUTTI
worker (Nvik)
one who works on a regular basis
/191

PINASUTTUQ
he/she works (Nvik)
strives to do something
/153

PINGASUNNGUTUQ
three o'clock
it becomes three
/98

PINGASUT (PL)
three
(linked to) *pingna*, this one up here
/186

PINGASUUJURTUT
six (Nvik)
they are three more than once
/186

PINGUQ
pimple, isolated hill
/165

PINNA
this one up here
/34

PINNGUAQ
toy, copy, imitation
something that has been imitated
/153

PINNGUA[R]TUQ
he/she plays, fakes
pretends to do something
/153

PIQALUJAQ
iceberg
(linked to) *paqu-*, bending, being bent
/24

PIQATI
friend
who does something with someone
/136

PIQUJAIT (PL)
rules, regulations
which are ordered
/195

PIQUJAQ
obligation, rule
that is ordered, that must be done
/94

PIQUTI
someone's possession
a possessed thing
/152

PIRQAJARTUQ
he/she can
he/she is able to do
/152

PIRTA[R]NIQ
back of the knee
/139

PIRURPALIANIQ
development
progressive growth
/195

PIRURTUQ (1)
he/she/it grows
becomes something
/153

PIRURTUQ (2)
plant
one that grows
/32

PISIQ
man's personal song
/95

PISUTTI/PISUKTI
land mammal
one that walks, a walker
/46

PISUTTIAPIK
small land mammal
small *pisutti* (walker)
/46

PISUTTUQ/PISUKTUQ
he/she/it walks
needs to do something
/153

PITATSAQ
sugar
something fit for being added (to food)
/192

PITITSI/PITIKSI
bow
that makes it receive something
/65

PITSI/PIPSI
dried fish
(linked to) *pipak-*, to split lengthwise
/67

PITSI-/PITTIULAAQ
black guillemot
*very small means for making it do
something
/51

PIUJUQ
he/she/it is good
is something
/3

PIULINIAGAIT (PL)
paraphernalia
those objects that will serve to do
something
/62

PIUNNGI[T]TUQ
he/she/it is bad
is not something
/3

PIUTSATUQ
finds nice/values one
considers someone to be something good
/86

PIVALLIAJUQ
it develops
does something more and more
/153

PIVALLIANIQ
development
the fact of doing something more and
more
/195

PUALULIK
bearded seal, one to two years old
one with mitts
/43

PUALUUK (D)
pair of mitts
(linked to) *puuq*, bag
/68

PUIJI
sea mammal
that has the habit of appearing (out of
water)
/42

PUIJJURARIAQ
swimming
swimming repeatedly
/196

PUIJJURARTUQ
a swimmer, he/she swims
one who swims repeatedly
/42

PUIJJUTUQ
appears once and for some time, swims
/42

PUJJUSIUTI
baking powder, yeast
means for making it rise
/67

PUJJUUTI
crustacean with claws
something used for pinching
/54

PUKAK
crystalline snow on ground
/23

PUKIQ
female animal *sila*'s child
white belly fur of an animal
/39

PULAARTUQ
he/she goes on a visit
enters somewhere frequently/for a long
time
/173

PULAARVIK
drawing-room, parlour
place for visiting
/183

PULIISI
police officer
(from the English "police")
/184

PULIISIKKUT (PL)
police station
group of police officers
/184

PULLAQ
bubble
/20

PUNNIQ
shortening (cooking)
coagulated fat floating on broth
/67

PUTUGUQ
big toe
*that becomes a hole
/151

PUUGUTAQ
plate
used for holding something
/67

PUUKULUK
biological mother (Nvik)
nice little pouch
/123

PUUSI
cat
(from the English "pussy [cat]")
/60

PUVAK
lung
(linked to) *puvi-*, to swell, be inflated
/143

PUVALLU[K]TUQ
has tuberculosis
has bad lungs
/165

QAAQ
bed sheets
that on top
/47

QAGGIQ
ceremonial snow house
/95

QAIJUQ
he/she comes
(linked to) *qaru*, dawn
/156

QAINNGUQ
ice adhering to the shore
(linked to) *qaəru[r]* (birch bark)
/24

QAIPPAA
he/she brings it
/156

QAIRARTUQ
that is smooth
is continually without anything on top
of it
/163

QAIRTUQ
high rock
that has nothing on top
/32

QAIRULIK
harp seal
that has bark (on it)
/43

QAJAQ
kayak
/66

QAJARIAQ
canvas canoe
that is like a kayak
/66

QAJUQ
meat or fish broth
/68

QAJUUTTAQ
cup
means for drinking *qajuq* (broth)
/68

QAKIRTUQ
bleached by sun and air
*that has wasted itself
/159

QAKUGU[Q]
when? (future) (Nvut)
(linked to) *-ku-*, conditional verbal ending
/177

QAKURTAQ
white, of a pale colour
that has been bleached
/159

QALASIQ
navel
(linked to) *qala*, swirl (hollow swirl)
/142

QALLU/QABLU
eyebrow
position for being inside
/148

QALLUNAANGAJUIT (PL)
mixed-blood Inuit
part-*Qallunaat* (part-Europeans)
/77

QALLUNAAQ
white European person
prominent eyebrows or who has been
bleached
/75

QALLUNAARTAQ
imported fabric
something related to *Qallunaat*
/69

QALLUNAATUINNAIT (PL)
anglophones
the only genuine *Qallunaat*
/77

QALLUNITTUQ
raises eyebrows briefly
/170

QAMANI
inside
/35

QAMUTIIK (D)
sled
the two (runners) used for pulling
/60

QANAAQ
shin
/152

QANGA
when? (past or general)
(linked to) -*nga*-, causative verbal ending
/177

QANGATTAJUUQ
airplane (NE Nvik)
that is in the habit of ascending
/185

QANGATTAJUURTI
airplane pilot (NE Nvik)
who operates a *qangattajuuq* (airplane)
/185

QANGATUINNAQ
whenever
a genuine *qanga* (when?)
/178

QANGIAQ
man's brother's child
*one getting, or brought, to the top
/111

QANIK
falling snow
/23

QANIQ
mouth
(linked to) *qalər*-, to utter, and *qatə*, loud
voice
/149

QANIUJAARPAIT (PL)
syllabic writing system
the big ones that look like snowflakes
/97

QANIUSINAA
lips
edge of the mouth
/149

QANNA
this one inside
/35

QANUINNGI[T]TUQ
is OK, it doesn't matter
he/she has no problem, there is no
problem
/163

QANUINNGITUNGA
I am OK
I do not have any problem
/164

QANUIPPIT?
how are you?
do you have a problem?
/163

QANUQ?
how?
/176

QANUTUINNAQ
anyhow
a genuine *qanuq* (how?)
/178

QAPUITTUQ
is wise (Inuinnaqtun)
is without foam (in the mind)
/240

QAQIARTUQ
feels humble, meek
(linked to) *qaqi[t]-*, to be hidden
/147

QAQILIRTUQ
tries dislodging animal
(linked to) *qaqi[t]-*, to be hidden
/146

QAQIVITTUQ
gets up/rises a bit
(linked to) *qaqi[t]-*, to be hidden
/147

QARIAQ
room, secondary igloo
place for coming up
/182

QARISARIIK (D)
a pair of twins
two who are brains for each other
/107

QARITAQ/QARISAQ
brain
*in a hidden position
/146

QARITAUJAQ
computer
that looks like a brain
/147

QARJUK
arrow
one that comes up or away
/65

QARLIIK (D)
pair of pants
/68

QARMAQ
semi-subterranean house
(linked to) *qarǝ-*, to come up
/45

QARQAQ
hill, mountain
high area
/32

QARQUJAQ
biscuit
piece of cooked and dried meat
/192

QARSAUQ
red-throated loon
/50

QASIGIAQ
harbour or freshwater seal
the fact of being speckled
/44

QATAAK!
Pal! (when addressing)
(from *qatanguti*, "sibling, cousin")
/126

QATANGUTI
sibling
a means for getting a chest *or
companions
/108

QATANGUTIGIIT (PL)
brothers and sisters
a group of siblings
/109

QATANGUTITSAQ
Ego's same-sex cousin
substitute sibling
/112

QATIGAAK (D)
upper trunk, thorax
(linked to) *qatǝ*, loud voice, *doing it
together
/141

293

QATSIRARPA?
how much is it?
how much does it get?
/190

QATSIT?
how much? how many?
/190

QATSITURPA?
how much is it?
how much does it eat?
/190

QATSIUGAQ
oatmeal, porridge
that has been made into a soup
/192

QAU
light
daylight, dawn
/26

QAUJIMANIQ
knowledge (ordinary)
the fact of having become aware
/26

QAUMANIQ
knowledge (shamanic)
the fact of diffusing light
/26

QAUMMALAK
lightning
which gives light once
/22

QAUMMAQ
skirt, dress
garment with an edge
/69

QAUPPAT
tomorrow
when there will be light
/26

QAUQ
forehead
*(linked to) qau-, light or qaa-, surface
/147

QAVANNGANIQ
south wind (NE Nvik)
coming from inside
/22

QAVVIK/QAGVIK
wolverine
(linked to) qatə, deep or loud voice
/48

QAVVITUQ
climbs
/48

QIAJUQ
he/she cries
/155

QIANNGUJUUQ
outboard motor
that sounds like crying
/66

QIILIK
white-haired
one who has qiit (white hair)
/148

QIIQ
a white hair
/148

QIJUGAIT (PL)
checkers, cards
little (pieces of) wood
/196

QIJUK
wood, solid fuel
/32

QIKIRTAQ
island
*(linked to) qikar-, to stay there doing nothing
/32

QILAK (1)
sky, igloo vault, heaven
*weaving, *tying
/26

QILAK (2)
roof of the mouth
vault, sky
/149

QILALUGAQ
narwhal, beluga whale
*(linked to) *qila*, a short period of time
/45

QILALUKKAANAQ
baby beluga/narwhal
something resembling a small beluga/
narwhal
/46

QILANIQ
string-pulling divination
the fact of invoking spirits
/94

QILATTAIT (PL)
matting on the bed
those bound together
/47

QILAUT[I]
traditional drum
a means for invoking spirits or *securing
links
/92

QILINGUJUQ
he/she is sullen, sulks
/87

QILLAQUTI
ritual gift to midwife
tie belonging to someone
/124

QILUTTUQ
it (dog) barks
/61

QIMIRIAQ
eyelash
place for examining something
/148

QIMIRLUK
backbone, stem (plant)
bad ridge
/140

QIMIRRUA[R]PAA
looks at it attentively
has a propensity to look at things
/159

QIMIUJAQ
nether world of the dead
*that looks like a net-line (under the sea)
/91

QIMMIJUAQ
horse (NE Nvik)
super-dog
/61

QIMMIQ
dog
one that is compelled to be shy or
respectful
/60

QIMMISUK
dog skin
lesser dog
/61

QIMUTSIIT (PL)
sledging equipage
those that move when they (dogs) pull
/60

QINGAAK (D)
nostrils
double nose
/148

QINGAQ
nose, igloo's vent hole
/148

QINNIQ/QINNIVIK
stone cache
(linked to) *qəngžur-*, to gather
/53

QIPIIT (PL)
blankets, sleeping bag
/47

QIRNITAIT (PL)
coloured people, blacks
black beings
/77

QIRNITAQ
black, of a dark colour
added *qirniq* (dark surface)
/159

QISIK
(outer) skin (man, seal)
/140

QITINNGUQ
Christmas
that becomes the middle (of the year)
/96

QITIQ
waist
the middle of something
/143

QITIRALIQ
noon, midnight
starting to be half of it
/98

QITIRSIQ/QITIR&IQ
middle finger
the middlemost one
/151

QITIRULLIQ
maggot
that has something associated with the
middle
/55

QITURNGAQ
someone's child
one who was recently soft and pliable
/107

QITURNGARIIT (PL)
nuclear family (children and parents)
a group including offspring
/109

QITURNGINGAUTI
eldest child, first child
means for giving birth for the first time
/122

QIUJAJUQ
he/she is cold
he/she freezes repeatedly
/25

QIUJANARTUQ
temperature is cold
that makes one being cold
/25

QIUJUQ
something freezing
/25

QIVIUQ
wool of the muskox
that curls back
/47

QUAQ
something deeply frozen
/25

QUAQAUTI
freezer
container for frozen things
/25

QUATSIAQ
child (shamanic language)
who is frozen hard
/140

QUIJARTUVIK
bathroom, toilet
place where one goes to urinate
/183

QUIJUQ
he/she urinates
*(linked to) *quik*, thighbone
/153

QUIK
thighbone, femur
/153

QUINATTUQ
he/she is ticklish
(linked to) *quiliqta-*, to tremble
/156

QUINGILITAQ
diaper
protection for the thighbone
/153

QUINIJUQ
is fat
(linked to) *quinattuq*, is ticklish
/156

QUIRTU[R]TUQ
he/she coughs
coughs repeatedly
/165

QUJANA[K]!
Never mind! Don't bother!
*don't be thankful! *how thankful!
(ironic)
/172

QUJANNAMIIK!
Thank you! (NE Nvut)
how thankful indeed
/171

QUJAQ
backbone, spine
/140

QUJATTUQ
he/she is thankful
/171

QUKIUTI
gun
means for producing a loud noise
/65

QULAAQ
ceiling
that reaches the upper side
/182

QULILLU ATAUSIRLU
eleven
and ten and one
/187

QULILLU MARRUULU
twelve
and ten and two
/187

QULILLU QULIUNNGIGARTULU
nineteen (Nvik)
and ten and nine
/187

QULIQANNGITUINNARTUT
nine (N Baffin)
they do not really have ten units
/187

QULIT (PL)
ten
the upper parts
/187

QULITTAQ
hooded parka
added upper part
/68

QULIUNNGIGARTUT
nine (Nvik)
they are not quite ten
/186

QULLIQ
soapstone seal-oil lamp
the uppermost one
/67

QULLISAJAQ
soapstone
that can be used for a seal-oil lamp
/3

QUNGA-/QUNGISIQ
neck
/141

QUNGATTUQ
he/she smiles
/154

QUNGULIQ
wild sorrel
being sour
/32

QUNIGUQ
eider down
that usually curls on itself
/52

QUPANUAQ
snow bunting, small bird
small fancy trim
/50

QUPIRRUAJUIT (PL)
rice
little bugs
/193

QUPIRRUALUK
crocodile
big bug
/56

QUPIRRUK
bug, insect, worm
that is associated with splitting lengthwise
/55

QURSUTAQ
yellow
added element that looks like urine
/160

QURTURAQ
thigh
/152

QURVIK
toilet bowl, chamber pot
place for watering something with urine
/183

QUVIANARTUQ
provokes joy
makes someone *quvia-* (rejoice)
/86

QUVIASUTTUQ
is happy, rejoices
/86

QUVIASUVVIK
Christmas
time for rejoicing
/96

QUVVIK
tear
(linked to) *qunik*, matter in eye
/155

SAA
table
what is in front of one
/183

SAAGIARTUQ
he/she converts
looks at it full face
/96

SAALA
a loser
/155

SAALAQARTUQ
he/she wins
has a *saala* (loser)
/155

SAAMA
salmon (Nvik)
(from the English "salmon")
/53

SAANGANI
facing
in a position facing him/her/it
/36

SAASIMATSIJUQ
he/she is guilty
faces (his/her crime)
/195

SAATANASI
Satan
(from the English "Satan")
/92

SAATTUQ
it is thin, flat
/156

SAGGALAK
young seal shedding fur
whose skin looks scratched out
/43

SAIMMAINIQ
peace
the fact of feeling consoled, appeased
/87

SAIMMAUTIGUTI
harmony-restoring measure
means for making people at peace
/195

SAIMMAUTIJUT (PL)
they enjoy peace
are in a state of mutual ease/consolation
/136

SAIMUURLUK! (D)
Let's shake hands! (Nvik)
let both of us do as in Chimo
/172

SAINISIIT (PL)
Chinese
(from the English "Chinese")
/77

SAKI
father-/mother-in-law
*(linked to) *sakiat*, rib cage
/117

SAKIAQ
wife's brother/husband's sister
little *saki* (in-law)
/118

SAKIAT (PL)
rib cage
*(linked to) *saa*, front part of something
/142

SAKILIRQIUTI
grandparent-in-law
means for being a *saki* (parent-in-law)
again
/117

SAKKU
bullet
projectile
/65

SÁLLU
a thin one
(linked to) *saattuq*, it is thin, flat
/156

SALLUTUJUQ
lies, is wrong
/85

SALUMAITTUQ
he/she/it is dirty, filthy
is not *saluma-* (clean)
/154

SALUMAJUQ
he/she/it is clean
has been swept or cleaned away
/154

SAMANI
down there
/34

SAMUNGA
downward, seaward
toward down there
/35

SANAJI
artisan, girl's midwife
one who fashions something
/191

SANAJUQ
makes, repairs, fashions something
/190

SANANNGUA[R]NIQ
carving figurines
the fact of pretending to fashion
something
/190

SANATTAILI
Sunday
forbidden to work!
/98

SANAUGAQ
flour (NE Nvik)
something (meat) that is manufactured
/66

SANGUJINIQ
root of the big toe
the fact of changing direction
/166

SANIANI
beside, near
at his/her/its side
/36

SANNA
that one down there (also the name of the
mistress of sea mammals)
/35

SANNGII[T]TUQ
he/she is weak
is not *sanngi-* (strong)
/156

SANNGIJUQ
is strong (Nvut, Labrador)
/156

SANNINGAJULIK
cross
that has a cross-piece on it
/96

SAPUTI
stone weir
used for blocking something
/65

SARPIK
whale tail
*that stands splay-footed
/45

SAUGAQ
sheep
(from the West Greenlandic "*sava*")
/61

SAUMIK
left side, left-handed
that makes something veer to the side
/150

SAUNAAQ
stone or pip of a fruit
small *sauniq* (bone)
/140

SAUNIIT (PL)
skeleton
the bones
/139

SAUNIQ
bone, fishbone, eggshell
*the fact of being buried
/140

SAUNIRIIK (D)
name-sharers (Nvik)
two who have each other as a bone
/125

SAUNIVINIQ
eponym (Nvik)
former *sauniq* (name-sharer)
/126

SAVAKTUQ
works (Alaska, W Arctic)
he/she works on something
/191

SAVIK
man's pointed knife
/68

SAVVIK/SAGVIK
chest
*(linked to) *saa*, front, and *sakiat*, rib cage
/142

SIARRIJARIAQ
ice skating
slipping continuously
/196

SIGGU[K]
beak, muzzle
/51

SIIJU!
See you!
(from the English "see you")
/175

SIIRNA[R]TUQ
it is sour
it provokes oozing out
/162

SIIRQUQ
knee
/152

SIJJALIJJAQ
old bearded seal
that makes waves repeatedly
/43

SIJJAQ (1)
beach
(linked to) *cingə-/cingig*, shoving/point
of land
/32

SIJJAQ (2)
fox den
big *siti* (animal hole)
/48

SIKIITU
snowmobile
(from the trademark "Skidoo")
/66

SIKKITAQ
square, rectangle, cube
made to be steep
/182

SIKU
sea ice
/24

SIKUTSAJAQ
sheet of paper
piece of future ice (freezing water)
/97

SILA
exterior, air, weather, intelligence
spirit of the cosmos
/19

SILAAQ
male animal child of *sila*
lesser *sila*
/39

SILAITTUQ
is stupid
has no *sila*
/20

SILAKITTUQ
is not very wise
has little *sila*
/20

SILALUTTUQ
weather is bad, it rains
sila is bad
/20

SILAPAAQ
outer upper garment
the outermost one
/69

SILAPPIAQ
outer set of clothing
most outside
/68

SILARJUAQ
world, universe
super-*sila* (all-embracing externality)
/20

SILARQI[R]TUQ
weather is good
sila is beautiful
/20

SILASIUTI
barometer
that is used in connection with *sila*
/236

SILATUJUQ
is wise, intelligent
has much *sila*
/20

SINAA
shoreline
its edge
/57

SINARNAQ
grey fur
/160

SINITTAVIK
hotel, guest house
place for sleeping repeatedly
/184

SINITTUQ/SINIKTUQ
he/she sleeps
/154

SINIVVIK
bedroom, bed (W Nvik)
place for sleeping
/183

SINNAJUQ
he/she is jealous
/87

SINNATUUMAJUQ
he/she dreams
gets repeatedly to sleep
/91

SIPINIQ
boy changing sex at birth
the action of splitting
/128

SIQININGA
south
its sun
/35

SIQINIQ
sun
splashing, exploding, sprinkling
/27

SIQINIUP NUIVINGA
east
where the sun appears
/36

SIQIRNGUJAQ
clock, watch
that looks like the sun
/98

SIRIJUQ
makes a cry of thanks
he/she is eager
/172

SIRMIQ
snow cementing an igloo
/23

SIRQITIQ
conversion ritual
crossing over to a more dangerous place
/97

SITAMAT (PL)
four
(linked to) *cita[g]*-, "to be hard"
/186

SITAMAUJUNNGIGARTUT
seven (Nvik)
they are not quite four more than once
/186

SITAMAUJURTUT
eight (Nvik)
they are four more than once
/186

SITI
lemming or mouse hole
/48

SITURARIAQ
skiing, tobogganing
sliding repeatedly
/196

SIUPIRUQ
periwinkle
*big ear
/54

SIURAQ
sand
*stable surface extending in front of
something
/31

SIUTI
ear
/148

SIVATAARVIK
Saturday (N Baffin)
time for getting biscuits
/98

SIVUANI
at the front, before
in his/her/its forepart
/36

SIVULIRTI
premier, mayor, head dog
the one who leads
/194

SIVUNIQ
vanguard, anteriority
the forepart of something, the time before
/211

SUATTUQ
abuses, quarrels with someone
raises voice
/87

SUITISI
candy
(from the English "sweets")
/193

SUKATTUQ
he/she/it is fast
/156

SUKKAI[T]TUQ
he/she/it is slow
is not *sukka-* (fast)
/156

SUKKAJUQ
he/she/it is fast (N Baffin)
/156

SULIATSAQAVUK
he/she works (Labrador)
he/she has something to be done
/191

SULIJUQ
speaks the truth, is right
it produces something
/85

SULIVUQ
he/she works (Greenland)
he/she is occupied at making something
/191

SULLUK
tube, elongated hole
something for blowing
/148

SUMUT?
why?
for what? because of what?
/176

SUNA?
what?
what is here/there?
/175

SUNATSAUJUQ
it is useful
that is fit for being or doing something
/209

SUNAUVVA
surprisingly
what else?
/175

SUNGUJUQ
he/she/it is strong (Nvik)
/156

SUNNGI[T]TUQ
he/she is not doing anything
/190

SUPUURUTIIT (PL)
cigarettes
means for blowing a long time
/192

SUPUURUTITUINNAQ
pipe (for smoking)
genuine *supuuruti* (cigarette)
/192

SURLULIRIJUQ
he/she deals with nostrils
rubs his/her nose
/148

SURLUUK (D)
cavities of the nostrils
(linked to) *sulluk*, tube
/148

SURQAQ
baleen
/45

SURUJUK
rain
(linked to) *sujuk-*, deteriorating
/22

SURUSIQ/TURUSIQ
boy
secondary (male) thing, or becoming
useful
/81

SURVATARTUQ
he/she knocks at the door
makes noise repeatedly
/173

SUVA?
what is he/she doing? what is going on?
/175

SUVAA?
is it not surprising?
what is going on indeed?
/175

SUVAK
fish roe
/54

SUVALLIJAQ
dish of roe, oil, and berries
made with *suvak* (fish roe)
/54

SUVIT?
what are you doing?
/175

TAALA
dollar
(from the English "dollar")
/189

TAAQ
darkness, obscurity
(linked to) *tau*, human (shamanic
language)
/26

TAAVAUVUSI!
Bye! (by hosts) (Nvut)
you people are out far away
/174

TAGATAGA
now (W Nvik)
(linked to) *tagga*, there it is!
/177

TAGVAUVUSI!
Bye! (by guests) (Nvut)
you people are right here
/174

TAITSUMANI
formerly, in the past
in that one (period of time) positioned
far away
/178

TAKIJUQ
he/she/it is tall, long
/156

TAKINIRPAAQ
the tallest
the utmost tall stature
/157

TAKINIRSAQ
taller than
liable to be a tall stature
/157

TAKKU
the gaze of someone
(linked to) *taku-*, to see
/159

TAKUJUQ
he/she sees
/158

TAKUNIQ
sight
the fact of seeing
/158

TAKUNNA[R]TUQ
he/she looks at something
makes oneself seeing
/158

TAKUNNATI
pupil of the eye
means for making oneself seeing
/159

TAKURNGA[R]TUQ
is scared by someone
sees for the first time
/159

TAKUVAA
he/she sees it
/158

TALIILAJUT (PL)
creatures on coastal reefs
those who hide frequently
/57

TALIQ
arm (anatomy)
(linked to) *tatə-*, jam in, and *tatyur-*, lead
by hand
/150

TALIRPIK
right side
the very best arm
/150

TALLIMAT (PL)
five
they (numbers) make an arm
/186

TALLIMAUJURTUT
ten (W Nvik)
they are five more than once
/187

TALLU/TABLU
chin
/149

TAMARMIK (D, PL)
two of them (Nvik), all
*(linked to) enclitic *-tamaat*, each of them
/189

TAMMARIIKKUTI
compass
means for preventing one from getting
lost
/36

TANASIQ
dance
(from the English "dance")
/196

TAP-/TAKPII[T]TUQ
he/she is short-sighted
does not see well
/158

TAP-/TAKPI[K]TUQ
he/she sees very well
sees a lot
/158

TAQAJUQ
he/she feels tired
stops or gives up
/154

TAQANARTUQ
it is tiring
makes one feel tired
/154

TAQAQ
vein, artery
/140

TAQUAT (PL)
travel provisions
/67

TARIUQ
the sea, table salt
the salty one
/28

TARNIQ
shadow soul
the fact of being dark
/90

TARQIQ
moon, month
light, *beautiful obscurity
/27

TARRALIJAARIAQ
cinema
making a reflection (projecting a movie)
/197

TARRANGA
north
its shadow
/35

TARRAQ
shadow, reflection
(linked to) *taaq*, darkness, obscurity
/26

TARRATUUTI
mirror
means for looking at one's own reflection
/183

TARRIATSUIT
invisible human beings
the hidden ones
/93

TARTUQ
kidney
*(linked to) *taaq-*, to be dark
/143

TASIJUAQ
sweater
that stretches
/69

TASIQ
lake
that stretches out
/32

TATSIQ
fog
/22

TAURSITURNIQ
barter, trade, exchange
the fact of providing frequently a
replacement
/185

TAUTTU
look, appearance, colour
(linked to) *tautuk-*, to look attentively
/159

TAUTUNNGI[T]TUQ
blind person
one who does not look attentively
/159

TAUTUTTUQ
he/she looks attentively
/159

TIGGAQ
rutting male seal
that is hard or stiff
/44

TIGUAQ
adoptee, adopted child
one who has been taken with the hands
/122

TIGULAURLUK! (D)
Let's shake hands!
let both of us hold each other's hand
/172

TIGUSINIQ
adoption
the fact of taking it with the hands
/122

TII
tea
(from the English "tea")
/192

TIIVI
television set
(from the English "TV")
/183

TIJJALUK
driftwood, flotsam
drifted ashore
/32

TIKAAGULLIK
orca-like whale, porpoise
which has a *tikaaguti* (peg or knob)
/44

TIKIPPAA
he/she comes to it, reaches it
/156

TIKIQ
forefinger, index, thimble
that points at something
/151

TIKIRAQ
point of land
that looks like an index finger
/32

TIKITTUQ
he/she arrives
/156

TILIJAUSIMAGUTI
mandate
means for doing something on command
/195

TILLI[K]TUQ
he/she steals something
/87

TIMI
body, public organization
(linked to) *timaa*, its centre (of a
periphery)
/139

TIMMIAQ
bird
that flies repeatedly
/50

TIMMIJUQ
it is flying
it takes off repeatedly
/50

TIMMIJUUQ
airplane (W Nvik)
that is in the habit of flying
/185

TINGUK
liver
/143

TININNIMIUTAQ
shellfish
that inhabits the *tininniq* (beach at low
tide)
/54

TININNIQ
beach at low tide
running-out tide
/54

TINITTUQ
the tide runs out
(linked to) *tanu-*, to push down
/33

TIPI
odour, flavour
/162

TIQITURAQ
adolescent animal
a small one that is alert
/44

TIRIAQ
weasel, ermine
that looks like a furtive game animal
/49

TIRIGA[N]NIAJAQ
fox skin
piece of fox
/49

TIRIGA[N]NIAQ
fox
*one trying to look like a furtive game
animal
/48

TIRILLU/TIRIGLU
bearded seal under one year old
*bad game animal
/43

TIRTITUQ
it boils
/25

TITIRARTUQ
he/she writes (Nvut)
marks something with repeated dots
/97

TITIRAUTI
pencil, pen (Nvut)
that is used for writing
/97

TUI
shoulder
/142

TUJURMIAQ
guest
one who has been sent away once again
/174

TUJURMINAK!
Be welcome! (Nvik)
do not feel bored or homesick
/174

TUJURMIUVIK
host
a place to be sent away again
/174

TUJURPAA
sends him/her something
/174

TUKIANI
in the axis of
in his/her/its axis
/36

TUKISIJUQ
he/she understands
encounters a lengthwise axis
/84

TULIMAAQ
human/small animal rib
small *tulimaq* (rib)
/140

TULIMAQ
rib of a large animal (e.g., whale)
/45

TULUGAQ
northern raven
one that gives repeated blows with its
beak
/51

TUNGASUGIT!
Be welcome!
do feel comfortable
/174

TUNGUJURTAQ
blue, green, purple
that looks like the dark sky or a ripe berry
/159

TUNIIT (PL)
Paleo-Eskimo people
(linked to) *tunər-*, strength, solidness
/74

TUNIJJUTI
gift
means for giving something
/95

TUNIJUQ
(animal) offers itself
it makes a gift of itself
/41

TUNIVAA
he/she gives it
/241

TUNNU
back fat of caribou
(linked to) *tunu*, the back
/47

TUNU
the back (anatomy)
the rear part of something
/142

TUNUANI
behind
at his/her/its rear
/36

TUNUSUK
nape of the neck
lesser *tunu* (back)
/142

TUPAAKI
tobacco
(from the English "tobacco")
/192

TUPAT-/TUPAKTUQ
he/she wakes up
is startled
/154

TUPIQ
tent
/66

TUQUJUQ
he/she/it dies
/91

TUQUNGAJUQ
he/she/it is dead
is in the situation of having died
/155

TURQUJAAQ
larynx
associated with choking on food
repeatedly
/141

TURSUAQ
tube
small windpipe
/142

TURSUK/TUR&UK
trachea, windpipe
/141

TURSURARTUQ
calls by a kinship term
calls someone out repeatedly
/142

TURSURAUTI
kinship term, nickname
means for addressing someone
/108

TURSUTAQ
stovepipe, chimney
added windpipe
/142

TURSUUK (D)
igloo tunnel, house porch
double windpipe
/142

TUSAAJI
interpreter, translator
one who understands what is said
/161

TUSAAJUQ
understands what is said
hears continually
/161

TUSARNIQ
the sense of hearing
the fact of hearing
/158

TUSARTUQ
hears, has heard about something
/161

TUSUJUQ
he/she is envious
/87

TUTITTUQ/TUTIKTUQ
sleeps with someone under the same
blanket
/162

TUTSIATITSIJI
lay preacher
who makes people pray
/96

TUTSIATUQ
he/she prays, begs
begs for something
/96

TUTSIAVIK
church
place for praying
/96

TUTSIMAJUQ
he/she feels sad
/87

TUTTU/TUKTU
caribou
much fat
/47

TUTTUJAQ
caribou hide
piece of caribou
/47

TUTTUSIURTUQ
goes looking for caribou
is in frequent contact with caribou
/63

TUTTUVAQ
cow (NE Nvik), moose
big caribou
/61

TUTTUVINIQ
caribou meat
former (dead) caribou
/67

TUTTUVINIRTUTUQ
he/she eats caribou meat
makes use of a dead caribou
/67

TUUGAAQ
walrus/narwhal tusk, ivory
that is poked head-on repeatedly
/44

TUUKKAQ
harpoon head
(linked to) *tuugaaq*, tusk, ivory
/44

TUULLIK
common loon
/50

TUURNGAQ
shaman's familiar spirit
one who has been secured
/91

TUURNGINIQ
casting a spell
resorting to *tuurngait* (spirits)
/95

TUVAQ
ice floe
/24

UANIUJAQ
onion
(from the English "onion")
/193

UANNIQ
northwest wind (NE Nvik)
from down there
/22

UASARTUQ
he/she washes (Nvut)
(from the English "wash")
/154

UI
husband
*swerving, protuberance
/113

UIGUIT (PL)
francophones
(those who say) *oui-oui*
/77

UIRNGA[R]TUQ
he/she feels sleepy
opens his/her eyes for the first time
/154

UIRSAQ
incubus spirit
would-be husband
/93

UISUK
male lover
lesser husband
/116

UITSIAQ
man sharing woman's midwife
good/nice husband (for the woman)
/125

UIVIITTUQ
is unruly, vicious
is without mental ability
/89

UJAMIK
medal
that is on the upper torso
/132

UJARAQ
rock
*what has been made to emerge, to protrude
/31

UJARATSIAQ
hammer
good stone
/65

UJJUK/UGJUK
bearded seal
(linked to) *ugat-*, to get up on something
/43

UJJUNAQ
shrew mouse
that looks like a bearded seal
/49

UJURUK
man's sister's child
(linked to) *ujuraq*, younger brother (in Yupik)
/111

UKALIQ
Arctic hare
/50

UKALIVINIQ
hare meat
former (dead) hare
/67

Words of the Inuit

UKIAQ
fall, autumn
lesser *ukiuq*
/21

UKIATSAQ
early fall
incoming *ukiaq*
/21

UKIUQ
winter, year
/21

UKIUQARNIQ
age
the fact of having winters (years)
/106

UKIURTA[R]TUQ
the Arctic
the one where winter lasts for a long time
/21

UKKUAQ
door
(linked to) *umag-*, to close up, to cover
/182

UKKUSIK
soapstone cooking pot
(linked to) *ugut-*, to cook something
/67

UKUAQ
daughter-/sister-in-law
*one who bends or is made to bend
/117

ULAAQ
woman's knife (Yupik)
lesser or *looking like *ulu[q]*, tongue
/150

ULIK
skirt, dress
that covers
/69

ULIMAUTI
adze, axe
means for fashioning something
/65

ULITTUQ
the tide rises
it becomes covered
/33

ULLAA[K]KUT!
Good morning!
during the morning
/171

ULLAAQ
morning
small *ullu[q]* (daylight)
/26

ULLAUTIGIAQ
racing
running together
/196

ULLU
nest
place for tying up
/52

ULLUIT (PL)
calendar
the days
/98

ULLUIT TAUJUT (PL)
days without sunrise
days that are dark
/237

ULLULIMAAQ
all day long
all of the day
/189

ULLUMI
today
during [this] day
/26

ULLU[Q]
daylight, day
/26

ULLURIAQ
star, planet
emission of daylight
/27

ULLUTAMAAT (PL)
every day
each of the days
/189

ULU
woman's rounded knife
(linked to) *ulu[q]*, tongue in Yupik
languages
/68

ULUAQ
cheek
/150

ULU[Q]
tongue (Yupik languages)
/149

UMIALITTAAQ
boat owner, ship captain
a given one who has an *umiaq* (boat)
/185

UMIAQ
open skin boat, any boat
something closed off (from water)
/65

UMIARAALUK
motorized schooner
big *umiaq* (boat)
/66

UMIARAAQ
rowboat
very small *umiaq* (boat)
/185

UMIARJUAQ
ship
super-*umiaq* (super-boat)
/185

UMIK/UMIIT
beard/facial hair
(linked to) *uməg-*, to cover something
/148

UMILIK
bearded man
who has an *umik* (beard)
/148

UMIMMAK
muskox
big whiskers
/47

UNA
this one close to me
/34

UNAAQ
harpoon
(linked to) *urnəg-*, to go toward
/64

UNALIQ
Cree person (W Arctic)
fearsome individual
/75

UNANI
down there
/34

UNATARTUQ
tries to kill, wages war
(linked to) *unaðmi-*, to challenge
/136

UNGAJUQ
wants to be with someone
/86

UNIKKAATUAT (PL)
stories
things told several times
/93

UNIKKATUQ
tells a story
it makes someone tell something
/94

UNIKKAUSIIT (PL)
myths, legends
things that are to be told
/93

UNNA
that one down there
/35

UNNGIJARTUQ
shaves his face
removes his facial hair
/148

UNNUAQ
night
small *unnuk* (daily darkness), early
morning
/26

UNNUATTAK
24-hour daylight
another [kind of] night, absence of night
/237

UNNUK
evening
daily period of darkness
/26

UNNU[K]KUT!
Good night!
during the evening
/171

UNNU[K]SAKKUT!
Good afternoon!
during the incoming evening (i.e.,
afternoon)
/171

UNUNGA
downward, seaward
toward down there
/35

UPIRNGAALAAQ
early summer (NE Nvik)
very small *upirngaaq* (summer)
/21

UPIRNGAAQ
summer (NE Nvik), springtime
surprised or surprising at first
/22

UPIRNGASA[A]Q
springtime (NE Nvik)
incoming *upirngaaq* (summer)
/21

UP-/UKPATIIK (D)
buttocks and upper thighs
used for bending repeatedly
/144

UPPIK/UKPIK
snowy owl
/51

UPPINIQ/UKPIRNIQ
religion
the fact of believing
/96

UPPITUQ/UKPIRTUQ
believer, finds credible
one who believes, finds something
credible
/96

UQALAUTI
telephone
means for talking for a long time
/169

UQAQ
tongue
the speaking one
/149

UQARTUQ
speaks, says
/85

UQAUSIIT (PL)
words, language
that are used for speaking
/85

UQAUSIRIVAA
confesses it
he/she has it as words
/95

UQUMMIASAJAQ
quid of chewing tobacco
stuff fit for being kept in the mouth
/192

UQUQU
animal (baby talk)
/82

URPIK
willow, shrub
real shelter
/32

URQU
leeward side
(a position) associated with a shelter
/25

URQUUJUQ
temperature is warm
it is a position sheltered from the wind
/25

URQUUQ!
How hot!
/25

URQUUSIURTUQ
he/she is hot
searches after warmth
/25

URSUALUK
petroleum, gasoline, oil
big blubber
/185

URSUQ
seal or whale blubber
/46

URVIUJAQ
spoon
that looks like an *urviq* (traditional
ornament)
/191

USUAPIK
clitoris (Nvik)
small penis
/145

USUK
penis
(linked to) *ucug*, sexual organ
/144

USUUJAQ (1)
pointed prow of a kayak
that looks like a penis
/71

USUUJAQ (2)
sausage, carrot
that looks like a penis
/193

UTSUK/UTTU[U]K
vagina, vulva
double *usuk* (sexual organ)
/145

UUGAQ
polar cod
/53

UUJUQ
boiled meat or fish
that has burned for a long time
/67

UUMAJJUTI
life goal
reason for being alive
/63

UUMAJUQ
animal
it is alive, one that is alive
/40

UUMAJURNIATUQ
relates to an animal
deals with an animal
/63

UUMAJURNIAVIGIJAQ
that has become a prey
is an occasion for dealing with an
uumajuq
/64

UUMAJURSIUTAQ
an animal that is hunted
that is searched for as an *uumajuq*
(animal)
/64

UUMAJURSIUTI
hunter
one who usually hunts
/62

UUMAJURSIUTUQ
he/she hunts
searches for animals
/62

UUMAJURTAQ
animal that was caught
one that was "*uumajuq*-ed"
/64

UUMAJUVINIQ
dead animal
former *uumajuq* (living being)
/63

UUMARTUQ
an animal that revives
one that comes to life again
/64

UUMISUTTUQ
dislikes, hates someone
(linked to) *ugu-*, heated up
/87

UUMMATI
heart
what gives life to a creature
/40

UUNARTUQ
hot thing, feverish person
makes one being burned
/25

UUTTUQ (1)
he/she is burnt
/65

UUTTUQ (2)
seal basking on ice
it (seal) is burnt
/65

UUTTU[R]PAA
tries/measures/tastes it
tries it repeatedly
/162

UUTTUUTI
measuring tool, example
used for testing or measuring something
/162

UUTTUUTIGILUGU
for example
having it as a means for testing
/162

UVANI
here very close
/34

[UVAT]SIARUQ
later on
/178

UVIKKAQ
teenager
*who has been lengthened
/79

UVILUQ
mussel
that opens like an eye
/54

UVINIK
human flesh and skin
/140

UVINIRUQ
shirt
that touches the skin
/69

UVIUQ
clitoris
*that swells or tilts for long
/145

UVVATUQ
washes body or something else (Nvik)
/154

UVVAUTI
soap, detergent (Nvik)
that is used for washing
/154

UVVAVIK
wash basin, sink
place for washing
/183

-VIK
place or time for
/177

References

Alasuaq, Davidialuk. 1981. *Unikkaatuat ujaranngutitait* [Stories turned into stone]. Edited by Bernard Saladin d'Anglure. Inuksiutiit allaniagait 3. Quebec City: Association Inuksiutiit Katimajiit.

Alia, Valerie. 1994. *Names, Numbers, and Northern Policy: Inuit, Project Surname, and the Politics of Identity*. Halifax: Fernwood.

Allen, Shanley E.M. 1996. *Aspects of Argument Structure Acquisition in Inuktitut*. Amsterdam: John Benjamins.

Annahatak, Betsy. 2014. "*Silatuniq*: Respectful State of Being in the World." *Études/Inuit/ Studies* 38 (1–2): 23–31.

Bach, Emmon. 2009. "On Morphosemantics: The Internal Meaning of Words." Copenhagen Linguistic Circle. http://people.umass.edu/ebach/papers/copenh.htm. Accessed 12 July 2015.

Baillargeon, Richard, Gérald Noelting, Louis-Jacques Dorais, and Bernard Saladin d'Anglure. 1977. "Aspects sémantiques et structuraux de la numération chez les Inuit." *Études/Inuit/ Studies* 1 (1): 93–128.

Ballantyne, Robert Michael. 1858. *Ungava: A Tale of Esquimaux Land*. London: Thomas Nelson and Sons.

Berge, Anna. 2018. "Re-Evaluating the Reconstruction of Proto-Eskimo-Aleut." *Journal of Historical Linguistics* 8 (2): 231–73.

Berge, Anna, and Lawrence D. Kaplan. 2005. "Contact-Induced Lexical Development in Yupik and Inuit Languages." *Études/Inuit/Studies* 29 (1–2): 285–305.

———. "Divine Inspiration." 2016. In "Questions de sémantique inuit/Topics in Inuit Semantics." Special issue, *Amerindia* 38: 3–24.

Bergsland, Knut. 1994. *Aleut Dictionary: Unangam Tunudgusii*. Fairbanks: Alaska Native Language Center.

Boas, Franz. 1964. *The Central Eskimo*. Lincoln: University of Nebraska Press. First published 1888.

Bordin, Guy. 2003. *Lexique analytique de l'anatomie humaine/Analytical Lexicon of Human Anatomy/Timiup ilangitta atingit Nunavimmilu Nunavummilu*. SELAF Arctique 6. Leuven and Paris: Peeters.

Briggs, Jean L. 1970. *Never in Anger: Portrait of an Eskimo Family*. Cambridge, MA: Harvard University Press.

Cancel, Carole. 2011. "Autorité, parole et pouvoir: Une approche anthropologique de l'activité néologique inuit au Nunavut." PhD diss., Université Laval.

Clément, Daniel. 2017. *L'écho des autres: L'analyse basique en anthropologie.* Quebec City: Presses de l'Université Laval.

Collis, Dermot R.F. 1971. *Pour une sémiologie de l'esquimau.* Paris: Université de Paris VI, Centre de linguistique quantitative.

Deer, Eva. 2015. *Eva Deer: An Inuit Leader and Educator/Eva Deer: Une leader et éducatrice inuit/Eva Deer: Sivulirti amma ilisaiji.* Translated and edited by Louis-Jacques Dorais. Quebec City: Université Laval, CIÉRA.

Denny, J. Peter. 1981. *Cultural Ecology of Mathematics: Ojibway and Inuit Hunters.* London, ON: University of Western Ontario, Department of Psychology.

Dorais, Louis-Jacques. 1974. "Petite introduction à la langue inuit." *Recherches amérindiennes au Québec* 4 (1): 23–32.

———. 1977. "La structure du vocabulaire moderne de la langue inuit du Québec-Labrador." *L'Homme* 17 (4): 35–63.

———. 1980. *The Inuit Language in Southern Labrador from 1694–1785.* National Museum of Man, Mercury Series, Canadian Ethnology Service Paper 66. Ottawa: National Museums of Canada.

———. 1983. *Uqausigusiqtaat: An Analytical Lexicon of Modern Inuktitut in Quebec-Labrador.* Quebec City: Presses de l'Université Laval.

———. 1984a. "Humiliation et harmonie: L'expression du droit coutumier chez les Inuit du Labrador." *Recherches amérindiennes au Québec* 14 (4): 3–8.

———. 1984b. "Sémantique des noms d'animaux en groenlandais de l'est." *Amerindia* 9: 7–23.

———. 1986. "Agiter l'homme pour attraper la femme: La sémantique des sexes en langue inuit." *Études/Inuit/Studies* 10 (1–2): 171–78.

———. 1988. *Tukilik: An Inuktitut Grammar for All.* Inuit Studies Occasional Papers 2. Quebec City: Association Inuksiutiit Katimajiit.

———. 1997. *Quaqtaq: Modernity and Identity in an Inuit Community.* Toronto: University of Toronto Press.

———. 2007. "La diaspora des esprits: Ancêtres et génies vietnamiens au Québec." In *La nature des esprits dans les cosmologies autochtones,* edited by Frédéric B. Laugrand and Jarich G. Oosten, 511–40. Quebec City: Presses de l'Université Laval.

———. 2010. *The Language of the Inuit: Syntax, Semantics, and Society in the Arctic.* Montreal and Kingston: McGill-Queen's University Press.

———. 2014. *Yawenda: Les Hurons-Wendat font revivre leur langue/The Huron-Wendat Revive Their Language.* Document de recherche Yawenda 11. Quebec City: Université Laval, CIÉRA.

———. 2016. "Morphosemantics and Their Limits: Three Inuit Examples." In "Questions de sémantique inuit/Topics in Inuit Semantics." Special issue, *Amerindia* 38: 47–86.

———. 2017a. *Inuit Languages and Dialects: Inuit Uqausiqatigiit.* Updated edition. Iqaluit: Nunavut Arctic College Media.

————. 2017b. "The Lexicon in Polysynthetic Languages." In *The Oxford Handbook of Polysynthesis*, edited by Michael Fortescue, Marianne Mithun, and Nicholas Evans, 135–57. Oxford: Oxford University Press.

————. 2017c. *Tuvaalummiut nunangat Quaqtaq/Quaqtaq, terre de la grande banquise 1960–1990*. 207 photos. Quebec City: Les Éditions GID.

————. 2018a. "A Marriage in Nunavik." In *The Hands' Measure: Essays Honouring Leah Aksaajuq Otak's Contribution to Arctic Science*, edited by John MacDonald and Nancy Wachowich, 225–35. Iqaluit: Nunavut Arctic College Media.

————. 2018b. *A Written Orality: The Canadian Inuit and Their Language*. With the collaboration of Hinrich Sachs and Fredrik Ehlin. Milan: Humboldt Books.

Eliade, Mircea. 1989. *Le mythe de l'éternel retour*. Paris: Gallimard. First published 1949.

Enel, Catherine. 1982. "Étude morphologique de quelques éléments de vocabulaire moderne ouest-groenlandais." DEA (Diplôme d'études supérieures) thesis, Université de Paris VII.

Fortescue, Michael. 1983. *A Comparative Manual of Affixes for the Inuit Dialects of Greenland, Canada and Alaska*. Man and Society 4. Copenhagen: Meddelelser om Grønland.

————. 1988. *Eskimo Orientation Systems*. Man and Society 11. Copenhagen: Meddelelser om Grønland.

————. 2016. "The Colours of the Arctic." In "Questions de sémantique inuit/Topics in Inuit Semantics." Special issue, *Amerindia* 38: 25–46.

Fortescue, Michael, Steven A. Jacobson, and Lawrence D. Kaplan. 2010. *Comparative Eskimo Dictionary with Aleut Cognates*. 2nd edition. Fairbanks: Alaska Native Language Center.

Gearheard, Shari Fox, Lene Kielsen Holm, Henry Huntington, Joe Mello Leavitt, and Andrew R. Mahoney, eds. 2013. *The Meaning of Ice*. Hanover, NH: University Press of New England.

Gombay, Nicole. 2010. *Making a Living: Place, Food and Economy in an Inuit Community*. Saskatoon: Purich Publishing.

Graburn, Nelson H.H. 1964. *Taqagmiut Eskimo Kinship Terminology*. Ottawa: Government of Canada, Department of Northern Affairs and National Resources, Northern Co-ordination and Research Centre.

————. 1965. "Some Aspects of Linguistic Acculturation in Northern Ungava Eskimo." *Kroeber Anthropological Society Papers* 32: 11–46.

Harnum, Betty. 1989. "Lexical Innovation in Inuktitut." MA thesis, University of Calgary.

Harper, Kenn. 1985. "The Early Development of Inuktitut Syllabic Orthography." *Études/Inuit/Studies* 9 (1): 141–62.

Hayashi, Midori. 2011. "The Structure of Multiple Tenses in Inuktitut." PhD diss., University of Toronto.

Heyes, Scott A. 2007. "Inuit Knowledge and Perceptions of the Land-Water Interface." PhD diss., McGill University.

Hot, Aurélie. 2009. "Language Rights and Language Choices: The Potential of Inuktitut Literacy." *Journal of Canadian Studies* 43 (2): 181–97.

Jeddore, Rose P., ed. 1976. *Labrador Inuit Uqausingit*. St. John's, NL: Inuit Committee on Literacy.

Jung, Carl C., and Charles Kerényi. 1968, *Introduction à l'essence de la mythologie*. Paris: Payot. First published 1941.

Kaplan, Lawrence D. 2003. "Inuit Snow Terms: How Many and What Does It Mean?" In *Building Capacity in Arctic Societies: Dynamics and Shifting*, edited by François Trudel, 263–69. Quebec City: Université Laval, CIÉRA.

Kublu, Alexina, and Jarich Oosten. 1999. "Changing Perspectives of Name and Identity among the Inuit of Northeast Canada." In *Arctic Identities*, edited by Jarich Oosten and Cornelius Remie, 56–78. Leiden: University of Leiden, CNWS Publications.

Kululaaq, Louisa. 2008–2009. *Pirurpalianirmuulingajut unikkaatuat* [Tales aimed at growing]. Quaqtaq, QC: Isummasaqvik School.

Kunuk, Zacharias, dir. 2002. *Arviq! (Bowhead!)*. Film, 52 minutes. Igloolik Isuma Productions.

———, and Norman Cohn, dirs. 2006. *The Journals of Knud Rasmussen*. Film, 112 minutes. Igloolik Isuma Productions, Kunuk Cohn Productions.

Laugrand, Frédéric B., and Jarich Oosten. 2008. *The Sea Woman: Sedna in Inuit Shamanism and Art in the Eastern Arctic*. Fairbanks: University of Alaska Press.

———. 2010. *Inuit Shamanism and Christianity: Transitions and Transformations in the Twentieth Century*. Montreal and Kingston: McGill-Queen's University Press.

———. 2012. "Maîtres de la vie et de la mort.: La grandeur des 'petites bêtes' du Grand Nord." *L'Homme* 202: 53–75.

———. 2015. *Hunters, Predators and Prey: Inuit Perceptions of Animals*. New York: Berghahn.

Le Goff, Jacques. 2003. *À la recherche du Moyen Âge*. Paris: Louis Audibert.

Macdonald, John. 1998. *The Arctic Sky: Inuit Astronomy, Star Lore, and Legend*. Toronto: Royal Ontario Museum; Igloolik: Nunavut Research Institute.

MacLean, Edna Ahgeak. 1990. "Culture and Change for Inupiat and Yupiks of Alaska." In *Arctic Languages: An Awakening*, edited by Dermot R.F. Collis, 159–75. Paris: Unesco.

———. 2014. *Iñupiaq to English Dictionary/Iñupiatun Uqaluit Taniktun Sivuniŋit*. Fairbanks: University of Alaska Press.

Markoosie. 1970. *Harpoon of the Hunter*. Montreal and Kingston: McGill-Queen's University Press.

———. 2011. *Angunasuttiup naukkutinga/Le harpon du chasseur*. Quebec City: Presses de l'Université du Québec.

Mattissen, Johanna. 2017. "Sub-Types of Polysynthesis." In *The Oxford Handbook of Polysynthesis*, edited by Michael Fortescue, Marianne Mithun, and Nicholas Evans, 70–98. Oxford: Oxford University Press.

Mithun, Marianne. 2009. "Polysynthesis in the Arctic." In *Variations in Polysynthesis, the Eskaleut Languages*, edited by Marc-Antoine Mahieu and Nicole Tersis, 3–18. Amsterdam: John Benjamins.

———. 2017. "Polysynthesis in North America." In *The Oxford Handbook of Polysynthesis*, edited by Michael Fortescue, Marianne Mithun, and Nicholas Evans, 235–59. Oxford: Oxford University Press.

Morantz, Toby. 2016. *Relations on Ungava Bay: An Illustrated History of Inuit, Naskapi, and Eurocanadian Interaction, 1800–1970*. Westmount, QC: Avataq Cultural Institute.

Morgan, Lewis Henry. 1997. *Systems of Consanguinity and Affinity of the Human Family*. Lincoln: University of Nebraska Press. First published 1870.

Namer, Fiammetta, and Pierre Zweigenbaum. 2004. "Acquiring Meaning for French Medical Terminology: Contribution of Morphosemantics." *Medinfo* 11 (1): 535–39.

Nappaaluk, Mitiarjuk. 1984. *Sanaaq unikkausinnguaq* [Sanaaq, an imaginary story]. Edited by Bernard Saladin d'Anglure. Inuksiutiit allaniagait 4. Quebec City: Association Inuksiutiit Katimajiit.

———. 2014. *Sanaaq: An Inuit Novel*. Translated by Bernard Saladin d'Anglure. Winnipeg: University of Manitoba Press.

Ootoova, Elisapee, John Tongak, Sam Erkloo, Sam Arnakallak, Nellie Sangoya, and Susie Pewatualuk. 2000. *Uqausiit tukingit inuktitut tununirmiutituungajuq* [The meanings of Inuktitut words, in the Tununiq dialect]. Iqaluit: Government of Nunavut, Qikiqtani School Operations.

Otak, Leah, and Peesee Pitsiulak-Stevens, eds. 2014. *Inuit Kinship and Naming Customs in Baffin Region*. Iqaluit: Nunavut Arctic College Media.

Ouellette, Nathalie. 2000. "Tuurngait et chamanes inuit dans le Nunavik occidental contemporain." MA thesis, Université Laval.

Qumaq, Taamusi. 1988. *Sivulitta piusituqangit* [The longstanding customs of our ancestors]. Inuksiutiit allaniagait 5. Quebec City: Association Inuksiutiit Katimajiit.

———. 1991. *Inuit uqausillaringit ulirnaisigutiit* [The genuine words of the Inuit, a dictionary]. Quebec City: Association Inuksiutiit Katimajiit; and Montreal: Avataq Cultural Institute.

Randa, Vladimir. 1986. *L'ours polaire et les Inuit*. Paris: SELAF.

———. 1994. "Inuillu uumajuillu: Les animaux dans les savoirs, les représentations et la langue des Iglulingmiut (Arctique oriental canadien)." PhD diss., École des Hautes Études en Sciences Sociales, Paris.

———. 2002. "'Qui se ressemble s'assemble': Logique de construction et d'organisation des zoonymes en langue inuit." *Études/Inuit/Studies* 26 (1): 71–108.

Rasing, Willem C.E. 2012. "Beyond Thule: Where Inuit and Aristotle Meet." In "Linguistic and Cultural Encounters in the Arctic: Essays in Memory of Susan Sammons." Supplementary issue, *Les Cahiers du CIÉRA*, 85–96.

Rasmussen, Knud. 1929. *Intellectual Culture of the Iglulik Eskimos*. Report of the Fifth Thule Expedition 1921–24, vol. 7. Copenhagen: Gyldendalske Boghandel.

———. 1931. *The Netsilik Eskimos: Social and Spiritual Culture*. Report of the Fifth Thule Expedition 1921–24, vol. 8. Copenhagen: Gyldendalske Boghandel.

———. 1932. *Intellectual Culture of the Copper Eskimos*. Report of the Fifth Thule Expedition 1921–24, vol. 9. Copenhagen: Gyldendalske Boghandel.

Robbe, Pierre, and Louis-Jacques Dorais. 1986. *Tunumiit oraasiat/Tunumiut oqaasi/Det østgrønlandske sprog/The East Greenlandic Inuit Language/La langue inuit du Groenland de l'Est*. Nordicana 49. Quebec City: Université Laval, Centre d'études nordiques.

Sadock, Jerold. 2017. "Affix Clusters and the Lexicon in Kalaallisut." In *Studies in Inuit Linguistics in Honor of Michael Fortescue*, edited by Lawrence D. Kaplan and Anna Berge, 1–25. Fairbanks: Alaska Native Language Center.

Saint-Aubin, Danièle. 1980. "English Loan-Verbs in the Inuktitut Speech of Inuit Bilinguals." MA thesis, McGill University.

Saladin d'Anglure, Bernard. 1977. "Iqallijuq ou les réminiscences d'une âme-nom inuit." *Études/Inuit/Studies* 1 (1): 33–63.

———. 1986. "Du foetus au chamane, la construction d'un 'troisième sexe' inuit." *Études/Inuit/Studies* 10 (1–2): 25–113.

———. 1993. "Sila, the Ordering Principle of the Inuit Cosmology." In *Shamans and Cultures*, edited by M. Hoppal and K. Howard, 210–25. Budapest: Hungarian Academy of Science.

———. 2000. "*Pijariurniq*: Performances et rituels inuit de la première fois." *Études/Inuit/Studies* 24 (2): 89–113.

———, ed. 2001. *Cosmology and Shamanism*. Interviewing Inuit Elders 4. Iqaluit: Nunavut Arctic College.

———. 2004. "Nanook, Super-Male: The Polar Bear in the Imaginary Space and Social Time of the Inuit of the Canadian Arctic." In *Signifying Animals: Human Meaning in the Natural World*, edited by Roy G. Willis, 381–414. London: Taylor and Francis e-Library. First published 1990. https://ebookcentral.proquest.com/docID=179420. Accessed 10 November 2018.

———. 2005. "The 'Third Gender' of the Inuit." *Diogenes* 52 (4): 134–44.

———. 2013. *L'organisation sociale traditionnelle des Inuit de Kangiqsujuaq, Nunavik*. Inukjuak, QC: Avataq Cultural Institute, Nunavik Publications.

———. 2018. *Inuit Stories of Being and Rebirth: Gender, Shamanism and the Third Sex*. Winnipeg: University of Manitoba Press.

Schneider, Lucien. 1970a. *Dictionnaire esquimau-français du parler de l'Ungava et contrées limitrophes*. Travaux et documents du Centre d'études nordiques 3. Quebec City: Presses de l'Université Laval.

———. 1970b. *Dictionnaire français-esquimau du parler de l'Ungava et contrées limitrophes*. Travaux et documents du Centre d'études nordiques 5. Quebec City: Presses de l'Université Laval.

———. 1972–76. *Inuktituorutit grammaire purement esquimaude*. Five vols. Quebec City: Government of Quebec, Ministry of Natural Resources.

———. 1979. *Dictionnaire des infixes de la langue esquimaude*. Dossier 43. Quebec City: Ministry of Cultural Affairs, Direction générale du Patrimoine.

———. 1985. *Ulirnaisigutiit: An Inuktitut-English Dictionary of Northern Quebec, Labrador and Eastern Arctic Dialects*. Quebec City: Presses de l'Université Laval.

Searles, Edmund N. 2016. "To Sell or Not to Sell: Country Food Markets and Inuit Identity in Nunavut." *Food and Foodways* 24 (3–4): 194–212.

Spalding, Alex. 1998. *Inuktitut: A Multi-Dialectal Outline Dictionary (with an Aivilingmiutaq Base)*. With the cooperation and help of Thomas Kusugaq. Iqaluit: Nunavut Arctic College.

Stairs, Arlene, and George Wenzel. 1992. "I Am I and the Environment: Inuit Hunting, Community, and Identity." *Journal of Indigenous Studies* 3 (1): 1–12.

Steckley, John. 2007. *Words of the Huron*. Waterloo, ON: Wilfrid Laurier University Press.

———. 2008. *White Lies about the Inuit*. Peterborough, ON: Broadview Press.

Tersis, Nicole, and Marc-Antoine Mahieu. 2006. "Sémantique des affixes incorporants en langue inuit (Groenland oriental)." *Études/Inuit/Studies* 30 (1): 157–81.

Therrien, Michèle. 1987. *Le corps inuit (Québec arctique)*. SELAF Arctique 1. Paris: SELAF; Bordeaux: Presses de l'Université de Bordeaux.

———. 1995. "Corps sain, corps malade chez les Inuit, une tension entre l'intérieur et l'extérieur: Entretiens avec Taamusi Qumaq." *Recherches amérindiennes au Québec* 25 (1): 71–84.

———. 1999. *Printemps inuit, naissance du Nunavut*. Arceaux, France: Indigène éditions.

———. 2000. "Nouvelles terminologies en inuktitut: Contraintes linguistiques, logiques, naturelles." In *La dynamique dans la langue et la culture inuit*, edited by Nicole Tersis and Michèle Therrien, 283–301. Leuven and Paris: Peeters.

———. 2002. "How Semantic Information Can Contribute to Shed Light on Concepts We Want to Investigate." In *Proceedings of the First IPSSAS Seminar*, edited by Michèle Therrien, 240–53. Nuuk, Greenland: Ilisimatusarfik.

Thibert, Arthur. 1955. *English-Eskimo, Eskimo-English Dictionary*. Ottawa: Canadian Research Centre for Anthropology.

Trott, Christopher G. 1989. "Structure and Pragmatics: Social Relations among the Tununirusirmiut." PhD diss., University of Toronto.

Turner, Lucien M. 1894. *Ethnology of the Ungava District, Hudson Bay Territory*. 11th Annual Report. Washington, DC: Bureau of American Ethnology.

Watt-Cloutier, Sheila. 2016. *The Right to Be Cold: One Woman's Story of Protecting Her Culture, the Arctic, and the Whole Planet*. Toronto: Penguin Random House Canada.

Weyapuk, Winton, and Igor Krupnik, eds. 2012. *Wales Inupiaq Sea Ice Dictionary/Kiŋikmi Sigum Qanuq Ilitaavut*. Washington, DC: Smithsonian Institution, Arctic Studies Center.

Woodbury, Anthony C. 2017. "Central Alaskan Yupik (Eskimo-Aleut): A Sketch of Morphologically Orthodox Polysynthesis." In *The Oxford Handbook of Polysynthesis*, edited by Michael Fortescue, Marianne Mithun, and Nicholas Evans, 536–59. Oxford: Oxford University Press.